Language Acts

RHETORIC AND WRITING I:
ACADEMIC READING AND ANALYTICAL WRITING

Second Edition

Ceil Malek, Editor

Kacey Ross, Managing Editor

Keri Hemenway and Andrea Wenker, Copy Editors

UCCS First-Year Rhetoric and Writing Program

University of Colorado, Colorado Springs

FOUNTAINHEAD
PRESS

Our green initiatives include:

Electronic Products

We deliver products in non-paper form whenever possible. This includes pdf downloadables, flash drives, & CDs.

Electronic Samples

We use Xample, a new electronic sampling system. Instructor samples are sent via a personalized web page that links to pdf downloads.

FSC Certified Printers

All of our printers are certified by the Forest Service Council which promotes environmentally and socially responsible management of the world's forests. This program allows consumer groups, individual consumers, and businesses to work together hand-in-hand to promote responsible use of the world's forests as a renewable and sustainable resource.

Recycled Paper

Most of our products are printed on a minimum of 30% post-consumer waste recycled paper.

Support of Green Causes

When we do print, we donate a portion of our revenue to green causes. Listed below are a few of the organizations that have received donations from Fountainhead Press. We welcome your feedback and suggestions for contributions, as we are always searching for worthy initiatives.

Rainforest 2 Reef

Environmental Working Group

Books may be purchased for educational purposes.

For information, please call or write:
1-800-586-0330
Fountainhead Press
Southlake, TX. 76092
Web site: www.fountainheadpress.com
Email: customerservice@fountainheadpress.com

ISBN 978-1-59871-989-5
Printed in the United States of America

A WORD TO THE ENGLISH 1310 STUDENT

The UCCS writing faculty worked collaboratively to develop the curriculum and reader for this first-year course in academic reading and analytical writing: both focus on the way *language acts* within the world. As a student in English 1310, you will move beyond the formulaic writing that may have been commonplace in previous writing classes, including five-paragraph essays, three-point thesis statements, and summary work. This writing class will extend purposely beyond these approaches by challenging you to read and engage with academic texts while supporting you to develop a new lens for understanding that is both analytically and rhetorically focused.

This course is multi-faceted as it hinges on your exposure to both writing process theory and rhetorical scholarship. You will be challenged to learn and apply rhetorical theory as a tool for unpacking, analyzing, and evaluating arguments from others. You will become familiar with rhetorical concepts, apply them to several kinds of texts, using them to develop and demonstrate your own analytical skills. At the same time, you will engage with writing classroom best practices, including inventing, drafting, conferences, peer review, and revision—the hallmarks of writing process theory.

The theoretical tools you will use in English 1310 will enable you to analyze and respond to arguments in a wide variety of contexts—the writing classroom, other coursework, and the world beyond the university. To succeed in the course, you will need to attend class regularly, engage intentionally in class discussion and collaborative work, consistently put forth your best effort, and take advantage of your instructor's office hours for additional support.

RHETORIC AND WRITING I

Academic Reading and Analytical Writing

Course Description

English 1310: Rhetoric and Writing I is the first course of a two-semester written communication sequence required of all UCCS students. The course introduces students to academic reading and writing processes. Students develop critical reading, writing, and thinking skills through class discussion, the rhetorical analysis of academic and civic texts, and the writing of documented analytical essays. Students analyze texts written for diverse purposes and audiences. The course focuses on writing process theory and rhetorical theory, which serves two complementary purposes—to prepare writers for academic reading and writing assignments at the university level and to introduce students to rhetoric and writing as a field. Signature features of the UCCS ENGL 1310 experience include writing instruction in a computer-mediated classroom; low course caps of 19 students; extensive small group and whole class discussion; and one-on-one writing conferences for all ENGL 1310 students.

Course Focus

English 1310 students learn a rhetorical approach to reading and writing in which they approach texts primarily as acts of communication rather than as static objects. English 1310 students concentrate on the elements of effective writing in academic and professional settings: understanding a writer's stance, developing a supportable argumentative purpose, discovering and using effective support strategies, making appropriate organizational and stylistic choices, and understanding the expectations of a wide range of audiences. The first few weeks of the semester are spent introducing the basics of rhetoric and analysis. The bulk of the course focuses on application of these rhetorical lenses to several kinds of texts, examining how each one makes an argument. It is the use of rhetorical theory that enables close reading and rigorous analysis of texts; students employ rhetorical concepts to define and evaluate how a text works in a particular situation and what impact it has on its audience.

Writing Assignments

All students will write four papers in English 1310 in which they practice academic analysis: two rhetorical analyses of written texts, one rhetorical analysis of either a written or visual text, and one additional analytical assignment. The fundamental kinds of texts are determined by the program—many are included in this book. A variety of nonfiction texts will be the subject of analysis in English 1310. Overall, the total amount of polished, final-draft writing each student should expect to complete per semester is between 6,000 and 7,500 words, or 20-25 pages (at 300 words per page).

Academic Reading, Responding, and Discussion

English 1310 incorporates critical reading activities as integral to academic work. Students read and annotate rhetorical theory, writing process theory, and argumentative texts in a variety of genres throughout the course. Class discussion and workshops will emphasize the close, critical analysis of the assigned texts. At the same time, English 1310 utilizes discussion as a necessary element to facilitate academic reading and writing. Students develop communication skills through large and small group discussions and writing conferences.

ENGLISH 1310 OUTCOMES

Rhetoric and Writing I at UCCS is aligned with the following outcomes, developed by the Council of Writing Program Administrators, the National Council of Teachers of English, and the National Writing Project.

Habits of mind refers to ways of approaching learning that are both intellectual and practical and that will support students' success in a variety of fields and disciplines. The eight habits of mind are essential for success in college writing:

- Curiosity – the desire to know more about the world.
- Openness – the willingness to consider new ways of being and thinking in the world.
- Engagement – a sense of investment and involvement in learning.
- Creativity – the ability to use novel approaches for generating, investigating, and representing ideas.
- Persistence – the ability to sustain interest in and attention to short- and long-term projects.
- Responsibility – the ability to take ownership of one's actions and understand the consequences of those actions for oneself and others.
- Flexibility – the ability to adapt to situations, expectations, or demands.
- Metacognition – the ability to reflect on one's own thinking as well as on the individual and cultural processes used to structure knowledge.

Students learn these habits of mind through **writing, reading, and critical analysis** experiences. These experiences aim to develop students'

- Rhetorical knowledge – the ability to analyze and act on understandings of audiences, purposes, and contexts in creating and comprehending texts;
- Critical thinking – the ability to analyze a situation or text and make thoughtful decisions based on that analysis, through writing and reading;
- Writing processes – multiple strategies to approach and undertake writing and research;
- Knowledge of conventions – the formal and informal guidelines that define what is considered to be correct and appropriate, or incorrect and inappropriate, in a piece of writing; and
- Ability to compose in multiple environments – from traditional pen and paper to electronic technologies.

Developing Rhetorical Knowledge

Rhetorical knowledge is the basis of good writing. Study of and practice with basic rhetorical concepts are important as writers learn to compose a variety of texts for different disciplines and purposes.

Students will

- Learn and practice key rhetorical concepts such as audience, purpose, context, and genre through writing and analysis of a variety of types of texts (nonfiction, informational, printed, visual, spatial, auditory, and otherwise)

- Write and analyze a variety of types of texts to identify
  - The audiences and purposes for which they are intended
  - The key choices of content, organization, evidence, and language use made by their author(s)
  - The relationships among these key choices and the ways that the text(s) appeal or speak to different audiences
- Write for different audiences, purposes, and contexts

Developing Critical Thinking Through Writing and Reading

Critical thinking is the ability to analyze a situation or text and make thoughtful decisions based on that analysis.

Writers may be asked to write about familiar or unfamiliar texts, examining assumptions about the texts held by different audiences. Through critical writing and reading, writers think through ideas, problems, and issues; identify and challenge assumptions; and explore multiple ways of understanding. This is important in college as writers are asked to move past obvious or surface-level interpretations and use writing to make sense of and respond to written, visual, verbal, and other texts that they encounter.

Students will

- Read texts from multiple points of view (e.g., sympathetic to a writer's position and critical of it) and in ways that are appropriate to the academic discipline or other contexts where the texts are being used
- Analyze diverse texts which responsibly articulate difference (gender, class, ethnicity, sexual orientation) as integral to the study of language theory and practice
- Write about texts for multiple purposes including (but not limited to) interpretation, synthesis, response, summary, critique, and analysis
- Understand the relationships among language, knowledge, and power

Developing Flexible Writing Processes

Writing processes are the multiple strategies writers use to approach and undertake writing tasks.

Writing processes are not linear. Successful writers use different processes that vary over time and depend on the particular task. Writers learn to move back and forth through different stages of writing, adapting those stages to the situation. This ability to employ flexible writing processes is important as students encounter different types of writing tasks that require them to work through the various stages independently to produce final, polished texts.

Students will learn to

- Understand writing assignments as a series of tasks, including finding, evaluating, analyzing, and synthesizing appropriate content and sources;
- Practice all aspects of writing processes including invention, drafting, sharing with others, revising in response to reviews, and editing;
- Generate ideas and texts using a variety of processes and situate those ideas within different academic disciplines and contexts;

- Incorporate evidence and ideas from written, visual, graphic, verbal, and other kinds of texts;
- Use feedback to revise texts to make them appropriate for the academic discipline or context for which the writing is intended;
- Work with others in various stages of writing; and
- Reflect on how different writing tasks and elements of the writing process contribute to their development as a writer.

Developing Knowledge of Conventions

Conventions are the formal rules and informal guidelines that define what is considered to be correct (or appropriate) and incorrect (or inappropriate) in a piece of writing. Conventions include the surface features of a text such as mechanics, spelling, and attribution of sources, as well as more global concerns such as content, tone, style, organization, and evidence. Conventions arise from a history of use and reflect the collected wisdom of the relevant readers and writers about the most effective ways of communicating in that area.

Conventions facilitate reading by making material easier to comprehend and creating common expectations between writer and reader. The ability to understand, analyze, and make decisions about using conventions appropriate for the purpose, audience, and genre is important in writing.

Students will learn to

- Write, read, and analyze a variety of texts from various disciplines and perspectives in order to
    - Investigate the logic and implications of different conventions,
    - Practice different conventions and analyze expectations for and effects on different audiences,
    - Practice editing and proofreading one's own writing and explore the implications of editing choices,
    - Explore the concept of intellectual property (i.e., ownership of ideas) as it is used in different disciplines and contexts, and
    - Identify differences between errors and intentional variations from expected conventions.
- Read and analyze print and multimodal texts composed in various styles, tones, and levels of formality;
- Use resources (such as print and online writing handbooks), with guidance, to edit drafts;
- Practice various approaches to the documentation and attribution of sources; and
- Examine the underlying logic in commonly used citation systems (e.g., MLA).

Composing in Multiple Environments

Composing in multiple environments refers to the ability to create writing using everything from traditional pen and paper to electronic technologies.

All forms of writing involve technologies, whether pen and paper, word processor, video recorder, or webpage. Research attests to the extensive writing that students produce electronically; composing in or outside of school, students and instructors can build on these experiences. As electronic technologies continue to spread and evolve, writers need to be thoughtful, effective users who are able to adapt to changing electronic environments.

Students will learn to

- Use a variety of electronic technologies intentionally to compose;
- Analyze print and electronic texts to determine how technologies affect reading and writing processes;
- Use technology strategically and with a clear purpose that enhances the writing for the audience;
- Analyze situations where print and electronic texts are used, examining why and how people have chosen to compose using different technologies; and
- Analyze electronic texts (their own and others') to explore and develop criteria for assessing the texts.

Outcomes developed by Council of Writing Program Administrators, National Council of Teachers of English, and National Writing Project. Published January 2011 by CWPA, NCTE and NWP.

ENGLISH 1310 ASSESSMENT CRITERIA

English 1310 core competencies in theoretical content, process skills, and critical reflection are assessed in multiple ways. Course outcomes are linked to competencies listed in the program's assessment rubric below. The Writing Program utilizes a rubric to assess documented analytical essays as the standard genre of the course. Instructors will adapt the writing program rubric to focus on particular criteria appropriate for each essay assignment.

Essays can be scored "HC" for highly competent, "C" for competent, "PC" for partially competent, and "NW" for needs work in each domain. Essays also receive a final rating using the same performance ranges: HC, C, PC, NW.

Criteria	Score	Feedback
Introduces topic and builds context Writer develops a context to guide the reader's entry into the topic. Rhetorical task is defined: texts, authors, and essential details.		
Conceptualizes purpose rhetorically Writer clearly states purpose/thesis.		
Chooses rhetorically appropriate evidence Writer selects effective evidence, details, or excerpts to substantively support stated aim.		
Integrates evidence Writer introduces and integrates evidence from the readings, mindful of syntactical options.		
Understands rhetorical concepts Writer's analysis reveals a solid understanding and effective application of rhetorical concepts and principles.		
Demonstrates analytical reasoning and development Writer interprets and analyzes evidence in support of stated aim.		
Organizes Writer effectively organizes essay to guide reader through the development of ideas.		

Follows language conventions Writer demonstrates control of language and may use language to enhance aim, including sentence boundaries, agreement, rhetorical effect.		
Adheres to MLA citations & formatting Writer follows MLA format, in-text source citations, and works cited.		
Shows understanding of topics and degree of insight Writer demonstrates understanding of the topic and offers insight beyond a reiterative account.		

TABLE OF CONTENTS

Alphabetical by Author

Sherman Alexie — The Joy of Reading and Writing: Superman and Me, *1*

Maya Angelou — Graduation, *4*

Susan B. Anthony — On Women's Right to Vote, *13*

Gloria Anzaldúa — How to Tame a Wild Tongue, *19*

Jonathan E. Barbur and Trischa Goodnow — The *Arete* of Amusement: An Aristotelian Perspective on the Ethos of *The Daily Show*, *28*

David Bartholomae — Inventing the University, *44*

George W. Bush — Address to a Joint Session of Congress and the American People, *50*

Nicholas Carr — Is Google Making Us Stupid?, *56*

Carrie Chapman Catt — Speech before Congress, *64*

Hillary Rodham Clinton — Women's Rights Are Human Rights, *68*

Mary Crow Dog and Richard Erdoes — Civilize Them with a Stick, *73*

Kevin Davis — Does Coming to College Mean Becoming Someone New?, *80*

Thomas de Zengotita — The Numbing of the American Mind, *86*

Frederick Douglass — How I Learned to Read and Write, *96*

Frederick Douglass — Letter to My Master, Thomas Auld, *101*

Frederick Douglass — What to the Slave Is the Fourth of July?, *107*

Eight Alabama Clergymen — Public Statement, *126*

Mort Gerberg — What Is a Cartoon?, *128*

Stuart Hirschberg — The Rhetoric of Advertising, *132*

L. Lennie Irvin — What Is Academic Writing?, *139*

Thomas Jefferson — The Declaration of Independence, *150*

John F. Kennedy — Cuban Missile Crisis, *155*

Jean Kilbourne — "Two Ways a Woman Can Get Hurt": Advertising and Violence, *161*

Martin Luther King, Jr.   Letter from Birmingham Jail, *174*

Stephen King   What Writing Is, *187*

Anne Lamott   Shitty First Drafts, *191*

Abraham Lincoln   The Gettysburg Address, *195*

William Lutz   With These Words, I Can Sell You Anything, *197*

Malcolm X   Discovering the Power of Language, *208*

Malcolm X   The Ballot or the Bullet, *211*

Michael Pollan   Why Bother?, *223*

Ronald Reagan   Address at Brandenburg Gate, *230*

Richard Rodriguez   Aria: A Memoir of a Bilingual Childhood, *236*

Franklin Delano Roosevelt   The Great Arsenal of Democracy, *246*

Karen Rosenberg   Reading Games: Strategies for Reading Scholarly Sources, *254*

Zadie Smith   Generation Why?, *262*

Luther Standing Bear   What the Indian Means to America, *273*

Elizabeth Cady Stanton   Seneca Falls Declaration, *281*

Richard Straub   Responding—Really Responding— to Other Students' Writing, *286*

Amy Tan   Mother Tongue, *298*

Deborah Tannen   Sex, Lies and Conversation: Why Is It So Hard for Men and Women to Talk to Each Other?, *303*

Sojourner Truth   Ain't I a Woman?, *308*

Elie Wiesel   The Perils of Indifference, *310*

About the Contributors, *315*

Credits, *318*

TOPICAL CLUSTERS

Language Acts to Develop Literacy and Identity

Sherman Alexie	The Joy of Reading and Writing: Superman and Me, *1*
Maya Angelou	Graduation, *4*
Gloria Anzaldúa	How to Tame a Wild Tongue, *19*
Kevin Davis	Does Coming to College Mean Becoming Someone New?, *80*
Mary Crow Dog and Richard Erdoes	Civilize Them with a Stick, *73*
Frederick Douglass	How I Learned to Read and Write, *96*
Malcolm X	Discovering the Power of Language, *208*
Richard Rodriguez	Aria: A Memoir of a Bilingual Childhood, *236*
Amy Tan	Mother Tongue, *298*
Sojourner Truth	Ain't I a Woman?, *308*

Language Acts in Public Spheres

Eight Alabama Clergymen	Public Statement, *126*
Frederick Douglass	Letter to My Master, Thomas Auld, *101*
Frederick Douglass	What to the Slave Is the Fourth of July?, *107*
Thomas Jefferson	Declaration of Independence, *150*
Martin Luther King, Jr.	Letter from Birmingham Jail, *174*
Michael Pollan	Why Bother?, *223*
Zadie Smith	Generation Why?, *262*
Elizabeth Cady Stanton	Seneca Falls Declaration, *281*

Language Acts to Address International Issues

George W. Bush	Address to a Joint Session of Congress and the American People, *50*
Hillary Rodham Clinton	Women's Rights Are Human Rights, *68*
Thomas Jefferson	The Declaration of Independence, *150*

John F. Kennedy   Cuban Missile Crisis, *155*

Michael Pollan   Why Bother?, *223*

Franklin Delano Roosevelt   The Great Arsenal of Democracy, *246*

Language Acts to Critique Culture

Jonathan E. Barbur and   The *Arete* of Amusement: An Aristotelian Perspective
Trischa Goodnow   on the Ethos of *The Daily Show*, *28*

Nicholas Carr   Is Google Making Us Stupid?, *56*

Thomas de Zengotita   The Numbing of the American Mind, *86*

Mort Gerberg   What Is a Cartoon?, *128*

Stuart Hirschberg   The Rhetoric of Advertising, *132*

Jean Kilbourne   "Two Ways a Woman Can Get Hurt":
                                    Advertising and Violence, *161*

William Lutz   With These Words, I Can Sell You Anything, *197*

Michael Pollan   Why Bother?, *223*

Zadie Smith   Generation Why?, *262*

Deborah Tannen   Sex, Lies and Conversation: Why Is It So Hard for
                                    Men and Women to Talk to Each Other?, *303*

Language Acts in Gender Arguments

Susan B. Anthony   On Women's Right to Vote, *13*

Gloria Anzaldúa   How to Tame a Wild Tongue, *19*

Carrie Chapman Catt   Speech before Congress, *64*

Hillary Rodham Clinton   Women's Rights Are Human Rights, *68*

Mary Crow Dog and   Civilize Them with a Stick, *73*
Richard Erdoes

Jean Kilbourne   "Two Ways a Woman Can Get Hurt": Advertising
                                    and Violence, *161*

Elizabeth Cady Stanton   Seneca Falls Declaration, *281*

Amy Tan   Mother Tongue, *298*

Deborah Tannen   Sex, Lies and Conversation: Why Is It So Hard for
                                    Men and Women to Talk to Each Other?, *303*

Sojourner Truth   Ain't I a Woman?, *308*

Language Acts in American History

Susan B. Anthony	On Women's Right to Vote, *13*
George W. Bush	Address to a Joint Session of Congress and the American People, *50*
Carrie Chapman Catt	Speech before Congress, *64*
Eight Alabama Clergymen	Public Statement, *126*
Frederick Douglass	What to the Slave Is the Fourth of July?, *107*
Thomas Jefferson	The Declaration of Independence, *150*
John F. Kennedy	Cuban Missile Crisis, *155*
Martin Luther King, Jr.	Letter from Birmingham Jail, *174*
Abraham Lincoln	The Gettysburg Address, *195*
Malcolm X	The Ballot or the Bullet, *211*
Franklin Delano Roosevelt	The Great Arsenal of Democracy, *246*
Luther Standing Bear	What the Indian Means to America, *273*
Elizabeth Cady Stanton	Seneca Falls Declaration, *281*
Sojourner Truth	Ain't I a Woman?, *308*
Elie Wiesel	The Perils of Indifference, *310*

Language Acts through Writing Process Theory

Sherman Alexie	The Joy of Reading and Writing: Superman and Me, *1*
David Bartholomae	Inventing the University, *44*
Kevin Davis	Does Coming to College Mean Becoming Someone New?, *80*
L. Lennie Irvin	What Is Academic Writing?, *139*
Stephen King	What Writing Is, *187*
Anne Lamott	Shitty First Drafts, *191*
Karen Rosenberg	Reading Games: Strategies for Reading Scholarly Sources, *254*
Richard Straub	Responding—Really Responding—to Other Students' Writing, *286*

Language Acts Examined through Rhetorical Theory

Jonathan E. Barbur and   The *Arete* of Amusement: An Aristotelian Perspective
Trischa Goodnow   on the Ethos of *The Daily Show* , 28

Mort Gerberg   What Is a Cartoon?, *128*

Stuart Hirschberg   The Rhetoric of Advertising, *132*

GENRE CLUSTERS

Analyses

Jonathan E. Barbur and Trischa Goodnow	The *Arete* of Amusement: An Aristotelian Perspective on the Ethos of *The Daily Show*, 28
David Bartholomae	Inventing the University, 44
Nicholas Carr	Is Google Making Us Stupid?, 56
Thomas de Zengotita	The Numbing of the American Mind, 86
Mort Gerberg	What Is a Cartoon?, 128
Stuart Hirschberg	The Rhetoric of Advertising, 132
L. Lennie Irvin	What Is Academic Writing?, 139
Jean Kilbourne	"Two Ways a Woman Can Get Hurt": Advertising and Violence, 161
William Lutz	With These Words, I Can Sell You Anything, 197
Michael Pollan	Why Bother?, 223
Zadie Smith	Generation Why?, 262
Deborah Tannen	Sex, Lies and Conversation: Why Is It So Hard for Men and Women to Talk to Each Other?, 303

Declarations, Proclamations, and Letters

Frederick Douglass	Letter to My Master, Thomas Auld, 101
Eight Alabama Clergymen	Public Statement, 126
Thomas Jefferson	The Declaration of Independence, 150
Martin Luther King, Jr.	Letter from Birmingham Jail, 174
Abraham Lincoln	The Gettysburg Address, 195
Luther Standing Bear	What the Indian Means to America, 273
Elizabeth Cady Stanton	Seneca Falls Declaration, 281

Global Addresses

George W. Bush — Address to a Joint Session of Congress and the American People, *50*

Hillary Rodham Clinton — Women's Rights Are Human Rights, *68*

Thomas Jefferson — The Declaration of Independence, *150*

John F. Kennedy — Cuban Missile Crisis, *155*

Franklin Delano Roosevelt — The Great Arsenal of Democracy, *246*

Literacy Autobiographies

Maya Angelou — Graduation, *4*

Gloria Anzaldúa — How to Tame a Wild Tongue, *19*

Mary Crow Dog and Richard Erdoes — Civilize Them with a Stick, *73*

Frederick Douglass — How I Learned to Read and Write, *96*

Malcolm X — Discovering the Power of Language, *208*

Richard Rodriguez — Aria: Memoir of a Bilingual Childhood, *236*

Amy Tan — Mother Tongue, *298*

Sojourner Truth — Ain't I a Woman?, *308*

Periodical Articles

Nicholas Carr — Is Google Making Us Stupid?, *56*

Thomas de Zengotita — The Numbing of the American Mind, *86*

Michael Pollan — Why Bother?, *223*

Richard Rodriguez — Aria: A Memoir of a Bilingual Childhood, *236*

Zadie Smith — Generation Why?, *262*

Deborah Tannen — Sex, Lies and Conversation: Why Is It So Hard for Men and Women to Talk to Each Other?, *303*

The Joy of Reading and Writing: Superman and Me

Sherman Alexie

One of the best-known Native American writers working today, Sherman Alexie (b. 1966) is a critically acclaimed author, poet, and filmmaker. Some of his more notable works include his collection of short stories, *The Lone Ranger and Tonto Fist Fight in Heaven* (1993), *The Absolutely True Diary of a Part-Time Indian (2007)*, and his screenplay for *Smoke Signals (1998)*. Born on the Spokane Indian Reservation in Washington, Alexie grew up surrounded by poverty, alcoholism, and abuse. A child of Spokane and Coeur d'Alene tribal descent who later left the reservation to attend an all-white high school, his writing is a product of his experience as both insider and outsider within American society. Often investigating the intersections of Native American culture with mainstream culture, Alexie's work attempts to reconstruct American Indian identity and disrupt the rampant mythologizing and stereotyping of Native American life commonly found in popular media. The following selection, originally published in *The Most Wonderful Books: Writers on Discovering the Pleasures of Reading*, recalls Alexie's childhood memory of learning to read alongside the hardships of reservation life.

—RT

1   I learned to read with a Superman comic book. Simple enough, I suppose. I cannot recall which particular Superman comic book I read, nor can I remember which villain he fought in that issue. I cannot remember the plot, nor the means by which I obtained the comic book. What I can remember is this: I was 3 years old, a Spokane Indian boy living with his family on the Spokane Indian Reservation in eastern Washington state. We were poor by most standards, but one of my parents usually managed to find some minimum-wage job or another, which made us middle-class by reservation standards. I had a brother and three sisters. We lived on a combination of irregular paychecks, hope, fear and government surplus food.

2   My father, who is one of the few Indians who went to Catholic school on purpose, was an avid reader of westerns, spy thrillers, murder mysteries, gangster epics, basketball player biographies and anything else he could find. He bought his books by the pound at Dutch's Pawn Shop, Goodwill, Salvation Army and Value Village. When he had extra money, he bought new novels at supermarkets, convenience stores and hospital gift shops. Our house was filled with books. They were stacked in crazy piles in the bathroom, bedrooms and living room. In a fit of unemployment-inspired creative energy, my father built a set of bookshelves and soon filled them with a random assortment of books about the Kennedy assassination, Watergate, the Vietnam War and the entire 23-book series of the Apache westerns. My father loved books, and since I loved my father with an aching devotion, I decided to love books as well.

3   I can remember picking up my father's books before I could read. The words themselves were mostly foreign, but I still remember the exact moment when I first understood,
with a sudden clarity, the purpose of a paragraph. I didn't have the vocabulary to say
"paragraph," but I realized that a paragraph was a fence that held words. The words inside
a paragraph worked together for a common purpose. They had some specific reason for
being inside the same fence. This knowledge delighted me. I began to think of everything
in terms of paragraphs. Our reservation was a small paragraph within the United States.
My family's house was a paragraph, distinct from the other paragraphs of the LeBrets to
the north, the Fords to our south and the Tribal School to the west. Inside our house, each
family member existed as a separate paragraph but still had genetics and common experiences to link us. Now, using this logic, I can see my changed family as an essay of seven
paragraphs: mother, father, older brother, the deceased sister, my younger twin sisters
and our adopted little brother.

4   At the same time I was seeing the world in paragraphs, I also picked up that Superman comic book. Each panel, complete with picture, dialogue and narrative was a three-
dimensional paragraph. In one panel, Superman breaks through a door. His suit is red, blue
and yellow. The brown door shatters into many pieces. I look at the narrative above the picture. I cannot read the words, but I assume it tells me that "Superman is breaking down the
door." Aloud, I pretend to read the words and say, "Superman is breaking down the door."
Words, dialogue, also float out of Superman's mouth. Because he is breaking down the
door, I assume he says, "I am breaking down the door." Once again, I pretend to read the
words and say aloud, "I am breaking down the door." In this way, I learned to read.

5   This might be an interesting story all by itself. A little Indian boy teaches himself to
read at an early age and advances quickly. He reads "Grapes of Wrath" in kindergarten
when other children are struggling through "Dick and Jane." If he'd been anything but
an Indian boy living on the reservation, he might have been called a prodigy. But he is
an Indian boy living on the reservation and is simply an oddity. He grows into a man who
often speaks of his childhood in the third-person, as if it will somehow dull the pain and
make him sound more modest about his talents.

6   A smart Indian is a dangerous person, widely feared and ridiculed by Indians and
non-Indians alike. I fought with my classmates on a daily basis. They wanted me to stay
quiet when the non-Indian teacher asked for answers, for volunteers, for help. We were
Indian children who were expected to be stupid. Most lived up to those expectations
inside the classroom but subverted them on the outside. They struggled with basic reading in school but could remember how to sing a few dozen powwow songs. They were
monosyllabic in front of their non-Indian teachers but could tell complicated stories and
jokes at the dinner table. They submissively ducked their heads when confronted by a
non-Indian adult but would slug it out with the Indian bully who was 10 years older. As
Indian children, we were expected to fail in the non-Indian world. Those who failed were
ceremonially accepted by other Indians and appropriately pitied by non-Indians.

7   I refused to fail. I was smart. I was arrogant. I was lucky. I read books late into the
night, until I could barely keep my eyes open. I read books at recess, then during lunch,
and in the few minutes left after I had finished my classroom assignments. I read books

in the car when my family traveled to powwows or basketball games. In shopping malls, I ran to the bookstores and read bits and pieces of as many books as I could. I read the books my father brought home from the pawnshops and secondhand. I read the books I borrowed from the library. I read the backs of cereal boxes. I read the newspaper. I read the bulletins posted on the walls of the school, the clinic, the tribal offices, the post office. I read junk mail. I read auto-repair manuals. I read magazines. I read anything that had words and paragraphs. I read with equal parts joy and desperation. I loved those books, but I also knew that love had only one purpose. I was trying to save my life.

8   Despite all the books I read, I am still surprised I became a writer. I was going to be a pediatrician. These days, I write novels, short stories, and poems. I visit schools and teach creative writing to Indian kids. In all my years in the reservation school system, I was never taught how to write poetry, short stories or novels. I was certainly never taught that Indians wrote poetry, short stories and novels. Writing was something beyond Indians. I cannot recall a single time that a guest teacher visited the reservation. There must have been visiting teachers. Who were they? Where are they now? Do they exist? I visit the schools as often as possible. The Indian kids crowd the classroom. Many are writing their own poems, short stories and novels. They have read my books. They have read many other books. They look at me with bright eyes and arrogant wonder. They are trying to save their lives. Then there are the sullen and already defeated Indian kids who sit in the back rows and ignore me with theatrical precision. The pages of their notebooks are empty. They carry neither pencil nor pen. They stare out the window. They refuse and resist. "Books," I say to them. "Books," I say. I throw my weight against their locked doors. The door holds. I am smart. I am arrogant. I am lucky. I am trying to save our lives.

Critical Reading Questions:

- **Interpretation:** Alexie explains that his love of books "had only one purpose." He later describes that purpose as "trying to save our lives." What does he mean by this statement?

- **Rhetorical analysis:** How does Sherman Alexie juxtapose popular cultural media with real-life hardships to enhance his ethos? How does this strategy reinforce his argument?

- **Rhetorical analysis:** Alexie explains that he "read with equal parts joy and desperation." Explore whether or not he is able to invoke these emotions throughout the essay. What effect is he trying to achieve by doing so?

Graduation

Maya Angelou

This piece originated as a chapter in Angelou's bestselling book *I Know Why the Caged Bird Sings* (1969), one of the first autobiographies by a twentieth century black woman to reach a wide readership. She enlarges the genre of autobiography by employing several techniques associated with fiction, such as dialogue, characterization, and lyricism. She features these elements in the following chapter, which focuses on Angelou's eighth grade graduation in Stamps, Arkansas. Ultimately, this is a story of growth—of recognition and appreciation for race and community, as well as an awakening to the power of language to construct and re-construct identities for self and others. Angelou died in 2014 at the age of 86.

—CG

1   The children in Stamps trembled visibly with anticipation. Some adults were excited too, but to be certain the whole young population had come down with graduation epidemic. Large classes were graduating from both the grammar school and the high school. Even those who were years removed from their own day of glorious release were anxious to help with preparations as a kind of dry run. The junior students who were moving into the vacating classes' chairs were tradition-bound to show their talents for leadership and management. They strutted through the school and around the campus exerting pressure on the lower grades. Their authority was so new that occasionally if they pressed a little too hard it had to be overlooked. After all, next term was coming, and it never hurt a sixth grader to have a play sister in the eighth grade, or a tenth-year student to be able to call a twelfth grader Bubba. So all was endured in a spirit of shared understanding. But the graduating classes themselves were the nobility. Like travelers with exotic destinations on their minds, the graduates were remarkably forgetful. They came to school without their books, or tablets or even pencils. Volunteers fell over themselves to secure replacements for the missing equipment. When accepted, the willing workers might or might not be thanked, and it was of no importance to the pregraduation rites. Even teachers were respectful of the now quiet and aging seniors, and tended to speak to them, if not as equals, as beings only slightly lower than themselves. After tests were returned and grades given, the student body, which acted like an extended family, knew who did well, who excelled, and what piteous ones had failed.

2   Unlike the white high school, Lafayette County Training School distinguished itself by having neither lawn, nor hedges, nor tennis court, nor climbing ivy. Its two buildings (main classrooms, the grade school and home economics) were set on a dirt hill with no fence to limit either its boundaries or those of bordering farms. There was a large expanse to the left of the school which was used alternately as a baseball diamond or a basketball court. Rusty hoops on the swaying poles represented the permanent recreational equipment,

although bats and balls could be borrowed from the P.E. teacher if the borrower was qualified and if the diamond wasn't occupied.

3   Over this rocky area relieved by a few shady tall persimmon trees the graduating class walked. The girls often held hands and no longer bothered to speak to the lower students. There was a sadness about them, as if this old world was not their home and they were bound for higher ground. The boys, on the other hand, had become more friendly, more outgoing. A decided change from the closed attitude they projected while studying for finals. Now they seemed not ready to give up the old school, the familiar paths and classrooms. Only a small percentage would be continuing on to college—one of the South's A & M (agricultural and mechanical) schools, which trained Negro youths to be carpenters, farmers, handymen, masons, maids, cooks and baby nurses. Their future rode heavily on their shoulders, and blinded them to the collective joy that had pervaded the lives of the boys and girls in the grammar school graduating class.

4   Parents who could afford it had ordered new shoes and ready-made clothes for themselves from Sears and Roebuck or Montgomery Ward. They also engaged the best seamstresses to make the floating graduating dresses and to cut down secondhand pants which would be pressed to a military slickness for the important event.

5   Oh, it was important, all right. Whitefolks would attend the ceremony, and two or three would speak of God and home, and the Southern way of life, and Mrs. Parsons, the principal's wife, would play the graduation march while the lower-grade graduates paraded down the aisles and took their seats below the platform. The high school seniors would wait in empty classrooms to make their dramatic entrance.

6   In the Store I was the person of the moment. The birthday girl. The center. Bailey had graduated the year before, although to do so he had had to forfeit all pleasures to make up for his time lost in Baton Rouge.

7   My class was wearing butter-yellow piqué dresses, and Momma launched out on mine. She smocked the yoke into tiny crisscrossing puckers, then shirred the rest of the bodice. Her dark fingers ducked in and out of the lemony cloth as she embroidered raised daisies around the hem. Before she considered herself finished she had added a crocheted cuff on the puff sleeves, and a pointy crocheted collar.

8   I was going to be lovely. A walking model of all the various styles of fine hand sewing and it didn't worry me that I was only twelve years old and merely graduating from the eighth grade. Besides, many teachers in Arkansas Negro schools had only that diploma and were licensed to impart wisdom.

9   The days had become longer and more noticeable. The faded beige of former times had been replaced with strong and sure colors. I began to see my classmates' clothes, their skin tones, and the dust that waved off pussy willows. Clouds that lazed across the sky were objects of great concern to me. Their shiftier shapes might have held a message that in my new happiness and with a little bit of time I'd soon decipher. During that period I looked at the arch of heaven so religiously my neck kept a steady ache. I had taken to smiling more often, and my jaws hurt from the unaccustomed activity. Between the two physical sore spots, I suppose I could have been uncomfortable, but that was not the case. As a member of the winning team (the graduating class of 1940) I had outdistanced unpleasant sensations by miles. I was headed for the freedom of the open fields.

10   Youth and social approval allied themselves with me and we trammeled memories of slights and insults. The wind of our swift passage remodeled my features. Lost tears were pounded to mud and then to dust. Years of withdrawal were brushed aside and left behind, as hanging ropes of parasitic moss.

11   My work alone had awarded me a top place and I was going to be one of the first called in the graduating ceremonies. On the classroom blackboard, as well as on the bulletin board in the auditorium, there were blue stars and white stars and red stars. No absences, no tardinesses, and my academic work was among the best of the year. I could say the preamble to the Constitution even faster than Bailey. We timed ourselves often: "WethepeopleoftheUnitedStatesinordertoformamoreperfectunion…" I had memorized the Presidents of the United States from Washington to Roosevelt in chronological as well as alphabetical order.

12   My hair pleased me too. Gradually the black mass had lengthened and thickened, so that it kept at last to its braided pattern, and I didn't have to yank my scalp off when I tried to comb it.

13   Louise and I had rehearsed the exercises until we tired out ourselves. Henry Reed was class valedictorian. He was a small, very black boy with hooded eyes, a long, broad nose and an oddly shaped head. I had admired him for years because each term he and I vied for the best grades in our class. Most often he bested me, but instead of being disappointed I was pleased that we shared top places between us. Like many Southern Black children, he lived with his grandmother, who was as strict as Momma and as kind as she knew how to be. He was courteous, respectful and soft-spoken to elders, but on the playground he chose to play the roughest games. I admired him. Anyone, I reckoned, sufficiently afraid or sufficiently dull could be polite. But to be able to operate at a top level with both adults and children was admirable.

14   His valedictory speech was entitled "To Be or Not To Be." The rigid tenth-grade teacher helped him to write it. He'd been working on the dramatic stresses for months.

15   The weeks until graduation were filled with heady activities. A group of small children were to be presented in a play about buttercups and daisies and bunny rabbits. They could be heard throughout the building practicing their hops and their little songs that sounded like silver bells. The older girls (non-graduates, of course) were assigned the task of making refreshments for the night's festivities. A tangy scent of ginger, cinnamon, nutmeg and chocolate wafted around the home economics building as the budding cooks made samples for themselves and their teachers.

16   In every corner of the workshop, axes and saws split fresh timber as the woodshop boys made sets and stage scenery. Only the graduates were left out of the general bustle. We were free to sit in the library at the back of the building or look in quite detachedly, naturally, on the measures being taken for our event.

17   Even the minister preached on graduation the Sunday before. His subject was, "Let your light so shine that men will see your good works and praise your Father, Who is in Heaven." Although the sermon was purported to be addressed to us, he used the occasion to speak to backsliders, gamblers, and general ne'er-do-wells. But since he had called our names at the beginning of the service we were mollified.

18   Among Negroes the tradition was to give presents to children going only from one grade to another. How much more important this was when the person was graduating at the top of the class. Uncle Willie and Momma had sent away for a Mickey Mouse watch like Bailey's. Louise gave me four embroidered handkerchiefs. (I gave her three crocheted doilies.) Mrs. Sneed, the minister's wife, made me an underskirt to wear for graduation, and nearly every customer gave me a nickel or maybe even a dime with the instruction "Keep on moving to higher ground," or some such encouragement.

19   Amazingly the great day finally dawned and I was out of bed before I knew it. I threw open the back door to see it more clearly, but Momma said, "Sister, come away from that door and put your robe on."

20   I hoped the memory of that morning would never leave me. Sunlight itself was still young, and the day had none of the insistence maturity would bring it in a few hours. In my robe and barefoot in the backyard, under cover of going to see about my new beans, I gave myself up to the gentle warmth and thanked God that no matter what evil I had done in my life He had allowed me to live to see this day. Somewhere in my fatalism I had expected to die, accidentally, and never have the chance to walk up the stairs in the auditorium and gracefully receive my hard-earned diploma. Out of God's merciful bosom I had won reprieve.

21   Bailey came out in his robe and gave me a box wrapped in Christmas paper. He said he had saved his money for months to pay for it. It felt like a box of chocolates, but I knew Bailey wouldn't save money to buy candy when we had all we could want under our noses.

22   He was as proud of the gift as I. It was a soft-leather-bound copy of a collection of poems by Edgar Allan Poe, or, as Bailey and I called him, "Eap." I turned to "Annabel Lee" and we walked up and down the garden rows, the cool dirt between our toes, reciting the beautifully sad lines.

23   Momma made a Sunday breakfast although it was only Friday. After we finished the blessing, I opened my eyes to find the watch on my plate. It was a dream of a day. Everything went smoothly and to my credit I didn't have to be reminded or scolded for anything. Near evening I was too jittery to attend to chores, so Bailey volunteered to do all before his bath.

24   Days before, we had made a sign for the Store and as we turned out the lights Momma hung the cardboard over the doorknob. It read clearly: CLOSED. GRADUATION.

25   My dress fitted perfectly and everyone said that I looked like a sunbeam in it. On the hill, going toward the school, Bailey walked behind with Uncle Willie, who muttered, "Go on, Ju." He wanted him to walk ahead with us because it embarrassed him to have to walk so slowly. Bailey said he'd let the ladies walk together, and the men would bring up the rear. We all laughed, nicely.

26   Little children dashed by out of the dark like fireflies. Their crepe-paper dresses and butterfly wings were not made for running and we heard more than one rip, dryly, and the regretful "uh uh" that followed.

27   The school blazed without gaiety. The windows seemed cold and unfriendly from the lower hill. A sense of ill-fated timing crept over me, and if Momma hadn't reached

for my hand I would have drifted back to Bailey and Uncle Willie, and possibly beyond. She made a few slow jokes about my feet getting cold, and tugged me along to the now-strange building.

28   Around the front steps, assurance came back. There were my fellow "greats," the graduating class. Hair brushed back, legs oiled, new dresses and pressed pleats, fresh pocket handkerchiefs and little hand-bags, all homesewn. Oh, we were up to snuff, all right. I joined my comrades and didn't even see my family go in to find seats in the crowded auditorium.

29   The school band struck up a march and all classes filed in as had been rehearsed. We stood in front of our seats, as assigned, and on a signal from the choir director, we sat. No sooner had this been accomplished than the band started to play the national anthem. We rose again and sang the song, after which we recited the pledge of allegiance. We remained standing for a brief minute before the choir director and the principal signaled to us, rather desperately I thought, to take our seats. The command was so unusual that our carefully rehearsed and smooth-running machine was thrown off. For a full minute we fumbled for our chairs and bumped into each other awkwardly. Habits change or solidify under pressure, so in our state of nervous tension we had been ready to follow our usual assembly pattern: the American National Anthem, then the pledge of allegiance, then the song every Black person I knew called the Negro National Anthem. All done in the same key, with the same passion and most often standing on the same foot.

30   Finding my seat at last, I was overcome with a presentiment of worse things to come. Something unrehearsed, unplanned, was going to happen, and we were going to be made to look bad. I distinctly remember being explicit in the choice of pronoun. It was "we," the graduating class, the unit, that concerned me then.

31   The principal welcomed "parents and friends" and asked the Baptist minister to lead us in prayer. His invocation was brief and punchy, and for a second I thought we were getting back on the high road to right action. When the principal came back to the dais, however, his voice had changed. Sounds always affected me profoundly and the principal's voice was one of my favorites. During assembly it melted and lowed weakly into the audience. It had not been in my plan to listen to him, but my curiosity was piqued and I straightened up to give him my attention.

32   He was talking about Booker T. Washington, our "late great leader," who said we can be as close as the fingers on the hand, etc....Then he said a few vague things about friendship and the friendship of kindly people to those less fortunate than themselves. With that his voice nearly faded, thin, away. Like a river diminishing to a stream and then to a trickle. But he cleared his throat and said, "Our speaker tonight, who is also our friend, came from Texarkana to deliver the commencement address, but due to the irregularity of the train schedule, he's going to, as they say, 'speak and run.'" He said that we understood and wanted the man to know that we were most grateful for the time he was able to give us and then something about how we were willing always to adjust to another's program, and without more ado—"I give you Mr. Edward Donleavy."

33   Not one but two white men came through the door offstage. The shorter one walked to the speaker's platform, and the tall one moved over to the center seat and sat down. But

that was our principal's seat, and already occupied. The dislodged gentleman bounced around for a long breath or two before the Baptist minister gave him his chair, then with more dignity than the situation deserved, the minister walked off the stage.

34   Donleavy looked at the audience once (on reflection, I'm sure that he wanted only to reassure himself that we were really there), adjusted his glasses and began to read from a sheaf of papers.

35   He was glad "to be here and to see the work going on just as it was in the other schools."

36   At the first "Amen" from the audience I willed the offender to immediate death by choking on the word. But Amen's and Yes, sir's began to fall around the room like rain through a ragged umbrella.

37   He told us of the wonderful changes we children in Stamps had in store. The Central School (naturally, the white school was Central) had already granted improvements that would be in use in the fall. A well-known artist was coming from Little Rock to teach art to them. They were going to have the newest microscopes and chemistry equipment for their laboratory. Mr. Donleavy didn't leave us long in the dark over who made these improvements available to Central High. Nor were we to be ignored in the general betterment scheme he had in mind.

38   He said that he had pointed out to people at a very high level that one of the first-line football tacklers at Arkansas Agricultural and Mechanical College had graduated from good old Lafayette County Training School. Here fewer Amen's were heard. Those few that did break through lay dully in the air with the heaviness of habit.

39   He went on to praise us. He went on to say how he had bragged that "one of the best basketball players at Fisk sank his first ball right here at Lafayette County Training School."

40   The white kids were going to have a chance to become Galileos and Madame Curies and Edisons and Gauguins, and our boys (the girls weren't even in on it) would try to be Jesse Owenses and Joe Louises.

41   Owens and the Brown Bomber were great heroes in our world, but what school official in the white-goddom of Little Rock had the right to decide that those two men must be our only heroes? Who decided that for Henry Reed to become a scientist he had to work like George Washington Carver, as a bootblack, to buy a lousy microscope? Bailey was obviously always going to be too small to be an athlete, so which concrete angel glued to what country seat had decided that if my brother wanted to become a lawyer he had first to pay penance for his skin by picking cotton and hoeing corn and studying correspondence books at night for twenty years?

42   The man's dead words fell like bricks around the auditorium and too many settled in my belly. Constrained by hand-learned manners I couldn't look behind me, but to my left and right the proud graduating class of 1940 had dropped their heads. Every girl in my row had found something new to do with her handkerchief. Some folded the tiny squares into love knots, some into triangles, but most were wadding them, then pressing them flat on their yellow laps.

43   On the dais, the ancient tragedy was being replayed. Professor Parsons sat, a sculptor's reject, rigid. His large, heavy body seemed devoid of will or willingness, and

his eyes said he was no longer with us. The other teachers examined the flag (which was draped stage right) or their notes, or the windows which opened on our now-famous playing diamond.

44   Graduation, the hush-hush of magic time of frills and gifts and congratulations and diplomas, was finished for me before my name was called. The accomplishment was nothing. The meticulous maps, drawn in three colors of ink, learning and spelling decasyl-labic words, memorizing the whole of The *Rape of Lucrece*—it was nothing. Donleavy had exposed us.

45   We were maids and farmers, handymen and washerwomen, and anything higher that we aspired to was farcical and presumptuous. Then I wished that Gabriel Prosser and Nat Turner had killed all white-folks in their beds and that Abraham Lincoln had been assas-sinated before the signing of the Emancipation Proclamation, and that Harriet Tubman had been killed by that blow on her head and Christopher Columbus had drowned in the *Santa Maria*.

46   It was awful to be Negro and have no control over my life. It was brutal to be young and already trained to sit quietly and listen to charges brought against my color and no chance of defense. We should all be dead. I thought I should like to see us all dead, one on top of the other. A pyramid of flesh with the whitefolks at the bottom, as the broad base, then the Indians with their silly tomahawks and teepees and wigwams and treaties, the Negroes with their mops and recipes and cotton sacks and spirituals sticking out of their mouths. The Dutch children should all stumble in their wooden shoes and break their necks. The French should choke to death on the Louisiana Purchase (1803) while silk-worms ate all the Chinese with their stupid pigtails. As a species, we were an abomination. All of us.

47   Donleavy was running for election, and assured our parents that if he won we could count on having the only colored paved playing field in that part of Arkansas. Also—he never looked up to acknowledge the grunts of acceptance—also, we were bound to get some new equipment for the home economics building and the workshop.

48   He finished, and since there was no need to give any more than the most perfunc-tory thank-you's, he nodded to the men on the stage, and the tall white man who was never introduced joined him at the door. They left with the attitude that now they were off to something really important. (The graduation ceremonies at Lafayette County Training School had been a mere preliminary.)

49   The ugliness they left was palpable. An uninvited guest who wouldn't leave. The choir was summoned and sang a modern arrangement of "Onward, Christian Soldiers," with new words pertaining to graduates seeking their place in the world. But it didn't work. Elouise, the daughter of the Baptist minister, recited "Invictus," and I could have cried at the impertinence of "I am the master of my fate, I am the captain of my soul."

50   My name had lost its ring of familiarity and I had to be nudged to go and receive my diploma. All my preparations had fled. I neither marched up to the stage like a conquering Amazon, nor did I look in the audience for Bailey's nod of approval. Marguerite Johnson, I heard the name again, my honors were read, there were noises in the audience of appre-ciation, and I took my place on stage as rehearsed.

51   I thought about colors I hated: ecru, puce, lavender, beige and black.

52   There was shuffling and rustling around me, then Henry Reed was giving his valedictory address, "To Be or Not to Be." Hadn't he heard the whitefolks? We couldn't be, so the question was a waste of time. Henry's voice came out clear and strong. I feared to look at him. Hadn't he got the message? There was no "nobler in the mind" for Negroes because the world didn't think we had minds, and they let us know it. "Outrageous fortune"? Now, that was a joke. When the ceremony was over I had to tell Henry Reed some things. That is, if I still cared. Not "rub," Henry, "erase." "Ah, there's the erase." Us.

53   Henry had been a good student in elocution. His voice rose on tides of promise and fell on waves of warnings. The English teacher had helped him to create a sermon winging through Hamlet's soliloquy. To be a man, a doer, a builder, a leader, or to be a tool, an unfunny joke, a crusher of funky toadstools. I marveled that Henry could go through with the speech as if we had a choice.

54   I had been listening and silently rebutting each sentence with my eyes closed; then there was a hush, which in an audience warns that something unplanned is happening. I looked up and saw Henry Reed, the conservative, the proper, the A student, turn his back to the audience and turn to us (the proud graduating class of 1940) and sing, nearly speaking,

55   *Lift ev'ry voice and sing*
Till earth and heaven ring
Ring with the harmonies of Liberty...

56   It was the poem written by James Weldon Johnson. It was the music composed by J. Rosamond Johnson. It was the Negro National Anthem. Out of habit we were singing it.

57   Our mothers and fathers stood in the dark hall and joined the hymn of encouragement. A kindergarten teacher led the small children onto the stage and the buttercups and daisies and bunny rabbits marked time and tried to follow:

58   *Stony the road we trod*
Bitter the chastening rod
Felt in the days when hop, unborn, had died.
Yet with a steady beat
Have not our weary feet
Come to the place for which our fathers sighed?

59   Every child I knew had learned that song with his ABC's and along with "Jesus Loves Me This I Know." But I personally had never heard it before. Never heard the words, despite the thousands of times I had sung them. Never thought they had anything to do with me.

60   On the other hand, the words of Patrick Henry had made such an impression on me that I had been able to stretch myself tall and trembling and say, "I know not what course others may take, but as for me, give me liberty or give me death."

61   *And now I heard, really for the first time:*
We have come over a way that with tears has been watered,
We have come, treading our path through the blood of the slaughtered.

62   While echoes of the song shivered in the air, Henry Reed bowed his head, said "Thank you," and returned to his place in the line. The tears that slipped down many faces were not wiped away in shame.

63   We were on top again. As always, again. We survived. The depths had been icy and dark, but now a bright sun spoke to our souls. I was no longer simply a member of the proud graduating class of 1940; I was a proud member of the wonderful, beautiful Negro race.

64   Oh, Black known and unknown poets, how often have your auctioned pains sustained us? Who will compute the lonely nights made less lonely by your songs, or the empty pots made less tragic by your tales?

65   If we were a people much given to revealing secrets, we might raise monuments and sacrifice to the memories of our poets, but slavery cured us of that weakness. It may be enough, however, to have it said that we survive in exact relationship to the dedication of our poets (include preachers, musicians and blues singers).

Critical Reading Questions:

- **Analysis:** Consider Angelou's excerpts from religious and/or historical texts. How do these excerpts define her as a Christian? As an African American woman? How do these excerpts and her disposition toward them affirm her American identity?

- **Analysis:** Review Edward Donleavy's speech. How does he use language to attempt to construct and constrain the black community's identity? Where can you see Angelou and/or the community responding directly to Donleavy?

On Women's Right to Vote

Susan B. Anthony

Susan B. Anthony was a leading suffragist in late 1800s America and played a key role in the fight for women's right to vote. In 1872, in a strategic move adopted by the National Woman Suffrage Association, she voted in the presidential election and was arrested and tried. At her trial, Justice Ward Hunt directed the jury to find her guilty, and she was fined. Anthony refused to pay the fine. Had further action been taken, Anthony could have taken her case to the Supreme Court, but Hunt did not order her to be taken into custody. Anthony used the event as motivation for a series of speeches throughout 1873. This speech attempts to prove that women already had the right to vote under U.S. law even though popular and judicial opinion agreed that they did not. Anthony applies the recently passed 14th Amendment (1868) and 15th Amendment (1870) to the U.S. Constitution as evidence supporting her claim. Even though these amendments were intended to give the right to vote to African American men, specifically men who had been freed from slavery after the Civil War, Anthony argues that the language of the amendments also applies to women. Although women in the U.S. were not granted the right to vote until 1918, Anthony's speeches were a vital part of the Women's Suffrage Movement.

—PH

1   I stand before you tonight under indictment for the alleged crime of having voted at the last presidential election, without having a lawful right to vote. It shall be my work this evening to prove to you that in thus voting, I not only committed no crime, but instead simply exercised my citizen's rights, guaranteed to me and all United States citizens by the National Constitution beyond the power of any State to deny.

2   Our democratic-republican government is based on the idea of the natural right of every individual member thereof to a voice and a vote in making and executing the laws. We assert the province of government to be to secure the people in the enjoyment of their inalienable rights. We throw to the winds the old dogma that government can give rights. No one denies that before governments were organized each individual possessed the right to protect his own life, liberty and property. When 100 to 1,000,000 people enter into a free government they do not barter away their natural rights; they simply pledge themselves to protect each other in the enjoyment of them through prescribed judicial and legislative tribunals. They agree to abandon the methods of brute force in the adjustment of their differences and adopt those of civilization.... The Declaration of Independence, the United States Constitution, the constitutions of the several States and the organic laws of the Territories, all alike propose to *protect* the people in the exercise of their God-given rights. Not one of them pretends to bestow rights.

3   All men are created equal, and endowed by their Creator with
certain inalienable rights. Among these are life, liberty and the pursuit of happiness. To secure these, governments are instituted among
men, deriving their just powers from the consent of the governed.

4   Here is no shadow of government authority over rights, or exclusion of any class
from their full and equal enjoyment. Here is pronounced the right of all men, and "con-
sequently," as the Quaker preacher said, "of all women," to a voice in the government.
And here, in this first paragraph of the Declaration, is the assertion of the natural right of
all to the ballot; for how can "the consent of the governed" be given, if the right to vote be
denied?... The women, dissatisfied as they are with this form of government, that enforces
taxation without representation—that compels them to obey laws to which they never
have given their consent—that imprisons and hangs them without a trial by a jury of their
peers—that robs them, in marriage, of the custody of their own persons, wages, and children—are this half of the people who are left wholly at the mercy of the other half, in direct
violation of the spirit and letter of the declarations of the framers of this government, every
one of which was based on the immutable principle of equal rights to all. By the declarations, kings, popes, priests, aristocrats, all were alike dethroned and placed on a common
level, politically, with the lowliest born subject or serf. By them, too, men, as such, were
deprived of their divine right to rule and placed on a political level with women. By the
practice of these declarations all class and caste distinctions would be abolished, and
slave, serf, plebeian, wife, woman, all alike rise from their subject position to the broader
platform of equality.

5   The preamble of the Federal Constitution says:

6   We, the people of the United States, in order to form a more
perfect union, establish justice, insure domestic tranquillity, provide
for the common defence, promote the general welfare, and secure
the blessings of liberty to ourselves and our posterity, do ordain
and establish this Constitution for the United States of America.

7   It was we, the people, not we, the white male citizens, nor we, the male citizens; but
we, the whole people, who formed this Union. We formed it not to give the blessings of liberty but to secure them; not to the half of ourselves and the half of our posterity, but to the
whole people—women as well as men. It is downright mockery to talk to women of their
enjoyment of the blessings of liberty while they are denied the use of the only means of
securing them provided by this democratic-republican government—the ballot....

8   When, in 1871, I asked [Senator Charles Sumner] to declare the power of the
United States Constitution to protect women in their right to vote—as he had done for
black men—he handed me a copy of all his speeches during that reconstruction period,
and said:

9   Put "sex" where I have "race" or "color," and you have here the best
and strongest argument I can make for woman. There is not a doubt but
women have the constitutional right to vote, and I will never vote for a Six-

teenth Amendment to guarantee it to them. I voted for both the Fourteenth and Fifteenth under protest; would never have done it but for the pressing emergency of that hour; would have insisted that the power of the original Constitution to protect all citizens in the equal enjoyment of their rights should have been vindicated through the courts. But the newly-made freedmen had neither the intelligence, wealth nor time to await that slow process. Women do possess all these in an eminent degree, and I insist that they shall appeal to the courts and through them establish the powers of our American magna carta to protect every citizen of the republic.

10   But, friends, when in accordance with Senator Sumner's counsel I went to the ballot-box, last November, and exercised my citizen's right to vote, the courts did not wait for me to appeal to them—they appealed to me, and indicted me on the charge of having voted illegally....

11   For any State to make sex a qualification that must ever result in the disfranchisement of one entire half of the people, is to pass a bill of attainder, an ex post facto law, and is therefore a violation of the supreme law of the land. By it the blessings of liberty are forever withheld from women and their female posterity. For them, this government has no just powers derived from the consent of the governed. For them, this government is not a democracy; it is not a republic. It is the most odious aristocracy ever established on the face of the globe. An oligarchy of wealth, where the rich govern the poor; an oligarchy of learning, where the educated govern the ignorant; or even an oligarchy of race, where the Saxon rules the African, might be endured; but this oligarchy of sex, which makes father, brothers, husband, sons, the oligarchs over the mother and sisters, the wife and daughters of every household; which ordains all men sovereigns, all women subjects—carries discord and rebellion into every home of the nation....

12   It is urged that the use of the masculine pronouns he, his and him in all the constitutions and laws, is proof that only men were meant to be included in their provisions. If you insist on this version of the letter of the law, we shall insist that you be consistent and accept the other horn of the dilemma, which would compel you to exempt women from taxation for the support of the government and from penalties for the violation of laws. There is no she or her or hers in the tax laws, and this is equally true of all the criminal laws.

13   Take for example, the civil rights law which I am charged with having violated; not only are all the pronouns in it masculine, but everybody knows that it was intended expressly to hinder the rebel men from voting. It reads, "If any person shall knowingly vote without his having a lawful right."... I insist if government officials may thus manipulate the pronouns to tax, fine, imprison and hang women, it is their duty to thus change them in order to protect us in our right to vote....

14   Though the words, persons, people, inhabitants, electors, citizens, are all used indiscriminately in the national and State constitutions, there was always a conflict of opinion, prior to the war, as to whether they were synonymous terms, but whatever room there was for doubt, under the old regime, the adoption of the Fourteenth Amendment settled that question forever in its first sentence:

15   All persons born or naturalized in the United States, and
        subject to the jurisdiction thereof, are citizens of the United
        States, and of the State wherein they reside.

16   The second settles the equal status of all citizens:

17   No State shall make or enforce any law which shall abridge the
        privileges or immunities of citizens of the United States; nor shall any State
        deprive any person of life, liberty or property without due process of law, or
        deny to any person within its jurisdiction the equal protection of the laws.

18   The only question left to be settled now is: Are women persons? I scarcely believe any
of our opponents will have the hardihood to say they are not. Being persons, then, women
are citizens, and no State has a right to make any new law, or to enforce any old law, which
shall abridge their privileges or immunities. Hence, every discrimination against women in
the constitutions and laws of the several States is today null and void, precisely as is every
one against negroes.

19   Is the right to vote one of the privileges or immunities of citizens? I think the disfran-
chised ex-rebels and ex-State prisoners all will agree that it is not only one of them, but
the one without which all the others are nothing. Seek first the kingdom of the ballot and all
things else shall be added, is the political injunction. . . .

20   However much the doctors of the law may disagree as to whether people and citizens, in the original Constitution, were one and the same, or whether the privileges and
immunities in the Fourteenth Amendment include the right of suffrage, the question of the
citizen's right to vote is forever settled by the Fifteenth Amendment. "The right of citizens
of the United States to vote shall not be denied or abridged by the United States, or by
any State, on account of race, color or previous condition of servitude." How can the State
deny or abridge the right of the citizen, if the citizen does not possess it? There is no
escape from the conclusion that to vote is the citizen's right, and the specifications of race,
color or previous condition of servitude can in no way impair the force of that emphatic
assertion that the citizen's right to vote shall not be denied or abridged. . . .

21   If, however, you will insist that the Fifteenth Amendment's emphatic interdiction
against robbing United States citizens of their suffrage "on account of race, color or previous condition of servitude," is a recognition of the right of either the United States or any
State to deprive them of the ballot for any or all other reasons, I will prove to you that the
class of citizens for whom I now plead are, by all the principles of our government and
many of the laws of the States, included under the term "previous conditions of servitude."

22   Consider first married women and their legal status. What is servitude? "The condition of a slave." What is a slave? "A person who is robbed of the proceeds of his labor; a
person who is subject to the will of another." By the laws of Georgia, South Carolina and
all the States of the South, the negro had no right to the custody and control of his person.
He belonged to his master. If he were disobedient, the master had the right to use correction. If the negro did not like the correction and ran away, the master had the right to use

coercion to bring him back. By the laws of almost every State in this Union today, North as well as South, the married woman has no right to the custody and control of her person. The wife belongs to the husband; and if she refuses obedience he may use moderate correction, and if she do not like his moderate correction and leave his "bed and board," the husband may use moderate coercion to bring her back. The little word "moderate," you see, is the saving clause for the wife, and would doubtless be overstepped should her offended husband administer his correction with the "cat-o'-nine-tails," or accomplish his coercion with blood-hounds.

23 Again the slave had no right to the earnings of his hands, they belonged to his master; no right to the custody of his children, they belonged to his master; no right to sue or be sued, or to testify in the courts. If he committed a crime, it was the master who must sue or be sued. In many of the States there has been special legislation, giving married women the right to property inherited or received by bequest, or earned by the pursuit of any avocation outside the home; also giving them the right to sue and be sued in matters pertaining to such separate property; but not a single State of this Union has ever secured the wife in the enjoyment of her right to equal ownership of the joint earnings of the marriage copartnership. And since, in the nature of things, the vast majority of married women never earn a dollar by work outside their families, or inherit a dollar from their fathers, it follows that from the day of their marriage to the day of the death of their husbands not one of them ever has a dollar, except it shall please her husband to let her have it. . . .

24 Is anything further needed to prove woman's condition of servitude sufficient to entitle her to the guarantees of the Fifteenth Amendment? Is there a man who will not agree with me that to talk of freedom without the ballot is mockery to the women of this republic, precisely as New England's orator, Wendell Phillips, at the close of the late war declared it to be to the newly emancipated black man? I admit that, prior to the rebellion, by common consent, the right to enslave, as well as to disfranchise both native and foreign born persons, was conceded to the States. But the one grand principle settled by the war and the reconstruction legislation, is the supremacy of the national government to protect the citizens of the United States in their right to freedom and the elective franchise, against any and every interference on the part of the several States; and again and again have the American people asserted the triumph of this principle by their overwhelming majorities for Lincoln and Grant.

25 The one issue of the last two presidential elections was whether the Fourteenth and Fifteenth Amendments should be considered the irrevocable will of the people; and the decision was that they should be, and that it is not only the right, but the duty of the national government to protect all United States citizens in the full enjoyment and free exercise of their privileges and immunities against the attempt of any State to deny or abridge. . . .

26 It is upon this just interpretation of the United States Constitution that our National Woman Suffrage Association, which celebrates the twenty-fifth anniversary of the woman's rights movement next May in New York City, has based all its arguments and action since the passage of these amendments. We no longer petition legislature or Congress to give us the right to vote, but appeal to women everywhere to exercise their too long

neglected "citizen's right." We appeal to the inspectors of election to receive the votes of all United States citizens, as it is their duty to do. We appeal to United States commissioners and marshals to arrest, as is their duty, the inspectors who reject the votes of United States citizens, and leave alone those who perform their duties and accept these votes. We ask the juries to return verdicts of "not guilty" in the cases of law-abiding United States citizens who cast their votes, and the inspectors of election who receive and count them. 27   We ask the judges to render unprejudiced opinions of the law, and wherever there is room for doubt to give the benefit to the side of liberty and equal rights for women, remembering that, as Sumner says, "The true rule of interpretation under our National Constitution, especially since its amendments, is that anything for human rights is constitutional, everything against human rights unconstitutional." It is on this line that we propose to fight our battle for the ballot—peaceably but nevertheless persistently—until we achieve complete triumph and all United States citizens, men and women alike, are recognized as equals in the government.

Critical Reading Questions:

- **Analysis:** Many readers have noted that there is little attempt to appeal directly to pathos in this speech and that Anthony intentionally downplays and weakens its emotional aspects. Do you agree with this claim? How might her decision to avoid pathos be related to the attitudes held about women and arguments made against women's suffrage?

- **Rhetorical analysis:** Anthony selects foundational texts from American history as sources of authority when making her argument. What type of audience might Anthony have been considering when she selected these texts? What logical techniques does she apply to show that these texts all apply to women as well as to men?

How to Tame a Wild Tongue

Gloria Anzaldúa

This following reading originates from Anzaldúa's most famous work, *Borderlands/La Frontera: The New Mestiza* (1999). As the title suggests, this text explores several boundaries, including those of culture, language, and genre. In this selection, Anzaldúa features autobiography, poetry, and cultural theory, using a range of languages and dialects. Her rhetorical choices come together to support several arguments; perhaps the central argument is the indelible connection between language and identity. Her strategic resistance to monolingual delivery highlights the tensions and dimensions of a multilingual experience. While readers may experience frustration with certain words or phrases, her strong claims regarding the interplay among language, culture, and identity remain accessible even without knowledge of Spanish or Mestiza. Anzaldúa provides profound insight into a multifaceted Mestiza ethos of woman, of lesbian, of Latina: of American.

—CG

1   "We're going to have to control your tongue," the dentist says, pulling out all the metal from my mouth. Silver bits plop and tinkle into the basin. My mouth is a motherlode.

2   The dentist is cleaning out my roots. I get a whiff of the stench when I gasp. "I can't cap that tooth yet, you're still draining," he says.

3   "We're going to have to do something about your tongue," I hear the anger rising in his voice. My tongue keeps pushing out the wads of cotton, pushing back the drills, the long thin needles. "I've never seen anything as strong or as stubborn," he says. And I think, how do you tame a wild tongue, train it to be quiet, how do you bridle and saddle it? How do you make it lie down?

4   *Who is to say that robbing a people of its language is less violent than war?*
        — Ray Gwyn Smith

5   I remember being caught speaking Spanish at recess—that was good for three licks on the knuckles with a sharp ruler. I remember being sent to the corner of the classroom for "talking back" to the Anglo teacher when all I was trying to do was tell her how to pronounce my name. "If you want to be American, speak 'American.' If you don't like it, go back to Mexico where you belong."

6   "I want you to speak English. *Pa' hallar buen trabajo tienes que saber hablar el inglés bien. Qué vale toda tu educación si todavía hablas inglés con un* 'accent,'" my mother would say, mortified that I spoke English like a Mexican. At Pan American University, I, and all Chicano students were required to take two speech classes. Their purpose: to get rid of our accents.

7   Attacks on one's form of expression with the intent to censor are a violation of the First Amendment. *El Anglo con cara de inocente nos arrancó la lengua.* Wild tongues can't be tamed, they can only be cut out.

Overcoming the Tradition of Silence

8   *Ahogadas, escupimos el oscuro.*
         Peleando con nuestra propia sombra el silencio nos sepulta.

9   *En boca cerrada no entran moscas.* "Flies don't enter a closed mouth" is a saying I kept hearing when I was a child. *Ser habladora* was to be a gossip and a liar, to talk too much. *Muchachitas bien criadas*, well-bred girls don't answer back. *Es una falta de respeto* to talk back to one's mother or father. I remember one of the sins I'd recite to the priest in the confession box the few times I went to confession: talking back to my mother, *hablar pa' 'tras, repelar. Hocicona, repelona, chismosa,* having a big mouth, questioning, carrying tales are all signs of being *mal criada*. In my culture they are all words that are derogatory if applied to women—I've never heard them applied to men.

10   The first time I heard two women, a Puerto Rican and a Cuban, say the word *"nosotras,"* I was shocked. I had not known the word existed. Chicanas use *nosotros* whether we're male or female. We are robbed of our female being by the masculine plural. Language is a male discourse.

11   *And our tongues have become dry the wilderness has dried out our tongue*
         and we have forgotten speech.
                                          — Irena Klepfisz

12   Even our own people, other Spanish speakers *nos quieren poner candados en la boca.* They would hold us back with their bag of *reglas de academia.*

Oyé como ladra: el lenguaje de la frontera

13   *Quien tiene boca se equivoca.*
                    — Mexican saying

14   *"Pocho,* cultural traitor, you're speaking the oppressor's language by speaking English, you're ruining the Spanish language," I have been accused by various Latinos and Latinas. Chicano Spanish is considered by the purist and by most Latinos deficient, a mutilation of Spanish.

15   But Chicano Spanish is a border tongue which developed naturally. Change, *evolución, enriquecimiento de palabras nuevas por invención o adopción* have created variants of Chicano Spanish, *un nuevo lenguauje. Un lenguaje que corresponde a un modo de vivir.* Chicano Spanish is not incorrect, it is a living language.

16   For a people who are neither Spanish nor live in a country in which Spanish is the first language; for a people who live in a country in which English is the reigning tongue

but who are not Anglo; for a people who cannot entirely identify with either standard (formal, Castilian) Spanish nor standard English, what recourse is left to them but to create their own language? A language which they can connect their identity to, one capable of communicating the realities and values true to themselves—a language with terms that are neither *español ni inglés*, but both. We speak a patois, a forked tongue, a variation of two languages.

17   Chicano Spanish sprang out of the Chicano's need to identify ourselves as a distinct people. We needed a language with which we could communicate with ourselves, a secret language. For some of us, language is a homeland closer than the Southwest—for many Chicanos today live in the Midwest and the East. And because we are a complex, heterogeneous people, we speak many languages. Some of the languages we speak are:

1.   Standard English
2.   Working class and slang English
3.   Standard Spanish
4.   Standard Mexican Spanish
5.   North Mexican Spanish dialect
6.   Chicano Spanish (Texas, New Mexico, Arizona and California have regional variations)
7.   Tex Mex
8.   Pachuco (called caló)

18   My "home" tongues are the languages I speak with my sister and brothers, with my friends. They are the last five listed, with 6 and 7 being closest to my heart. From school, the media and job situations, I've picked up standard and working class English. From Mamagrande Locha and from reading Spanish and Mexican literature, I've picked up Standard Spanish and Standard Mexican Spanish. From *los recién llegados*, Mexican immigrants, and *braceros*, I learned the North Mexican dialect. With Mexicans I'll try to speak either Standard Mexican Spanish or the North Mexican dialect. From my parents and Chicanos living in the Valley, I picked up Chicano Texas Spanish, and I speak it with my mom, younger brother (who married a Mexican and who rarely mixes Spanish with English), aunts and older relatives.

19   With Chicanas from *Nuevo México* or *Arizona* I will speak Chicano Spanish a little, but often they don't understand what I'm saying. With most California Chicanas I speak entirely in English (unless I forget). When I first moved to San Francisco, I'd rattle off something in Spanish, unintentionally embarrassing them. Often it is only with another Chicana *tejana* that I can talk freely.

20   Words distorted by English are known as anglicisms or *pochismos*. The *pocho* is an anglicized Mexican or American of Mexican origin who speaks Spanish with an accent characteristic of North Americans and who distorts and reconstructs the language according to the influence of the English. Tex-Mex, or Spanglish, comes most naturally to me. I may switch back and forth from English to Spanish in the same sentence or in the same word. With my sister and my brother Nune and with Chicano *tejano* contemporaries I speak in Tex-Mex.

21   From kids and people my own age I picked up *Pachuco. Pachuco* (the language of the zoot suiters) is a language of rebellion, both against Standard Spanish and Standard English. It is a secret language. Adults of the culture and outsiders cannot understand it. It is made up of slang words from both English and Spanish. *Ruca* means girl or woman, *vato* means guy or dude, *chale* means no, *simón* means yes, *churro* is sure, talk is *periquiar, pigionear* means petting, *que gacho* means how nerdy, *ponte águila* means watch out, death is called *la pelona.* Through lack of practice and not having others who speak it, I've lost most of the *Pachuco* tongue.

Chicano Spanish

22   Chicanos, after 250 years of Spanish/Anglo colonization, have developed significant differences in the Spanish we speak. We collapse two adjacent vowels into a single syllable and sometimes shift the stress in certain words such as *maíz/maiz, cohete/cuete.* We leave out certain consonants when they appear between vowels: *lado/lao, mojado/mojao.* Chicanos from South Texas pronounce *f* as *j* as in *jue (fue).* Chicanos use "archaisms," words that are no longer in the Spanish language, words that have been evolved out. We say *semos, truje, haiga, ansina,* and *naiden.* We retain the "archaic" *j,* as in *jalar,* that derives from an earlier *h,* (the French *halar* or the Germanic *halon* which was lost to standard Spanish after the 16th century), but which is still found in several regional dialects such as the one spoken in South Texas. (Due to geography, Chicanos from the Valley of South Texas were cut off linguistically from other Spanish speakers. We tend to use words that the Spaniards brought over from Medieval Spain. The majority of the Spanish colonizers in Mexico and the Southwest came from Extremadura—Hernán Cortés was one of them—and Andalucía. Andalucians pronounce *ll* like a *y,* and their *d*'s tend to be absorbed by adjacent vowels: *tirado* becomes *tirao.* They brought *el lenguaje popular, dialectos y regionalismos.*)

23   Chicanos and other Spanish speakers also shift *ll* to *y* and *z* to *s.* We leave out initial syllables, saying *tar* for *estar, toy* for *estoy, hora* for *ahora* (*cubanos* and *puertorriqueños* also leave out initial letters of some words). We also leave out the final syllable such as *pa* for *para.* The intervocalic *y,* the *ll* as in *tortilla, ella, botella,* gets replaced by *tortia* or *tortiya, ea, botea.* We add an additional syllable at the beginning of certain words: *atocar* for *tocar, agastar* for *gastar.* Sometimes we'll say *lavaste las vacijas,* other times *lavates* (substituting the *ates* verb endings for the *aste*).

24   We use anglicisms, words borrowed from English: *bola* from ball, *carpeta* from carpet, *máchina de lavar* (instead of *lavadora*) from washing machine. Tex-Mex argot, created by adding a Spanish sound at the beginning or end of an English word such as *cookiar* for cook, *watchar* for watch, *parkiar* for park, and *rapiar* for rape, is the result of the pressures on Spanish speakers to adapt to English.

25   We don't use the word *vosotros/as* or its accompanying verb form. We don't say *claro* (to mean yes), *imagínate,* or *me emociona,* unless we picked up Spanish from Latinas, out of a book, or in a classroom. Other Spanish-speaking groups are going through the same, or similar, development in their Spanish.

Linguistic Terrorism

26   *Deslenguadas. Somos los del español deficiente.* We are your linguistic nightmare, your linguistic aberration, your linguistic *mestizaje*, the subject of your *burla*. Because we speak with tongues of fire we are culturally crucified. Racially, culturally and linguistically *somos huérfanos*—we speak an orphan tongue.

27   Chicanas who grew up speaking Chicano Spanish have internalized the belief that we speak poor Spanish. It is illegitimate, a bastard language. And because we internalize how our language has been used against us by the dominant culture, we use our language differences against each other.

28   Chicana feminists often skirt around each other with suspicion and hesitation. For the longest time I couldn't figure it out. Then it dawned on me. To be close to another Chicana is like looking into the mirror. We are afraid of what we'll see there. *Pena.* Shame. Low estimation of self. In childhood we are told that our language is wrong. Repeated attacks on our native tongue diminish our sense of self. The attacks continue throughout our lives.

29   Chicanas feel uncomfortable talking in Spanish to Latinas, afraid of their censure. Their language was not outlawed in their countries. They had a whole lifetime of being immersed in their native tongue; generations, centuries in which Spanish was a first language, taught in school, heard on radio and TV, and read in the newspaper.

30   If a person, Chicana or Latina, has a low estimation of my native tongue, she also has a low estimation of me. Often with *mexicanas y latinas* we'll speak English at parties or conferences. Yet, at the same time, we're afraid the other will think we're *agringadas* because we don't speak Chicano Spanish. We oppress each other trying to out-Chicano each other, vying to be the "real" Chicanas, to speak like Chicanos. There is no one Chicano language just as there is no one Chicano experience. A monolingual Chicana whose first language is English or Spanish is just as much a Chicana as one who speaks variants of Spanish. A Chicana from Michigan or Chicago or Detroit is just as much a Chicana as one from the Southwest. Chicano Spanish is as diverse linguistically as it is regionally.

31   By the end of this century, Spanish speakers will comprise the biggest minority group in the U.S., a country where students in high school and colleges are encouraged to take French classes because French is considered more "cultured." But for a language to remain alive it must be used. By the end of this century English, and not Spanish, will be the mother tongue of most Chicanos and Latinos.

32   So, if you want to really hurt me, talk badly about my language. Ethnic identity is twin skin to linguistic identity—I am my language. Until I can take pride in my language, I cannot take pride in myself. Until I can accept as legitimate Chicano Texas Spanish, Tex-Mex and all the other languages I speak, I cannot accept the legitimacy of myself. Until I am free to write bilingually and switch to codes without having to translate, while I still have to speak English or Spanish when I would rather speak Spanglish, and as long as I have to accommodate the English speakers rather than having them accommodate me, my tongue will be illegitimate.

33   I will no longer be made to feel ashamed of existing. I will have my voice: Indian, Spanish, white. I will have my serpent's tongue—my woman's voice, my sexual voice, my poet's voice. I will overcome the tradition of silence.

34   *My fingers move sly against your palm*
Like women everywhere, we speak in code....
                    — Melanie Kaye/Kantrowitz

"Vistas," corridos, y comida: My Native Tongue

35   In the 1960s, I read my first Chicano novel. It was *City of Night* by John Rechy, a gay Texan, son of a Scottish father and a Mexican mother. For days I walked around in stunned amazement that a Chicano could write and could get published. When I read *I Am Joaquín* I was surprised to see a bilingual book by a Chicano in print. When I saw poetry written in Tex-Mex for the first time, a feeling of pure joy flashed through me. I felt like we really existed as a people. In 1971, when I started teaching High School English to Chicano students, I tried to supplement the required texts with works by Chicanos, only to be reprimanded and forbidden to do so by the principal. He claimed that I was supposed to teach "American" and English literature. At the risk of being fired, I swore my students to secrecy and slipped in Chicano short stories, poems, a play. In graduate school, while working toward a Ph.D., I had to "argue" with one advisor after the other, semester after semester, before I was allowed to make Chicano literature an area of focus.

36   Even before I read books by Chicanos or Mexicans, it was the Mexican movies I saw at the drive-in—the Thursday night special of $1.00 a carload—that gave me a sense of belonging. *"Vámonos a las vistas,"* my mother would call out and we'd all—grandmother, brothers, sister and cousins—squeeze into the car. We'd wolf down cheese and bologna white bread sandwiches while watching Pedro Infante in melodramatic tearjerkers like *Nosotros los pobres*, the first "real" Mexican movie (that was not an imitation of European movies). I remember seeing *Cuando los hijos se van* and surmising that all Mexican movies played up the love a mother has for her children and what ungrateful sons and daughters suffer when they are not devoted to their mothers. I remember the singing-type "westerns" of Jorge Negrete and Miquel Aceves Mejía. When watching Mexican movies, I felt a sense of homecoming as well as alienation. People who were to amount to something didn't go to Mexican movies, or *bailes* or tune their radios to *bolero, rancherita*, and *corrido* music.

37   The whole time I was growing up, there was *norteño* music sometimes called North Mexican border music, or Tex-Mex music, or Chicano music, or *cantina* (bar) music. I grew up listening to *conjuntos*, three-or four-piece bands made up of folk musicians playing guitar, *bajo sexto*, drums and button accordion, which Chicanos had borrowed from the German immigrants who had come to Central Texas and Mexico to farm and build breweries. In the Rio Grande Valley, Steve Jordan and Little Joe Hernández were popular, and Flaco Jiménez was the accordion king. The rhythms of Tex-Mex music are those of the polka, also adapted from the Germans, who in turn had borrowed the polka from the Czechs and Bohemians.

38   I remember the hot, sultry evenings when *corridos*—songs of love and death on the Texas-Mexican borderlands—reverberated out of cheap amplifiers from the local *cantinas* and wafted in through my bedroom window.

39   *Corridos* first became widely used along the South Texas/Mexican border during the early conflict between Chicanos and Anglos. The *corridos* are usually about Mexican heroes who do valiant deeds against the Anglo oppressors. Pancho Villa's song, *"La cucaracha,"* is the most famous one. *Corridos* of John F. Kennedy and his death are still very popular in the Valley. Older Chicanos remember Lydia Mendoza, one of the great border *corrido* singers who was called *la Gloria de Tejas.* Her *"El tango negro,"* sung during the Great Depression, made her a singer of the people. The everpresent *corridos* narrated one hundred years of border history, bringing news of events as well as entertaining. These folk musicians and folk songs are our chief cultural mythmakers, and they made our hard lives seem bearable.

40   I grew up feeling ambivalent about our music. Country-western and rock-and-roll had more status. In the 50s and 60s, for the slightly educated and *agringado* Chicanos, there existed a sense of shame at being caught listening to our music. Yet I couldn't stop my feet from thumping to the music, could not stop humming the words, nor hide from myself the exhilaration I felt when I heard it.

41   There are more subtle ways that we internalize identification, especially in the forms of images and emotions. For me food and certain smells are tied to my identity, to my homeland. Woodsmoke curling up to an immense blue sky; woodsmoke perfuming my grandmother's clothes, her skin. The stench of cow manure and the yellow patches on the ground; the crack of a .22 rifle and the reek of cordite. Homemade white cheese sizzling in a pan, melting inside a folded *tortilla.* My sister Hilda's hot, spicy *menudo, chile colorado* making it a deep red, pieces of *panza* and hominy floating on top. My brother Carito barbequing *fajitas* in the backyard. Even now and 3,000 miles away, I can see my mother spicing the ground beef, pork and venison with *chile.* My mouth salivates at the thought of the hot steaming *tamales* I would be eating if I were home.

Si le preguntas a mi mamá, "¿Qué eres?"

10   *Identity is the essential core of who we are as individuals,*
the conscious experience of the self inside.

— Kaufman

43   *Nosotros los Chicanos* straddle the borderlands. On one side of us, we are constantly exposed to the Spanish of the Mexicans, on the other side we hear the Anglos' incessant clamoring so that we forget our language. Among ourselves we don't say *nosotros los americanos, o nosotros los españoles, o nosotros los hispanos.* We say *nosotros los mexicanos* (by *mexicanos* we do not mean citizens of Mexico; we do not mean a national identity, but a racial one). We distinguish between *mexicanos del otro lado* and *mexicanos de este lado.* Deep in our hearts we believe that being Mexican has nothing to do with which country one lives in. Being Mexican is a state of soul—not one of mind, not one of citizenship. Neither eagle nor serpent, but both. And like the ocean, neither animal respects borders.

44   *Dime con quien andas y te diré quien eres.*
(Tell me who your friends are and I'll tell you who you are.)
— Mexican saying

45   *Si le preguntas a mi mamá, "¿Qué eres?" te dirá, "Soy mexicana."* My brothers and sisters say the same. I sometimes will answer *"soy mexicana"* and at others will say *"soy Chicana" o "soy tejana."* But I identified as *"Raza"* before I ever identified as *"mexicana"* or "Chicana."

46   As a culture, we call ourselves Spanish when referring to ourselves as a linguistic group and when copping out. It is then that we forget our predominant Indian genes. We are 70–80% Indian. We call ourselves Hispanic or Spanish-American or Latin American or Latin when linking ourselves to other Spanish-speaking peoples of the Western hemisphere and when copping out. We call ourselves Mexican-American to signify we are neither Mexican nor American, but more the noun "American" than the adjective "Mexican" (and when copping out).

47   Chicanos and other people of color suffer economically for not acculturating. This voluntary (yet forced) alienation makes for psychological conflict, a kind of dual identity—we don't identify with the Anglo-American cultural values and we don't totally identify with the Mexican cultural values. We are a synergy of two cultures with various degrees of Mexicanness or Angloness. I have so internalized the borderland conflict that sometimes I feel like one cancels out the other and we are zero, nothing, no one. *A veces no soy nada ni nadie. Pero hasta cuando no lo soy, lo soy.*

48   When not copping out, when we know we are more than nothing, we call ourselves Mexican, referring to race and ancestry; *mestizo* when affirming both our Indian and Spanish (but we hardly ever own our Black ancestry); Chicano when referring to a politically aware people born and/or raised in the U.S.; *Raza* when referring to Chicanos; *tejanos* when we are Chicanos from Texas.

49   Chicanos did not know we were a people until 1965 when Céasar Chavez and the farmworkers united and *I Am Joaquín* was published and *La Raza Unida* party was formed in Texas. With that recognition, we became a distinct people. Something momentous happened to the Chicano soul—we became aware of our reality and acquired a name and a language (Chicano Spanish) that reflected that reality. Now that we had a name, some of the fragmented pieces began to fall together—who we were, what we were, how we had evolved. We began to get glimpses of what we might eventually become.

50   Yet the struggle of identities continues, the struggle of borders is our reality still. One day the inner struggle will cease and a true integration will take place. In the meantime, *tenémos que hacer la lucha. ¿Quién está protegiendo los ranchos de mi gente? ¿Quién está tratando de cerrar la fisura entre la india y el blanco en nuestra sangre? El Chicano, sí, el Chicano que anda como un ladrón en su propia casa.*

51   *Los Chicanos,* how patient we seem, how very patient. There is the quiet of the Indian about us. We know how to survive. When other races have given up their tongue, we've kept ours. We know what it is to live under the hammer blow of the dominant *norteamericano* culture. But more than we count the blows, we count the days the weeks the

years the centuries the eons until the white laws and commerce and customs will rot in the deserts they've created, lie bleached. *Humildos* yet proud, *quietos* yet wild; *nosotros los mexicanos-Chicanos* will walk by the crumbling ashes as we go about our business. Stubborn, persevering, impenetrable as stone, yet possessing a malleability that renders us unbreakable, we, the *mestizas* and *mestizos,* will remain.

Critical Reading Questions:

- **Interpretation:** Identify at least two passages in which Anzaldúa focuses on her relationship with language. What do these passages suggest about the relationship between language and power?

- **Interpretation:** Consider Anzaldúa's multiple uses of "tongue" as a metaphor for a locus of power. What is at stake in her taking control of her own "tongue"? How is it used to resist oppression?

- **Reflection:** Follow your reactions to Anzaldúa's integration of diverse languages throughout the essay. How does the language disrupt or engage your understanding? Reflect on why, as a rhetor, Anzaldúa would make the stylistic choice to deviate from Standard Written English.

The *Arete* of Amusement:
An Aristotelian Perspective on the Ethos of *The Daily Show*

Jonathan E. Barbur and Trischa Goodnow

Barbur and Goodnow demonstrate the power of applying classical rhetorical concepts to a popular culture phenomenon, *The Daily Show*, focusing on how this Comedy Central news show establishes credibility in the eyes of its viewers. The writers argue that this political satire outperforms conventional news programs as a forum for serious public discussion. This essay by academic rhetoricians models a way of structuring and developing a rhetorical analysis. They first establish a context for their essay, published in 2011, in which they examine how conventional news media have lost credibility as "a legitimate source of information." Then they offer explicit and detailed definitions of the rhetorical terms they will employ, focusing on three elements of ethos defined by Aristotle: good sense, good moral character, and goodwill, before offering their thesis that "although *The Daily Show* may also be an entertaining spectacle, it has gained its viewers' trust." The core of the essay focuses on how and why *The Daily Show* merits credibility by looking closely at the program and its recent scholarship. The writers conclude by reinforcing their evaluation argument that the show "elevates the quality of reasoned discourse."

—CM

1   Once upon a time, there was great trust in the news media establishment. Though the American media has always produced both partisan and yellow journalism, it was also shaped by individuals such as Edward R. Murrow and Walter Cronkite who stood for courageous and probing investigations into the powerful, practiced civility and fair-mindedness, and envisioned the role of journalist as a public servant. Television news was shaped by such attitudes during its first three decades, and Murrow and Cronkite's most prominent successors (e.g., Dan Rather, Peter Jennings) seemed to live up to their standards.

2   Thus, even if it was never perfect, for many years national television news at least aspired to high ideals. Early broadcast journalists "saw their profession as a mission," filling a critical social and political role by functioning as "a *searchlight*—a light of public inquiry and political accountability, dedicated to providing citizens the informational resources they needed to participate in a political public sphere" (Baym, 2004, p. 2). But all Golden Ages end, and in contrast to the ideal of yesterday, "today's television news, absorbed into the portfolios of the giant media conglomerates, has become a *floodlight*—a hyper-mediated, theatrical light of exposure, a commodity packaged to sell" (Baym, 2004, p. 2).

3   There are undoubtedly many reasons for this change—though as the passage above notes, a major factor has been consolidation of ownership and the new media conglomerates' treatment of news as a commoditized, profit-centered business rather than a unique, public-centered profession. Today, the news is expected to turn a profit. Meanwhile, an explosion in the number of competing radio and television channels, and the birth of the twenty-four-hour news cycle (i.e., CNN and the Internet) act to pressure journalists to run stories without time for adequate investigation and background research (Baym, 2005). Moreover—particularly since the terrorist attacks of 2001—the news media has increasingly abandoned its role as "watchdog"—that is, as a critic of government and corporate abuse—functioning instead as a defender of the powerful, or at the least as an uncritical conduit for powerful institutions to spread their messages (Holbert, et al., 2007); indeed, McKain (2005) notes that three-quarters of the content of most news broadcasts originate from government statements.

4   But these trends have coincided with—arguably, they have caused—a severe decline in viewership for traditional news media, particularly among younger viewers (Morris, 2008). In rhetorical terms, in other words, these trends have caused the traditional news media to lose its *credibility* as a legitimate source of information, while at the same time they have given citizens other options to get information about the world. Increasingly, people find little of merit in either the traditional news' content or its judgment, and cynicism about the media is rampant.

5   In contrast however, shows that mix news with entertainment, such as late-night talk shows, have gained viewers (Baym, 2005; Coe, et al., 2008). Such "soft news programs are those that package political information in an entertaining form, often through the use of an interview format wherein the interaction between host and guest provides ample comedy or conflict" (Coe, et al., 2008, pp. 201-202). Besides the entertainment factor, such programs avoid accusations of bias because they never claim to be objective or serious; they never aspire to the calling of a "journalist" in the mold of Murrow or Cronkite, and thus they lose nothing if they fail to reach journalistic ideals.

6   *The Daily Show*, Comedy Central's "fake news" show, is of course one of the best examples of this hybrid genre, mixing entertainment with an insightful critique of the media. Baym describes it as an experiment in journalistic practices in that its hybrid of parody, satire and serious discussion presented in an entertaining way moves beyond the limits of traditional television genres such as "news" and "entertainment," forming a "profound phenomenon of discursive integration, a way of speaking about, understanding, and acting within the world defined by the permeability of form and the fluidity of content" (2005, p. 262). And despite concerns that its comedic approach to news would negatively affect its audience's understanding of the world, *The Daily Show*'s audience is actually among the most informed segments of the population, though also typically quite cynical about both media and government (Long, 2004; McKain, 2005; Baumgartner and Morris, 2006).

7   Moreover, *The Daily Show* (and particularly Jon Stewart as an individual) has emerged as a source that its viewing audience trusts—it has developed credibility even as the "serious" media has lost it. The show has garnered Emmys, Peabodys, and numerous other accolades for the quality of its coverage ("Awards," n.d.); and Jon Stewart tied with Dan Rather, Tom Brokaw, Anderson Cooper, and Brian Williams as the most admired and trusted journalist in America—a significant achievement for someone who repeatedly insists that he is not a journalist at all (Pew, 2008).

8   Presumably, *The Daily Show* has not achieved this status simply because of a vacuum in credible news media, but rather because the show exhibits qualities that lead its viewers to see it as trustworthy in its own right—in rhetorical terminology, qualities that lead its audience to judge it as possessing ethos, a trait that "brings to mind a person's moral character, [and] communal existence," exhibited through their skillful use of rhetoric (Hyde, 2004, p. xvii). Over the rest of this chapter we briefly review the concept of ethos, then turn to consider how *The Daily Show* exhibits its ethos.

Ethos

9   From the earliest discussions of rhetoric in classical Greece, persuasion has been understood as centered on "a speaker's knowledge of the varieties and complexities of human character," such that "this knowledge enables the speaker to project a favorable self-image and to shape arguments in ways that accommodate differing audiences and occasions" (Baumlin, 2006, "Ethos" section). In more modern terminology then, rhetorical effectiveness might be seen as grounded on a practical application of psychology as the speaker makes judgments about and adapts to their audience's outlook, prejudices, and emotions.

10   For some classical theorists, such as Isocrates and Plato, the projection of self-image seems inherently interwoven with the speaker's actual moral character and role in the larger community (Hyde, 2004; Baumlin, 2006). But ethos is most commonly associated with Aristotle's theory of rhetoric; for him, what is of interest is the audience's judgment of a source's character and the strategies that the speaker uses in order to be perceived positively (Hyde, 2004; Baumlin, 2006).

11   For Aristotle, ethos is "persuasion [that] is achieved by the speaker's personal character when the speech is so spoken as to make us think him credible," and it fits with logos (the evidence and arguments advanced by a speaker) and pathos (the speaker's evocation of emotions) as one of the three basic means by which a speaker can seek to persuade (Aristotle, 1954/1984, p. 25). It is, however, the most powerful of the three artistic proofs because

12   We believe good men more fully and more readily than others;
        this is true generally whatever the question is, and absolutely true
        where exact certainty is impossible and opinions are divided....
        [The speaker's] character may almost be called the most effective
        means of persuasion he possesses. (Aristotle, 1954/1984, p. 25)

13   The Aristotelian concept of ethos can be considered as composed of three elements exhibited by speakers during their rhetorical acts: phronesis, or good sense, intelligence, capability, and practical wisdom; arete, or excellence, virtue, and good moral character; and eunoia, or benevolence and goodwill towards the audience (Aristotle, 1954/1984, p. 91; Baumlin, 2006, "Aristotelian ethos" section).

14   Good sense encompasses all knowledge and capabilities that are relevant to the topic the speaker is discussing. This includes sound reasoning abilities, knowledge of theory, science, history, and other fields, practical and technical skills when relevant, and so on; as Smith summarizes, "what is clear from early on in the Rhetoric is that a public speaker must know a great deal to be successful" (2004, p. 10). Phronesis, however, goes beyond any specific list of knowledge to encompass "a capacity for discerning in the sphere of action the intermediate point where right conduct lies in any given situation" (Smith, 2004, pp. 10-11). In the end, it is the speaker's overall capacity for judgment that matters, and specific knowledge is merely grist for the mill of a soundly reasoning mind.

15   Beyond good sense, a source must exhibit sound moral character—they should be an excellent person. While it is beyond the scope of this chapter to discuss Aristotle's ethical theories in great detail, it is useful to note here that—in keeping with the general classical Greek notion of the Golden Mean—he articulates virtues as character traits that consistently exhibit a happy medium between two undesirable extremes (Kraut, 2010).

16   For example, when describing someone as "courageous," one is speaking of how a person routinely deals with experiences of fear and danger. A cowardly person is ruled by their fear, while a rash individual tends toward taking unnecessary risks; but a courageous person overcomes their fear to take reasonable risks as the situation warrants them. Aristotle's ethics are primarily concerned with such habitually exhibited traits, such as courage, honesty, friendliness, and generosity, rather than with rigid rules that dictate whether to consider a given act right or wrong. Such balanced and consistent virtues are the "character traits that human beings need in order to live life at its best" (Kraut, 2010, "Preliminaries" section, para. 1): to exhibit excellence in their endeavors (arete), and to live in such a way as to promote their own and others' happiness (*eudaimonia*) (Kraut, 2010).

17   The final element of Aristotelian ethos is benevolence or goodwill directed towards the audience. This can be considered something like friendship, in that the speaker's behavior conveys that they have the audience's best interests in mind and that they are on the audience's side. It differs from friendship, however, in that it does not imply reciprocity or the expectation that the audience will necessarily care for the speaker in the same way (Smith, 2004).

18   As a speaker exhibits (or fails to exhibit) these three elements, they interweave to shape how the audience will likely judge the speaker's overall character and trustworthiness—their ethos. Aristotle notes that they build on each other because

19   Men either form a false opinion through want of good sense; or they form
        a true opinion, but because of their moral badness do not say what they
        really think; or finally, they are both sensible and upright, but not well dis-
        posed to their hearers, and may fail in consequence to recommend what

they know to be the best course. These are the only possible cases. It
follows that any one who is thought to have all three of these good qualities will inspire trust in his audience. (Aristotle, 1954/1984, p. 91)

20   Moreover the three elements function to reinforce each other, as when a speaker's
apparent practical wisdom suggests to an audience that the speaker also possesses a
virtue of fair-mindedness, because to exercise good judgment implies the capacity to
weigh all the available information and consider all reasonable viewpoints (Smith, 2004).
Conversely, a source that seems fair-minded to an audience will be more likely to seem to
have good sense, because their willingness to consider others' viewpoints is likely to lead
to more well-reasoned decisions.

21   In the following pages we will consider some of the ways in which *The Daily Show*
exhibits these traits of good sense, good character, and goodwill. Before doing so, we
pause to reflect again on the loss of trust in traditional news in light of the constituent qualities of ethos. The profession's traditional mission to serve as a means of informing a nation
so that it could function effectively as a democracy seems to mirror the quality of goodwill toward the audience, while traditional journalistic ideals such as objectivity and the
questioning of sources parallel the quality of good sense. Conversely however, the com-
mercialized spectacle of modern broadcast news and partisan punditry is the antithesis
of ethos: in failing, for example, to investigate a government statement before airing it to
the public it fails to express wisdom and good sense; and it pursues profit at the expense
of sound information, indicating a lack of concern for its audience's interests. Thus, most
attempts to recapture viewers by increasing the spectacle are likely doomed to failure
so long as they ignore the basic nature of what makes a source credible. In contrast,
although *The Daily Show* may also be an entertaining spectacle it has gained its viewers'
trust, and in the next section we turn to examine why.

The Ethos of *The Daily Show*

22   *The Daily Show* is first a comedy, and the audience is in their seats because they
expect to laugh. Whether on or off the show, Stewart adamantly maintains that he is not
a journalist, nor a social or media critic, but a "comedian who has the pleasure of writing
jokes about things that I actually care about. And that's really it" ("Bill Moyers interviews
Jon Stewart," 2003, n.p.).

23   Yet, unlike other hybrids of news and entertainment—e.g., late-night variety show
monologues or *Saturday Night Live's Weekend Update*—the show's discursive integration
of news and entertainment clearly involves more than just punch lines that happen to be
based on current events. It is frequently referred to not only as one of the funniest shows
on television but also as one of the most intelligent and intellectual. For example, Smolkin
(2007) notes how the show has become a favorite among media scholars and professional journalists, Trier claims *The Daily Show* is arguably "the best critical media literacy
program on television" (2008, p. 424), and Colletta calls the show's "informed satire…
some of the most bracing and engaging commentary on the television landscape" (2009,

p. 872). Moreover, the show arguably "not only assumes, but even requires, previous and significant knowledge of the news on the part of viewers if they want to get the joke" (Pew, 2008, n.p.).

24   In addition, the show's approach is typically ironic and satirical. Colletta reminds us that

25   Traditionally, irony has been a means to expose the space between what is real and what is appearance, or what is meant and what is said, revealing incoherence and transcending it through the aesthetic form and meaning of a work of art. (2009, p. 856)

26   Satire, moreover, differs from the strictly comedic because it uses humor not merely as an end to itself but as a "weapon," "hold[ing] up human vices and follies to ridicule and scorn" in an attempt to improve society (Colletta, 2009, p. 859). We can thus begin our assessment of *The Daily Show* by keeping in mind that much of its display of good sense, good morals, and goodwill will revolve around the manner in which it uses humor intelligently to expose the gaps between reality and appearance, and the way in which its strategies critique follies and attempt to improve society.

Good Sense

27   The first element of Aristotelian ethos is intelligence and good sense, and in this section we consider four key ways in which *The Daily Show* exhibits this trait: first, through the type of news that it covers; second, through its strategy of remediating clips drawn from other media; third, through its exaggerated parodies of news reports and journalistic conventions; and fourth, in its interview segment, particularly its selection of guests.

28   Turning first to its selection of stories and the content of its news coverage, we note that as a proportion of its airtime *The Daily Show* incorporates roughly the same amount of "substance"—actual information—as does mainstream broadcast journalism (Fox, et al., 2007). A key difference, however, is that where the remainder of *The Daily Show*'s content—the non-substantive portion—is humorous, in conventional news broadcasts the non-substantive content tends to be "hype"—i.e., political election coverage that focuses on the horse race or on candidate image over issues (Fox, et al., 2007).

29   In common with mainstream broadcast journalism, particularly the network evening newscasts that it parodies, *The Daily Show* focuses most heavily on U.S. foreign affairs, national elections, and politics; it differs from them, however, in that a significant portion of its coverage focuses on the media itself (Pew, 2008). Moreover, *The Daily Show*'s coverage is more heavily concentrated on these subjects, and it tends to entirely ignore subjects that consume a significant portion of conventional news, such as crime and disasters (Pew, 2008).

30   Perhaps most important, although *The Daily Show* offers a more focused selection of news that arguably sacrifices breadth, it also tends to devote far more time to each story. Conventional news, as well as comedy like Jay Leno or *Weekend Update*, emphasizes a "now this" format in which each story is given very little time (Baym, 2005). For the comedy shows, each topic serves only as the premise for a quick punch line, while for

network news broadcasts brevity is an ostensible necessity as it allows the inclusion of more topics; but in either case, it is rare for any topic to be dealt with in detail. *The Daily Show*, in contrast, tends to develop stories to much greater depth even as it incorporates humor throughout the delivery—in some cases, single stories consume up to eight minutes of a broadcast, far exceeding most conventional news (Baym, 2005). Moreover, its segments include far more extensive discussion of an event's background than would ever be present on a network or cable news broadcast, situating the event within a historical context (even if this context is often presented through parody) (Baym, 2005). Finally, not only is the subject matter more completely contextualized in terms of individual stories, it is also in the case of events that are part of major ongoing stories, such as the Iraq War, often constituted as part of a long-running series of stories (e.g., *The Daily Show*'s "Mess-O-Potamia" series discussing Middle East affairs) that further imply continuity and contextualization.

31   When we put together these aspects of the show's selection and treatment of news, we can see the first element of *The Daily Show*'s phronesis. The show suggests superior judgment and thoughtfulness in comparison to conventional news simply because it develops context for its stories, a practice that is enabled by its more selective choices about what to cover. At the same time, by replacing hype and sensationalism with humor, it performatively criticizes the conventional news' emphasis on non-substantive material even as it entertains its audience.

32   Next, we turn from the show's subject matter to its strategy of using clips drawn from other media, particularly network and cable news, congressional hearings, and press conferences. McKain (2005) labels this an example of "remediation," the constantly self-referential practice of media borrowing and re-contextualizing each other's content and formal practices. Ironically, in its heavy emphasis on directly showing politicians' soundbites, the show hearkens to an earlier era of broadcast journalism, but *The Daily Show* has developed its use of clips into a new art form, which "its choices of soundbites turn[ing] contemporary conventions on their head" (Baym, 2005, p. 264).

33   By placing a politician's statements—often a dozen or more statements stretching over months—directly next to one another, contradictions and hypocrisy are made self-evident. By playing clips drawn from many different news or punditry broadcasts, it becomes easy to observe the otherwise subtle way in which the media's self-referencing enables the chaining out (in the sense used by Bormann [1972]) of simplistic reactions or calculated issue framing—i.e., it becomes easy to see how, somehow, nearly everyone on television uses the same language and assumptions to discuss issues.

34   McKain (2005) describes an example that highlights this technique's ability to effectively demonstrate the government's attempts at "message control" (i.e., spin or propaganda), when the show compares footage of National Security Advisor Condoleezza Rice and White House Press Secretary Scott McClelland speaking separately to the media about Bush Administration war plans. By cutting back and forth between them, *The Daily Show* reveals that both speakers are using almost exactly the same (rehearsed) phrasing, with the segment "culminat[ing] in 'the money shot': an intersplicing of the two voices as

they recite the same line, 'at the meeting it was a map of Afghanistan that was rolled out on the table'" (McKain, 2005, pp. 421-422).

35   *The Daily Show* does not rely only on juxtaposition of clips. Sometimes simply playing a clip that would otherwise be edited for brevity and clarity places its subject in an entirely different light. For example, Baym (2005) considers the coverage of George W. Bush's statement on the resignation of CIA Director George Tenet. In the *New York Times* and on ABC News brief quotes are drawn from Bush's speech, which, in and of themselves, suggest clear speech and thought. In contrast, *The Daily Show* plays a lengthy clip that shows Bush speaking haltingly and searching for something positive to say about Tenet. The news media's conventions demand clarity, but without the full context of the delivery such conventions produce a misleading image (Baym, 2005).

36   The use of clip remediation, in its various forms, thus serves as both a direct way of holding the powerful accountable for their statements and actions and as a central element of the show's effectiveness in terms of media criticism. The strategy "consistently disrupts government officials' cultivated images of assurance and knowledge" (McKain, 2005, p. 419), while also laying bare the illusions created by, and the limitations of, the news media's professional conventions. Moreover, simply by making use of publicly available clips from other media *The Daily Show* positions itself as an intellectual (and possibly moral) superior in relation to other media. In principle, any news or editorial show could use clips in the same way. That they do not (despite the ease of doing so and the abundance of material that illustrates, for example, a politician's direct contradiction of previous statements) suggests, in and of itself, that the conventional news media are either lazy, inept, or intentionally colluding in the concealment of the truth—and that *The Daily Show* possesses the good sense to be able to recognize and demonstrate this effectively to its audience.

37   The third aspect of the show we treat in this section is its parody news segments—skits, sketches and discussions with its "correspondents." For example, many of these sketches involve green-screened reports with backdrops that suggest on-the-scene reporting from the White House to Baghdad to outer space. In these parodies, the show mocks and deconstructs the news media's long-standing practice of sending reporters to read statements in front of the White House or at the scene of a crime, a convention that aims to create the illusion of immediacy and construct the news media as a (falsely) transparent medium that enables viewers to experience the reality of a situation (McKain, 2005). In the show's self-evidently fake-on-the-scene reports

38   the satiric payoff is that calling attention to...the clichéd use of "on the
           scene" reporters demonstrates how ludicrous they are as gestures of
           immediacy. After all, that ABC News's John Gibson stands in front of the
           White House when he recites news about the president does not mean
           that he has particular, unique, or even useful access to the president. Most
           likely, the news he delivers came down through the same channels of gate-
           keeping that it did for the other News networks. (McKain, 2005, p. 418)

39   Perhaps the most ubiquitous aspect of the show's parody of news media conventions are the absurdly inflated (and constantly varying) titles borne by the comedian-correspondents and the arrogant, condescending tone struck by most of them—every correspondent on *The Daily Show* is a "senior correspondent," whether Senior Baghdad Correspondent or Senior Black Correspondent. Like fake-on-the-scene reports, self-important titles and demeanors undermine the traditional news' claim of authority; in claiming obviously unfounded expertise, the show is suggesting that conventional broadcast journalists likewise lack such expertise. *The Daily Show* thus highlights how merely appearing on television confers the appearance of expertise, rather than expertise justifying one's appearance, and thus

40   The ultimate target of *The Daily Show*'s parody pieces, then, may be the
          myth of the contemporary journalist as a credentialed pro-
          fessional who commands some specialized ability to deter-
          mine the truth of a situation. (Baym, 2004, p. 15)

41   Guest interviews constitute another critical element of *The Daily Show*'s phronesis, but rather than focusing on satire or parody, the interviews are typically played straight. Humor during the interviews emerges mostly from Stewart's self-deprecation and quipping asides; indeed, "the interviews are entirely incongruous with the 'fake news' portions of the show" (McKain, 2005, p. 425). The interviews' core, instead, is substantive discussion of public affairs. With the occasional exception of a Hollywood celebrity, the majority of guests are politicians (recent guests included Tony Blair, Sept. 14, 2010, and Bill Clinton, Sept. 16, 2010), non-fiction authors, historians, social critics and others who would rarely (if ever) appear on other late-night talk shows. Stewart invariably engages with the substance of the book being promoted, or pushes a politician to move past spin and give straight answers to questions.

42   The interview segments, therefore, function directly to emphasize the show's phronesis first by constructing the show as a place where serious discussion can occur—and where books on classical history can co-exist with high elected officials; and second, by demonstrating Stewart to be a thoughtful, widely-read and articulate individual committed to the serious exploration and consideration of wide-ranging topics. Thus, the mere presence of guests of the caliber that *The Daily Show* routinely garners, and the manner in which Stewart engages with them, grant the show intellectual authority.

43   Much of the literature discussing *The Daily Show* has focused on how these characteristic elements innovate in terms of integrating previously separated genres of discourse, or in dissecting media norms. But through the lens of Aristotelian ethos, we can also understand these practices as strategies that illustrate the show's reasoning ability, its broad knowledge base, its cleverness and its good judgment. Through satire and parody, *The Daily Show* not only deconstructs the traditional media's claim of authority and holds the powerful accountable, but also actively constructs itself as an

44   authority predicated on knowledge—knowledge of what actually lies outside
          the window, of what the reporters/producers of what is going on cannot say,
          of the immediacy that their remediations obstruct. (McKain, 2005, p. 427)

45   At the same time the guest interviews take an entirely different tack, positioning the show not merely as a national court jester using humor to expose absurdity and folly, but also as a forum for serious discourse. We will return to this last point when discussing how the show conveys its sense of goodwill; first, however, we turn to the show's exhibition of virtues and good moral character.

Good Moral Character

46   In this section, we focus on two key virtues exhibited by *The Daily Show*: wittiness and good temper. This is hardly an exhaustive discussion of the show's exhibited virtues, and equally strong cases can be made for its exhibition of those virtues labeled by Aristotle as friendliness or honesty about oneself, among others; but limitations of space and the primacy of wit and good temper in establishing the show's overall ethos lead to our focus here.

47   First, and most obviously, the show is centered on the exhibition of wittiness. In his discussion of the virtue of wittiness, Aristotle defines it as the golden mean between the excess of buffoonery and deficiency of boorishness. At first glance (or if one does not find its humor to their taste) *The Daily Show* might be accused of buffoonery—of "striving after humour at all costs, and aiming rather at raising a laugh than at saying what is becoming and at avoiding pain to the object of their fun" (Aristotle, 1925/1998, p. 103). But its nature as a comedy show, and its deployment of humor for the purposes of social improvement through satire should alleviate such criticisms; certainly, the show cannot be accused of a deficiency in its attempts at humor.

48   Aristotle also distinguishes between types of humor suitable to the educated and the ignorant—for example, innuendo to the former and indecent language to the latter—and *The Daily Show* practices the entire spectrum, from the most immature to the sophisticated. Indeed, its use of (bleeped) profanity and crude humor plays an important role because it deconstructs the convention of television and implies that the show is willing to say even that which has been condemned by the conservative standards of government and network censors (McKain, 2005)—it thus conveys a sense of casual honesty and lack of concern for the limitations imposed by social convention. Conversely, the fact that so much of its humor comes from, for example, nothing more than the juxtaposition of politicians' contradictory statements and Stewart's raised eyebrow, or from parodies that cleverly highlight faulty media conventions, means that the show operates at least as much (actually, more so) at the level of educated, intellectual humor.

49   Next, there is the virtue of gentleness or good temper, terms that Aristotle uses primarily to refer to one's demeanor with regards to the emotion of anger. An excess of anger is irascibility or irritability, while the undesirable deficiency is spiritlessness, the failure to feel anger even when sufficiently provoked. Indeed, in Aristotle's phrasing, "to endure being insulted and put up with insult to one's friends is slavish" and "those who are not angry at the things they should be angry at are thought to be fools"; but anger can be virtuous so long as "we are angry with the right people, at the right things, in the right way" (Aristotle, 1925/1998, p. 97).

50   In relation to its competitors in the media, *The Daily Show* strikes a virtuous balance in its expression of anger. The partisan punditry of Rush Limbaugh or Bill O'Reilly, by comparison, is effectively a trade in anger, while conventional news media seems spiritless as it passively conveys government spin and acts as a conduit for hypocrisy. On *The Daily Show*, anger at hypocrisy or other vices is of course primarily expressed through satire, and most overt expressions of anger are feigned and exaggerated for comic effect, nonetheless, the emotional core of the show might well be considered a restrained anger at injustice and hypocrisy that is expressed through humor as a form of catharsis and release. Indeed, Stewart has described himself as "a tiny, neurotic man, standing in the back of the room throwing tomatoes at the chalk board" ("Bill Moyers interview," 2003).

51   But on occasion Stewart will drop the intellectual detachment necessary for satire and simply express anger and disgust openly, as when after the former CEO of Tyco was acquitted he called the holdout juror a "cunt" to the audience's shocked surprise (McKain, 2005), or when he ranted against conservatives seeking to shift blame during Hurricane Katrina. Invariably, such eruptions by Stewart are in response to unusually blatant injustices, and as a form of emotional honesty they function rhetorically (though probably not in a calculated way) to generate credibility because they expose the essential decency of a human who is overwhelmed by cavalierly unjust or cruel behavior, and, moreover, because they fit with "the audience's desire"—and arguably, emotional need—for "this view be articulated and its belief that this view is ethical, or just, or valid" (McKain, 2005, pg. 427).

Goodwill

52   We turn finally to consider *The Daily Show*'s goodwill toward its audience. Of course, this trait is expressed implicitly, for example, in its use of good sense to expose hypocrisy, hold elites accountable, and deconstruct illusions fostered by other media, and through expressions of anger at injustices. In this section, however, we touch on how the show overtly indicates goodwill through the advocacy of deliberative democracy and commitment to the public interest on the part of politicians, media and common citizens.

53   Deliberative democracy, as Baym (2005) notes, is an ideal centered on open, free dialogue in which citizens engage with each other to find answers to common challenges together and it necessarily requires a strong commitment on the part of civic participants to each others' welfare and to norms of dialogue and debate not as competition or verbal combat but as a means of collective truth- and solution-seeking. Outside the confines of *The Daily Show*, Stewart frequently exhibits his commitment to this ideal as he did by chastising Crossfire hosts Tucker Carlson and Paul Begala for practicing political theater rather than debate and dialogue ("Stewart appearance," 2004), or when he expressed his frustration with the dominance of partisan punditry when interviewed by Bill Moyers:

54   The whole idea that political discourse has degenerated into shows
            that have to be entitled *Crossfire* and *Hardball*, and you know,
            "I'm Gonna Beat Your Ass" or whatever...is mind-boggling...

> I don't understand how issues can be dissected from the left
> and from the right as though…even cartoon characters have
> more than left and right. ("Bill Moyers interview," 2003, n.p.)

55   But this ideal also permeates the show itself, especially during its interview segments. Beyond enhancing the show's apparent intelligence, as discussed above, they position the show as an integral part of a larger cultural dialogue, a Habermasian public sphere. The goal of the interview is not to score points on the guest or tear them down, nor even to make predictions that imply superior knowledge or insight (as with, e.g., The McLaughlin Group), but rather a genuine struggle on Stewart's part—both as an individual and as a delegate for the audience—to better understand the world, including national/global problems and possible courses of action (Baym, 2005).

56   When the guest is an author, Stewart often falls back on his trademark self-deprecating humor, implying the guest's superior knowledge, and to some degree playing the fool as he asks questions and makes quips to personalize the often erudite guests and make their work accessible to the general public without watering it down. It is, however, when his guests are politicians that Stewart's commitment to the public sphere and the demands of deliberative democracy become most evident. His interview style becomes more assertive as he uses both straight questions and jokes to cut through spin and demand answers.

57   For example, former U.K. Prime Minister Tony Blair appeared as his guest on September 14, 2010; Blair maintained his characteristic emphasis on the need to employ all possible means to combat terrorism while downplaying consideration of social and economic costs. Rather than contesting this position openly, Stewart employed insightful humor by making an analogy to cockroaches in New York City, noting that as a rich person he could certainly seal his apartment and bug-bomb it daily—but who wants to live that way? In this way, Stewart highlights the single-minded approach of "message control" and opens up the possibility for discussion outside the confines dictated by elites.

58   Conversely, however, politicians who have expressed desire for and commitment to reasonable and fair-minded discourse often become repeat guests and "friends" of the show. John McCain, for example, made many appearances, often agreeing with Stewart on the need for more reasonable dialogue in politics—though after adopting a more hard-line position in the 2010 Republican Senate primary in Arizona, and being ridiculed and chastised during *The Daily Show*'s news segments for his turnabout behavior, he has not returned.

59   And the show has recently made a further step in rekindling the public sphere. What began as a typical—for *The Daily Show*—satire of pundit Glenn Beck's "Restoring Honor" rally quickly snowballed into something much larger. The "Rally to Restore Sanity" (planned for the Washington Mall on October 30, 2010) is "Woodstock, but with the nudity and drugs replaced by respectful disagreement" ("Rally, 2010). In this most recent move, as throughout Stewart's tenure, *The Daily Show* continues to champion principles of ideological moderation, dialogue and civic participation.

60   Thus, the counterpoint to *The Daily Show*'s cynical and satirical dissection of spin, propaganda and illusory media norms is the show's elevation of reasoned discourse and its expectation that both politicians and citizens should abide by this standard, ideals that are arguably increasingly rare in contemporary media. In the show's vision of society, "dialogue...is the locus of democracy, the public process through which citizens determine their preferences and define the public will" (Baym, 2005, p. 273). In its implicit and explicit advocacy of this ideal, the show confirms its commitment to the well-being of its audience, the nation, and humanity at large.

Conclusion

61   Undoubtedly, there are many other aspects of *The Daily Show* with Jon Stewart that enhance its ethos. The show's inherent fair-mindedness, attacking absurdity regardless of the source, qualifies as an intellectual and moral virtue itself, although it permeates the show and is suggested in all the areas we discussed. Over the last decade it has evolved within the larger social milieu while maintaining constancy in terms of quality; its viewers have grown older with Stewart and seen correspondents come and go (including Stephen Colbert to his own wildly successful sibling parody show)—its simple longevity thus also serves to build credibility. And, as the show has become a cultural institution it is increasingly referenced by other media as a source, which further enhances its credibility and legitimacy (McKain, 2005).

62   Though there are many other aspects of the show which might be discussed in relation to its credibility, it should, however, be clear why *The Daily Show* has risen to hold such a significant status among many well-informed citizens: it exhibits all the traits of ethos—good sense and judgment, good moral character, and goodwill towards its audience. It exemplifies the classical ideal of arete (virtue and excellence) in the execution of its twin missions of satire and the advocacy of deliberative democracy and achieves a level of consistent quality rarely seen on contemporary television in either news or entertainment even as it creatively integrates the two realms.

63   And while it can be said to promote cynicism and disenchantment with politics and the media, it in fact seems to enhance people's sense of internal political efficacy, the feeling that one can understand politics, and engage in the political process to make a difference in the world (Baumgartner and Morris, 2006). Arguably this is because, as it dismantles the carefully constructed illusion of the superior—or for that matter, even tolerable—competence, knowledge and decency of elites in politics and the media, it helps return public affairs to the realm of non-elite citizens. It thus also furthers eudaimonia: the happiness, well-being and beautiful flourishing of individuals living in self-determined community with each other that for Aristotle and many other classical philosophers is the ultimate end-goal of human life.

64   Thus, while this essay has viewed the show through the framework of Aristotle's understanding of ethos, we close by drawing on Isocrates, whose conception of ethos maintained an integration of practical persuasive effects with the speaker's actual inner soul, and suggest that *The Daily Show* exemplifies these qualities as well:

65   For Isocrates, ethos is both a legitimating source for and a praiseworthy
effect of the ethical practice of the orator's art…[and] the orator is necessarily both a student and a teacher of the dynamics of civic responsibility. Heeding the call of *public* service as a person of "good repute," his
presence and rhetorical competence are a "showing-forth" (*epi-deixis*)
of an *ethos*, a principled self, that instructs the moral consciousness
and actions of others and thereby serves as a possible catalyst for them
to do the same for the good of their community. (Hyde, 2004, p. xv)

References

Aristotle. (1998). *The Nichomachean Ethics*. (D. Ross, Trans.). New York: Oxford University
Press, Inc. (Original work published 1925.)

———. (1984). *Rhetoric*. (W.R. Roberts, Trans.). In *The Rhetoric and Poetics of Aristotle*.
New York: McGraw-Hill, Inc. (Original work published 1954.)

Awards for "The Daily Show with Jon Stewart" (n.d.). *The Internet Movie Database*.
Retrieved from http://www.imdb.com/title/tt0115147/awards.

Baumgartner, J., and Morris, J.S. (2006). *The Daily Show* effect: candidate evaluations,
efficacy, and American youth. *American Politics Research*, 34(3), 341-367.

Baumlin, J.S. (2006). Ethos. In T.O. Sloane (Ed.), *Encyclopedia of Rhetoric*. Oxford University Press (E-reference edition).

Baym, G. (2004). *The Daily Show* and the reinvention of political journalism. Paper presented at "Faith, Fun, and Futuramas," Third Annual Pre-APSA Conference on
Political Communication Wednesday, September 1, 2004, Chicago, Illinois.

———. (2005). *The Daily Show*: discursive integration and the reinvention of political journalism. *Political Communication, 22*(3), 259-276.

Bill Moyers interviews Jon Stewart. (2003, July 11). *NOW with Bill Moyers*. (2003, July
11). [Television program transcript]. Retrieved from http://www.pbs.org/now/tran-
script/transcript_stewart.html.

Bormann, E. (1972). Fantasy and rhetorical vision: the rhetorical criticism of social reality.
Quarterly Journal of Speech, 58, 396-407.

Coe, K., Tewksbury, D., Bond, B.J., Drogos, K.L., Porter, R.W., Yahn, A., and Zhang, Y.
(2008). Hostile news: partisan use and perceptions of cable news programming.
Journal of Communication 58, 201-219.

Colletta, L. (2009). "Political Satire and Postmodern Irony in the Age of Stephen Colbert
and Jon Stewart." *Journal of Popular Culture* 42(5), 856-874.

Fox, J.R., Koloen, G., and Sahin, V. (2007). No joke: A comparison of substance in *The
Daily Show with Jon Stewart* and broadcast network television coverage of the
2004 Presidential Election campaign. *Journal of Broadcasting and Electronic
Media* 51(2), 213-227.

Holbert, R.L., Lambe, J.L., Dudo, A.D., and Carlton, K.A. (2007). Primacy effects of *The Daily Show* and national TV news viewing: young viewers, political gratifications, and internal political self-efficacy. *Journal of Broadcasting and Electronic Media* 51(1), 20-38.

Hyde, M.J. (2004). Introduction. In M.J. Hyde (Ed.), *The Ethos of Rhetoric* (pp. xiii-xxviii). Columbia: South Carolina: University of South Carolina Press.

Kraul, R. (2010, March 29). Aristotle's Ethics. In E.W. Zalta (Ed.), *The Stanford Encyclopedia of Philosophy (Summer 2010 Edition)*. Retrieved from http://plato.stanford.edu/entries/aristotle-ethics/.

Long, B. (2004, September 29). "'*Daily Show*' viewers ace political quiz." Retrieved from http://www.cnn.com/2004/SHOWBIZ/TV/09/28/comedy.politics/.

McKain, A. (2005). Not necessarily not the news: gatekeeping, remediation, and *The Daily Show*. *The Journal of American Culture*, 28(4), 415-430.

Morris, J. (2008). *The Daily Show with Jon Stewart* and audience attitude change during the 2004 party conventions. *Political Behavior* 31, 79-102.

Pew Research Center. (2008, May 8). *The Daily Show*: Journalism, satire, or just laughs? Retrieved from http://pewresearch.org/pubs/829/the-daily-show-journalism-satire-or-just-laughs.

Rally to Restore Sanity. (2010). Retrieved from http://www.rallytorestoresanity.com/.

Smith, C.R. (2004). *Ethos* dwells pervasively: A hermeneutic reading of Aristotle on credibility. In M.J. Hyde (Ed.), *The Ethos of Rhetoric* (pp. 1-19). Columbia, South Carolina: University of South Carolina Press.

Smolkin, R. (2007). What the mainstream media can learn from Jon Stewart: No, not to be funny and snarky, but to be bold and to do a better job of cutting through the fog. *American Journalism Review* 29(3), 18-25.

Stewart, appearance on Crossfire. (2004, October 15). *Crossfire*. [Television program transcript]. Retrieved from http://politicalhumor.about.com/library/bljonstewartcrossfire.htm.

Trier, J. (2008). *The Daily Show* with Jon Stewart: Part 1. *Journal of Adolescent and Adult Literacy* 51(5), 424-427.

Critical Reading Questions:

- **Summary:** Barbur and Goodnow offer nuanced definitions of the rhetorical appeal ethos, focusing on how Aristotle understood the concept. These definitions form the foundation of their rhetorical analysis. Indicate in some detail how Barbur and Goodnow define the essence of ethos in Aristotle's view, and define the three elements of good sense, good moral character, and goodwill, using summary and paraphrase, citing the essay.

- **Analysis:** The rhythm of rhetorical analysis is to make claims about how a text works and then to offer evidence supporting them. Look at the paragraphs on pages 8-16, quickly examining the rhetorical analysis. What kinds of evidence from *The Daily Show* do the authors use to make their points about how ethos works?

Inventing the University

David Bartholomae

The following selection from David Bartholomae's "Inventing the University" offers insight into the concept of academic discourse communities and reasons why it is difficult for students to enter them. Bartholomae is a professor of English at the University of Pittsburgh whose work is foundational to the field of Rhetoric and Composition. In this piece, originally published in 1986, Bartholomae recognizes that student writers must think, reason, and write in unfamiliar ways as they enter the world of academic writing. Bartholomae suggests that a student must "learn to speak our language. Or . . . carry off the bluff, since speaking and writing will most certainly be required long before the skill is 'learned.'" After establishing that universities ask students to write in unfamiliar ways, Bartholomae offers ways to help students navigate the unfamiliar waters of academic discourse communities. Primarily, he recommends that students "imagine and conform to a reader's goals," which might be a fancy way of suggesting that students "fake it until they make it."

—KGR

1 Education may well be, as of right, the instrument whereby every individual, in a society like our own, can gain access to any kind of discourse. But we well know that in its distribution, in what it permits and in what it prevents, it follows the well-trodden battle-lines of social conflict. Every educational system is a political means of maintaining or of modifying the appropriation of discourse, with the knowledge and the powers to carry it out.

2 —FOCAULT, *The Discourse on Language*

...the text is the form of the social relationships made visible, palpable, material.

3 —BERNSTEIN, *Codes, Modalities and the Process of Cultural Reproduction: A Model*

4 Every time a student sits down to write for us, he has to invent the university for the occasion—invent the university, that is, or a branch of it, like history or anthropology or economics or English. The student has to learn to speak our language, to speak as we do, to try on the peculiar ways of knowing, selecting, evaluating, reporting, concluding, and arguing that define the discourse of our community. Or perhaps I should say the various discourses of our community, since it is in the nature of a liberal arts education that a student, after the first year or two must learn to try on a variety of voices and interpre-

tive schemes—to write, for example, as a literary critic one day and as an experimental psychologist the next; to work within fields where the rules governing the presentation of examples or the development of an argument are both distinct and, even to a professional mysterious.

5   The student has to appropriate (or be appropriated by) a specialized discourse, and he has to do this as though he were easily and comfortably one with his audience, as though he were a member of the academy or an historian or anthropologist or an economist; he has to invent the university by assembling and mimicking its language while finding some compromise between idiosyncrasy, a personal history, on the one hand, and the requirements of convention, the history of a discipline, on the other. He must learn to speak our language. Or he must dare to speak it or to carry off the bluff, since speaking and writing will most certainly be required long before the skill is "learned." And this, understandably, causes problems.

6   Let me look quickly at an example. Here is an essay, written by a college freshman.

7   In the past time I thought that an incident was creative was when I had
         to make a clay model of the earth, but not of the classical or your every-
         day model of the earth which consists of the two cores, the mantle and
         the crust. I thought of these things in a dimension of which it would be
         unique, but easy to comprehend. Of course, your materials to work
         with were basic and limited at the same time, but thought help to put
         this limit into a right attitude or frame of mind to work with the clay.

         In the beginning of the clay model, I had to research and learn
         the different dimensions of the earth (in magnitude, quantity, state
         of matter, etc.) After this, I learned how to put this into the clay
         and come up with something different than any other person in
         my class at the time. In my opinion, color coordination and shape
         was the key to my creativity of the clay model of the earth.

         Creativity is the venture of the mind at work with the mechanics relay to
         the limbs from the cranium, which stores and triggers this action. It can
         be a burst of energy released at a precise time a thought is being trans-
         mitted. This can cause a frenzy of the human body, but it depends on
         the characteristics of the individual and how they can relay the message
         clearly enough through mechanics of the body to us as an observer. Then
         we must determine if it is creative or a learned process varied by the indi-
         viduals thought process. Creativity is indeed a tool which has to exist, or
         our world will not succeed into the future and progress like it should.

8   I am continually impressed by the patience and goodwill of our students. This student was writing a placement essay during freshman orientation. (The problem set to him was; "Describe a time when you did something you felt to be creative. Then, on the basis of the

incident you have described go on to draw some general conclusions about 'creativity.'") He knew that university faculty would be reading and evaluating this essay, and so he wrote for them.

9   In some ways it is a remarkable performance. He is trying on the discourse even though he doesn't have the knowledge that would make the discourse more than a routine, a set of conventional rituals and gestures. And he is doing this, I think, even though he *knows* he doesn't have the knowledge that would make the discourse more than a routine. He defines himself as a researcher working systematically, and not as a kid in a high school class: "I thought of these things in a dimension of ..."; "I had to research and learn the different dimensions of the earth (in magnitude, quantity, state of matter, etc.)." He moves quickly into a specialized language (his approximation of our jargon) and draws both a general, textbook-like conclusion—"Creativity is the venture of the mind at work..."—and a resounding peroration—"Creativity is indeed a tool which has to exist, or our world will not succeed into the future and progress like it should." The writer has even picked up the rhythm of our prose with that last "indeed" and with the qualifications and the parenthetical expressions of the opening paragraphs. And through it all he speaks with an impressive air of authority.

10   There is an elaborate but, I will argue, a necessary and enabling fiction at work here as the student dramatizes his experience in a "setting"—the setting required by the discourse—where he can speak to us as a companion, a fellow researcher. As I read the essay, there is only one moment when the fiction is broken, when we are addressed differently. The student says, "Of course, your materials to work with were basic and limited at the same time, but thought help to put this limit into a right attitude or frame of mind to work with the clay." At this point, I think, we become students and he the teacher giving us a lesson (as in, "You take your pencil in your right hand and put your paper in front of you"). This is, however, one of the most characteristic slips of basic writers. (I use the term *basic writers* to refer to university students traditionally placed in remedial composition courses.) It is very hard for them to take on the role—the voice, the persona—of an authority whose authority is rooted in scholarship, analysis, or research. They slip, then, into a more immediately available and realizable voice of authority, the voice of a teacher giving a lesson or the voice of a parent lecturing at the dinner table. They offer advice or homilies rather than "academic" conclusions. There is a similar break in the final paragraph, where the conclusion that pushes for a definition ("Creativity is the venture of the mind at work with the mechanics relay to the limbs from the cranium") is replaced by a conclusion that speaks in the voice of an elder ("Creativity is indeed a tool which has to exist, or our world will not succeed into the future and progress like it should").

11   It is not uncommon, then, to find such breaks in the concluding sections of essays written by basic writers. Here is the concluding section of essay written by a student about his work as a mechanic. He had been asked to generalize about work after reviewing an on-the-job experience or incident that "stuck in his mind" as somehow significant.

12   How could two repairmen miss a leak? Lack of pride? No incentive? Lazy? I don't know.

13   At this point the writer is in a perfect position to speculate, to move from the problem to an analysis of the problem. Here is how the paragraph continues, however (and notice the change in pronoun reference).

14   From this point on, I take my time, do it right, and don't let customers get
         under your skin. If they have a complaint, tell them to call your boss and
         he'll be more than glad to handle it. Most important, worry about your-
         self, and keep a clear eye on everyone, for there's always someone try-
         ing to take advantage of you, anytime and anyplace. (Emphasis added)

15   We get neither a technical discussion nor an "academic" discussion but a Lesson on Life.(1) This is the language he uses to address the general question, "How could two repairmen miss a leak?" The other brand of conclusion, the more academic one, would have required him to speak of his experience in our terms; it would, that is, have required a special vocabulary, a special system of presentation, and an interpretive scheme (or a set of commonplaces) he could have used to identify and talk about the mystery of human error. The writer certainly had access to the range of acceptable commonplaces for such an explanation: "lack of pride," "no incentive," "lazy." Each commonplace would dictate its own set of phrases, examples, and conclusions; and we, his teachers, would know how to write out each argument, just as we know how to write out more specialized arguments of our own. A "commonplace" then, is a culturally or institutionally authorized concept or statement that carries with it its own necessary elaboration. We all use commonplaces to orient ourselves in the world; they provide points of reference and a set of "prearticulated" explanations that are readily available to organize and interpret experience. The phrase "lack of pride" carries with it its own account of the repairman's error, just as at another point in time a reference to "original sin" would have provided an explanation, or just as in certain university classrooms a reference to "alienation" would enable writers to continue and complete the discussion. While there is a way in which these terms are interchange-able, they are not all permissible. A student in a composition class would most likely be turned away from a discussion of original sin. Commonplaces are the "controlling ideas" of our composition textbooks, textbooks that not only insist on a set form for expository writing but a set view of public life.(2)

16   When the writer says, "I don't know," then, he is not saying that he has nothing to say. He is saying that he is not in a position to carry on this discussion. And so we are addressed as apprentices rather than as teachers or scholars. In order to speak as a per-son of status or privilege, the writer can either speak to us in our terms—in the privileged language of university discourse—or, in default (or in defiance) of that, he can speak to us as though we were children, offering us the wisdom of experience.

17   I think it is possible to say that the language of the "Clay Model" paper has come *through* the writer and not from the writer. The writer has located himself (more precisely, he has located the self that is represented by the "I" on the page) in a context that is finally beyond him, not his own and not available to his immediate procedures for inventing and arranging text. I would not, that is, call this essay an example of "writer-based" prose. I

would not say that it is egocentric or that it represents the "interior monologue or a writer thinking and talking to himself" (Flower, 1981, p. 63). It is, rather, the record of a writer who has lost himself in the discourse of his readers. There is a context beyond the intended reader that is not the world but a way of talking about the world, a way of talking that determines the use of examples, the possible conclusions, acceptable commonplaces, and key words for an essay on the construction of a clay model of the earth. This writer has entered the discourse without successfully approximating it.

18   Linda Flower (1981) has argued that the difficulty inexperienced writers have with writing can be understood as a difficulty in negotiating the transition between "writer-based" and "reader-based" prose. Expert writers, in other words, can better imagine how a reader will respond to a text and can transform or restructure what they have to say around a goal shared with a reader. Teaching students to revise for readers, then, will better prepare them to write initially with a reader in mind. The success of this pedagogy depends on the degree to which a writer can imagine and conform to a reader's goals. The difficulty of this act of imagination and the burden of such conformity are so much at the heart of the problem that a teacher must pause and take stock before offering revision as a solution. A student like the one who wrote the "Clay Model" paper is not so much trapped in a private language as he is shut out from one of the privileged languages of public life, a language he is aware of but cannot control.

Notes

1. David Olson (1981) has made a similar observation about school-related problems of language learning in younger children. Here is his conclusion: "Hence, depending upon whether children assumed language was primarily suitable for making assertions and conjectures or primarily for making direct or indirect commands, they will either find school texts easy or difficult" (p. 107).

2. For Aristotle, there were both general and specific commonplaces. A speaker, says Aristotle, has a "stock of arguments to which he may turn for a particular need."

    > If he knows the *topoi* (regions, places, lines of argument)—and a skilled speaker will know them—he will know where to find what he wants for a special case. The general topics, or *commonplaces,* are regions containing arguments that are common to all branches of knowledge... But there are also special topics (regions, places, *loci*) in which one looks for arguments appertaining to particular branches of knowledge, special sciences, such as ethics or politics. (1932, pp. 154-55).

    And, he says, "the topics or places, then, may be indifferently thought of as in the science that is concerned or in the mind of the speaker." But the question of location is "indifferent" *only* if the mind of the speaker is in line with set opinion, general assumption.

For the speaker (or writer) who is not situated so comfortably in the privileged public realm, this is indeed not an indifferent matter at all. If he does not have the commonplace at hand, he will not, in Aristotle's terms, know where to go at all.

References

Aristotle. (1932). *The Rhetoric of Aristotle* (L. Cooper, Trans.). Englewood Cliffs, NJ: Prentice-Hall.

Flower, L.S. (1981). Revising writer-based prose. *Journal of Basic Writing 3,* 62-74.

Olson, D.R. (1981). Writing: The divorce of the author from the text. In B.M. Kroll and R.J. Vann (Eds.) *Exploring speaking-writing relationships: Connections and contrasts.* Urbana, IL: National Council of Teachers of English.

Critical Reading Questions:

- **Reflection:** What are the differences in the ways you are asked to think, reason, and write in your current classes? How does the university get "invented" differently in psychology as opposed to biology or in history as opposed to English?

- **Interpretation:** Even though the university primarily exists to teach students, Bartholomae seems to suggest that students don't "belong" in the discourse community of the university. Does he satisfactorily reconcile this conflict? If so, how?

Address to a Joint Session of Congress and the American People

George W. Bush

The stakeholders for what some consider to be the most important speech made on September 20, of the early twenty-first century include a worldwide audience of many nations but most importantly, and obviously, a nation of fearful Americans faced with a national tragedy: the destruction of the World Trade Center towers on September 11th, 2001. Bush's speech, the rhetorical product of presidential speechwriters, offers many opportunities to explore the pisteis—ethos, logos, and pathos. Definitionally, Bush's speech seeks to name the events of 9/11 as both a tragedy and a terrorist attack. By labeling the events this way, Bush attempts to offer assurances and comfort to victims and observers while clearly offering a targeted threat to those behind the attacks.

—WCM

1   Mr. Speaker, Mr. President *Pro Tempore,* members of Congress, and fellow Americans:

2   In the normal course of events, Presidents come to this chamber to report on the state of the Union. Tonight, no such report is needed. It has already been delivered by the American people.

3   We have seen it in the courage of passengers, who rushed terrorists to save others on the ground—passengers like an exceptional man named Todd Beamer. And would you please help me to welcome his wife, Lisa Beamer, here tonight.

4   We have seen the state of our Union in the endurance of rescuers, working past exhaustion. We have seen the unfurling of flags, the lighting of candles, the giving of blood, the saying of prayers—in English, Hebrew, and Arabic. We have seen the decency of a loving and giving people who have made the grief of strangers their own.

5   My fellow citizens, for the last nine days, the entire world has seen for itself the state of our Union—and it is strong.

6   Tonight we are a country awakened to danger and called to defend freedom. Our grief has turned to anger, and anger to resolution. Whether we bring our enemies to justice, or bring justice to our enemies, justice will be done.

7   I thank the Congress for its leadership at such an important time. All of America was touched on the evening of the tragedy to see Republicans and Democrats joined together on the steps of this Capitol, singing "God Bless America." And you did more than sing; you acted, by delivering $40 billion to rebuild our communities and meet the needs of our military.

8   Speaker Hastert, Minority Leader Gephardt, Majority Leader Daschle and Senator Lott, I thank you for your friendship, for your leadership and for your service to our country.

9   And on behalf of the American people, I thank the world for its outpouring of support. America will never forget the sounds of our National Anthem playing at Buckingham Palace, on the streets of Paris, and at Berlin's Brandenburg Gate.

10   We will not forget South Korean children gathering to pray outside our embassy in Seoul, or the prayers of sympathy offered at a mosque in Cairo. We will not forget moments of silence and days of mourning in Australia and Africa and Latin America.

11   Nor will we forget the citizens of 80 other nations who died with our own: dozens of Pakistanis; more than 130 Israelis; more than 250 citizens of India; men and women from El Salvador, Iran, Mexico and Japan; and hundreds of British citizens. America has no truer friend than Great Britain.

12   Once again, we are joined together in a great cause—so honored the British Prime Minister has crossed an ocean to show his unity of purpose with America. Thank you for coming, friend.

13   On September the 11th, enemies of freedom committed an act of war against our country. Americans have known wars—but for the past 136 years, they have been wars on foreign soil, except for one Sunday in 1941. Americans have known the casualties of war—but not at the center of a great city on a peaceful morning. Americans have known surprise attacks—but never before on thousands of civilians. All of this was brought upon us in a single day—and night fell on a different world, a world where freedom itself is under attack.

14   Americans have many questions tonight. Americans are asking: Who attacked our country? The evidence we have gathered all points to a collection of loosely affiliated terrorist organizations known as al Qaeda. They are the same murderers indicted for bombing American embassies in Tanzania and Kenya, and responsible for bombing the USS Cole.

15   Al Qaeda is to terror what the mafia is to crime. But its goal is not making money; its goal is remaking the world—and imposing its radical beliefs on people everywhere.

16   The terrorists practice a fringe form of Islamic extremism that has been rejected by Muslim scholars and the vast majority of Muslim clerics—a fringe movement that perverts the peaceful teachings of Islam. The terrorists' directive commands them to kill Christians and Jews, to kill all Americans, and make no distinction among military and civilians, including women and children.

17   This group and its leader—a person named Osama bin Laden—are linked to many other organizations in different countries, including the Egyptian Islamic Jihad and the Islamic Movement of Uzbekistan. There are thousands of these terrorists in more than 60 countries. They are recruited from their own nations and neighborhoods and brought to camps in places like Afghanistan, where they are trained in the tactics of terror. They are sent back to their homes or sent to hide in countries around the world to plot evil and destruction.

18   The leadership of al Qaeda has great influence in Afghanistan and supports the Taliban regime in controlling most of that country. In Afghanistan, we see al Qaeda's vision for the world.

19   Afghanistan's people have been brutalized—many are starving and many have fled. Women are not allowed to attend school. You can be jailed for owning a television. Religion can be practiced only as their leaders dictate. A man can be jailed in Afghanistan if his beard is not long enough.

20   The United States respects the people of Afghanistan—after all, we are currently its largest source of humanitarian aid—but we condemn the Taliban regime. It is not only repressing its own people, it is threatening people everywhere by sponsoring and sheltering and supplying terrorists. By aiding and abetting murder, the Taliban regime is committing murder.

21   And tonight, the United States of America makes the following demands on the Taliban: Deliver to United States authorities all the leaders of al Qaeda who hide in your land. Release all foreign nationals, including American citizens, you have unjustly imprisoned. Protect foreign journalists, diplomats and aid workers in your country. Close immediately and permanently every terrorist training camp in Afghanistan, and hand over every terrorist, and every person in their support structure, to appropriate authorities. Give the United States full access to terrorist training camps, so we can make sure they are no longer operating.

22   These demands are not open to negotiation or discussion. The Taliban must act, and act immediately. They will hand over the terrorists, or they will share in their fate.

23   I also want to speak tonight directly to Muslims throughout the world. We respect your faith. It's practiced freely by many millions of Americans, and by millions more in countries that America counts as friends. Its teachings are good and peaceful, and those who commit evil in the name of Allah blaspheme the name of Allah. The terrorists are traitors to their own faith, trying, in effect, to hijack Islam itself. The enemy of America is not our many Muslim friends; it is not our many Arab friends. Our enemy is a radical network of terrorists, and every government that supports them.

24   Our war on terror begins with al Qaeda, but it does not end there. It will not end until every terrorist group of global reach has been found, stopped and defeated.

25   Americans are asking, why do they hate us? They hate what we see right here in this chamber—a democratically elected government. Their leaders are self-appointed. They hate our freedoms—our freedom of religion, our freedom of speech, our freedom to vote and assemble and disagree with each other.

26   They want to overthrow existing governments in many Muslim countries, such as Egypt, Saudi Arabia, and Jordan. They want to drive Israel out of the Middle East. They want to drive Christians and Jews out of vast regions of Asia and Africa.

27   These terrorists kill not merely to end lives, but to disrupt and end a way of life. With every atrocity, they hope that America grows fearful, retreating from the world and forsaking our friends. They stand against us, because we stand in their way.

28   We are not deceived by their pretenses to piety. We have seen their kind before. They are the heirs of all the murderous ideologies of the 20th century. By sacrificing human life to serve their radical visions—by abandoning every value except the will to power—they follow in the path of fascism, and Nazism, and totalitarianism. And they will follow that path all the way, to where it ends: in history's unmarked grave of discarded lies.

29   Americans are asking: How will we fight and win this war? We will direct every resource at our command—every means of diplomacy, every tool of intelligence, every instrument of law enforcement, every financial influence, and every necessary weapon of war—to the disruption and to the defeat of the global terror network

30   This war will not be like the war against Iraq a decade ago, with a decisive liberation of territory and a swift conclusion. It will not look like the air war above Kosovo two years ago, where no ground troops were used and not a single American was lost in combat.

31   Our response involves far more than instant retaliation and isolated strikes. Americans should not expect one battle, but a lengthy campaign, unlike any other we have ever seen. It may include dramatic strikes, visible on TV, and covert operations, secret even in success. We will starve terrorists of funding, turn them one against another, drive them from place to place, until there is no refuge or no rest. And we will pursue nations that provide aid or safe haven to terrorism. Every nation, in every region, now has a decision to make. Either you are with us, or you are with the terrorists. From this day forward, any nation that continues to harbor or support terrorism will be regarded by the United States as a hostile regime.

32   Our nation has been put on notice: We are not immune from attack. We will take defensive measures against terrorism to protect Americans. Today, dozens of federal departments and agencies, as well as state and local governments, have responsibilities affecting homeland security. These efforts must be coordinated at the highest level. So tonight I announce the creation of a Cabinet-level position reporting directly to me—the Office of Homeland Security.

33   And tonight I also announce a distinguished American to lead this effort, to strengthen American security: a military veteran, an effective governor, a true patriot, a trusted friend—Pennsylvania's Tom Ridge. He will lead, oversee and coordinate a comprehensive national strategy to safeguard our country against terrorism, and respond to any attacks that may come.

34   These measures are essential. But the only way to defeat terrorism as a threat to our way of life is to stop it, eliminate it, and destroy it where it grows. Many will be involved in this effort, from FBI agents to intelligence operatives to the reservists we have called to active duty. All deserve our thanks, and all have our prayers. And tonight, a few miles from the damaged Pentagon, I have a message for our military: Be ready. I've called the Armed Forces to alert, and there is a reason. The hour is coming when America will act, and you will make us proud.

35   This is not, however, just America's fight. And what is at stake is not just America's freedom. This is the world's fight. This is civilization's fight. This is the fight of all who believe in progress and pluralism, tolerance and freedom.

36   We ask every nation to join us. We will ask, and we will need, the help of police forces, intelligence services, and banking systems around the world. The United States is grateful that many nations and many international organizations have already responded—with sympathy and with support. Nations from Latin America, to Asia, to Africa, to Europe, to the Islamic world. Perhaps the NATO Charter reflects best the attitude of the world: An attack on one is an attack on all.

37   The civilized world is rallying to America's side. They understand that if this terror goes unpunished, their own cities, their own citizens may be next. Terror, unanswered, can not only bring down buildings, it can threaten the stability of legitimate governments. And you know what—we're not going to allow it.

38   Americans are asking: What is expected of us? I ask you to live your lives, and hug your children. I know many citizens have fears tonight, and I ask you to be calm and resolute, even in the face of a continuing threat.

39   I ask you to uphold the values of America, and remember why so many have come here. We are in a fight for our principles, and our first responsibility is to live by them. No one should be singled out for unfair treatment or unkind words because of their ethnic background or religious faith.

40   I ask you to continue to support the victims of this tragedy with your contributions. Those who want to give can go to a central source of information, *libertyunites.org,* to find the names of groups providing direct help in New York, Pennsylvania, and Virginia.

41   The thousands of FBI agents who are now at work in this investigation may need your cooperation, and I ask you to give it.

42   I ask for your patience, with the delays and inconveniences that may accompany tighter security; and for your patience in what will be a long struggle.

43   I ask your continued participation and confidence in the American economy. Terrorists attacked a symbol of American prosperity. They did not touch its source. America is successful because of the hard work, and creativity, and enterprise of our people. These were the true strengths of our economy before September 11th, and they are our strengths today.

44   And, finally, please continue praying for the victims of terror and their families, for those in uniform, and for our great country. Prayer has comforted us in sorrow, and will help strengthen us for the journey ahead.

45   Tonight I thank my fellow Americans for what you have already done and for what you will do. And ladies and gentlemen of the Congress, I thank you, their representatives, for what you have already done and for what we will do together.

46   Tonight, we face new and sudden national challenges. We will come together to improve air safety, to dramatically expand the number of air marshals on domestic flights, and take new measures to prevent hijacking. We will come together to promote stability and keep our airlines flying, with direct assistance during this emergency.

47   We will come together to give law enforcement the additional tools it needs to track down terror here at home. We will come together to strengthen our intelligence capabilities to know the plans of terrorists before they act, and find them before they strike.

48   We will come together to take active steps that strengthen America's economy, and put our people back to work.

49   Tonight we welcome two leaders who embody the extraordinary spirit of all New Yorkers: Governor George Pataki, and Mayor Rudolph Giuliani. As a symbol of America's resolve, my administration will work with Congress, and these two leaders, to show the world that we will rebuild New York City.

50   After all that has just passed—all the lives taken, and all the possibilities and hopes that died with them—it is natural to wonder if America's future is one of fear. Some speak of an age of terror. I know there are struggles ahead, and dangers to face. But this country will define our times, not be defined by them. As long as the United States of America is determined and strong, this will not be an age of terror; this will be an age of liberty, here and across the world.

51   Great harm has been done to us. We have suffered great loss. And in our grief and anger we have found our mission and our moment. Freedom and fear are at war. The advance of human freedom—the great achievement of our time, and the great hope of every time—now depends on us. Our nation—this generation—will lift a dark threat of violence from our people and our future. We will rally the world to this cause by our efforts, by our courage. We will not tire, we will not falter, and we will not fail.

52   It is my hope that in the months and years ahead, life will return almost to normal. We'll go back to our lives and routines, and that is good. Even grief recedes with time and grace. But our resolve must not pass. Each of us will remember what happened that day, and to whom it happened. We'll remember the moment the news came—where we were and what we were doing. Some will remember an image of a fire, or a story of rescue. Some will carry memories of a face and a voice gone forever.

53   And I will carry this: It is the police shield of a man named George Howard, who died at the World Trade Center trying to save others. It was given to me by his mom, Arlene, as a proud memorial to her son. This is my reminder of lives that ended, and a task that does not end.

54   I will not forget this wound to our country or those who inflicted it. I will not yield; I will not rest; I will not relent in waging this struggle for freedom and security for the American people.

55   The course of this conflict is not known, yet its outcome is certain. Freedom and fear, justice and cruelty, have always been at war, and we know that God is not neutral between them.

56   Fellow citizens, we'll meet violence with patient justice—assured of the rightness of our cause, and confident of the victories to come. In all that lies before us, may God grant us wisdom, and may He watch over the United States of America.

57   Thank you.

Critical Reading Questions:

- **Rhetorical analysis:** Are the places where Bush uses "American" values as rhetorical appeals effective? How, why, and for what audiences?

- **Rhetorical analysis:** What rhetorical strategies does Bush use to secure the trust, confidence, and goodwill of his audience?

Is Google Making Us Stupid?

Nicholas Carr

**American writer Nicholas Carr initially generated conversation and contro-
versy with his insights on the outsourcing of information technology, and
debate over his ideas came to new heights in the media and blogosphere
when the following article appeared in *The Atlantic Monthly*. Originally entitled "Is Google Making Us Stoopid?" this work's primary assertion is that
the Internet may be adversely affecting human concentration and cognition. Carr also argues that, in many ways, we are a creation of our machines
as much as they are our creations. He describes how the clock standard-
ized human experience into discrete moments of time and how profoundly
Friedrich Nietzsche's writing was transformed when he had to shift from
handwriting to typing. Similarly, in this computerized age, it is only natural
that we think in computer terms. Carr expanded the themes in this article
into his book *The Shallows: What the Internet Is Doing to Our Brains*, which
was a 2011 Pulitzer Prize finalist.**

—BLS

1   "Dave, stop. Stop, will you? Stop, Dave. Will you stop, Dave?" So the supercomputer
HAL pleads with the implacable astronaut Dave Bowman in a famous and weirdly poignant scene toward the end of Stanley Kubrick's *2001: A Space Odyssey*. Bowman, having nearly been sent to a deep-space death by the malfunctioning machine, is calmly,
coldly disconnecting the memory circuits that control its artificial brain. "Dave, my mind is
going," HAL says, forlornly. "I can feel it. I can feel it."

2   I can feel it, too. Over the past few years I've had an uncomfortable sense that someone, or something, has been tinkering with my brain, remapping the neural circuitry, reprogramming the memory. My mind isn't going—so far as I can tell—but it's changing. I'm not
thinking the way I used to think. I can feel it most strongly when I'm reading. Immersing
myself in a book or a lengthy article used to be easy. My mind would get caught up in the
narrative or the turns of the argument, and I'd spend hours strolling through long stretches
of prose. That's rarely the case anymore. Now my concentration often starts to drift after
two or three pages. I get fidgety, lose the thread, begin looking for something else to do.
I feel as if I'm always dragging my wayward brain back to the text. The deep reading that
used to come naturally has become a struggle.

3   I think I know what's going on. For more than a decade now, I've been spending a
lot of time online, searching and surfing and sometimes adding to the great databases of
the Internet. The Web has been a godsend to me as a writer. Research that once required
days in the stacks or periodical rooms of libraries can now be done in minutes. A few
Google searches, some quick clicks on hyperlinks, and I've got the telltale fact or pithy
quote I was after. Even when I'm not working, I'm as likely as not to be foraging in the

Web's info-thickets—reading and writing e-mails, scanning headlines and blog posts, watching videos and listening to podcasts, or just tripping from link to link to link. (Unlike footnotes, to which they're sometimes likened, hyperlinks don't merely point to related works; they propel you toward them.)

4   For me, as for others, the Net is becoming a universal medium, the conduit for most of the information that flows through my eyes and ears and into my mind. The advantages of having immediate access to such an incredibly rich store of information are many, and they've been widely described and duly applauded. "The perfect recall of silicon memory," *Wired*'s Clive Thompson has written, "can be an enormous boon to thinking." But that boon comes at a price. As the media theorist Marshall McLuhan pointed out in the 1960s, media are not just passive channels of information. They supply the stuff of thought, but they also shape the process of thought. And what the Net seems to be doing is chipping away my capacity for concentration and contemplation. My mind now expects to take in information the way the Net distributes it: in a swiftly moving stream of particles. Once I was a scuba diver in the sea of words. Now I zip along the surface like a guy on a Jet Ski.

5   I'm not the only one. When I mention my troubles with reading to friends and acquaintances—literary types, most of them—many say they're having similar experiences. The more they use the Web, the more they have to fight to stay focused on long pieces of writing. Some of the bloggers I follow have also begun mentioning the phenomenon. Scott Karp, who writes a blog about online media, recently confessed that he has stopped reading books altogether. "I was a lit major in college, and used to be [a] voracious book reader," he wrote. "What happened?" He speculates on the answer: "What if I do all my reading on the Web not so much because the way I read has changed, i.e. I'm just seeking convenience, but because the way I THINK has changed?"

6   Bruce Friedman, who blogs regularly about the use of computers in medicine, also has described how the Internet has altered his mental habits. "I now have almost totally lost the ability to read and absorb a longish article on the Web or in print," he wrote earlier this year. A pathologist who has long been on the faculty of the University of Michigan Medical School, Friedman elaborated on his comment in a telephone conversation with me. His thinking, he said, has taken on a "staccato" quality, reflecting the way he quickly scans short passages of text from many sources online. "I can't read *War and Peace* anymore," he admitted. "I've lost the ability to do that. Even a blog post of more than three or four paragraphs is too much to absorb. I skim it."

7   Anecdotes alone don't prove much. And we still await the long-term neurological and psychological experiments that will provide a definitive picture of how Internet use affects cognition. But a recently published study of online research habits, conducted by scholars from University College London, suggests that we may well be in the midst of a sea change in the way we read and think. As part of the five-year research program, the scholars examined computer logs documenting the behavior of visitors to two popular research sites, one operated by the British Library and one by a U.K. educational consortium, that provide access to journal articles, e-books, and other sources of written information. They found that people using the sites exhibited "a form of skimming activity," hopping from one source to another and rarely returning to any source they'd already visited. They typically

read no more than one or two pages of an article or book before they would "bounce" out to another site. Sometimes they'd save a long article, but there's no evidence that they ever went back and actually read it. The authors of the study report:

8   It is clear that users are not reading online in the traditional sense;
           indeed there are signs that new forms of "reading" are emerg-
           ing as users "power browse" horizontally through titles, con-
           tents pages and abstracts going for quick wins. It almost seems
           that they go online to avoid reading in the traditional sense.

9   Thanks to the ubiquity of text on the Internet, not to mention the popularity of text-messaging on cell phones, we may well be reading more today than we did in the 1970s or 1980s, when television was our medium of choice. But it's a different kind of reading, and behind it lies a different kind of thinking—perhaps even a new sense of the self. "We are not only *what* we read," says Maryanne Wolf, a developmental psychologist at Tufts University and the author of *Proust and the Squid: The Story and Science of the Reading Brain.* "We are *how* we read." Wolf worries that the style of reading promoted by the Net, a style that puts "efficiency" and "immediacy" above all else, may be weakening our capacity for the kind of deep reading that emerged when an earlier technology, the printing press, made long and complex works of prose commonplace. When we read online, she says, we tend to become "mere decoders of information." Our ability to interpret text, to make the rich mental connections that form when we read deeply and without distraction, remains largely disengaged.

10   Reading, explains Wolf, is not an instinctive skill for human beings. It's not etched into our genes the way speech is. We have to teach our minds how to translate the symbolic characters we see into the language we understand. And the media or other technologies we use in learning and practicing the craft of reading play an important part in shaping the neural circuits inside our brains. Experiments demonstrate that readers of ideograms, such as the Chinese, develop a mental circuitry for reading that is very different from the circuitry found in those of us whose written language employs an alphabet. The variations extend across many regions of the brain, including those that govern such essential cognitive functions as memory and the interpretation of visual and auditory stimuli. We can expect as well that the circuits woven by our use of the Net will be different from those woven by our reading of books and other printed works.

11   Sometime in 1882, Friedrich Nietzsche bought a typewriter—a Malling-Hansen Writing Ball, to be precise. His vision was failing, and keeping his eyes focused on a page had become exhausting and painful, often bringing on crushing headaches. He had been forced to curtail his writing, and he feared that he would soon have to give it up. The typewriter rescued him, at least for a time. Once he had mastered touch-typing, he was able to write with his eyes closed, using only the tips of his fingers. Words could once again flow from his mind to the page.

12   But the machine had a subtler effect on his work. One of Nietzsche's friends, a composer, noticed a change in the style of his writing. His already terse prose had become even tighter, more telegraphic. "Perhaps you will through this instrument even take to a

new idiom," the friend wrote in a letter, noting that, in his own work, his "'thoughts' in music and language often depend on the quality of pen and paper."

13   "You are right," Nietzsche replied, "our writing equipment takes part in the forming of our thoughts." Under the sway of the machine, writes the German media scholar Friedrich A. Kittler, Nietzsche's prose "changed from arguments to aphorisms, from thoughts to puns, from rhetoric to telegram style."

14   The human brain is almost infinitely malleable. People used to think that our mental meshwork, the dense connections formed among the 100 billion or so neurons inside our skulls, was largely fixed by the time we reached adulthood. But brain researchers have discovered that that's not the case. James Olds, a professor of neuroscience who directs the Krasnow Institute for Advanced Study at George Mason University, says that even the adult mind "is very plastic." Nerve cells routinely break old connections and form new ones. "The brain," according to Olds, "has the ability to reprogram itself on the fly, altering the way it functions."

15   As we use what the sociologist Daniel Bell has called our "intellectual technologies"— the tools that extend our mental rather than our physical capacities—we inevitably begin to take on the qualities of those technologies. The mechanical clock, which came into common use in the 14th century, provides a compelling example. In *Technics and Civilization,* the historian and cultural critic Lewis Mumford described how the clock "disassociated time from human events and helped create the belief in an independent world of mathematically measurable sequences." The "abstract framework of divided time" became "the point of reference for both action and thought."

16   The clock's methodical ticking helped bring into being the scientific mind and the scientific man. But it also took something away. As the late MIT computer scientist Joseph Weizenbaum observed in his 1976 book, *Computer Power and Human Reason: From Judgment to Calculation,* the conception of the world that emerged from the widespread use of timekeeping instruments "remains an impoverished version of the older one, for it rests on a rejection of those direct experiences that formed the basis for, and indeed constituted, the old reality." In deciding when to eat, to work, to sleep, to rise, we stopped listening to our senses and started obeying the clock.

17   The process of adapting to new intellectual technologies is reflected in the changing metaphors we use to explain ourselves to ourselves. When the mechanical clock arrived, people began thinking of their brains as operating "like clockwork." Today, in the age of software, we have come to think of them as operating "like computers." But the changes, neuroscience tells us, go much deeper than metaphor. Thanks to our brain's plasticity, the adaptation occurs also at a biological level.

18   The Internet promises to have particularly far-reaching effects on cognition. In a paper published in 1936, the British mathematician Alan Turing proved that a digital computer, which at the time existed only as a theoretical machine, could be programmed to perform the function of any other information-processing device. And that's what we're seeing today. The Internet, an immeasurably powerful computing system, is subsuming most of our other intellectual technologies. It's becoming our map and our clock, our printing press and our typewriter, our calculator and our telephone, and our radio and TV.

19   When the Net absorbs a medium, that medium is re-created in the Net's image. It injects the medium's content with hyperlinks, blinking ads, and other digital gewgaws, and it surrounds the content with the content of all the other media it has absorbed. A new e-mail message, for instance, may announce its arrival as we're glancing over the latest headlines at a newspaper's site. The result is to scatter our attention and diffuse our concentration.

20   The Net's influence doesn't end at the edges of a computer screen, either. As people's minds become attuned to the crazy quilt of Internet media, traditional media have to adapt to the audience's new expectations. Television programs add text crawls and pop-up ads, and magazines and newspapers shorten their articles, introduce capsule summaries, and crowd their pages with easy-to-browse info-snippets. When, in March of this year, *The New York Times* decided to devote the second and third pages of every edition to article abstracts, its design director, Tom Bodkin, explained that the "shortcuts" would give harried readers a quick "taste" of the day's news, sparing them the "less efficient" method of actually turning the pages and reading the articles. Old media have little choice but to play by the new-media rules.

21   Never has a communications system played so many roles in our lives—or exerted such broad influence over our thoughts—as the Internet does today. Yet, for all that's been written about the Net, there's been little consideration of how, exactly, it's reprogramming us. The Net's intellectual ethic remains obscure.

22   About the same time that Nietzsche started using his typewriter, an earnest young man named Frederick Winslow Taylor carried a stopwatch into the Midvale Steel plant in Philadelphia and began a historic series of experiments aimed at improving the efficiency of the plant's machinists. With the approval of Midvale's owners, he recruited a group of factory hands, set them to work on various metalworking machines, and recorded and timed their every movement as well as the operations of the machines. By breaking down every job into a sequence of small, discrete steps and then testing different ways of performing each one, Taylor created a set of precise instructions—an "algorithm," we might say today—for how each worker should work. Midvale's employees grumbled about the strict new regime, claiming that it turned them into little more than automatons, but the factory's productivity soared.

23   More than a hundred years after the invention of the steam engine, the Industrial Revolution had at last found its philosophy and its philosopher. Taylor's tight industrial choreography—his "system," as he liked to call it—was embraced by manufacturers throughout the country and, in time, around the world. Seeking maximum speed, maximum efficiency, and maximum output, factory owners used time-and-motion studies to organize their work and configure the jobs of their workers. The goal, as Taylor defined it in his celebrated 1911 treatise, *The Principles of Scientific Management,* was to identify and adopt, for every job, the "one best method" of work and thereby to effect "the gradual substitution of science for rule of thumb throughout the mechanic arts." Once his system was applied to all acts of manual labor, Taylor assured his followers, it would bring about a restructuring not only of industry but of society, creating a utopia of perfect efficiency. "In the past the man has been first," he declared; "in the future the system must be first."

24   Taylor's system is still very much with us; it remains the ethic of industrial manufacturing. And now, thanks to the growing power that computer engineers and software coders wield over our intellectual lives, Taylor's ethic is beginning to govern the realm of the mind as well. The Internet is a machine designed for the efficient and automated collection, transmission, and manipulation of information, and its legions of programmers are intent on finding the "one best method"—the perfect algorithm—to carry out every mental movement of what we've come to describe as "knowledge work."

25   Google's headquarters, in Mountain View, California—the Googleplex—is the Internet's high church, and the religion practiced inside its walls is Taylorism. Google, says its chief executive, Eric Schmidt, is "a company that's founded around the science of measurement," and it is striving to "systematize everything" it does. Drawing on the terabytes of behavioral data it collects through its search engine and other sites, it carries out thousands of experiments a day, according to the *Harvard Business Review,* and it uses the results to refine the algorithms that increasingly control how people find information and extract meaning from it. What Taylor did for the work of the hand, Google is doing for the work of the mind.

26   The company has declared that its mission is "to organize the world's information and make it universally accessible and useful." It seeks to develop "the perfect search engine," which it defines as something that "understands exactly what you mean and gives you back exactly what you want." In Google's view, information is a kind of commodity, a utilitarian resource that can be mined and processed with industrial efficiency. The more pieces of information we can "access" and the faster we can extract their gist, the more productive we become as thinkers.

27   Where does it end? Sergey Brin and Larry Page, the gifted young men who founded Google while pursuing doctoral degrees in computer science at Stanford, speak frequently of their desire to turn their search engine into an artificial intelligence, a HAL-like machine that might be connected directly to our brains. "The ultimate search engine is something as smart as people—or smarter," Page said in a speech a few years back. "For us, working on search is a way to work on artificial intelligence." In a 2004 interview with *Newsweek,* Brin said, "Certainly if you had all the world's information directly attached to your brain, or an artificial brain that was smarter than your brain, you'd be better off." Last year, Page told a convention of scientists that Google is "really trying to build artificial intelligence and to do it on a large scale."

28   Such an ambition is a natural one, even an admirable one, for a pair of math whizzes with vast quantities of cash at their disposal and a small army of computer scientists in their employ. A fundamentally scientific enterprise, Google is motivated by a desire to use technology, in Eric Schmidt's words, "to solve problems that have never been solved before," and artificial intelligence is the hardest problem out there. Why wouldn't Brin and Page want to be the ones to crack it?

29   Still, their easy assumption that we'd all "be better off" if our brains were supplemented, or even replaced, by an artificial intelligence is unsettling. It suggests a belief that intelligence is the output of a mechanical process, a series of discrete steps that can be isolated, measured, and optimized. In Google's world, the world we enter when we go

online, there's little place for the fuzziness of contemplation. Ambiguity is not an opening for insight but a bug to be fixed. The human brain is just an outdated computer that needs a faster processor and a bigger hard drive.

30   The idea that our minds should operate as high-speed data-processing machines is not only built into the workings of the Internet, it is the network's reigning business model as well. The faster we surf across the Web—the more links we click and pages we view—the more opportunities Google and other companies gain to collect information about us and to feed us advertisements. Most of the proprietors of the commercial Internet have a financial stake in collecting the crumbs of data we leave behind as we flit from link to link—the more crumbs, the better. The last thing these companies want is to encourage leisurely reading or slow, concentrated thought. It's in their economic interest to drive us to distraction.

31   Maybe I'm just a worrywart. Just as there's a tendency to glorify technological progress, there's a countertendency to expect the worst of every new tool or machine. In Plato's *Phaedrus,* Socrates bemoaned the development of writing. He feared that, as people came to rely on the written word as a substitute for the knowledge they used to carry inside their heads, they would, in the words of one of the dialogue's characters, "cease to exercise their memory and become forgetful." And because they would be able to "receive a quantity of information without proper instruction," they would "be thought very knowledgeable when they are for the most part quite ignorant." They would be "filled with the conceit of wisdom instead of real wisdom." Socrates wasn't wrong—the new technology did often have the effects he feared—but he was shortsighted. He couldn't foresee the many ways that writing and reading would serve to spread information, spur fresh ideas, and expand human knowledge (if not wisdom).

32   The arrival of Gutenberg's printing press, in the 15th century, set off another round of teeth gnashing. The Italian humanist Hieronimo Squarciafico worried that the easy availability of books would lead to intellectual laziness, making men "less studious" and weakening their minds. Others argued that cheaply printed books and broadsheets would undermine religious authority, demean the work of scholars and scribes, and spread sedition and debauchery. As New York University professor Clay Shirky notes, "Most of the arguments made against the printing press were correct, even prescient." But, again, the doomsayers were unable to imagine the myriad blessings that the printed word would deliver.

33   So, yes, you should be skeptical of my skepticism. Perhaps those who dismiss critics of the Internet as Luddites or nostalgists will be proved correct, and from our hyperactive, data-stoked minds will spring a golden age of intellectual discovery and universal wisdom. Then again, the Net isn't the alphabet, and although it may replace the printing press, it produces something altogether different. The kind of deep reading that a sequence of printed pages promotes is valuable not just for the knowledge we acquire from the author's words but for the intellectual vibrations those words set off within our own minds. In the quiet spaces opened up by the sustained, undistracted reading of a book, or by any other act of contemplation, for that matter, we make our own associations, draw our own inferences and analogies, foster our own ideas. Deep reading, as Maryanne Wolf argues, is indistinguishable from deep thinking.

34 If we lose those quiet spaces, or fill them up with "content," we will sacrifice something important not only in our selves but in our culture. In a recent essay, the playwright Richard Foreman eloquently described what's at stake:

35   I come from a tradition of Western culture, in which the ideal (my ideal) was the complex, dense and "cathedral-like" structure of the highly educated and articulate personality—a man or woman who carried inside themselves a personally constructed and unique version of the entire heritage of the West. [But now] I see within us all (myself included) the replacement of complex inner density with a new kind of self—evolving under the pressure of information overload and the technology of the "instantly available."

36 As we are drained of our "inner repertory of dense cultural inheritance," Foreman concluded, we risk turning into "'pancake people'—spread wide and thin as we connect with that vast network of information accessed by the mere touch of a button."

37 I'm haunted by that scene in *2001*. What makes it so poignant, and so weird, is the computer's emotional response to the disassembly of its mind: its despair as one circuit after another goes dark, its childlike pleading with the astronaut—"I can feel it. I can feel it. I'm afraid"—and its final reversion to what can only be called a state of innocence. HAL's outpouring of feeling contrasts with the emotionlessness that characterizes the human figures in the film, who go about their business with an almost robotic efficiency. Their thoughts and actions feel scripted, as if they're following the steps of an algorithm. In the world of *2001*, people have become so machinelike that the most human character turns out to be a machine. That's the essence of Kubrick's dark prophecy: as we come to rely on computers to mediate our understanding of the world, it is our own intelligence that flattens into artificial intelligence.

Critical Reading Questions:

- **Reflection:** In this work, Carr relies primarily on his personal experience with the Internet to make generalizations about the way people have come to think. How does Carr's experience parallel your own personal experience with the Internet? Carr was born in 1959. Would his experience necessarily be different from someone born decades later?

- **Rhetorical analysis:** Emotions are a major theme in Carr's work, especially in his conclusion in which he juxtaposes feeling machines with automaton people. How does his exploration of these feelings work to elicit *pathos* from his audience? What emotions might Carr's title invoke? Is this hyperbole, *pathemata*, or both?

Speech before Congress

Carrie Chapman Catt

Carrie Chapman Catt delivered this speech to Congress in 1917 in Washington, D.C. Catt was a leader of the Women's Suffrage Movement; her activism helped orchestrate the grass roots efforts of the National American Woman Suffrage Association. Eventually, she founded the League of Women Voters. At the time Catt delivered this speech, women's suffrage was determined at the state level. Her speech was given to an entirely male audience since women were not yet a recognized part of government; some of her audience were supporters of women's suffrage, but others were indifferent or even anti-suffrage. Despite her mixed audience and her position as an outsider because of her gender, Catt's strong plea to Congress is for the immediate passage of the Federal Suffrage Amendment. She argues, primarily through historical precedence and America's global influence, for ratification of the amendment which was eventually adopted in 1920.

—KGR

1   Woman suffrage is inevitable. Suffragists knew it before November 4, 1917; opponents afterward. Three distinct causes made it inevitable.

2   First, the history of our country. Ours is a nation born of revolution, of rebellion against a system of government so securely entrenched in the customs and traditions of human society that in 1776 it seemed impregnable. From the beginning of things, nations had been ruled by kings and for kings, while the people served and paid the cost. The American Revolutionists boldly proclaimed the heresies: "Taxation without representation is tyranny." "Governments derive their just powers from the consent of the governed." The colonists won, and the nation which was established as a result of their victory has held unfailingly that these two fundamental principles of democratic government are not only the spiritual source of our national existence but have been our chief historic pride and at all times the sheet anchor of our liberties.

3   Eighty years after the Revolution, Abraham Lincoln welded those two maxims into a new one: "Ours is a government of the people, by the people, and for the people." Fifty years more passed and the president of the United States, Woodrow Wilson, in a mighty crisis of the nation, proclaimed to the world: "We are fighting for the things which we have always carried nearest to our hearts: for democracy, for the right of those who submit to authority to have a voice in their own government."

4   All the way between these immortal aphorisms political leaders have declared unabated faith in their truth. Not one American has arisen to question their logic in the 141 years of our national existence. However stupidly our country may have evaded the logical application at times, it has never swerved from its devotion to the theory of democracy as expressed by those two axioms. . . .

5   With such a history behind it, how can our nation escape the logic it has never failed to follow, when its last unenfranchised class calls for the vote? Behold our Uncle Sam floating the banner with one hand, "Taxation without representation is tyranny," and with the other seizing the billions of dollars paid in taxes by women to whom he refuses "representation." Behold him again, welcoming the boys of twenty-one and the newly made immigrant citizen to "a voice in their own government" while he denies that fundamental right of democracy to thousands of women public school teachers from whom many of these men learn all they know of citizenship and patriotism, to women college presidents, to women who preach in our pulpits, interpret law in our courts, preside over our hospitals, write books and magazines, and serve in every uplifting moral and social enterprise. Is there a single man who can justify such inequality of treatment, such outrageous discrimination? Not one. . . .

6   Second, the suffrage for women already established in the United States makes women suffrage for the nation inevitable. When Elihu Root, as president of the American Society of International Law, at the eleventh annual meeting in Washington, April 26, 1917, said, "The world cannot be half democratic and half autocratic. It must be all democratic or all Prussian. There can be no compromise," he voiced a general truth. Precisely the same intuition has already taught the blindest and most hostile foe of woman suffrage that our nation cannot long continue a condition under which government in half its territory rests upon the consent of half of the people and in the other half upon the consent of all the people; a condition which grants representation to the taxed in half of its territory and denies it in the other half; a condition which permits women in some states to share in the election of the president, senators, and representatives and denies them that privilege in others. It is too obvious to require demonstration that woman suffrage, now covering half our territory, will eventually be ordained in all the nation. No one will deny it. The only question left is when and how will it be completely established.

7   Third, the leadership of the United States in world democracy compels the enfranchisement of its own women. The maxims of the Declaration were once called "fundamental principles of government." They are now called "American principles" or even "Americanisms." They have become the slogans of every movement toward political liberty the world around, of every effort to widen the suffrage for men or women in any land. Not a people, race, or class striving for freedom is there anywhere in the world that has not made our axioms the chief weapon of the struggle. More, all men and women the world around, with farsighted vision into the verities of things, know that the world tragedy of our day is not now being waged over the assassination of an archduke, nor commercial competition, nor national ambitions, nor the freedom of the seas. It is a death grapple between the forces which deny and those which uphold the truths of the Declaration of Independence. . . .

8   Do you realize that in no other country in the world with democratic tendencies is suffrage so completely denied as in a considerable number of our own states? There are thirteen black states where no suffrage for women exists, and fourteen others where suffrage for women is more limited than in many foreign countries.

9   Do you realize that when you ask women to take their cause to state referendum you compel them to do this: that you drive women of education, refinement, achievement, to beg men who cannot read for their political freedom?

10   Do you realize that such anomalies as a college president asking her janitor to give her a vote are overstraining the patience and driving women to desperation?

11   Do you realize that women in increasing numbers indignantly resent the long delay in their enfranchisement?

12   Your party platforms have pledged women suffrage. Then why not be honest, frank friends of our cause, adopt it in reality as your own, make it a party program, and "fight with us"? As a party measure—a measure of all parties—why not put the amendment through Congress and the legislatures? We shall all be better friends, we shall have a happier nation, we women will be free to support loyally the party of our choice, and we shall be far prouder of our history.

13   "There is one thing mightier than kings and armies"—aye, than Congresses and political parties—"the power of an idea when its time has come to move." The time for woman suffrage has come. The woman's hour has struck. If parties prefer to postpone action longer and thus do battle with this idea, they challenge the inevitable. The idea will not perish; the party which opposes it may. Every delay, every trick, every political dishonesty from now on will antagonize the women of the land more and more, and when the party or parties which have so delayed woman suffrage finally let it come, their sincerity will be doubted and their appeal to the new voters will be met with suspicion. This is the psychology of the situation. Can you afford the risk? Think it over.

14   We know you will meet opposition. There are a few "women haters" left, a few "old males of the tribe," as Vance Thompson calls them, whose duty they believe it to be to keep women in the places they have carefully picked out for them. Treitschke, made world famous by war literature, said some years ago, "Germany, which knows all about Germany and France, knows far better what is good for Alsace-Lorraine than that miserable people can possibly know." A few American Treitschkes we have who know better than women what is good for them. There are women, too, with "slave souls" and "clinging vines" for backbones. There are female dolls and male dandies. But the world does not wait for such as these, nor does liberty pause to heed the plaint of men and women with a grouch. She does not wait for those who have a special interest to serve, nor a selfish reason for depriving other people of freedom. Holding her torch aloft, liberty is pointing the way onward and upward and saying to America, "Come."

15   To you and the supporters of our cause in Senate and House, and the number is large, the suffragists of the nation express their grateful thanks. This address is not meant for you. We are more truly appreciative of all you have done than any words can express. We ask you to make a last, hard fight for the amendment during the present session. Since last we asked a vote on this amendment, your position has been fortified by the addition to suffrage territory of Great Britain, Canada, and New York.

16   Some of you have been too indifferent to give more than casual attention to this question. It is worthy of your immediate consideration. A question big enough to engage the attention of our allies in wartime is too big a question for you to neglect.

17   Some of you have grown old in party service. Are you willing that those who take your places by and by shall blame you for having failed to keep pace with the world and thus having lost for them a party advantage? Is there any real gain for you, for your party, for your nation by delay? Do you want to drive the progressive men and women out of your party?

18   Some of you hold to the doctrine of states' rights as applying to woman suffrage. Adherence to that theory will keep the United States far behind all other democratic nations upon this question. A theory which prevents a nation from keeping up with the trend of world progress cannot be justified.

19   Gentlemen, we hereby petition you, our only designated representatives, to redress our grievances by the immediate passage of the Federal Suffrage Amendment and to use your influence to secure its ratification in your own state, in order that the women of our nation may be endowed with political freedom before the next presidential election, and that our nation may resume its world leadership in democracy.

20   Woman suffrage is coming—you know it. Will you, Honorable Senators and Members of the House of Representatives, help or hinder it?

Critical Reading Questions:

- **Rhetorical analysis:** How does Catt create a sense of urgency for the issue of women's suffrage? Why would/wouldn't her various argumentative techniques be effective for her audience?

- **Analysis:** How do Catt's rhetorical strategies present her plea as bigger and of more importance than women's suffrage? Why is/isn't this effective?

Women's Rights Are Human Rights

Hillary Rodham Clinton

Hillary Rodham Clinton (then the First Lady of the United States) was invited to speak at the United Nations Fourth World Conference on Women held in Beijing, China. She delivered this address on September 5, 1995, to an international audience of women's rights advocates from across the globe, including representatives from 189 governments and over 5,000 representatives from non-governmental organizations. Clinton faced an interesting kairotic moment as the keynote speaker at the conference. Her speech attempts to create a sense of energy and positive momentum for the audience, to express to a global audience many of the shared views of the conference attendees, and to offer a strategic call for a redefinition of women's rights. By placing women's rights within the larger framework of human rights, she was able both to signify the importance of the issue and to give supporters of the Women's Rights Movement access to the broad network of economic, social, and political support that has already been created to support and defend human rights in general.

—PH

1   Thank you very much, Gertrude Mongella, for your dedicated work that has brought us to this point, distinguished delegates, and guests:

2   I would like to thank the Secretary General for inviting me to be part of this important United Nations Fourth World Conference on Women. This is truly a celebration, a celebration of the contributions women make in every aspect of life: in the home, on the job, in the community, as mothers, wives, sisters, daughters, learners, workers, citizens, and leaders.

3   It is also a coming together, much the way women come together every day in every country. We come together in fields and factories, in village markets and supermarkets, in living rooms and board rooms. Whether it is while playing with our children in the park, or washing clothes in a river, or taking a break at the office water cooler, we come together and talk about our aspirations and concerns. And time and again, our talk turns to our children and our families. However different we may appear, there is far more that unites us than divides us. We share a common future, and we are here to find common ground so that we may help bring new dignity and respect to women and girls all over the world, and in so doing bring new strength and stability to families as well.

4   By gathering in Beijing, we are focusing world attention on issues that matter most in our lives—the lives of women and their families: access to education, health care, jobs and credit, the chance to enjoy basic legal and human rights and to participate fully in the political life of our countries.

5   There are some who question the reason for this conference. Let them listen to the voices of women in their homes, neighborhoods, and workplaces. There are some who wonder whether the lives of women and girls matter to economic and political progress

around the globe. Let them look at the women gathered here and at Huairou—the home-makers and nurses, the teachers and lawyers, the policymakers and women who run their own businesses. It is conferences like this that compel governments and peoples every-where to listen, look, and face the world's most pressing problems. Wasn't it after all—after the women's conference in Nairobi ten years ago that the world focused for the first time on the crisis of domestic violence?

6   Earlier today, I participated in a World Health Organization forum. In that forum, we talked about ways that government officials, NGOs, and individual citizens are working to address the health problems of women and girls. Tomorrow, I will attend a gathering of the United Nations Development Fund for Women. There, the discussion will focus on local—and highly successful—programs that give hard-working women access to credit so they can improve their own lives and the lives of their families.

7   What we are learning around the world is that if women are healthy and educated, their families will flourish. If women are free from violence, their families will flourish. If women have a chance to work and earn as full and equal partners in society, their families will flourish. And when families flourish, communities and nations do as well. That is why every woman, every man, every child, every family, and every nation on this planet does have a stake in the discussion that takes place here.

8   Over the past 25 years, I have worked persistently on issues relating to women, chil-dren, and families. Over the past two-and-a half years, I've had the opportunity to learn more about the challenges facing women in my own country and around the world.

9   I have met new mothers in Indonesia, who come together regularly in their village to discuss nutrition, family planning, and baby care. I have met working parents in Denmark who talk about the comfort they feel in knowing that their children can be cared for in safe, and nurturing after-school centers. I have met women in South Africa who helped lead the struggle to end apartheid and are now helping to build a new democracy. I have met with the leading women of the Western Hemisphere who are working every day to promote literacy and better health care for children in their countries. I have met women in India and Bangladesh who are taking out small loans to buy milk cows, or rickshaws, or thread in order to create a livelihood for themselves and their families. I have met the doctors and nurses in Belarus and Ukraine who are trying to keep children alive in the aftermath of Chernobyl.

10   The great challenge of this conference is to give voice to women everywhere whose experiences go unnoticed, whose words go unheard. Women comprise more than half the world's population, 70% of the world's poor, and two-thirds of those who are not taught to read and write. We are the primary caretakers for most of the world's children and elderly. Yet much of the work we do is not valued—not by economists, not by historians, not by popular culture, not by government leaders.

11   At this very moment, as we sit here, women around the world are giving birth, raising children, cooking meals, washing clothes, cleaning houses, planting crops, working on assembly lines, running companies, and running countries. Women also are dying from diseases that should have been prevented or treated. They are watching their children succumb to malnutrition caused by poverty and economic deprivation. They are being

denied the right to go to school by their own fathers and brothers. They are being forced into prostitution, and they are being barred from the bank lending offices and banned from the ballot box.

12   Those of us who have the opportunity to be here have the responsibility to speak for those who could not. As an American, I want to speak for those women in my own country, women who are raising children on the minimum wage, women who can't afford health care or child care, women whose lives are threatened by violence, including violence in their own homes.

13   I want to speak up for mothers who are fighting for good schools, safe neighborhoods, clean air, and clean airwaves; for older women, some of them widows, who find that, after raising their families, their skills and life experiences are not valued in the marketplace; for women who are working all night as nurses, hotel clerks, or fast food chefs so that they can be at home during the day with their children; and for women everywhere who simply don't have time to do everything they are called upon to do each and every day.

14   Speaking to you today, I speak for them, just as each of us speaks for women around the world who are denied the chance to go to school, or see a doctor, or own property, or have a say about the direction of their lives, simply because they are women. The truth is that most women around the world work both inside and outside the home, usually by necessity.

15   We need to understand there is no one formula for how women should lead our lives. That is why we must respect the choices that each woman makes for herself and her family. Every woman deserves the chance to realize her own God-given potential. But we must recognize that women will never gain full dignity until their human rights are respected and protected.

16   Our goals for this conference, to strengthen families and societies by empowering women to take greater control over their own destinies, cannot be fully achieved unless all governments—here and around the world—accept their responsibility to protect and promote internationally recognized human rights. The international community has long acknowledged and recently reaffirmed at Vienna that both women and men are entitled to a range of protections and personal freedoms, from the right of personal security to the right to determine freely the number and spacing of the children they bear. No one—No one should be forced to remain silent for fear of religious or political persecution, arrest, abuse, or torture.

17   Tragically, women are most often the ones whose human rights are violated. Even now, in the late 20th century, the rape of women continues to be used as an instrument of armed conflict. Women and children make up a large majority of the world's refugees. And when women are excluded from the political process, they become even more vulnerable to abuse. I believe that now, on the eve of a new millennium, it is time to break the silence. It is time for us to say here in Beijing, and for the world to hear, that it is no longer acceptable to discuss women's rights as separate from human rights.

18   These abuses have continued because, for too long, the history of women has been a history of silence. Even today, there are those who are trying to silence our words. But the voices of this conference and of the women at Huairou must be heard loudly and clearly:

19   It is a violation of human rights when babies are denied food, or drowned, or suffo-
cated, or their spines broken, simply because they are born girls.

20   It is a violation of human rights when women and girls are sold into the slavery of prostitution for human greed—and the kinds of reasons that are used to justify this practice
should no longer be tolerated.

21   It is a violation of human rights when women are doused with gasoline, set on fire,
and burned to death because their marriage dowries are deemed too small.

22   It is a violation of human rights when individual women are raped in their own communities and when thousands of women are subjected to rape as a tactic or prize of war.

23   It is a violation of human rights when a leading cause of death worldwide among
women ages 14 to 44 is the violence they are subjected to in their own homes by their own
relatives.

24   It is a violation of human rights when young girls are brutalized by the painful and
degrading practice of genital mutilation.

25   It is a violation of human rights when women are denied the right to plan their own
families, and that includes being forced to have abortions or being sterilized against
their will.

26   If there is one message that echoes forth from this conference, let it be that human
rights are women's rights and women's rights are human rights once and for all. Let us not
forget that among those rights are the right to speak freely—and the right to be heard.

27   Women must enjoy the rights to participate fully in the social and political lives of their
countries, if we want freedom and democracy to thrive and endure. It is indefensible that
many women in nongovernmental organizations who wished to participate in this conference have not been able to attend—or have been prohibited from fully taking part.

28   Let me be clear. Freedom means the right of people to assemble, organize, and
debate openly. It means respecting the views of those who may disagree with the views
of their governments. It means not taking citizens away from their loved ones and jailing
them, mistreating them, or denying them their freedom or dignity because of the peaceful
expression of their ideas and opinions.

29   In my country, we recently celebrated the 75th anniversary of Women's Suffrage. It
took 150 years after the signing of our Declaration of Independence for women to win the
right to vote. It took 72 years of organized struggle, before that happened, on the part of
many courageous women and men. It was one of America's most divisive philosophical
wars. But it was a bloodless war. Suffrage was achieved without a shot being fired.

30   But we have also been reminded, in V-J Day observances last weekend, of the good
that comes when men and women join together to combat the forces of tyranny and to
build a better world. We have seen peace prevail in most places for a half century. We
have avoided another world war. But we have not solved older, deeply-rooted problems
that continue to diminish the potential of half the world's population.

31   Now it is the time to act on behalf of women everywhere. If we take bold steps to better the lives of women, we will be taking bold steps to better the lives of children and families too. Families rely on mothers and wives for emotional support and care. Families rely
on women for labor in the home. And increasingly, everywhere, families rely on women for
income needed to raise healthy children and care for other relatives.

32   As long as discrimination and inequities remain so commonplace everywhere in the world, as long as girls and women are valued less, fed less, fed last, overworked, underpaid, not schooled, subjected to violence in and outside their homes—the potential of the human family to create a peaceful, prosperous world will not be realized.

33   Let this conference be our—and the world's—call to action. Let us heed that call so we can create a world in which every woman is treated with respect and dignity, every boy and girl is loved and cared for equally, and every family has the hope of a strong and stable future. That is the work before you. That is the work before all of us who have a vision of the world we want to see—for our children and our grandchildren.

34   The time is now. We must move beyond rhetoric. We must move beyond recognition of problems to working together, to have the common efforts to build that common ground we hope to see.

35   God's blessing on you, your work, and all who will benefit from it.

36   Godspeed and thank you very much.

Critical Reading Questions:

- **Rhetorical analysis:** Because Clinton is the First Lady of the United States when she gives this speech, her audience may come to the speech with certain preconceptions about her that may positively or negatively affect her ethos. How might being a white, wealthy, and powerful American hurt her ethos with this audience? How might it help her ethos? In what ways does she manage, overcome, or make use of this ethos within the speech?

- **Interpretation:** Clinton uses a strategic repetition of the phrase "it is a violation of human rights" to reinforce her primary argument for the speech. How is this strategy affected by the nature of her argument, the genre of her text (public keynote address), and her direct (conference attendees) and indirect (global) audience?

Civilize Them with a Stick

Mary Crow Dog and Richard Erdoes

Mary Crow Dog is one name of many—including Mary Brave Bird and Mary Ellen Moore-Richard—reflecting Crow Dog's complex cultural and racial background. Crow Dog used writing, from starting an underground newspaper at sixteen to writing books as an adult, to expose the realities and inequities of reservation life. "Civilize Them with a Stick" is a chapter from *Lakota Woman*, written with author Richard Erdoes and published in 1990, that graphically describes her experiences at the St. Francis Mission School, a 1960s "typical old Indian boarding school." She writes to a "sympathetic white audience," but evokes much stronger emotions than sympathy through detailed, shocking descriptions of devastating childhood experiences that span generations to provide evidence that an "outward appearance of civilized life" can obscure inhuman savagery. Crow Dog's use of imagery helps the reader see her growth from a kitten whose "claws were still small" to a strong, confident young woman who fights to embrace her heritage. "Civilize Them with a Stick" takes readers with Crow Dog as she learns that she doesn't have to "[hate and mistrust] every white person on sight," an insightful journey of self-discovery for both Crow Dog and her readers.

—DG

1   Gathered from the cabin, the wickiup,
       and the tepee, partly by cajolery and partly by threats,
       partly by bribery and partly by force,
       they are induced to leave their kindred to enter these schools
       and take upon themselves the outward appearance of civilized life.
              — Annual Report of the Department of Interior, 1901

2   It is almost impossible to explain to a sympathetic white person what a typical old Indian boarding school was like; how it affected the Indian child suddenly dumped into it like a small creature from another world, helpless, defenseless, bewildered, trying desperately and instinctively to survive and sometimes not surviving at all. I think such children were like the victims of Nazi concentration camps trying to tell average, middleclass Americans what their experience had been like. Even now, when these schools are much improved, when the buildings are new, all gleaming steel and glass, the food tolerable, the teachers well trained and well intentioned, even trained in child psychology—unfortunately the psychology of white children, which is different from ours—the shock to the child upon arrival is still tremendous. Some just seem to shrivel up, don't speak for days on end, and have an empty look in their eyes. I know of an eleven-year-old on another reservation who hanged herself, and in our school, while I was there, a girl jumped out of the window, trying to kill herself to escape an unbearable situation. That first shock is always there....

3   The mission school at St. Francis was a curse for our family for generations. My grandmother went there, then my mother, then my sisters and I. At one time or other every one of us tried to run away. Grandma told me once about the bad times she had experienced at St. Francis. In those days they let students go home only for one week every year. Two days were used up for transportation, which meant spending just five days out of three hundred and sixty-five with her family. And that was an improvement. Before grandma's time, on many reservations they did not let the students go home at all until they had finished school. Anybody who disobeyed the nuns was severely punished. The building in which my grandmother stayed had three floors, for girls only. Way up in the attic were little cells, about five by five by ten feet. One time she was in church and instead of praying she was playing jacks. As punishment they took her to one of those little cubicles where she stayed in darkness because the windows had been boarded up. They left her there for a whole week with only bread and water for nourishment. After she came out she promptly ran away, together with three other girls. They were found and brought back. The nuns stripped them naked and whipped them. They used a horse buggy whip on my grandmother. Then she was put back into the attic for two weeks.

4   My mother had much the same experiences but never wanted to talk about them, and then there I was, in the same place. The school is now run by the BIA—the Bureau of Indian Affairs—but only since about fifteen years ago. When I was there, during the 1960s, it was still run by the Church. The Jesuit father ran the boys' wing and the Sisters of the Sacred Heart ran us—with the help of the strap. Nothing had changed since my grandmother's days. I have been told recently that even in the '70s they were still beating children at that school. All I got out of school was being taught how to pray. I learned quickly that I would be beaten if I failed in my devotions or, God forbid, prayed the wrong way, especially prayed in Indian to Wakan Tanka, the Indian Creator.

5   The girls' wing was built like an F and was run like a penal institution. Every morning at five o'clock the sisters would come into our large dormitory to wake us up, and immediately we had to kneel down at the sides of our beds and recite the prayers. At six o'clock we were herded into the church for more of the same. I did not take kindly to the discipline and to marching by the clock, left-right, left-right. I was never one to like being forced to do something. I do something because I feel like doing it. I felt this way always, as far as I can remember, and my sister Barbara felt the same way. An old medicine man once told me: "Us Lakotas are not like dogs who can be trained, who can be beaten and keep on wagging their tails, licking the hand that whipped them. We are like cats, little cats, big cats, wildcats, bobcats, mountain lions. It doesn't matter what kind, but cats who can't be tamed, who scratch if you step on their tails." But I was only a kitten and my claws were still small.

6   Barbara was still in the school when I arrived and during my first year or two she could still protect me a little bit. When Barb was a seventh-grader, she ran away together with five other girls, early in the morning before sunrise. They brought them back in the evening. The girls had to wait for two hours in front of the mother superior's office. They were hungry and cold, frozen through. It was wintertime and they had been running the whole day without food, trying to make good their escape. The mother superior asked

each girl, "Would you do this again?" She told them that as punishment they would not be allowed to visit home for a month and that she'd keep them busy on work details until the skin on their knees and elbows had worn off. At the end of her speech she told each girl, "Get up from this chair and lean over it." She then lifted the girls' skirts and pulled down their underpants. Not little girls either, but teenagers. She had a leather strap about a foot long and four inches wide fastened to a stick, and beat the girls, one after another, until they cried. Barb did not give her that satisfaction but just clenched her teeth. There was one girl, Barb told me, the nun kept on beating and beating until her arm got tired.

7   I did not escape my share of the strap. Once, when I was thirteen years old, I refused to go to Mass. I did not want to go to church because I did not feel well. A nun grabbed me by the hair, dragged me upstairs, made me stoop over, pulled my dress up (we were not allowed at the time to wear jeans), pulled my panties down, and gave me what they called "swats"—twenty-five swats with a board around which Scotch tape had been wound. She hurt me badly.

8   My classroom was right next to the principal's office and almost every day I could hear him swatting the boys. Beating was the common punishment for not doing one's homework, or for being late to school. It had such a bad effect upon me that I hated and mistrusted every white person on sight, because I met only one kind. It was not until much later that I met sincere white people I could relate to and be friends with. Racism breeds racism in reverse.

9   The routine at St. Francis was dreary. Six a.m., kneeling in church for an hour or so; seven o'clock, breakfast; eight o'clock, scrub the floor, peel spuds, make classes. We had to mop the dining room twice every day and scrub the tables. If you were caught taking a rest, doodling on the bench with a fingernail or knife, or just rapping, the nun would come up with a dish towel and just slap it across your face, saying, "You're not supposed to be talking, you're supposed to be working!" Monday mornings we had cornmeal mush, Tuesday oatmeal, Wednesday rice and raisins, Thursday cornflakes, and Friday all the leftovers mixed together or sometimes fish. Frequently the food had bugs or rocks in it. We were eating hot dogs that were weeks old, while the nuns were dining on ham, whipped potatoes, sweet peas, and cranberry sauce. In winter our dorm was icy cold while the nuns' rooms were always warm.

10   I have seen little girls arrive at the school, first-graders, just fresh from home and totally unprepared for what awaited them, little girls with pretty braids, and the first thing the nuns did was chop their hair off and tie up what was left behind their ears. Next they would dump the children into tubs of alcohol, a sort of rubbing alcohol, "to get the germs off." Many of the nuns were German immigrants, some from Bavaria, so that we sometimes speculated whether Bavaria was some sort of Dracula country inhabited by monsters. For the sake of objectivity I ought to mention that two of the German fathers were great linguists and that the only Lakota-English dictionaries and grammars which are worth anything were put together by them.

11   At night some of the girls would huddle together for comfort and reassurance. Then the nun in charge of the dorm would come in and say, "What are the two of you doing in bed together? I smell evil in this room. You girls are evil incarnate. You are sinning. You are

going to hell and burn forever. You can act that way in the devil's frying pan." She would get them out of bed in the middle of the night, making them kneel and pray until morning. We had not the slightest idea what it was all about. At home we slept two and three in a bed for animal warmth and a feeling of security.

12   The nuns and the girls in the two top grades were constantly battling it out physically with fists, nails, and hair-pulling. I myself was growing from a kitten into an undersized cat. My claws were getting bigger and were itching for action. About 1969 or 1970 a strange young white girl appeared on the reservation. She looked about eighteen or twenty years old. She was pretty and had long, blond hair down to her waist, patched jeans, boots, and a backpack. She was different from any other white person we had met before. I think her name was Wise. I do not know how she managed to overcome our reluctance and distrust, getting us into a corner, making us listen to her, asking us how we were treated. She told us that she was from New York. She was the first real hippie or Yippie we had come across. She told us of people called the Black Panthers, Young Lords, and Weathermen. She said, "Black people are getting it on. Indians are getting it on in St. Paul and California. How about you?" She also said, "Why don't you put out an underground paper, mimeograph it. It's easy. Tell it like it is. Let it all hang out." She spoke a strange lingo but we caught on fast.

13   Charlene Left Hand Bull and Gina One Star were two full-blood girls I used to hang out with. We did everything together. They were willing to join me in a Sioux uprising. We put together a newspaper which we named the Red Panther. In it we wrote how bad the school was, what kind of slop we had to eat—slimy, rotten, blackened potatoes for two weeks—the way we were beaten. I think I was the one who wrote the worst article about our principal of the moment, Father Keeler. I put all my anger and venom into it. I called him a goddam wasicun son of a bitch. I wrote that he knew nothing about Indians and should go back to where he came from, teaching white children whom he could relate to. I wrote that we knew which priests slept with which nuns and that all they ever could think about was filling their bellies and buying a new car. It was the kind of writing which foamed at the mouth, but which also lifted a great deal of weight from one's soul.

14   On Saint Patrick's Day, when everybody was at the big powwow, we distributed our newspapers. We put them on windshields and bulletin boards, in desks and pews, in dorms and toilets. But someone saw us and snitched on us. The shit hit the fan. The three of us were taken before a board meeting. Our parents, in my case my mother, had to come. They were told that ours was a most serious matter, the worst thing that had ever happened in the school's long history. One of the nuns told my mother, "Your daughter really needs to be talked to." "What's wrong with my daughter?" my mother asked. She was given one of our Red Panther newspapers. The nun pointed out its name to her and then my piece, waiting for mom's reaction. After a while she asked, "Well, what have you got to say to this? What do you think?"

15   My mother said, "Well, when I went to school here, some years back, I was treated a lot worse than these kids are. I really can't see how they can have any complaints, because we was treated a lot stricter. We could not even wear skirts halfway up our knees. These girls have it made. But you should forgive them because they are young. And it's

supposed to be a free country, free speech and all that. I don't believe what they done is wrong." So all I got out of it was scrubbing six flights of stairs on my hands and knees, every day. And no boy-side privileges.

10   The boys and girls were still pretty much separated. The only time one could meet a member of the opposite sex was during free time, between four and five-thirty, in the study hall or on benches or the volleyball court outside, and that was strictly supervised. One day Charlene and I went over to the boys' side. We were on the ball team and they had to let us practice. We played three extra minutes, only three minutes more than we were supposed to. Here was the nuns' opportunity for revenge. We got twenty-five swats. I told Charlene, "We are getting too old to have our bare asses whipped that way. We are old enough to have babies. Enough of this shit. Next time we fight back." Charlene only said, "Hoka-hay!"

17   We had to take showers every evening. One little girl did not want to take her panties off and one of the nuns told her, "You take those underpants off—or else!" But the child was ashamed to do it. The nun was getting her swat to threaten the girl. I went up to the sister, pushed her veil off, and knocked her down. I told her that if she wanted to hit a little girl she should pick on me, pick one her own size. She got herself transferred out of the dorm a week later.

18   In a school like this there is always a lot of favoritism. At St. Francis it was strongly tinged with racism. Girls who were near-white, who came from what the nuns called "nice families," got preferential treatment. They waited on the faculty and got to eat ham or eggs and bacon in the morning. They got the easy jobs while the skins, who did not have the right kind of background—myself among them—always wound up in the laundry room sorting out ten bushel baskets of dirty boys' socks every day. Or we wound up scrubbing the floors and doing all the dishes. The school therefore fostered fights and antagonism between whites and breeds, and between breeds and skins. At one time Charlene and I had to iron all the robes and vestments the priests wore when saying Mass. We had to fold them up and put them into a chest in the back of the church. In a corner, looking over our shoulders, was a statue of the crucified Savior, all bloody and beaten up. Charlene looked up and said, "Look at that poor Indian. The pigs sure worked him over." That was the closest I ever came to seeing Jesus.

19   I was held up as a bad example and didn't mind. I was old enough to have a boyfriend and promptly got one. At the school we had an hour and a half for ourselves. Between the boys' and the girls' wings were some benches where one could sit. My boyfriend and I used to go there just to hold hands and talk. The nuns were very uptight about any boy-girl stuff. They had an exaggerated fear of anything having even the faintest connection with sex. One day in religion class, an all-girl class, Sister Bernard singled me out for some remarks, pointing me out as a bad example, an example that should be shown. She said that I was too free with my body. That I was holding hands which meant that I was not a good example to follow. She also said that I wore unchaste dresses, skirts which were too short, too suggestive, shorter than regulations permitted, and for that I would be punished. She dressed me down before the whole class, carrying on and on about my unchastity.

20   I stood up and told her, "You shouldn't say any of those things, miss. You people are a lot worse than us Indians. I know all about you, because my grandmother and my aunt told me about you. Maybe twelve, thirteen years ago you had a water stoppage here in St. Francis. No water could get through the pipes. There are water lines right under the mission, underground tunnels and passages where in my grandmother's time only the nuns and priests could go, which were off-limits to everybody else. When the water backed up they had to go through all the water lines and clean them out. And in those huge pipes they found the bodies of newborn babies. And they were white babies. They weren't Indian babies. At least when our girls have babies, they don't do away with them that way, like flushing them down the toilet, almost.

21   "And that priest they sent here from Holy Rosary in Pine Ridge because he molested a little girl. You couldn't think of anything better than dump him on us. All he does is watch young women and girls with that funny smile on his face. Why don't you point him out for an example?"

22   Charlene and I worked on the school newspaper. After all we had some practice. Every day we went down to Publications. One of the priests acted as the photographer, doing the enlarging and developing. He smelled of chemicals which had stained his hands yellow. One day he invited Charlene into the darkroom. He was going to teach her developing. She was developed already. She was a big girl compared to him, taller too. Charlene was nicely built, not fat, just rounded. No sharp edges anywhere: All of a sudden she rushed out of the darkroom, yelling to me, "Let's get out of here! He's trying to feel me up. That priest is nasty." So there was this too to contend with—sexual harassment. We complained to the student body. The nuns said we just had a dirty mind.

23   We got a new priest in English. During one of his first classes he asked one of the boys a certain question. The boy was shy. He spoke poor English, but he had the right answer. The priest told him, "You did not say it right. Correct yourself. Say it over again." The boy got flustered and stammered. He could hardly get out a word. But the priest kept after him: "Didn't you hear? I told you to do the whole thing over. Get it right this time." He kept on and on.

24   I stood up and said, "Father, don't be doing that. If you go into an Indian's home and try to talk Indian, they might laugh at you and say, 'Do it over correctly. Get it right this time!'"

25   He shouted at me, "Mary, you stay after class. Sit down right now!"

26   I stayed after class, until after the bell. He told me, "Get over here!"

27   He grabbed me by the arm, pushing me against the blackboard, shouting. "Why are you always mocking us? You have no reason to do this."

28   I said, "Sure I do. You were making fun of him. You embarrassed him. He needs strengthening, not weakening. You hurt him. I did not hurt you."

29   He twisted my arm and pushed real hard. I turned around and hit him in the face, giving him a bloody nose. After that I ran out of the room, slamming the door behind me. He and I went to Sister Bernard's office. I told her, "Today I quit school. I'm not taking any more of this, none of this shit anymore. None of this treatment. Better give me my diploma. I can't waste any more time on you people."

30 Sister Bernard looked at me for a long, long time. She said, "All right, Mary Ellen, go home today. Come back in a few days and get your diploma." And that was that. Oddly enough, that priest turned out okay. He taught a class in grammar, orthography, com-position, things like that. I think he wanted more respect in class. He was still young and unsure of himself. But I was in there too long. I didn't feel like hearing it. Later he became a good friend of the Indians, a personal friend of myself and my husband. He stood up for us during Wounded Knee and after he stood up to his superiors, stuck his neck way out, became a real people priest. He even learned our language. He died prematurely of cancer. It is not only the good Indians who die young, but the good whites, too. It is the timid ones who know how to take care of themselves who grow old. I am still grateful to that priest for what he did for us later and for the quarrel he picked with me—or did I pick it with him?—because it ended a situation which had become unendurable for me. The day of my fight with him was my last day in school.

Critical Reading Questions:

* **Rhetorical analysis:** Consider the evidence Crow Dog offers to support the claim that "Racism breeds racism in reverse." How do Crow Dog's pathetic appeals support her case?

* **Rhetorical analysis:** "Racism breeds racism in reverse" is one main argument Crow Dog explicitly articulates, but she makes other, more implicit, arguments. Trace evidence for another argument in the text.

* **Rhetorical analysis:** Crow Dog specifically names her audience: "a sympathetic white audience." For what other audiences might the rhetorical appeals be more or less effective?

Does Coming to College Mean Becoming Someone New?

Kevin Davis

Kevin Davis is a professor and Writing Center Director at East Central University in Ada, Oklahoma, and received teaching excellence awards from the university in 1991, 1996, and 2003. In this essay, published in *The Subject is Writing: Essays by Teachers and Students*, 2003, Davis explores the moves and changes students need to make in order to succeed in college. Using personal experiences supported by scholarly research, Davis argues that students must be willing to make a personal commitment to learning the forms of writing and ways of thinking valued by their chosen disciplines. While he never explicitly answers the question the title of his essay poses, Davis clearly illustrates changes that he and others were willing to make in order to be successful in their chosen fields. In the end, coming to college only means becoming someone new if the student is willing and committed to internalizing both the formalistic and the epistemic aspects of a new, academic discourse community.

—DG

1   As an undergraduate English major, I felt like an outsider. I originally chose to major in English because of my love for reading and writing, but the reading and writing college expected of me was not the reading and writing I was prepared to do. Sure, I could read the assigned literature, and I could make my own good sense of it. Yet that was not enough for my English professors. They wanted me to make their sense of the literature, to understand the texts as they understood them. Not only that, they expected me to write about this alien sense-making in turgid, impersonal, passive-voiced prose. When I became an English major, I didn't just learn certain understandings of what I read; I also had to learn a particular way of reading and writing. Right from the start, it was clear that if I was to become a member of the English-majors community, I had to do more than read and think and write; I had to turn into someone new.

2   Perhaps that is why I was never a very successful English major and why, eventually, I left the academic world and joined the business community. I was living on the boundary between academic and home communities, between maintaining my identity and accepting another. I found I didn't like the someone new I was being asked to become.

3   Eventually, I returned to the academic world and discovered I fit into the community of outsiders known as rhetoricians (people who study the way other people effectively communicate). I'm not sure if I fit into this community because I wanted to join it more than I had wanted to join the English studies community, because it was willing to accept me as I already was, or because I had matured enough to be willing to become someone new. I do know, however, that this second attempt at entrance into the academic community has been as successful as my earlier attempt was a flop.

4   As a rhetorician and because of my past experience, I have become interested in issues of community membership. Everyone is a member of several discourse communities (the term rhetoricians use to describe groups of people who share patterns and strategies of communications). We're all members of a home discourse community, based on our family's regional, social, and economic lifestyles. And many of us are members of other discourse communities because we are familiar with particular language communities through experience such as jobs and hobbies. But entering the academic discourse communities present on college campuses can produce problems and anxieties of students who are attempting the transition.

5   In the rest of this essay, I want to use my own experiences and research to answer several questions. What happens as students try to become members of new academic discourse communities? What special writing and thinking abilities are required? What personal investments must be made?

6   When I was eighteen, my writing was an extremely personal activity. I didn't just throw words on pages; I invested myself into the work. Everything I wrote was full of personal insights, personal style, and voice. A good writer, I was regularly praised and rewarded for my high school writing efforts. I was totally unprepared for the shocking comments that my college professors would place on my writing.

7   Part of the problem came from a natural maturing process: The valued and original insights of a high school senior were suddenly the trite and common repetitions of a college student. And part of the problem came from style. The original, personal, whimsical voice of a young writer was not enough to assure my spot in the academic community.

8   I have now discovered that rhetoricians have an insightful way of looking at the split I experienced (North 1986). "Formalists," people who think that the most important aspect of a particular discourse community is the forms the community's writers use, would suggest that I didn't know the appropriate forms for academic writing. I didn't know what academic writing sounded like, and I didn't know how to present my ideas in the lingo that would bring the ideas recognition and acceptance. On the other hand, "epistemics," people who think that the most important aspect of a particular discourse community is the way the community thinks and solves problems, would suggest that I was not thinking like members of the academic world are supposed to think. I didn't process my thoughts in appropriate academic ways, according to the epistemics, and I wasn't positively involved with my studies.

9   Several composition scholars have completed research studies that try to understand more fully what happens with students trying to enter academic discourse communities. Recently, for example, Stephen North (1986) investigated the ways three students changed during one philosophy course. He relied solely on his readings of papers the students wrote in order to describe three contexts in which the students changed: the *rhetorical* (the students' sense of their audience and their purpose for writing), the *intellectual or epistemic* (how the students struggled to understand the ideas they were studying), and the *disciplinary or formalistic* (how the students used language to show membership in the discourse community). By looking at papers similar to those that I wrote as an under-

graduate, North was able to ascertain these three changes in writing for students entering new discourse communities.

10   Another research project, completed by Lucille McCarthy (1987), studied one student as he learned to negotiate his way through new discourse communities in several different freshman and sophomore courses. McCarthy made several conclusions from her work. First, she found that her subject used the same writing process to figure out how to complete a variety of writing tasks; this would imply that a student who can write in one situation, like I could, can extrapolate a process for writing into other situations. Second, she found that the purpose for the writing task and the student's involvement with the task were important to the writer's success; this implies that students write better if they are actively involved in the topic they are writing about, which is certainly true in my own experience. Finally, McCarthy concluded that writing tasks that are familiar in one situation were considered different when the student encountered them in a different situation; this implies that epistemic knowledge of a discourse community is important for a writer to succeed.

11   These adaptations writers make to new discourse communities are not limited, of course, to undergraduate college students. Everyone enters new communities throughout life. Carol Berkenkotter, Thomas Hucklin, and John Ackerman (1988) verified this when they examined the experiences of a teacher who returned to graduate school after several years of teaching. In their study, they ended up agreeing with both the formalists and the epistemics. They concluded that student writers have to assimilate both the forms and the thoughts of an academic discourse community to function within it. Their subject had to change the nature of his writing, from personal exploration to impersonal declaration, but he also had to change his community allegiance: he had to learn to think like a member of the community.

12   By looking at these studies and at my experience, then I can begin to make some conclusions about how students have to adapt their writing and thinking to succeed in college's unfamiliar academic discourse community. First, we have to recognize and accept the forms of the community, we have to make our writing look and sound like that of the field. Second, we have to learn to think in the ways that are valued by the field we are entering; we have to be personal or impersonal, focused on ideas or numbers, as the field demands. Third, we have to have a reliable comfortable writing process that we can take with us from task to task, community to community; once established, the process will probably serve us in a variety of settings. Finally, we have to become personally and intellectually involved with the community, wanting to be a part of it; without personal involvement, the formalistic and epistemic changes are merely window dressing.

13   As I look back on my own experience, I can clearly identify that last change as the most problematic for me. As an undergraduate English major, I never completed the personal commitment important for my success in the field. Eventually, I learned to mimic the writing and thinking activities that the field valued, but I remained unwilling to submit to the authority of those form and thought patterns. To personally endorse the English studies discourse community I would have had to abandon much of what I believed about life.

Later, when I returned to graduate school to study rhetoric, however, I easily endorsed the field, finding it more palatable to my native ways of being.

14   As I began my own research into discourse community membership, I was particularly interested in the personal involvement issues. Did other people reject communities, as I had done, because they were hesitant to make the personal commitments necessary for success? Could individuals only join communities that endorsed their native ways of thinking? Or did other people accept the communities and, in the process, give up something of their native ways of being in the world?

15   To investigate the personal changes students make as they enter new discourse communities, I interviewed, several times over six months, two undergraduates who were taking their first courses toward a degree and eventual licenses in social work.

16   Stella (the names are changed) was in her early twenties and in college for the second time, having delayed her education for a marriage. As Stella engaged the social work community, she became more accepting of differences in others, developing a new sense of open-mindedness. As she put it, "I try to see people as they are and not make judgments....Through my social work classes, I've learned that everybody should be treated that way." But sometimes this open, nonjudgmental attitude caused problems for Stella who suddenly found that her husband was prejudiced in several ways. "My husband is racially prejudiced, and I'm real open and have no problem with that"; "My husband's family thinks welfare people are lazy. I really stand up for people they don't understand." Through her entrance into the new community, her attitudes toward others changed, and she adopted a socially accepting worldview even when the new worldview was in direct conflict with her family. In the process, she became more committed to the community of social workers.

17   The other participant in the study, Charlotte, had graduated from high school in 1957. After raising a family and working as both a cosmetologist and a practical nurse, Charlotte was finally returning to college to get the degree she had long cherished. Charlotte, too, was willing to make the personal commitment that membership in the social work community required. As she put it, "The course is really making a difference in my thoughts; I had not recognized that I was biased in my way of thinking." Further, Charlotte suggested that self awareness and open-mindedness were mandatory for a social worker; "If you don't understand yourself, you can't help anyone else. Not in the way that will help people take control of a situation." Her studies in social work, she said, changed her overall view of people and communities and culture. And, like Stella, Charlotte tried to become a change agent for those around her: "Just this weekend my husband made a comment, and I said, 'Now just a minute, that's not the way it is at all.'"

18   In attempting to enter the social work discourse community, both Stella and Charlotte underwent a great deal of self-realization. Both acknowledged their native social worldview, critiqued it, began to develop new social worldviews, and even tried to become change agents for their spouses' worldviews. Through this progression, both women began to develop what their instructor described as the "social work frame of reference," a socially accepting worldview that is necessary for an individual to help members of

diverse social groups try to improve their position in life. In the process, they became increasingly estranged from their home communities.

19   Research—my own and others'—exploring discourse communities verified what my personal experiences taught me. Learning to write within an academic discourse community is not a simple procedure.

20   First, we have to learn to put down words and ideas in community acceptable ways. We have to internalize and apply the form limitations of the discourse community; our writing has to look like writing in the community is supposed to look. In my own experience, this formalistic community entrance was easy to master, quick to develop; I learned to sound like an English major early in my education.

21   But there is more. We also have to learn to explore ideas by exploring the intellectual manners that are important to a particular field. We have to accept and use the epistemic process of the discourse community. This can be more difficult than the other forms, but new ways of thinking usually develop easily through repeated contact. In my own experience, the epistemic knowledge developed a bit more slowly than the formalistic, but it, too, grew rapidly; I was soon thinking and sounding like an English major.

22   Finally—and I think most importantly—personal commitment to a particular community is involved in entering that new discourse community. Students can develop the sound of a community and apply the thought process of the community without adopting the worldviews of the community, without truly accepting membership in that community. In my own case, I was unwilling to become the person the literary studies community required me to be and to develop the worldview the community expected. As a result, I pursued careers in two different communities, business and rhetoric. Literary studies expected me to become somebody new, somebody I was unwilling to become. I was willing to become a business manager and, later, a rhetorician.

23   In my research, however, I found that Stella and Charlotte were willing to make the total transition, to write in social worker ways, to solve problems using social worker methods, and finally to adopt a social worker worldview, no matter how alien it was to their native communities. In the process of coming to college, Stella and Charlotte found themselves becoming someone new.

Works Cited

Berkenkotter, Carol; Hucklin, Thomas; and John Ackerman (1988), "Conventions, Conversations, and the Writer: Case Study of a Student in a Rhetoric PhD. Program," *Research in the Teaching of English, 22,* 9-44.

McCarthy, Lucille (1987), "A Stranger in Strange Lands; A College Student Writing Across the Curriculum," *Research in the Teaching of English, 21,* 233-265.

---. (1985), *The Making of Knowledge in Composition: Portrait of an Emerging Field.* Upper Montclair, NJ; Boynton/Cook.

North, Stephen (1986), "Writing in a Philosophy Class: Three Case Studies." *Research in the Teaching of English, 20,* 225-262.

Critical Reading Questions:

- **Rhetorical analysis:** What different kinds of evidence does Davis provide in support of his argument? Why are these differing kinds of evidence effective for his target audience?

- **Rhetorical analysis:** Note the structure of Davis' essay. How does he engage the reader? How does he articulate his argument? How does he support that argument and bring the essay to a conclusion? Is this structure effective and why?

The Numbing of the American Mind

Thomas de Zengotita

Months after the events of 9/11, writer Thomas de Zengotita reflects on the modern lives of Americans in this article published in *Harper's Magazine*. He claims the reactions to 9/11 (or lack thereof) mirror changes in society's thinking. He believes there is so much happening in America today, repeatedly reported upon or constantly advertised by channel after channel. Based on this continual flow of information, de Zengotita suggests that our culture has a hard time distinguishing what is real and what is not. The author faults the number of media and choices on hand for the "numbing of the American mind." There are not just three news channels to choose from anymore but hundreds; they now play, repeat, and hype the news twenty-four hours a day. De Zengotita explores the argument that everything is designed for effect and that Americans have become dependent upon that. De Zengotita's cultural critique recognizes that pathos is incessant in media; he argues that in order to protect ourselves and our mental capacity, we never stay involved in the emotion too long but quickly search for the next one. It's easier that way.

—KH

1   ... the massive influx of impressions is so great; surprising, barbaric, and violent things press so overpoweringly—"balled up into hideous clumps"—win the youthful soul; that it can save itself only by taking recourse in premeditated stupidity.

        —Friedrich Nietzsche

2   It was to have been the end of irony, remember? Superficial celebrity culture was over; a new age of seriousness was upon us. Of course, the way media celebrities focused on their own mood as the consequence of September 11 was in itself an irony so marvelous you knew immediately how wrong they were. And sure enough, the spotlight never wavered. It went on shining as it always had, on those it was meant for—on them. A guarantee of continuing superficiality right there, quite apart from unintended irony.

3   So we shared Dan Rather's pain, marveled at intrepid Ashleigh Banfield, scrutinizing those ferocious tribal fighters through her designer specs, and Tom Brokaw, arbiter of greatness among generations, took us on a tour of the real West Wing. But these iconic moments swam into focus only momentarily, soon to be swept away in a deluge of references, references so numerous, so relentlessly repeated, that they came at last to constitute a solid field, a new backdrop for all our public performances. How often did you hear, how often did you say, "Since the events of 9/11"? A new idiom had been deposited in the language, approaching the same plane of habituality as "by the way" or "on the other

86

hand." And in the process we got past it after all. Six months or so was all it took. The holidays came and went, and—if you were not personally stricken by the terror of September—chances are you got over it. You moved on.

4   How is that possible?

5   Nietzsche was not thinking I.Q. or ignorance when he used the word "stupidity." He meant stupidity as in clogged, anesthetized. Numb. He thought people at the end of the nineteenth century were suffocating in a vast goo of meaningless stimulation. Ever notice how, when your hand is numb, everything feels thin? Even a solid block of wood lacks depth and texture. You can't feel the wood; your limb just encounters the interrupting surface. Well, numb is to the soul as thin is to a mediated world. Our guiding metaphor. And it isn't just youthful souls either.

6   Here's the basic situation. On the one hand: the Web, satellite cable TV, PalmPilot, DVD, Ethernet—Virtual Environments everywhere. On the other hand: cloning, genetic engineering, artificial intelligence, robotics—Virtual Beings everywhere. Someday, when people (or whatever they are) look back on our time, all this will appear as a single development, called something like "The Information Revolution," and the lesson of that revolution will have been this: what counts is the code. Silicon- or carbon-based. Artifact or animate. The difference between them is disappearing. This is not science fiction. This is really happening. Right now, in an Atlanta hospital, there is a quadriplegic with his brain directly wired to a computer. He can move the cursor with his thoughts.

7   The moving cursor doesn't really need explaining—it comes down to digital bytes and neurochemical spikes. What needs explaining is our equanimity in the face of staggering developments. How can we go about our business when things like this are happening? How can we just read the article, shake our heads, turn the page ? If creatures from outer space sent a diplomatic mission to the U.N., how long would it be before we were taking that in stride? Before Comedy Central send-ups were more entertaining than the actual creatures? About six months?

8   Soap-opera politics. The therapy industry. Online communities. Digital effects. Workshops for every workplace. Viagra, Prozac, Ritalin. Reality TV. Complete makeovers. Someday, it will be obvious that all the content on our information platforms converges on this theme: there is no important difference between fabrication and reality, between a chemical a pill introduces and one your body produces, between role-playing in marital therapy and playing your role as a spouse, between selling and making, campaigning and governing, expressing and existing. And that is why we moved on after September 11, after an event that seemed so enormous, so horrific, so stark, that even the great blob of virtuality that is our public culture would be unable to absorb it. But it could. It has. Here's how.

Fabrication

9   Some people refuse to believe that reality has become indistinguishable from fabrication. But beliefs are crude reflections of the psychological processes that actually determine how we function. Fat people believe they are on the stocky side. Abject drunks believe they are poetical free spirits. Malicious prudes believe they are selfless do-good-

ers. And a lot of people still believe that, with some obvious exceptions involving hoaxes and errors, we know what's real and what's not. We can tell the difference between the Kursk and the Titanic (meaning the movie, of course), for example.

10   And maybe we can—when specifically focused on the issue. It might take a while, of course, because there are so many gradations when you stop to think about it. For example:

- Real real: You fall down the stairs. Stuff in your life that's so familiar you've forgotten the statement it makes.
- Observed real: You drive by a car wreck. Stuff in your life in which the image-statement is as salient as the function.
- Between real real and observed real: Stuff that oscillates between the first two categories. Like you're wearing something you usually take for granted but then you meet someone attractive.
- Edited real real: Shtick you have down so pat you don't know it's shtick anymore, but you definitely only use it in certain situations. Documentaries and videos in which people are unaware of the camera, though that's not easy to detect, actually. Candid photographs.
- Edited observed real: Other people's down-pat shtick. Shtick you are still working on. Documentaries in which people are accommodating the camera, which is actually a lot of the time, probably.
- Staged real: Formal events like weddings. Retail-clerk patter.
- Edited staged real: Pictures of the above. Homemade porn.
- Staged observed real unique: Al kisses Tipper. Survivor.
- Staged observed real repeated: Al kisses Tipper again and again. Anchor-desk and talk-show intros and segues. Weather Channel behavior.
- (In the interests of time, we can skip the subtler middle range of distinctions and go to the other end of the spectrum:)
- Staged realistic: The English Patient and NYPD Blue.
- Staged hyperreal: Oliver Stone movies and Malcolm in the Middle.
- Overtly unreal realistic: S.U.V.'s climbing buildings. Digitized special effects in general, except when they are more or less undetectable.
- Covertly unreal realistic: Hair in shampoo ads. More or less undetectable digital effects, of which there are more every day.
- Between overtly and covertly unreal realistic: John Wayne in a beer ad (you have to know he's dead to know he isn't "really" in the ad).
- Real unreal: Robo-pets.
- Unreal real: Strawberries that won't freeze because they have fish genes in them.

11   See? No problem. The differences are perfectly clear.

12   But the issue isn't can we do it; it's do we do it—and the answer is, of course not. Our minds are the product of total immersion in a daily experience saturated with fabrications to a degree unprecedented in human history. People have never had to cope with so much stuff, so many choices. In kind and number.

Flood

13   And sheer quantity really matters, because here we collide with a real limit, one of the few that remain—namely, how much a person can register at a given instant. No innovation in techno access or consationalism can overcome this bottleneck. It determines the fundamental dynamic, the battle to secure attention, in every domain of our lives.

14   Compare, say, the cereal and juice sections of a supermarket today with those of years ago. For you youngsters out there, take it from Dad: it used to be Wheaties, Corn Flakes, Cheerios (oats), Rice Krispies—and that was about it. One for each grain, see? Same for fruit juice. But now? Pineapple/Banana/Grape or Strawberry/Orange/Kiwi anyone? And that's just a sample from Tropicana—check out Nantucket Nectars. Makes of cars? Types of sunglasses? Sneaker species? Pasta possibilities? On and on. It's all about options, as they say.

15   Umbrella brands toss off diverse and evolving lines of market-researched products for niches of Self-inventing customers with continual access to every representational fabrication ever produced in the whole of human history. That's "the environment." You like Vedic ankle tattoos? 1930s cockney caps? Safari jackets? Inca ponchos? Victorian lace-up high-heel booties? Whatever.

16   No wonder that word caught on.

17   The moreness of everything ascends inevitably to a threshold in psychic life. A change of state takes place. The discrete display melts into a pudding, and the mind is forced to certain adaptations if it is to cohere at all.

18   When you find out about the moving cursor, or hear statistics about AIDS in Africa, or see your 947th picture of a weeping fireman, you can't help but become fundamentally indifferent because you are exposed to things like this all the time, just as you are to the rest of your options. Over breakfast. In the waiting room. Driving to work. At the checkout counter. All the time. I know you know this already. I'm just reminding you.

19   Which is not to say you aren't moved. On the contrary, you are moved, often deeply, very frequently—never more so, perhaps, than when you saw the footage of the towers coming down on 9/11. But you are so used to being moved by footage, by stories, by representations of all kinds—that's the point. It's not your fault that you are so used to being moved, you just are.

20   So it's not surprising that you have learned to move on so readily to the next, sometimes moving, moment. It's sink or surf. Spiritual numbness guarantees that your relations with the moving will pass. And the stuffed screen accommodates you with moving surfaces that assume you are numb enough to accommodate them. And so on, back and forth. The dialectic of postmodern life.

21   One might say, "Well, people didn't respond deeply to every development in the world 200 years ago either." And that's true, but it isn't an objection, it's a confirmation. Until the new media came along, people didn't even know about such developments, or not as quickly, and above all not as dramatically or frequently. Also, there weren't as many developments, period. This is crucial, another aspect of sheer moreness that gets overlooked. Less was happening.

22   The contrast is stark with, say, the Middle Ages. By the industrial era, a lot more was happening, and numbness became an issue then. Think of Baudelaire, adrift in the crowd, celebrating the artist for resisting numbness, for maintaining vulnerability—thus setting the standard for the genius of modernism. But a qualitative threshold has since been breached. Cities no longer belong to the soulful flaneur but to the wired-up voyeur in his soundproofed Lexus. Behind his tinted windows, with his cell phone and CD player, he gets more input, with less static, from more and different channels, than Baudelaire ever dreamed of. But it's all insulational—as if the deities at Dreamworks were invisibly at work around us, touching up the canvas of reality with existential airbrushes. Everything has that edgeless quality, like the lobby of a high-end Marriott/Ramada/Sheraton. Whole neighborhoods feel like that now. And you can be sure that whatever they do at "the site" will feel like that, too. Even if they specifically set out to avoid having it feel like that—it will still feel like that. They can't control themselves. They can't stop.

23   Take the new Times Square, everybody's icon for this process. All the usual observations apply—and each contributes its iota to muffling what it meant to expose. But the point here is the way everything in that place is aimed. Everything is firing message modules, straight for your gonads, your taste buds, your vanities, your fears. These modules seek to penetrate, but in a passing way. A second of your attention is all they ask. Nothing is firing that rends or cuts. It's a massage, really, if you just go with it. And why not? Some of the most talented people on the planet have devoted their lives to creating this psychic sauna, just for you.

24   And it's not just the screens and billboards, the literal signs; it's absolutely everything you encounter. Except for the eyes of the people, shuffling along, and the poignant imperfections of their bodies; they are so manifestly unequal to the solicitations lavished upon them. No wonder they stuff themselves with junk—or, trying to live up to it all, enslave themselves to regimes of improvement.

25   Yes, there were ersatz environments and glitzy ads back in the fifties, but this is a new order of quality and saturation. Saying that it's just more of what we had before is like saying a hurricane is just more breeze. For here, too, there is a psychological threshold. Today, your brain is, as a matter of brute fact, full of stuff that was designed to affect you. As opposed to the scattered furniture of nature and history that people once registered just because it happened to be there. September 11 had to accommodate the fact that our inner lives are now largely constituted by effects.

26   To get relief, you have to stumble into the Greyhound bus station in Albany, or some old side-street barbershop that time forgot, into someplace not yet subjected to the renovating ministrations of the International Red Brick and Iron Filigree Restoration Corporation. And "stumble" is the key concept here. Accidental places are the only real places left.

27   That's why a couple of weeks out in Nature doesn't make it anymore. Even if you eschew the resonant clutter of The Tour and The Gear, you will virtualize everything you encounter anyway, all by yourself. You won't see wolves, you'll see "wolves." You'll be murmuring to yourself, at some level, "Wow, look, a real wolf, not in a cage, not on TV, I can't believe it."

28   That's right, you can't. Natural things have become their own icons.

29   And you will get restless really fast if that "wolf" doesn't do anything. The kids will start squirming in, like, five minutes; you'll probably need to pretend you're not getting bored for a while longer. But if that little smudge of canine out there in the distance continues to just loll around in the tall grass, and you don't have a really powerful tripod-supported telelens gizmo to play with, you will get bored. You will begin to appreciate how much technology and editing goes into making those nature shows. The truth is that if some no-account chipmunk just happens to come around your campsite every morning for crumbs from your picnic table, it will have meant more to you than any "wolf."

30   Precious accidents.

31   Back to the new Times Square—do you parse out the real from the fabricated in that melange? Not can you, but do you. The Fox screen is showing Elian in his Cuban school uniform on the side of a building—real or not? Some glorious babe in her underwear is sprawled across 35 percent of your visual field. She's looking you right in the eye. You feel that old feeling—real or not? A fabulous man, sculpted to perfection by more time in the health club than most parents have for their kids, is gliding by on Day-Glo Rollerblades eight inches high. He's wearing Tex-tex gear so tight it looks like it's under his skin, and the logos festooning his figure emit meaning-beeps from every angle—real or not? What about the pumped-up biceps? If he uses steroids? But, once again, the issue isn't what you can do when I call your attention to it. The real issue is do you do it as a matter of routine processing? Or do you rely instead on a general immunity that only numbness can provide, an immunity that puts the whole flood in brackets and transforms it all into a play of surfaces— over which you hover and glide like a little god, dipping in here and there for the moving experience of your choice, with the ultimate reaches of your soul on permanent remote?

Finitude

32   What about that feeling that it's all been done? Not in the techie department, of course; there, the possibility of novelty seems to be unlimited. But in those areas occupied by what platform proprietors call "content providers." What a phrase! Could anything register devastation of the spirit more completely than that little generic? Could meaning suffer more complete evacuation? Not since we landed on the moon and found nothing has our cultural unconscious encountered so traumatic a void.

33   Maybe the postmodern taste for recycling and pastiche is more than a phase? Maybe it's necessity. Maybe more or less everything that can be done in the plastic arts, say, has been done? How many different ways can a finite set of shapes and colors be arranged in a finite space? We aren't talking infinitely divisible Platonic geometry here. Maybe there just isn't any really new way to put x shapes and y colors into z permutations. Maybe some day it will be obvious that the characteristic gestures of twentieth-century art were flailing against this fact. Cezanne's planes, Magritte's pipe, Pollock's swirls, Warhol's soup can, Christo's draperies, Serrano's piss, the "installations"—so many desperate efforts to elude the end of originality?

34   Likewise with music? How many distinguishable sounds can be put in how many patterns? There has to be some limit. After you've integrated techno and Brazilian-Afro and Tibetan monko and Hump-backed Whalo, at some point, surely, there's going to be noth-

ing left but play it again, Sam. Maybe that's why it's the age of the mix. And characters and plots, in stories and shows? What's the raw material? Sex, outlaws, illness, death, master villains, guilt, the fall of giants, fate, just desserts, the dark side, redemption by the little things, a few other themes—we all know the repertoire. Maybe it's just impossible to think of anything that couldn't be described, after the fashion of all contemporary pitches, as "It's To the Lighthouse meets Married with Children" or "It's Hannibal Lecter meets Peter Pan."

35   The prospect of finitude helps to account for the turn to sensation, as if intensity of presentation could make up for repetition. Of course, sensation is also a response to sheer clutter on the screen, a way to grab the most possible attention in the least amount of time. But that clutter also accounts for why everything's already been done, and so it cycles on relentlessly—fill the pages, fill the time slots, fill the channels, the websites, the roadsides, the building facades, the fronts and backs of shirts and caps, everything, everything must be saying something, every minute. But what? What's left to say? It doesn't matter. Cut to the response.

36   Zap. Whimper. Flinch. Cringe. Melt. Assert! Exult! Weep. Subside. Ahhh ...

37   Eventually we can just wire our glands directly to a console of sensation buttons, plat-form to platform, and be done with this tiresome content altogether. Call it P2P communi-cation. Talk about interactive. Thus will the human soul be compensated for the despair of finitude.

Fast

38   Remember that T-shirt from the eighties that said "High on Stress"? It was sort of true and sort of a way to bluff it out and sort of a protest—it had that "any number of mean-ings" quality we now prefer to depth. That's because the any-number-of-meanings quality keeps you in motion, but depth asks you to stop. Depth is to your life what dead air is to a talk show.

39   Being numb isn't antithetical to being totally stressed, 24-7—and asking for more. Over-scheduled busyness might seem like the opposite of numbness, but it is just the active aspect of living in a flood of fabricated surfaces. Consider the guiding metaphor again. The (absence of) sensation that is physical numbness is constituted by a multitude of thrills and tingles at a frequency beyond which you feel nothing. The numbness of busy-ness works on the same principle, but it relies upon its agents to abide by an agreement they must keep secret, even from themselves. The agreement is this: we will so conduct ourselves that everything becomes an emergency.

40   Under that agreement, stress is how reality feels. People addicted to busyness, peo-ple who don't just use their cell phones in public but display in every nuance of cell-phone deportment their sense of throbbing connectedness to Something Important—these peo-ple would suffocate like fish on a dock if they were cut off from the Flow of Events they have conspired with their fellows to create. To these plugged-in players, the rest of us look like zombies, coasting on fumes. For them, the feeling of being busy is the feeling of being alive.

41   Partly, it's a function of speed, like in those stress dramas that television provides to keep us virtually busy, even in our downtime. The bloody body wheeled into the ER, every personjack on the team yelling numbers from monitors, screaming for meds and equipment, especially for those heart-shocker pads—that's the paradigm scene. All the others derive from it: hostage-negotiator scenes, staffers pulling all-nighters in the West Wing, detectives sweeping out of the precinct, donning jackets, adjusting holsters, snapping wisecracks. Sheer speed and Lives on the Line. That's the recipe for feeling real.

42   The irony is that after we have worked really hard on something urgent for a long time, we do escape numbness for a while—stepping out of the building, noticing the breeze, the cracks in the sidewalk, the stillness of things in the shop window. During those accidental and transitional moments, we actually get the feeling of the real we were so frantically pursuing when we were busy. But we soon get restless. We can't take the input reduction. Our psychic metabolism craves more.

43   Actually, stress dramas are about the lives of the media people who make them. They purport to be about hospitals or law firms, but they are actually about what it is like to make TV shows, about high-stakes teamwork in the land of celebrity, where, by definition, everything matters more than it does anywhere else, a land that welcomes diversity and foibles as long as The Job Gets Done, a land where everything personal, unconditional, intimate—everything unbounded by the task—takes place on the side. That's why, in these shows through which the celebrated teach the rest of us how to be like them, the moments of heartfelt encounter that make it all worthwhile are stolen in the corridors of power, while the verdict is awaited. If we get that real-folks-rushing-to-get-out-of-the-house-in-the-morning scene, it's just to underscore the priority of the Flow of Events that protects the busy from being left alone in the stillness with what makes it all worthwhile. Lest direction be lost, motion must be maintained.

Moving On

44   So life in a flood of surfaces means a life of perpetual motion, and TV provides the model in other modes as well. Take the transitions from story to story in newscasts, that finishing-with-a-topic moment. "Whether these supplies, still piling up after weeks of intense effort by these humanitarian workers, will actually reach the victims (pause) remains to be seen." A hint of a sigh, a slight shake of the head, eyes down-turning; the note of seasoned resignation. Profound respect is conveyed for the abandoned topic even as a note of anticipation rises to greet the (also interesting, but less burdensome) next topic—and the new camera angle at the anchor desk makes it clear that stern and external necessity, rather than any human agency, governs the shift from two minutes on mass starvation to the next episode of The Fall of the House of Enron.

45   Judy Woodruff is especially good at this, her particular little head nod, or shake, as the case may be, and the way her lips tighten up a tad. "If it were up to me as a human being I would never leave this coverage of thousands of dying innocents, but, as a newscaster, of course, I have to." And her speaking voice says, "All right, Jim, we have to go to a break now, but we will be following this story as it develops—and thanks again." "Thank

you, Judy," says Jim, echoing her gesture, and we understand that he, too, as a human being, would never allow us to move on from so ghastly and demanding a reality, but it isn't up to him as a human being either. It isn't up to anybody, actually. That's the one real reality. Moving on.

46   It would be irrelevant to object by asking, "Well, how else are we supposed to do it?" There isn't any other way to do it. That's the point. This isn't a consultant's memo. This is a serious diagnosis of a serious condition. Would we rather not know about it because it happens to be incurable ? This goes much deeper than subject matter, or political bias, the usual fodder. It determines the way we frame everything. Like all that is most profound in human custom, this agreement is almost physical, an attunement, more music than semantics. It instills and expresses, moment by moment, the attitude we bring to living in this world of surfaces.

47   So, for example, you don't have to wait for the anchorperson to change the topic. You can change it yourself, and you don't have to sigh or tighten your lips as you make the transition. But you do. Monitor yourself next time you zap away from some disturbing something on Lehrer to catch the action on the Law & Order reruns. You mime those little gestures as you punch the buttons. These are the constituting habit structures of our culture.

48   And we've touched already on what awaits you when you join the gang on Law & Order. The stress drama re-creating, more elaborately, the basic gesture of the news show, the one you just performed when you slid away from those refugee visuals. Everything's in motion, elliptical, glancing, fungible. You see the sides of faces, the slope of shoulders, the beginnings of expressions but not the ends, the ends of expressions but not the beginnings. No matter the horror, no matter the injustice, no matter how passionate McCoy may feel, no matter how angry Bratt gets at Briscoe (actors or characters?), no matter how obnoxious the defense attorney or impatient the judge (especially in chambers), they all keep moving. And the camera keeps moving, too, gliding, peeking, glimpsing. Frightened witnesses, incoming lawyers, outgoing suspects, they're all moving—as is the traffic, the doors, hands, phones, everything. Meaningful personal encounters are bound to be interrupted, and the performers, like would-be fighters in a bar relying on friends to keep them apart, anticipate the interruption. Ferociously or tenderly, they emote in transitional interlude, awaiting inevitable rescue by events, and, gratefully regretting the passing of the moment of communion, they watch the D.A. step into the elevator and deliver the homily as the door slides shut across his grizzled visage, a homily that is never merely upbeat or despairing, never final or conclusive in any way. Because the one thing people in a TV series know is that tomorrow is another show, and they will be ready to roll. For they are pros, and pros know how to deal. It's not that they're indifferent or cynical. They care. Sometimes they win, sometimes they lose—but, either way, they move on. That's the lesson, the ultimate homily of all shows. The way we live now.

49   So, if we were spared a gaping wound in the flesh and blood of personal life, we inevitably moved on after September 11. We were carried off by endlessly proliferating representations of the event, and by an ever expanding horizon of associated stories and characters, and all of them, in their turn, represented endlessly, and the whole sweep of

it driven by the rhythms of The Show—anthrax, postal workers, the Bronx lady, the Saddam connection, Osama tapes, Al Jazeera's commentary on Osama tapes, Christiane Amanpour's commentary on Al Jazeera's commentary on Osama tapes, a magazine story about Christiane Amanpour ...

50   And that's just one thread in this tapestry of virtuality. The whole is so densely woven and finely stranded that no mind could possibly comprehend it, escape it, govern it. It's the dreamwork of culture. It just proceeds and we with it, each of us exposed to thousands, probably millions of 9/11-related representations—everything from the layout of the daily paper to rippling-flag logos to NYPD caps on tourists to ads for Collateral Damage. Conditioned thus relentlessly to move from representation to representation, we got past the thing itself as well; or rather, the thing itself was transformed into a sea of signs and upon it we were borne away from every shore, moving on, moving on.

51   What else could we do?

Critical Reading Questions:

- **Reflection:** What role does "reality" TV play in the lives of Americans today? According to de Zengotita, how does this shape culture?

- **Reflection:** Why does the author claim Americans can't sustain emotional response? With this in mind, why is pathos so important in American culture?

How I Learned to Read and Write

Frederick Douglass

"How I Learned to Read and Write," written by Fredrick Douglass, was originally published in 1845 in the *Narrative of the Life of Fredrick Douglass, An American Slave*. In this rich and detailed narrative, he portrays himself as a highly educated slave who was able to overcome the racial injustices of the time by learning to read and write. At only twelve years of age, he had a great desire to learn and began to self-educate. Recognizing that the path to freedom and racial equality is in the ability to communicate through words and phrases, he argues that language enables the writer to recognize his/her position in life. In his deeply moving and emotional narrative, Douglass effectively calls attention to the plight of fellow slaves and the racial injustices of slavery, seeking to persuade and empower others with this knowledge.

—OM

1   I lived in Master Hugh's family about seven years. During this time, I succeeded in learning to read and write. In accomplishing this, I was compelled to resort to various stratagems. I had no regular teacher. My mistress, who had kindly commenced to instruct me, had, in compliance with the advice and direction of her husband, not only ceased to instruct, but had set her face against my being instructed by anyone else. It is due, however, to my mistress to say of her, that she did not adopt this course of treatment immediately. She at first lacked the depravity indispensable to shutting me up in mental darkness. It was at least necessary for her to have some training in the exercise of irresponsible power, to make her equal to the task of treating me as though I were a brute.

2   My mistress was, as I have said, a kind and tender hearted woman; and in the simplicity of her soul she commenced, when I first went to live with her, to treat me as she supposed one human being ought to treat another. In entering upon the duties of a slaveholder, she did not seem to perceive that I sustained to her the relation of a mere chattel, and that for her to treat me as a human being was not only wrong, but dangerously so. Slavery proved as injurious to her as it did to me. When I went there, she was a pious, warm, and tender-hearted woman. There was no sorrow or suffering for which she had not a tear. She had bread for the hungry, clothes for the naked, and comfort for every mourner that came within her reach. Slavery soon proved its ability to divest her of these heavenly qualities. Under its influence, the tender heart became stone, and the lamblike disposition gave way to one of tiger-like fierceness. The first step in her downward course was in her ceasing to instruct me. She now commenced to practice her husband's precepts. She finally became even more violent in her opposition than her husband himself. She was not satisfied with simply doing as well as he had commanded; she seemed anxious to do better. Nothing seemed to make her more angry than to see me with a newspaper. She seemed to think that here lay the danger. I have had her rush at me with a face made all

up of fury, and snatch from me a newspaper, in a manner that fully revealed her apprehension. She was an apt woman; and a little experience soon demonstrated, to her satisfaction, that education and slavery were incompatible with each other.

3   From this time I was most narrowly watched. If I was in a separate room any considerable length of time, I was sure to be suspected of having a book, and was at once called to give an account of myself. All this, however, was too late. The first step had been taken. Mistress, in teaching me the alphabet, had given me the *inch,* and no precaution could prevent me from taking the *ell.*

4   The plan which I adopted, and the one by which I was most successful, was that of making friends of all the little white boys whom I met in the street. As many of these as I could, I converted into teachers. With their kindly aid, obtained at different times and in different places, I finally succeeded in learning to read. When I was sent on errands, I always took my book with me, and by going one part of my errand quickly, I found time to get a lesson before my return. I used also to carry bread with me, enough of which was always in the house, and to which I was always welcome; for I was much better off in this regard than many of the poor white children in our neighborhood. This bread I used to bestow upon the hungry little urchins, who, in return, would give me that more valuable bread of knowledge. I am strongly tempted to give the names of two or three of those little boys, as a testimonial of the gratitude and affection I bear them; but prudence forbids;— not that it would injure me, but it might embarrass them; for it is almost an unpardonable offense to teach slaves to read in this Christian country. It is enough to say of the dear little fellows, that they lived on Philpot Street, very near Durgin and Bailey's ship-yard. I used to talk this matter of slavery over with them. I would sometimes say to them, I wished I could be as free as they would be when they got to be men. "You will be free as soon as you are twenty-one, *but I am a slave for life!* Have not I as good a right to be free as you have?" These words used to trouble them; they would express for me the liveliest sympathy, and console me with the hope that something would occur by which I might be free.

5   I was now about twelve years old, and the thought of being *a slave for life* began to bear heavily upon my heart. Just about this time, I got hold of a book entitled "The Columbian Orator." Every opportunity I got, I used to read this book. Among much of other interesting matter, I found in it a dialogue between a master and his slave. The slave was represented as having run away from his master three times. The dialogue represented the conversation which took place between them, when the slave was retaken the third time. In this dialogue, the whole argument in behalf of slavery was brought forward by the master, all of which was disposed of by the slave. The slave was made to say some very smart as well as impressive things in reply to his master—things which had the desired though unexpected effect; for the conversation resulted in the voluntary emancipation of the slave on the part of the master.

6   In the same book, I met with one of Sheridan's mighty speeches on and in behalf of Catholic emancipation. These were choice documents to me. I read them over and over again with unabated interest. They gave tongue to interesting thoughts of my own soul, which had frequently flashed through my mind, and died away for want of utterance. The moral which I gained from the dialogue was the power of truth over the conscience of

even a slaveholder. What I got from Sheridan was a bold denunciation of slavery, and a powerful vindication of human rights. The reading of these documents enabled me to utter my thoughts, and to meet the arguments brought forward to sustain slavery; but while they relieved me of one difficulty, they brought on an other even more painful than the one of which I was relieved. The more I read, the more I was led to abhor and detest my enslavers. I could regard them in no other light than a band of successful robbers, who had left their homes, and gone to Africa, and stolen us from our homes, and in a strange land reduced us to slavery. I loathed them as being the meanest as well as the most wicked of men. As I read and contemplated the subject, behold that very discontentment which Master Hugh had predicted would follow my learning to read had already come, to torment and sting my soul to unutterable anguish. As I writhed under it, I would at times feel that learning to read had been a curse rather than a blessing. It had given me a view of my wretched condition, without the remedy. It opened my eyes to the horrible pit, but to no ladder upon which to get out. In moments of agony, I envied my fellow-slaves for their stupidity. I have often wished myself a beast. I preferred the condition of the meanest reptile to my own. Anything, no matter what, to get rid of thinking! It was this everlasting thinking of my condition that tormented me. There was no getting rid of it. It was pressed upon me by every object within sight or hearing, animate or inanimate. The silver trump of freedom had roused my soul to eternal wakefulness. Freedom now appeared, to disappear no more forever. It was heard in every sound, and seen in every thing. It was ever present to torment me with a sense of my wretched condition. I saw nothing without seeing it, I heard nothing without hearing it, and felt nothing without feeling it. It looked from every star, it smiled in every calm, breathed in every wind, and moved in every storm.

7   I often found myself regretting my own existence, and wishing myself dead; and but for the hope of being free, I have no doubt but that I should have killed myself, or done something for which I should have been killed. While in this state of mind, I was eager to hear any one speak of slavery. I was a ready listener. Every little while, I could hear something about the abolitionists. It was some time before I found what the word meant. It was always used in such connections as to make it an interesting word to me. If a slave ran away and succeeded in getting clear, or if a slave killed his master, set fire to a barn, or did any thing very wrong in the mind of a slaveholder, it was spoken of as the fruit of *abolition*. Hearing the word in this connection very often, I set about learning what it meant. The dictionary afforded me little or no help. I found it was "the act of abolishing;" but then I did not know what was to be abolished. Here I was perplexed. I did not dare to ask anyone about its meaning, for I was satisfied that it was something they wanted me to know very little about. After a patient waiting, I got one of our city papers, containing an account of the number of petitions from the north, praying for the abolition of slavery in the District of Columbia, and of the slave trade between the States. From this time I understood the words *abolition* and *abolitionist,* and always drew near when that word was spoken, expecting to hear something of importance to myself and fellow-slaves. The light broke in upon me by degrees. I went one day down on the wharf of Mr. Waters; and seeing two Irishmen unloading a scow of stone, I went, unasked, and helped them. When we had finished, one of them came to me and asked me if I were a slave. I told him I was.

He asked, "Are ye a slave for life?" I told him that I was. The good Irishman seemed to be deeply affected by the statement. He said to the other that it was a pity so fine a little fellow as myself should be a slave for life. He said it was a shame to hold me. They both advised me to run away to the north; that I should find friends there, and that I should be free. I pretended not to be interested in what they said, and treated them as if I did not understand them; for I feared they might be treacherous. White men have been known to encourage slaves to escape, and then, to get the reward, catch them and return them to their masters. I was afraid that these seemingly good men might use me so; but I nevertheless remembered their advice, and from that time I resolved to run away. I looked forward to a time at which it would be safe for me to escape. I was too young to think of doing so immediately; besides, I wished to learn how to write, as I might have occasion to write my own pass. I consoled myself with the hope that I should one day find a good chance. Meanwhile, I would learn to write.

[margin note: that is messed up!]

8   The idea as to how I might learn to write was suggested to me by being in Durgin and Bailey's ship-yard, and frequently seeing the ship carpenters, after hewing, and getting a piece of timber ready for use, write on the timber the name of that part of the ship for which it was intended. When a piece of timber was intended for the larboard side, it would be marked thus—"L." When a piece was for the starboard side, it would be marked thus—"S." A piece for the larboard side forward, would be marked thus—"L. F." When a piece was for starboard side forward, it would be marked thus—"S. F." For larboard aft, it would be marked thus—"L. A." For starboard aft, it would be marked thus—"S. A." I soon learned the names of these letters, and for what they were intended when placed upon a piece of timber in the ship-yard. I immediately commenced copying them, and in a short time was able to make the four letters named. After that, when I met with any boy who I knew could write, I would tell him I could write as well as he. The next word would be, "I don't believe you. Let me see you try it." I would then make the letters which I had been so fortunate as to learn, and ask him to beat that. In this way I got a good many lessons in writing which it is quite possible I should never have gotten in any other way. During this time, my copy-book was the board fence, brick wall, and pavement; my pen and ink was a lump of chalk. With these, I learned mainly how to write. I then commenced and continued copying the Italics in Webster's Spelling Book, until I could make them all without looking on the book. By this time, my little Master Thomas had gone to school, and learned how to write, and had written over a number of copy-books. These had been brought home, and shown to some of our near neighbors, and then laid aside. My mistress used to go to class meeting at the Wilk Street meetinghouse every Monday afternoon, and leave me to take care of the house. When left thus, I used to spend the time in writing in the spaces left in Master Thomas's copy-book, copying what he had written. I continued to do this until I could write a hand very similar to that of Master Thomas. Thus, after a long, tedious effort for years, I finally succeeded in learning how to write.

[margin note: good idea]

Critical Reading Questions:

- **Rhetorical analysis:** How does Douglass use definitional claims as an appeal to logos to characterize slavery and thereby persuade his audience of his values and beliefs?

- **Analysis:** What are some counterarguments that Douglass offers regarding the dangers of learning to read and write? How might they reinforce anti-abolitionist ideals?

Letter to My Master, Thomas Auld

Frederick Douglass

Commemorating the tenth anniversary of his escape to the North, Frederick Douglass wrote a deeply emotional public letter to his master, Captain Thomas Auld, on September 3, 1848. In it, he proclaimed his individual personhood and love of freedom while simultaneously denouncing the sins of slaveholders and the inhumane practice of slavery. Later published in his anti-slavery newspaper, the *North Star*, Douglass' letter was intended as a "weapon with which to assail the system of slavery." Throughout the writing, he scathingly attacks Auld for his "wickedness and cruelty" by recounting brutal beatings, broken families, and forced degradation. By directly addressing a slaveholder instead of Northern sympathizers, this letter departs from traditional abolitionist rhetoric. It acts as a powerful indictment of slavery while offering a compelling argument for freedom and equality for all human beings.

—RT

1   SIR—The long and intimate, though by no means friendly, relation which unhappily subsisted between you and myself, leads me to hope that you will easily account for the great liberty which I now take in addressing you in this open and public manner. The same fact may possibly remove any disagreeable surprise which you may experience on again finding your name coupled with mine, in any other way than in an advertisement, accurately describing my person, and offering a large sum for my arrest. In thus dragging you again before the public, I am aware that I shall subject myself to no inconsiderable amount of censure. I shall probably be charged with an unwarrantable, if not wanton and reckless disregard of the rights and properties of private life. There are those north as well as south who entertain a much higher respect for rights which are merely conventional, than they do for rights which are personal and essential. Not a few there are in our country, who, while they have no scruples against robbing the laborer of the hard earned results of his patient industry, will be shocked by the extremely indelicate manner of bringing your name before the public. Believing this to be the case, and wishing to meet every reasonable or plausible objection to my conduct, I will frankly state the ground upon which I justify myself in this instance, as well as on former occasions when I have thought proper to mention your name in public. All will agree that a man guilty of theft, robbery, or murder, has forfeited the right to concealment and private life; that the community have a right to subject such persons to the most complete exposure. However much they may desire retirement, and aim to conceal themselves and their movements from the popular gaze, the public have a right to ferret them out, and bring their conduct before the proper tribunals of the country for investigation. Sir, you will undoubtedly make the proper application of these generally admitted principles, and will easily see the light in which you are regarded by me; I will not therefore manifest ill temper, by calling you hard names. I know you to

be a man of some intelligence, and can readily determine the precise estimate which I entertain of your character. I may therefore indulge in language which may seem to others indirect and ambiguous, and yet be quite well understood by yourself.

2   I have selected this day on which to address you, because it is the anniversary of my emancipation; and knowing no better way, I am led to this as the best mode of celebrating that truly important event. Just ten years ago this beautiful September morning, yon bright sun beheld me a slave—a poor degraded chattel—trembling at the sound of your voice, lamenting that I was a man, and wishing myself a brute. The hopes which I had treasured up for weeks of a safe and successful escape from your grasp, were powerfully confronted at this last hour by dark clouds of doubt and fear, making my person shake and my bosom to heave with the heavy contest between hope and fear. I have no words to describe to you the deep agony of soul which I experienced on that never-to-be-forgotten morning—for I left by daylight. I was making a leap in the dark. The probabilities, so far as I could by reason determine them, were stoutly against the undertaking. The preliminaries and precautions I had adopted previously, all worked badly. I was like one going to war without weapons—ten chances of defeat to one of victory. One in whom I had confided, and one who had promised me assistance, appalled by fear at the trial hour, deserted me, thus leaving the responsibility of success or failure solely with myself. You, sir, can never know my feelings. As I look back to them, I can scarcely realize that I have passed through a scene so trying. Trying, however, as they were, and gloomy as was the prospect, thanks be to the Most High, who is ever the God of the oppressed, at the moment which was to determine my whole earthly career, His grace was sufficient; my mind was made up. I embraced the golden opportunity, took the morning tide at the flood, and a free man, young, active, and strong, is the result.

3   I have often thought I should like to explain to you the grounds upon which I have justified myself in running away from you. I am almost ashamed to do so now, for by this time you may have discovered them yourself. I will, however, glance at them. When yet but a child about six years old, I imbibed the determination to run away. The very first mental effort that I now remember on my part, was an attempt to solve the mystery—why am I a slave? and with this question my youthful mind was troubled for many days, pressing upon me more heavily at times than others. When I saw the slave-driver whip a slave-woman, cut the blood out of her neck, and heard her piteous cries, I went away into the corner of the fence, wept and pondered over the mystery. I had, through some medium, I know not what, got some idea of God, the Creator of all mankind, the black and the white, and that he had made the blacks to serve the whites as slaves. How he could do this and be *good*, I could not tell. I was not satisfied with this theory, which made God responsible for slavery, for it pained me greatly, and I have wept over it long and often. At one time, your first wife, Mrs. Lucretia, heard me sighing and saw me shedding tears, and asked of me the matter, but I was afraid to tell her. I was puzzled with this question, till one night while sitting in the kitchen, I heard some of the old slaves talking of their parents having been stolen from Africa by white men, and were sold here as slaves. The whole mystery was solved at once. Very soon after this, my Aunt Jinny and Uncle Noah ran away, and the great noise made about it by your father-in-law, made me for the first time acquainted with the fact,

that there were free states as well as slave states. From that time, I resolved that I would some day run away. The morality of the act I dispose of as follows: I am myself; you are yourself; we are two distinct persons, equal persons. What you are, I am. You are a man, and so am I. God created both, and made us separate beings. I am not by nature bound to you, or you to me. Nature does not make your existence depend upon me, or mine to depend upon yours. I cannot walk upon your legs, or you upon mine. I cannot breathe for you, or you for me; I must breathe for myself, and you for yourself. We are distinct persons, and are each equally provided with faculties necessary to our individual existence. In leaving you, I took nothing but what belonged to me, and in no way lessened your means for obtaining an *honest* living. Your faculties remained yours, and mine became useful to their rightful owner. I therefore see no wrong in any part of the transaction. It is true, I went off secretly; but that was more your fault than mine. Had I let you into the secret, you would have defeated the enterprise entirely; but for this, I should have been really glad to have made you acquainted with my intentions to leave.

[handwritten margin note: Its not his fault]

4   You may perhaps want to know how I like my present condition. I am free to say, I greatly prefer it to that which I occupied in Maryland. I am, however, by no means prejudiced against the state as such. Its geography, climate, fertility, and products, are such as to make it a very desirable abode for any man; and but for the existence of slavery there, it is not impossible that I might again take up my abode in that state. It is not that I love Maryland less, but freedom more. You will be surprised to learn that people at the north labor under the strange delusion that if the slaves were emancipated at the south, they would flock to the north. So far from this being the case, in that event, you would see many old and familiar faces back again to the south. The fact is, there are few here who would not return to the south in the event of emancipation. We want to live in the land of our birth, and to lay our bones by the side of our fathers; and nothing short of an intense love of personal freedom keeps us from the south. For the sake of this, most of us would live on a crust of bread and a cup of cold water.

5   Since I left you, I have had a rich experience. I have occupied stations which I never dreamed of when a slave. Three out of the ten years since I left you, I spent as a common laborer on the wharves of New Bedford, Massachusetts. It was there I earned my first free dollar. It was mine. I could spend it as I pleased. I could buy hams or herring with it, without asking any odds of anybody. That was a precious dollar to me. You remember when I used to make seven, or eight, or even nine dollars a week in Baltimore, you would take every cent of it from me every Saturday night, saying that I belonged to you, and my earnings also. I never liked this conduct on your part—to say the best, I thought it was a little mean. I would not have served you so. But let that pass. I was a little awkward about counting money in New England fashion when I first landed in New Bedford. I came near betraying myself several times. I caught myself saying phip, for fourpence; and at one time a man actually charged me with being a runaway, whereupon I was silly enough to become one by running away from him, for I was greatly afraid he might adopt measures to get me again into slavery, a condition I then dreaded more than death.

[handwritten margin note: Nobody looked for him? they hired runaways?]

6   I soon learned, however, to count money, as well as to make it, and got on swimmingly. I married soon after leaving you; in fact, I was engaged to be married before I left

you; and instead of finding my companion a burden, she was truly a helpmate. She went to live at service, and I to work on the wharf, and though we toiled hard the first winter, we never lived more happily. After remaining in New Bedford for three years, I met with William Lloyd Garrison, a person of whom you have *possibly* heard, as he is pretty generally known among slaveholders. He put it into my head that I might make myself serviceable to the cause of the slave, by devoting a portion of my time to telling my own sorrows, and those of other slaves, which had come under my observation. This was the commencement of a higher state of existence than any to which I had ever aspired. I was thrown into society the more pure, enlightened, and benevolent, that the country affords. Among these I have never forgotten you, but have invariably made you the topic of conversation—thus giving you all the notoriety I could do. I need not tell you that the opinion formed of you in these circles is far from being favorable. They have little respect for your honesty, and less for your religion.

7   But I was going on to relate to you something of my interesting experience. I had not long enjoyed the excellent society to which I have referred, before the light of its excellence exerted a beneficial influence on my mind and heart. Much of my early dislike of white persons was removed, and their manners, habits, and customs, so entirely unlike what I had been used to in the kitchen-quarters on the plantations of the south, fairly charmed me, and gave me a strong disrelish for the coarse and degrading customs of my former condition. I therefore made an effort so to improve my mind and deportment, as to be somewhat fitted to the station to which I seemed almost providentially called. The transition from degradation to respectability was indeed great, and to get from one to the other without carrying some marks of one's former condition, is truly a difficult matter. I would not have you think that I am now entirely clear of all plantation peculiarities, but my friends here, while they entertained the strongest dislike of them, regard me with that charity to which my past life somewhat entitles me, so that my condition in this respect is exceedingly pleasant. So far as my domestic affairs are concerned, I can boast of as comfortable a dwelling as your own. I have an industrious and neat companion, and four dear children—the oldest a girl of nine years, and three fine boys, the oldest eight, the next six, and the youngest four years old. The three oldest are now going regularly to school—two can read and write, and the other can spell, with tolerable correctness, words of two syllables. Dear fellows! they are all in comfortable beds, and are sound asleep, perfectly secure under my own roof. There are no slaveholders here to rend my heart by snatching them from my arms, or blast a mother's dearest hopes by tearing them from her bosom. These dear children are ours—not to work up into rice, sugar, and tobacco, but to watch over, regard, and protect, and to rear them up in the nurture and admonition of the gospel—to train them up in the paths of wisdom and virtue, and, as far as we can, to make them useful to the world and to themselves. Oh! sir, a slaveholder never appears to me so completely an agent of hell, as when I think of and look upon my dear children. It is then that my feelings rise above my control. I meant to have said more with respect to my own prosperity and happiness, but thoughts and feelings which this recital has quickened, unfits me to proceed further in that direction. The grim horrors of slavery rise in all their ghastly terror before me; the wails of millions pierce my heart and chill my blood. I remember the chain, the gag, the bloody

[handwritten annotations: "restrain" with arrow pointing to word, "slave" with arrow, "thats horrible"]

whip; the death-like gloom overshadowing the broken spirit of the fettered bondman; the appalling liability of his being torn away from wife and children, and sold like a beast in the market. Say not that this is a picture of fancy. You well know that I wear stripes on my back, inflicted by your direction; and that you, while we were brothers in the same church, caused this right hand, with which I am now penning this letter, to be closely tied to my left, and my person dragged, at the pistol's mouth, fifteen miles, from the Bay Side to Easton, to be sold like a beast in the market, for the alleged crime of intending to escape from your possession. All this, and more, you remember, and know to be perfectly true, not only of yourself, but of nearly all of the slaveholders around you.

8   At this moment, you are probably the guilty holder of at least three of my own dear sisters, and my only brother, in bondage. These you regard as your property. They are recorded on your ledger, or perhaps have been sold to human flesh-mongers, with a view to filling your own ever-hungry purse. Sir, I desire to know how and where these dear sisters are. Have you sold them? or are they still in your possession? What has become of them? are they living or dead? And my dear old grandmother, whom you turned out like an old horse to die in the woods—is she still alive? Write and let me know all about them. If my grandmother be still alive, she is of no service to you, for by this time she must be nearly eighty years old—too old to be cared for by one to whom she has ceased to be of service; send her to me at Rochester, or bring her to Philadelphia, and it shall be the crowning happiness of my life to take care of her in her old age. Oh! she was to me a mother and a father, so far as hard toil for my comfort could make her such. Send me my grandmother! that I may watch over and take care of her in her old age. And my sisters—let me know all about them. I would write to them, and learn all I want to know of them, without disturbing you in any way, but that, through your unrighteous conduct, they have been entirely deprived of the power to read and write. You have kept them in utter ignorance, and have therefore robbed them of the sweet enjoyments of writing or receiving letters from absent friends and relatives. Your wickedness and cruelty, committed in this respect on your fellow-creatures, are greater than all the stripes you have laid upon my back or theirs. It is an outrage upon the soul, a war upon the immortal spirit, and one for which you must give account at the bar of our common Father and Creator.

[handwritten annotation: "slave are allowed to be old?"]

9   The responsibility which you have assumed in this regard is truly awful, and how you could stagger under it these many years is marvelous. Your mind must have become darkened, your heart hardened, your conscience seared and petrified, or you would have long since thrown off the accursed load, and sought relief at the hands of a sin-forgiving God. How, let me ask, would you look upon me, were I, some dark night, in company with a band of hardened villains, to enter the precincts of your elegant dwelling, and seize the person of your own lovely daughter, Amanda, and carry her off from your family, friends, and all the loved ones of her youth—make her my slave—compel her to work, and I take her wages—place her name on my ledger as property—disregard her personal rights—fetter the powers of her immortal soul by denying her the right and privilege of learning to read and write—feed her coarsely—clothe her scantily, and whip her on the naked back occasionally; more, and still more horrible, leave her unprotected—a degraded victim to the brutal lust of fiendish overseers, who would pollute, blight, and blast her frail soul—rob

[handwritten annotation: "cruel"]

her of all dignity—destroy her virtue, and annihilate in her person all the graces that adorn the character of virtuous womanhood? I ask, how would you regard me, if such were my conduct? Oh! the vocabulary of the damned would not afford a word sufficiently infernal to express your idea of my God-provoking wickedness. Yet, sir, your treatment of my beloved sisters is in all essential points precisely like the case I have now supposed. Damning as would be such a deed on my part, it would be no more so than that which you have committed against me and my sisters.

10   I will now bring this letter to a close; you shall hear from me again unless you let me hear from you. I intend to make use of you as a weapon with which to assail the system of slavery—as a means of concentrating public attention on the system, and deepening the horror of trafficking in the souls and bodies of men. I shall make use of you as a means of exposing the character of the American church and clergy—and as a means of bringing this guilty nation, with yourself, to repentance. In doing this, I entertain no malice toward you personally. There is no roof under which you might need for your comfort, which I would not readily grant. Indeed, I should esteem it a privilege to set you an example as to how mankind ought to treat each other.

11   I am your fellow-man, but not your slave.

powerful

Critical Reading Questions:

- **Rhetorical analysis:** Select excerpts where Douglass attacks slaveholders or slavery in general. How does Douglass substantiate these condemnations? What purposes do these attacks serve?

- **Rhetorical analysis:** How do Douglass' emotional experiences help him establish his ethos and his right to condemn slavery?

- **Analysis:** Follow how Douglass employs religion both to condemn slavery and to illustrate his individual manhood. How does he use religion for both of these motives?

- **Rhetorical analysis:** Trace Douglass' use of pathetic appeals. Explain why he often surrounds happy memories with painful ones. What rhetorical purposes does this serve?

- **Analysis:** One of Douglass' motives in this letter is to advance a definitional claim for what it means to be a person. What is his definition, and how does he support it?

What to the Slave Is the Fourth of July?

Frederick Douglass

This speech was delivered by Fredrick Douglass on July 5, 1852, at an Independence Day celebration hosted by the Ladies Anti-Slavery Society of Rochester, New York. Invited to speak at the event, Douglass recognized the potential for his speech to persuade others to join the abolition movement and end slavery. In his speech, he eloquently challenges the white audience in attendance to examine the contrast that exists between the true beneficiaries of the Declaration of Independence—white Americans—and those who are largely ignored or omitted from the document—slaves. His speech portrays racial injustices and the suffering of slaves to support his argument that the continuance of racial slavery denies enslaved people the freedom and benefits given to white Americans. He thus constructs his argument that the Fourth of July celebration is merely a celebration for a select few.

—OM

1   Mr. President, Friends and Fellow Citizens:

2   He who could address this audience without a quailing sensation, has stronger nerves than I have. I do not remember ever to have appeared as a speaker before any assembly more shrinkingly, nor with greater distrust of my ability, than I do this day. A feeling has crept over me, quite unfavorable to the exercise of my limited powers of speech. The task before me is one which requires much previous thought and study for its proper performance. I know that apologies of this sort are generally considered flat and unmeaning. I trust, however, that mine will not be so considered. Should I seem at ease, my appearance would much misrepresent me. The little experience I have had in addressing public meetings, in country schoolhouses, avails me nothing on the present occasion.

3   The papers and placards say, that I am to deliver a 4th [of] July oration. This certainly sounds large, and out of the common way, for it is true that I have often had the privilege to speak in this beautiful Hall, and to address many who now honor me with their presence. But neither their familiar faces, nor the perfect gage I think I have of Corinthian Hall, seems to free me from embarrassment.

4   The fact is, ladies and gentlemen, the distance between this platform and the slave plantation, from which I escaped, is considerable—and the difficulties to be overcome in getting from the latter to the former, are by no means slight. That I am here to-day is, to me, a matter of astonishment as well as of gratitude. You will not, therefore, be surprised, if in what I have to say, I evince no elaborate preparation, nor grace my speech with any high sounding exordium. With little experience and with less learning, I have been able to throw my thoughts hastily and imperfectly together; and trusting to your patient and generous indulgence, I will proceed to lay them before you.

5   This, for the purpose of this celebration, is the 4th of July. It is the birthday of your National Independence, and of your political freedom. This, to you, is what the Passover was to the emancipated people of God. It carries your minds back to the day, and to the act of your great deliverance; and to the signs, and to the wonders, associated with that act, and that day. This celebration also marks the beginning of another year of your national life; and reminds you that the Republic of America is now 76 years old. I am glad, fellow-citizens, that your nation is so young. Seventy-six years, though a good old age for a man, is but a mere speck in the life of a nation. Three score years and ten is the allotted time for individual men; but nations number their years by thousands. According to this fact, you are, even now, only in the beginning of your national career, still lingering in the period of childhood. I repeat, I am glad this is so. There is hope in the thought, and hope is much needed, under the dark clouds which lower above the horizon. The eye of the reformer is met with angry flashes, portending disastrous times; but his heart may well beat lighter at the thought that America is young, and that she is still in the impressible stage of her existence. May he not hope that high lessons of wisdom, of justice and of truth, will yet give direction to her destiny? Were the nation older, the patriot's heart might be sadder, and the reformer's brow heavier. Its future might be shrouded in gloom, and the hope of its prophets go out in sorrow. There is consolation in the thought that America is young. Great streams are not easily turned from channels, worn deep in the course of ages. They may sometimes rise in quiet and stately majesty, and inundate the land, refreshing and fertilizing the earth with their mysterious properties. They may also rise in wrath and fury, and bear away, on their angry waves, the accumulated wealth of years of toil and hardship. They, however, gradually flow back to the same old channel, and flow on as serenely as ever. But, while the river may not be turned aside, it may dry up, and leave nothing behind but the withered branch, and the unsightly rock, to howl in the abyss-sweeping wind, the sad tale of departed glory. As with rivers so with nations.

6   Fellow-citizens, I shall not presume to dwell at length on the associations that cluster about this day. The simple story of it is that, 76 years ago, the people of this country were British subjects. The style and title of your "sovereign people" (in which you now glory) was not then born. You were under the British Crown. Your fathers esteemed the English Government as the home government; and England as the fatherland. This home government, you know, although a considerable distance from your home, did, in the exercise of its parental prerogatives, impose upon its colonial children, such restraints, burdens and limitations, as, in its mature judgment, it deemed wise, right and proper.

7   But, your fathers, who had not adopted the fashionable idea of this day, of the infallibility of government, and the absolute character of its acts, presumed to differ from the home government in respect to the wisdom and the justice of some of those burdens and restraints. They went so far in their excitement as to pronounce the measures of government unjust, unreasonable, and oppressive, and altogether such as ought not to be quietly submitted to. I scarcely need say, fellow-citizens, that my opinion of those measures fully accords with that of your fathers. Such a declaration of agreement on my part would not be worth much to anybody. It would, certainly, prove nothing, as to what part I might have taken, had I lived during the great controversy of 1776. To say now that America was

right, and England wrong, is exceedingly easy. Everybody can say it; the dastard, not less than the noble brave, can flippantly discant on the tyranny of England towards the American Colonies. It is fashionable to do so; but there was a time when to pronounce against England, and in favor of the cause of tho colonies, tried men's souls. They who did so were accounted in their day, plotters of mischief, agitators and rebels, dangerous men. To side with the right, against the wrong, with the weak against the strong, and with the oppressed against the oppressor! here lies the merit, and the one which, of all others, seems unfashionable in our day. The cause of liberty may be stabbed by the men who glory in the deeds of your fathers. But, to proceed.

8   Feeling themselves harshly and unjustly treated by the home government, your fathers, like men of honesty, and men of spirit, earnestly sought redress. They petitioned and remonstrated; they did so in a decorous, respectful, and loyal manner. Their conduct was wholly unexceptionable. This, however, did not answer the purpose. They saw themselves treated with sovereign indifference, coldness and scorn. Yet they persevered. They were not the men to look back.

9   As the sheet anchor takes a firmer hold, when the ship is tossed by the storm, so did the cause of your fathers grow stronger, as it breasted the chilling blasts of kingly displeasure. The greatest and best of British statesmen admitted its justice, and the loftiest eloquence of the British Senate came to its support. But, with that blindness which seems to be the unvarying characteristic of tyrants, since Pharaoh and his hosts were drowned in the Red Sea, the British Government persisted in the exactions complained of.

10   The madness of this course, we believe, is admitted now, even by England; but we fear the lesson is wholly lost on our present ruler.

11   Oppression makes a wise man mad. Your fathers were wise men, and if they did not go mad, they became restive under this treatment. They felt themselves the victims of grievous wrongs, wholly incurable in their colonial capacity. With brave men there is always a remedy for oppression. Just here, the idea of a total separation of the colonies from the crown was born! It was a startling idea, much more so than we, at thio diotance of time, regard it. The timid and the prudent (as has been intimated) of that day, were, of course, shocked and alarmed by it.

12   Such people lived then, had lived before, and will, probably, ever have a place on this planet; and their course, in respect to any great change, (no matter how great the good to be attained, or the wrong to be redressed by it), may be calculated with as much precision as can be the course of the stars. They hate all changes, but silver, gold and copper change! Of this sort of change they are always strongly in favor.

13   These people were called Tories in the days of your fathers; and the appellation, probably, conveyed the same idea that is meant by a more modern, though a somewhat less euphonious term, which we often find in our papers, applied to some of our old politicians.

14   Their opposition to the then dangerous thought was earnest and powerful; but, amid all their terror and affrighted vociferations against it, the alarming and revolutionary idea moved on, and the country with it.

15   On the 2nd of July, 1776, the old Continental Congress, to the dismay of the lovers of ease, and the worshipers of property, clothed that dreadful idea with all the authority

of national sanction. They did so in the form of a resolution; and as we seldom hit upon resolutions, drawn up in our day whose transparency is at all equal to this, it may refresh your minds and help my story if I read it. "Resolved, That these united colonies are, and of right, ought to be free and Independent States; that they are absolved from all allegiance to the British Crown; and that all political connection between them and the State of Great Britain is, and ought to be, dissolved."

16   Citizens, your fathers made good that resolution. They succeeded; and to-day you reap the fruits of their success. The freedom gained is yours; and you, therefore, may properly celebrate this anniversary. The 4th of July is the first great fact in your nation's history—the very ring-bolt in the chain of your yet undeveloped destiny.

17   Pride and patriotism, not less than gratitude, prompt you to celebrate and to hold it in perpetual remembrance. I have said that the Declaration of Independence is the ring-bolt to the chain of your nation's destiny; so, indeed, I regard it. The principles contained in that instrument are saving principles. Stand by those principles, be true to them on all occasions, in all places, against all foes, and at whatever cost.

18   From the round top of your ship of state, dark and threatening clouds may be seen. Heavy billows, like mountains in the distance, disclose to the leeward huge forms of flinty rocks! That bolt drawn, that chain broken, and all is lost. Cling to this day—cling to it, and to its principles, with the grasp of a storm-tossed mariner to a spar at midnight.

19   The coming into being of a nation, in any circumstances, is an interesting event. But, besides general considerations, there were peculiar circumstances which make the advent of this republic an event of special attractiveness.

20   The whole scene, as I look back to it, was simple, dignified and sublime.

21   The population of the country, at the time, stood at the insignificant number of three millions. The country was poor in the munitions of war. The population was weak and scattered, and the country a wilderness unsubdued. There were then no means of concert and combination, such as exist now. Neither steam nor lightning had then been reduced to order and discipline. From the Potomac to the Delaware was a journey of many days. Under these, and innumerable other disadvantages, your fathers declared for liberty and independence and triumphed.

22   Fellow Citizens, I am not wanting in respect for the fathers of this republic. The signers of the Declaration of Independence were brave men. They were great men too—great enough to give fame to a great age. It does not often happen to a nation to raise, at one time, such a number of truly great men. The point from which I am compelled to view them is not, certainly, the most favorable; and yet I cannot contemplate their great deeds with less than admiration. They were statesmen, patriots and heroes, and for the good they did, and the principles they contended for, I will unite with you to honor their memory.

23   They loved their country better than their own private interests; and, though this is not the highest form of human excellence, all will concede that it is a rare virtue, and that when it is exhibited, it ought to command respect. He who will, intelligently, lay down his life for his country, is a man whom it is not in human nature to despise. Your fathers staked their lives, their fortunes, and their sacred honor, on the cause of their country. In their admiration of liberty, they lost sight of all other interests.

24   They were peace men; but they preferred revolution to peaceful submission to bondage. They were quiet men; but they did not shrink from agitating against oppression. They showed forbearance; but that they knew its limits. They believed in order; but not in the order of tyranny. With them, nothing was "settled" that was not right. With them, justice, liberty and humanity were "final;" not slavery and oppression. You may well cherish the memory of such men. They were great in their day and generation. Their solid manhood stands out the more as we contrast it with these degenerate times.

25   How circumspect, exact and proportionate were all their movements! How unlike the politicians of an hour! Their statesmanship looked beyond the passing moment, and stretched away in strength into the distant future. They seized upon eternal principles, and set a glorious example in their defense. Mark them!

26   Fully appreciating the hardship to be encountered, firmly believing in the right of their cause, honorably inviting the scrutiny of an on-looking world, reverently appealing to heaven to attest their sincerity, soundly comprehending the solemn responsibility they were about to assume, wisely measuring the terrible odds against them, your fathers, the fathers of this republic, did, most deliberately, under the inspiration of a glorious patriotism, and with a sublime faith in the great principles of justice and freedom, lay deep the corner-stone of the national superstructure, which has risen and still rises in grandeur around you.

27   Of this fundamental work, this day is the anniversary. Our eyes are met with demonstrations of joyous enthusiasm. Banners and pennants wave exultingly on the breeze. The din of business, too, is hushed. Even Mammon seems to have quitted his grasp on this day. The ear-piercing fife and the stirring drum unite their accents with the ascending peal of a thousand church bells. Prayers are made, hymns are sung, and sermons are preached in honor of this day; while the quick martial tramp of a great and multitudinous nation, echoed back by all the hills, valleys and mountains of a vast continent, bespeak the occasion one of thrilling and universal interests nation's jubilee.

28   Friends and citizens, I need not enter further into the causes which led to this anniversary. Many of you understand them better than I do. You could instruct me in regard to them. That is a branch of knowledge in which you feel, perhaps, a much deeper interest than your speaker. The causes which led to the separation of the colonies from the British ' crown have never lacked for a tongue. They have all been taught in your common schools, narrated at your firesides, unfolded from your pulpits, and thundered from your legislative halls, and are as familiar to you as household words. They form the staple of your national poetry and eloquence.

29   I remember, also, that, as a people, Americans are remarkably familiar with all facts which make in their own favor. This is esteemed by some as a national trait—perhaps a national weakness. It is a fact, that whatever makes for the wealth or for the reputation of Americans, and can be had cheap! will be found by Americans. I shall not be charged with slandering Americans, if I say I think the American side of any question may be safely left in American hands.

30   I leave, therefore, the great deeds of your fathers to other gentlemen whose claim to have been regularly descended will be less likely to be disputed than mine!

31   The Present.

32   My business, if I have any here to-day, is with the present. The accepted time with God and his cause is the ever-living now.

33   Trust no future, however pleasant,
         Let the dead past bury its dead;
         Act, act in the living present,
         Heart within, and God overhead.

34   We have to do with the past only as we can make it useful to the present and to the future. To all inspiring motives, to noble deeds which can be gained from the past, we are welcome. But now is the time, the important time. Your fathers have lived, died, and have done their work, and have done much of it well. You live and must die, and you must do your work. You have no right to enjoy a child's share in the labor of your fathers, unless your children are to be blest by your labors. You have no right to wear out and waste the hard-earned fame of your fathers to cover your indolence. Sydney Smith tells us that men seldom eulogize the wisdom and virtues of their fathers, but to excuse some folly or wickedness of their own. This truth is not a doubtful one. There are illustrations of it near and remote, ancient and modern. It was fashionable, hundreds of years ago, for the children of Jacob to boast, we have "Abraham to our father," when they had long lost Abraham's faith and spirit. That people contented themselves under the shadow of Abraham's great name, while they repudiated the deeds which made his name great. Need I remind you that a similar thing is being done all over this country to-day? Need I tell you that the Jews are not the only people who built the tombs of the prophets, and garnished the sepulchres of the righteous? Washington could not die till he had broken the chains of his slaves. Yet his monument is built up by the price of human blood, and the traders in the bodies and souls of men, shout—"We have Washington to our father." Alas! that it should be so; yet so it is.

35   The evil that men do, lives after them,
         The good is oft' interred with their bones.

36   What have I, or those I represent, to do with your national independence?

37   Fellow-citizens, pardon me, allow me to ask, why am I called upon to speak here to-day? What have I, or those I represent, to do with your national independence? Are the great principles of political freedom and of natural justice, embodied in that Declaration of Independence, extended to us? and am I, therefore, called upon to bring our humble offering to the national altar, and to confess the benefits and express devout gratitude for the blessings resulting from your independence to us?

38   Would to God, both for your sakes and ours, that an affirmative answer could be truthfully returned to these questions! Then would my task be light, and my burden easy and delightful. For who is there so cold, that a nation's sympathy could not warm him? Who so obdurate and dead to the claims of gratitude, that would not thankfully acknowledge such priceless benefits? Who so stolid and selfish, that would not give his voice to swell the hallelujahs of a nation's jubilee, when the chains of servitude had been torn from his limbs? I

am not that man. In a case like that, the dumb might eloquently speak, and the "lame man leap as an hart."

39   But, such is not the state of the case. I say it with a sad sense of the disparity between us. I am not included within the pale of this glorious anniversary! Your high Independence only reveals the immeasurable distance between us. The blessings in which you, this day, rejoice, are not enjoyed in common. The rich inheritance of justice, liberty, prosperity and independence, bequeathed by your fathers, is shared by you, not by me. The sunlight that brought life and healing to you, has brought stripes and death to me. This Fourth [of] July is yours, not mine. You may rejoice, I must mourn. To drag a man in fetters into the grand illuminated temple of liberty, and call upon him to join you in joyous anthems, were inhuman mockery and sacrilegious irony. Do you mean, citizens, to mock me, by asking me to speak to-day? If so, there is a parallel to your conduct. And let me warn you that it is dangerous to copy the example of a nation whose crimes, lowering up to heaven, were thrown down by the breath of the Almighty, burying that nation in irrecoverable ruin! I can to-day take up the plaintive lament of a peeled and woe-smitten people!

40   "By the rivers of Babylon, there we sat down. Yea! we wept when we remembered Zion. We hanged our harps upon the willows in the midst thereof. For there, they that carried us away captive, required of us a song; and they who wasted us required of us mirth, saying, 'Sing us one of the songs of Zion.' How can we sing the Lord's song in a strange land? If I forget thee, O Jerusalem, let my right hand forget her cunning. If I do not remember thee, let my tongue cleave to the roof of my mouth."

41   Fellow-citizens; above your national, tumultuous joy, I hear the mournful wail of millions! whose chains, heavy and grievous yesterday, are, to-day, rendered more intolerable by the jubilee shouts that reach them. If I do forget, if I do not faithfully remember those bleeding children of sorrow this day, "may my right hand forget her cunning, and may my tongue cleave to the roof of my mouth!" To forget them, to pass lightly over their wrongs, and to chime in with the popular theme, would be treason most scandalous and shocking, and would make me a reproach before God and the world. My subject, then fellow-citizens, is AMERICAN SLAVERY. I shall see, this day, and its popular characteristics, from the slave's point of view. Standing, there, identified with the American bondman, making his wrongs mine, I do not hesitate to declare, with all my soul, that the character and conduct of this nation never looked blacker to me than on this 4th of July! Whether we turn to the declarations of the past, or to the professions of the present, the conduct of the nation seems equally hideous and revolting. America is false to the past, false to the present, and solemnly binds herself to be false to the future. Standing with God and the crushed and bleeding slave on this occasion, I will, in the name of humanity which is outraged, in the name of liberty which is fettered, in the name of the constitution and the Bible, which are disregarded and trampled upon, dare to call in question and to denounce, with all the emphasis I can command, everything that serves to perpetuate slavery—the great sin and shame of America! "I will not equivocate; I will not excuse;" I will use the severest language I can command; and yet not one word shall escape me that any man, whose judgment is not blinded by prejudice, or who is not at heart a slaveholder, shall not confess to be right and just.

42   But I fancy I hear some one of my audience say, it is just in this circumstance that you and your brother abolitionists fail to make a favorable impression on the public mind. Would you argue more, and denounce less, would you persuade more, and rebuke less, your cause would be much more likely to succeed. But, I submit, where all is plain there is nothing to be argued. What point in the anti-slavery creed would you have me argue? On what branch of the subject do the people of this country need light? Must I undertake to prove that the slave is a man? That point is conceded already. Nobody doubts it. The slaveholders themselves acknowledge it in the enactment of laws for their government. They acknowledge it when they punish disobedience on the part of the slave. There are seventy-two crimes in the State of Virginia, which, if committed by a black man, (no matter how ignorant he be), subject him to the punishment of death; while only two of the same crimes will subject a white man to the like punishment. What is this but the acknowledgement that the slave is a moral, intellectual and responsible being? The manhood of the slave is conceded. It is admitted in the fact that Southern statute books are covered with enactments forbidding, under severe fines and penalties, the teaching of the slave to read or to write. When you can point to any such laws, in reference to the beasts of the field, then I may consent to argue the manhood of the slave. When the dogs in your streets, when the fowls of the air, when the cattle on your hills, when the fish of the sea, and the reptiles that crawl, shall be unable to distinguish the slave from a brute, then will I argue with you that the slave is a man!

43   For the present, it is enough to affirm the equal manhood of the Negro race. Is it not astonishing that, while we are ploughing, planting and reaping, using all kinds of mechanical tools, erecting houses, constructing bridges, building ships, working in metals of brass, iron, copper, silver and gold; that, while we are reading, writing and cyphering, acting as clerks, merchants and secretaries, having among us lawyers, doctors, ministers, poets, authors, editors, orators and teachers; that, while we are engaged in all manner of enterprises common to other men, digging gold in California, capturing the whale in the Pacific, feeding sheep and cattle on the hill-side, living, moving, acting, thinking, planning, living in families as husbands, wives and children, and, above all, confessing and worshipping the Christian's God, and looking hopefully for life and immortality beyond the grave, we are called upon to prove that we are men!

44   Would you have me argue that man is entitled to liberty? that he is the rightful owner of his own body? You have already declared it. Must I argue the wrongfulness of slavery? Is that a question for Republicans? Is it to be settled by the rules of logic and argumentation, as a matter beset with great difficulty, involving a doubtful application of the principle of justice, hard to be understood? How should I look to-day, in the presence of Americans, dividing, and subdividing a discourse, to show that men have a natural right to freedom? speaking of it relatively, and positively, negatively, and affirmatively. To do so, would be to make myself ridiculous, and to offer an insult to your understanding. There is not a man beneath the canopy of heaven, that does not know that slavery is wrong for him.

45   What, am I to argue that it is wrong to make men brutes, to rob them of their liberty, to work them without wages, to keep them ignorant of their relations to their fellow men,

to beat them with sticks, to flay their flesh with the lash, to load their limbs with irons, to hunt them with dogs, to sell them at auction, to sunder their families, to knock out their teeth, to burn their flesh, to starve them into obedience and submission to their masters? Must I argue that a system thus marked with blood, and stained with pollution, is wrong? No! I will not. I have better employments for my time and strength than such arguments would imply.

46   What, then, remains to be argued? Is it that slavery is not divine; that God did not establish it; that our doctors of divinity are mistaken? There is blasphemy in the thought. That which is inhuman, cannot be divine! Who can reason on such a proposition? They that can, may; I cannot. The time for such argument is past.

47   At a time like this, scorching irony, not convincing argument, is needed. O! had I the ability, and could I reach the nation's ear, I would, to-day, pour out a fiery stream of biting ridicule, blasting reproach, withering sarcasm, and stern rebuke. For it is not light that is needed, but fire; it is not the gentle shower, but thunder. We need the storm, the whirlwind, and the earthquake. The feeling of the nation must be quickened; the conscience of the nation must be roused; the propriety of the nation must be startled; the hypocrisy of the nation must be exposed; and its crimes against God and man must be proclaimed and denounced.

48   What, to the American slave, is your 4th of July? I answer: a day that reveals to him, more than all other days in the year, the gross injustice and cruelty to which he is the constant victim. To him, your celebration is a sham; your boasted liberty, an unholy license; your national greatness, swelling vanity; your sounds of rejoicing are empty and heartless; your denunciations of tyrants, brass fronted impudence; your shouts of liberty and equality, hollow mockery; your prayers and hymns, your sermons and thanksgivings, with all your religious parade, and solemnity, are, to him, mere bombast, fraud, deception, impiety, and hypocrisy—a thin veil to cover up crimes which would disgrace a nation of savages. There is not a nation on the earth guilty of practices, more shocking and bloody, than are the people of these United States, at this very hour.

49   Go where you may, search where you will, roam through all the monarchies and despotisms of the old world, travel through South America, search out every abuse, and when you have found the last, lay your facts by the side of the everyday practices of this nation, and you will say with me, that, for revolting barbarity and shameless hypocrisy, America reigns without a rival.

Internal Slave-Trade

50   Take the American slave-trade, which, we are told by the papers, is especially prosperous just now. Ex-Senator Benton tells us that the price of men was never higher than now. He mentions the fact to show that slavery is in no danger. This trade is one of the peculiarities of American institutions. It is carried on in all the large towns and cities in one-half of this confederacy; and millions are pocketed every year, by dealers in this horrid traffic. In several states, this trade is a chief source of wealth. It is called (in contradistinction to the foreign slave-trade) "the internal slave-trade." It is, probably, called so, too,

in order to divert from it the horror with which the foreign slave-trade is contemplated. That trade has long since been denounced by this government, as piracy. It has been denounced with burning words, from the high places of the nation, as an execrable traffic. To arrest it, to put an end to it, this nation keeps a squadron, at immense cost, on the coast of Africa. Everywhere, in this country, it is safe to speak of this foreign slave-trade, as a most inhuman traffic, opposed alike to the laws of God and of man. The duty to extirpate and destroy it, is admitted even by our DOCTORS OF DIVINITY. In order to put an end to it, some of these last have consented that their colored brethren (nominally free) should leave this country, and establish themselves on the western coast of Africa! It is, however, a notable fact that, while so much execration is poured out by Americans upon those engaged in the foreign slave-trade, the men engaged in the slave-trade between the states pass without condemnation, and their business is deemed honorable.

51   Behold the practical operation of this internal slave-trade, the American slave-trade, sustained by American politics and America religion. Here you will see men and women reared like swine for the market. You know what is a swine-drover? I will show you a man-drover. They inhabit all our Southern States. They perambulate the country, and crowd the highways of the nation, with droves of human stock. You will see one of these human flesh-jobbers, armed with pistol, whip and bowie-knife, driving a company of a hundred men, women, and children, from the Potomac to the slave market at New Orleans. These wretched people are to be sold singly, or in lots, to suit purchasers. They are food for the cotton-field, and the deadly sugar-mill. Mark the sad procession, as it moves wearily along, and the inhuman wretch who drives them. Hear his savage yells and his blood-chilling oaths, as he hurries on his affrighted captives! There, see the old man, with locks thinned and gray. Cast one glance, if you please, upon that young mother, whose shoulders are bare to the scorching sun, her briny tears falling on the brow of the babe in her arms. See, too, that girl of thirteen, weeping, yes! weeping, as she thinks of the mother from whom she has been torn! The drove moves tardily. Heat and sorrow have nearly consumed their strength; suddenly you hear a quick snap, like the discharge of a rifle; the fetters clank, and the chain rattles simultaneously; your ears are saluted with a scream, that seems to have torn its way to the center of your soul! The crack you heard, was the sound of the slave-whip; the scream you heard, was from the woman you saw with the babe. Her speed had faltered under the weight of her child and her chains! that gash on her shoulder tells her to move on. Follow the drove to New Orleans. Attend the auction; see men examined like horses; see the forms of women rudely and brutally exposed to the shocking gaze of American slave-buyers. See this drove sold and separated forever; and never forget the deep, sad sobs that arose from that scattered multitude. Tell me citizens, WHERE, under the sun, you can witness a spectacle more fiendish and shocking. Yet this is but a glance at the American slave-trade, as it exists, at this moment, in the ruling part of the United States.

52   I was born amid such sights and scenes. To me the American slave-trade is a terrible reality. When a child, my soul was often pierced with a sense of its horrors. I lived on Philpot Street, Fell's Point, Baltimore, and have watched from the wharves, the slave ships in the Basin, anchored from the shore, with their cargoes of human flesh, waiting

for favorable winds to waft them down the Chesapeake. There was, at that time, a grand slave mart kept at the head of Pratt Street, by Austin Woldfolk. His agents were sent into every town and county in Maryland, announcing their arrival, through the papers, and on flaming "hand-bills," headed CASH FOR NEGROES. Those men were generally well dressed men, and very captivating in their manners. Ever ready to drink, to treat, and to gamble. The fate of many a slave has depended upon the turn of a single card; and many a child has been snatched from the arms of its mother by bargains arranged in a state of brutal drunkenness.

53   The flesh-mongers gather up their victims by dozens, and drive them, chained, to the general depot at Baltimore. When a sufficient number have been collected here, a ship is chartered, for the purpose of conveying the forlorn crew to Mobile, or to New Orleans. From the slave prison to the ship, they are usually driven in the darkness of night; for since the antislavery agitation, a certain caution is observed.

54   In the deep still darkness of midnight, I have been often aroused by the dead heavy footsteps, and the piteous cries of the chained gangs that passed our door. The anguish of my boyish heart was intense; and I was often consoled, when speaking to my mistress in the morning, to hear her say that the custom was very wicked; that she hated to hear the rattle of the chains, and the heart-rending cries. I was glad to find one who sympathized with me in my horror.

55   Fellow-citizens, this murderous traffic is, to-day, in active operation in this boasted republic. In the solitude of my spirit, I see clouds of dust raised on the highways of the South; I see the bleeding footsteps; I hear the doleful wail of fettered humanity, on the way to the slave-markets, where the victims are to be sold like horses, sheep, and swine, knocked off to the highest bidder. There I see the tenderest ties ruthlessly broken, to gratify the lust, caprice and rapacity of the buyers and sellers of men. My soul sickens at the sight.

56   Is this the land your Fathers loved,
           The freedom which they toiled to win?
           Is this the earth whereon they moved?
           Are these the graves they slumber in?

57   But a still more inhuman, disgraceful, and scandalous state of things remains to be presented.

58   By an act of the American Congress, not yet two years old, slavery has been nationalized in its most horrible and revolting form. By that act, Mason & Dixon's line has been obliterated; New York has become as Virginia; and the power to hold, hunt, and sell men, women, and children as slaves remains no longer a mere state institution, but is now an institution of the whole United States. The power is co-extensive with the Star-Spangled Banner and American Christianity. Where these go, may also go the merciless slave-hunter. Where these are, man is not sacred. He is a bird for the sportsman's gun. By that most foul and fiendish of all human decrees, the liberty and person of every man are put in peril. Your broad republican domain is hunting ground for men. Not for thieves and robbers, enemies of society, merely, but for men guilty of no crime. Your lawmakers have

commanded all good citizens to engage in this hellish sport. Your President, your Secretary of State, your lords, nobles, and ecclesiastics, enforce, as a duty you owe to your free and glorious country, and to your God, that you do this accursed thing. Not fewer than forty Americans have, within the past two years, been hunted down and, without a momont's warning, hurried away in chains, and consigned to slavery and excruciating torture. Some of these have had wives and children, dependent on them for bread; but of this, no account was made. The right of the hunter to his prey stands superior to the right of marriage, and to all rights in this republic, the rights of God included! For black men there are neither law, justice, humanity, nor religion. The Fugitive Slave Law makes MERCY TO THEM, A CRIME; and bribes the judge who tries them. An American JUDGE GETS TEN DOLLARS FOR EVERY VICTIM HE CONSIGNS to slavery, and five, when he fails to do so. The oath of any two villains is sufficient, under this hell-black enactment, to send the most pious and exemplary black man into the remorseless jaws of slavery! His own testimony is nothing. He can bring no witnesses for himself. The minister of American justice is bound by the law to hear but one side; and that side, is the side of the oppressor. Let this damning fact be perpetually told. Let it be thundered around the world, that, in tyrant-killing, king-hating, people-loving, democratic, Christian America, the seats of justice are filled with judges, who hold their offices under an open and palpable bribe, and are bound, in deciding in the case of a man's liberty, hear only his accusers!

59   In glaring violation of justice, in shameless disregard of the forms of administering law, in cunning arrangement to entrap the defenseless, and in diabolical intent, this Fugitive Slave Law stands alone in the annals of tyrannical legislation. I doubt if there be another nation on the globe, having the brass and the baseness to put such a law on the statute-book. If any man in this assembly thinks differently from me in this matter, and feels able to disprove my statements, I will gladly confront him at any suitable time and place he may select.

Religious Liberty

60   I take this law to be one of the grossest infringements of Christian Liberty, and, if the churches and ministers of our country were not stupidly blind, or most wickedly indifferent, they, too, would so regard it.

61   At the very moment that they are thanking God for the enjoyment of civil and religious liberty, and for the right to worship God according to the dictates of their own consciences, they are utterly silent in respect to a law which robs religion of its chief significance, and makes it utterly worthless to a world lying in wickedness. Did this law concern the "mint, anise and cummin"—abridge the right to sing psalms, to partake of the sacrament, or to engage in any of the ceremonies of religion, it would be smitten by the thunder of a thousand pulpits. A general shout would go up from the church, demanding repeal, repeal, instant repeal! And it would go hard with that politician who presumed to solicit the votes of the people without inscribing this motto on his banner. Further, if this demand were not complied with, another Scotland would be added to the history of religious liberty, and the stern old Covenanters would be thrown into the shade. A John Knox would be seen at every church door, and heard from every pulpit, and Fillmore would have no more quarter than was shown by Knox, to the beautiful, but treacherous queen Mary of

Scotland. The fact that the church of our country, (with fractional exceptions), does not esteem "the Fugitive Slave Law" as a declaration of war against religious liberty, implies that that church regards religion simply as a form of worship, an empty ceremony, and not a vital principle, requiring active benevolence, justice, love and good will towards man. It esteems sacrifice above mercy; psalm-singing above right doing; solemn meetings above practical righteousness. A worship that can be conducted by persons who refuse to give shelter to the houseless, to give bread to the hungry, clothing to the naked, and who enjoin obedience to a law forbidding these acts of mercy, is a curse, not a blessing to mankind. The Bible addresses all such persons as "scribes, Pharisees, hypocrites, who pay tithe of mint, anise, and cummin, and have omitted the weightier matters of the law, judgment, mercy and faith."

The Church Responsible

62   But the church of this country is not only indifferent to the wrongs of the slave, it actu-ally takes sides with the oppressors. It has made itself the bulwark of American slavery, and the shield of American slave-hunters. Many of its most eloquent Divines, who stand as the very lights of the church, have shamelessly given the sanction of religion and the Bible to the whole slave system. They have taught that man may, properly, be a slave; that the relation of master and slave is ordained of God; that to send back an escaped bond-man to his master is clearly the duty of all the followers of the Lord Jesus Christ; and this horrible blasphemy is palmed off upon the world for Christianity.

63   For my part, I would say, welcome infidelity! welcome atheism! welcome anything! in preference to the gospel, as preached by those Divines! They convert the very name of religion into an engine of tyranny, and barbarous cruelty, and serve to confirm more infi-dels, in this age, than all the infidel writings of Thomas Paine, Voltaire, and Bolingbroke, put together, have done! These ministers make religion a cold and flinty-hearted thing, having neither principles of right action, nor bowels of compassion. They strip the love of God of its beauty, and leave the throng of religion a huge, horrible, repulsive form. It is a religion for oppressors, tyrants, man stealers, and thugs. It is not that "pure and undefiled religion" which is from above, and which is "first pure, then peaceable, easy to be entreated, full of mercy and good fruits, without partiality, and without hypocrisy." But a religion which favors the rich against the poor; which exalts the proud above the humble; which divides mankind into two classes, tyrants and slaves; which says to the man in chains, stay there; and to the oppressor, oppress on; it is a religion which may be professed and enjoyed by all the robbers and enslavers of mankind; it makes God a respecter of persons, denies his fatherhood of the race, and tramples in the dust the great truth of the brotherhood of man. All this we affirm to be true of the popular church, and the popular worship of our land and nation—a religion, a church, and a worship which, on the authority of inspired wisdom, we pronounce to be an abomination in the sight of God. In the language of Isaiah, the Ameri-can church might be well addressed, "Bring no more vain ablations; incense is an abomi-nation unto me: the new moons and Sabbaths, the calling of assemblies, I cannot away with; it is iniquity even the solemn meeting. Your new moons and your appointed feasts my soul hateth. They are a trouble to me; I am weary to bear them; and when ye spread forth your hands I will hide mine eyes from you. Yea! when ye make many prayers, I will not

hear. YOUR HANDS ARE FULL OF BLOOD; cease to do evil, learn to do well; seek judgment; relieve the oppressed; judge for the fatherless; plead for the widow."

64   The American church is guilty, when viewed in connection with what it is doing to uphold slavery; but it is superlatively guilty when viewed in connection with its ability to abolich slavery. The sin of which it is guilty is one of omission as well as of commission. Albert Barnes but uttered what the common sense of every man at all observant of the actual state of the case will receive as truth, when he declared that "There is no power out of the church that could sustain slavery an hour, if it were not sustained in it."

65   Let the religious press, the pulpit, the Sunday school, the conference meeting, the great ecclesiastical, missionary, Bible and tract associations of the land array their immense powers against slavery and slave-holding; and the whole system of crime and blood would be scattered to the winds; and that they do not do this involves them in the most awful responsibility of which the mind can conceive.

66   In prosecuting the anti-slavery enterprise, we have been asked to spare the church, to spare the ministry; but how, we ask, could such a thing be done? We are met on the threshold of our efforts for the redemption of the slave, by the church and ministry of the country, in battle arrayed against us; and we are compelled to fight or flee. From what quarter, I beg to know, has proceeded a fire so deadly upon our ranks, during the last two years, as from the Northern pulpit? As the champions of oppressors, the chosen men of American theology have appeared—men, honored for their so-called piety, and their real learning. The LORDS of Buffalo, the SPRINGS of New York, the LATHROPS of Auburn, the COXES and SPENCERS of Brooklyn, the GANNETS and SHARPS of Boston, the DEWEYS of Washington, and other great religious lights of the land, have, in utter denial of the authority of Him, by whom they professed to be called to the ministry, deliberately taught us, against the example of the Hebrews and against the remonstrance of the Apostles, they teach "that we ought to obey man's law before the law of God."

67   My spirit wearies of such blasphemy; and how such men can be supported, as the "standing types and representatives of Jesus Christ," is a mystery which I leave others to penetrate. In speaking of the American church, however, let it be distinctly understood that I mean the great mass of the religious organizations of our land. There are exceptions, and I thank God that there are. Noble men may be found, scattered all over these Northern States, of whom Henry Ward Beecher of Brooklyn, Samuel J. May of Syracuse, and my esteemed friend on the platform, are shining examples; and let me say further, that upon these men lies the duty to inspire our ranks with high religious faith and zeal, and to cheer us on in the great mission of the slave's redemption from his chains.

Religion in England and Religion in America

68   One is struck with the difference between the attitude of the American church towards the anti-slavery movement, and that occupied by the churches in England towards a similar movement in that country. There, the church, true to its mission of ameliorating, elevating, and improving the condition of mankind, came forward promptly, bound up the wounds of the West Indian slave, and restored him to his liberty. There, the question of emancipation was a high[ly] religious question. It was demanded, in the name of human-

ity, and according to the law of the living God. The Sharps, the Clarksons, the Wilberforces, the Buxtons, and Burchells and the Knibbs, were alike famous for their piety, and for their philanthropy. The anti-slavery movement there was not an anti-church movement, for the reason that the church took its full share in prosecuting that movement: and the anti-slavery movement in this country will cease to be an anti-church movement, when the church of this country shall assume a favorable, instead of a hostile position towards that movement. Americans! your republican politics, not less than your republican religion, are flagrantly inconsistent. You boast of your love of liberty, your superior civilization, and your pure Christianity, while the whole political power of the nation (as embodied in the two great political parties), is solemnly pledged to support and perpetuate the enslavement of three millions of your countrymen. You hurl your anathemas at the crowned headed tyrants of Russia and Austria, and pride yourselves on your Democratic institutions, while you yourselves consent to be the mere tools and bodyguards of the tyrants of Virginia and Carolina. You invite to your shores fugitives of oppression from abroad, honor them with banquets, greet them with ovations, cheer them, toast them, salute them, protect them, and pour out your money to them like water; but the fugitives from your own land you advertise, hunt, arrest, shoot and kill. You glory in your refinement and your universal education yet you maintain a system as barbarous and dreadful as ever stained the character of a nation—a system begun in avarice, supported in pride, and perpetuated in cruelty. You shed tears over fallen Hungary, and make the sad story of her wrongs the theme of your poets, statesmen and orators, till your gallant sons are ready to fly to arms to vindicate her cause against her oppressors; but, in regard to the ten thousand wrongs of the American slave, you would enforce the strictest silence, and would hail him as an enemy of the nation who dares to make those wrongs the subject of public discourse! You are all on fire at the mention of liberty for France or for Ireland; but are as cold as an iceberg at the thought of liberty for the enslaved of America. You discourse eloquently on the dignity of labor; yet, you sustain a system which, in its very essence, casts a stigma upon labor. You can bare your bosom to the storm of British artillery to throw off a threepenny tax on tea; and yet wring the last hard earned farthing from the grasp of the black laborers of your country. You profess to believe "that, of one blood, God made all nations of men to dwell on the face of all the earth," and hath commanded all men, everywhere to love one another; yet you notoriously hate, (and glory in your hatred), all men whose skins are not colored like your own. You declare, before the world, and are understood by the world to declare, that you "hold these truths to be self evident, that all men are created equal; and are endowed by their Creator with certain inalienable rights; and that, among these are, life, liberty, and the pursuit of happiness;" and yet, you hold securely, in a bondage which, according to your own Thomas Jefferson, "is worse than ages of that which your fathers rose in rebellion to oppose," a seventh part of the inhabitants of your country.

69   Fellow-citizens! I will not enlarge further on your national inconsistencies. The existence of slavery in this country brands your republicanism as a sham, your humanity as a base pretense, and your Christianity as a lie. It destroys your moral power abroad; it corrupts your politicians at home. It saps the foundation of religion; it makes your name a hissing, and a by word to a mocking earth. It is the antagonistic force in your government,

the only thing that seriously disturbs and endangers your Union. It fetters your progress; it is the enemy of improvement, the deadly foe of education; it fosters pride; it breeds insolence; it promotes vice; it shelters crime; it is a curse to the earth that supports it; and yet, you cling to it, as if it were the sheet anchor of all your hopes. Oh! be warned! be warned! a horrible reptile is coiled up in your nation's bosom; the venomous creature is nursing at the tender breast of your youthful republic; for the love of God, tear away, and fling from you the hideous monster, and let the weight of twenty millions crush and destroy it forever!

The Constitution

70   But it is answered in reply to all this, that precisely what I have now denounced is, in fact, guaranteed and sanctioned by the Constitution of the United States; that the right to hold and to hunt slaves is a part of that Constitution framed by the illustrious Fathers of this Republic.

71   Then, I dare to affirm, notwithstanding all I have said before, your fathers stooped, basely stooped "To palter with us in a double sense: And keep the word of promise to the ear, But break it to the heart."

72   And instead of being the honest men I have before declared them to be, they were the veriest imposters that ever practiced on mankind. This is the inevitable conclusion, and from it there is no escape. But I differ from those who charge this baseness on the framers of the Constitution of the United States. It is a slander upon their memory, at least, so I believe. There is not time now to argue the constitutional question at length—nor have I the ability to discuss it as it ought to be discussed. The subject has been handled with masterly power by Lysander Spooner, Esq., by William Goodell, by Samuel E. Sewall, Esq., and last, though not least, by Gerritt Smith, Esq. These gentlemen have, as I think, fully and clearly vindicated the Constitution from any design to support slavery for an hour.

73   "[L]et me ask, if it be not somewhat singular that, if the Constitution were intended to be, by its framers and adopters, a slave-holding instrument, why neither slavery, slaveholding, nor slave can anywhere be found in it."

74   Fellow-citizens! there is no matter in respect to which, the people of the North have allowed themselves to be so ruinously imposed upon, as that of the pro-slavery character of the Constitution. In that instrument I hold there is neither warrant, license, nor sanction of the hateful thing; but, interpreted as it ought to be interpreted, the Constitution is a GLORIOUS LIBERTY DOCUMENT. Read its preamble, consider its purposes. Is slavery among them? Is it at the gateway? or is it in the temple? It is neither. While I do not intend to argue this question on the present occasion, let me ask, if it be not somewhat singular that, if the Constitution were intended to be, by its framers and adopters, a slave-holding instrument, why neither slavery, slaveholding, nor slave can anywhere be found in it. What would be thought of an instrument, drawn up, legally drawn up, for the purpose of entitling the city of Rochester to a tract of land, in which no mention of land was made? Now, there are certain rules of interpretation, for the proper understanding of all legal instruments. These rules are well established. They are plain, common-sense rules, such as you and I, and all of us, can understand and apply, without having passed years in the study of law.

I scout the idea that the question of the constitutionality or unconstitutionality of slavery is not a question for the people. I hold that every American citizen has a right to form an opinion of the constitution, and to propagate that opinion, and to use all honorable means to make his opinion the prevailing one. Without this right, the liberty of an American citizen would be as insecure as that of a Frenchman. Ex-Vice-President Dallas tells us that the constitution is an object to which no American mind can be too attentive, and no American heart too devoted. He further says, the constitution, in its words, is plain and intelligible, and is meant for the home-bred, unsophisticated understandings of our fellow-citizens. Senator Berrien tells us that the Constitution is the fundamental law, that which controls all others. The charter of our liberties, which every citizen has a personal interest in understanding thoroughly. The testimony of Senator Breese, Lewis Cass, and many others that might be named, who are everywhere esteemed as sound lawyers, so regard the constitution. I take it, therefore, that it is not presumption in a private citizen to form an opinion of that instrument.

75   Now, take the constitution according to its plain reading, and I defy the presentation of a single pro-slavery clause in it. On the other hand it will be found to contain principles and purposes, entirely hostile to the existence of slavery.

76   I have detained my audience entirely too long already. At some future period I will gladly avail myself of an opportunity to give this subject a full and fair discussion.

77   Allow me to say, in conclusion, notwithstanding the dark picture I have this day presented of the state of the nation, I do not despair of this country. There are forces in operation, which must inevitably work the downfall of slavery. "The arm of the Lord is not shortened," and the doom of slavery is certain. I, therefore, leave off where I began, with hope. While drawing encouragement from the Declaration of Independence, the great principles it contains, and the genius of American Institutions, my spirit is also cheered by the obvious tendencies of the age. Nations do not now stand in the same relation to each other that they did ages ago. No nation can now shut itself up from the surrounding world, and trot round in the same old path of its fathers without interference. The time was when such could be done. Long established customs of hurtful character could formerly fence themselves in, and do their evil work with social impunity. Knowledge was then confined and enjoyed by the privileged few, and the multitude walked on in mental darkness. But a change has now come over the affairs of mankind. Walled cities and empires have become unfashionable. The arm of commerce has borne away the gates of the strong city. Intelligence is penetrating the darkest corners of the globe. It makes its pathway over and under the sea, as well as on the earth. Wind, steam, and lightning are its chartered agents. Oceans no longer divide, but link nations together. From Boston to London is now a holiday excursion. Space is comparatively annihilated. Thoughts expressed on one side of the Atlantic are, distinctly heard on the other. The far off and almost fabulous Pacific rolls in grandeur at our feet. The Celestial Empire, the mystery of ages, is being solved. The fiat of the Almighty, "Let there be Light," has not yet spent its force. No abuse, no outrage whether in taste, sport or avarice, can now hide itself from the all-pervading light. The iron shoe, and crippled foot of China must be seen, in contrast with nature. Africa

must rise and put on her yet unwoven garment. "Ethiopia shall stretch out her hand unto God." In the fervent aspirations of William Lloyd Garrison, I say, and let every heart join in saying it:

78   God speed the year of jubilee
           The wide world o'er!
           When from their galling chains set free,
           Th' oppress'd shall vilely bend the knee,
           And wear the yoke of tyranny
           Like brutes no more.
           That year will come, and freedom's reign,
           To man his plundered rights again
           Restore.

79   God speed the day when human blood
           Shall cease to flow!
           In every clime be understood,
           The claims of human brotherhood,
           And each return for evil, good,
           Not blow for blow;
           That day will come all feuds to end.
           And change into a faithful friend
           Each foe.

80   God speed the hour, the glorious hour,
           When none on earth
           Shall exercise a lordly power,
           Nor in a tyrant's presence cower;
           But all to manhood's stature tower,
           By equal birth!
           THAT HOUR WILL COME, to each, to all,
           And from his prison-house, the thrall
           Go forth.

81   Until that year, day, hour, arrive,
           With head, and heart, and hand I'll strive,
           To break the rod, and rend the gyve,
           The spoiler of his prey deprive—
           So witness Heaven!
           And never from my chosen post,
           Whate'er the peril or the cost,
           Be driven.

Critical Reading Questions:

- **Rhetorical analysis:** How does Douglass' framing of the abolition movement as American help to encourage his audience to identify with him or elicit emotions that might motivate them to them to join the movement?

- **Analysis:** How does Douglass' narrative invite the audience to affirm the struggle of other slaves, and how does it establish a need for change and function as a call to action?

Public Statement

Eight Alabama Clergymen

Although he is never mentioned by name, Martin Luther King, Jr., is the obvious target of this epistolary denouncement of the non-violent protests in Birmingham, Alabama, in April of 1963. In fact, it is this statement that prompted King's own "Letter from Birmingham Jail," just four days later. The white clergymen who attached their names to this document represent a variety of Christian denominations, Baptist, Catholic, Episcopal, Methodist, and Presbyterian, as well as Judaism. The majority of these religious leaders were responsible for a previous letter in January of the same year that, while broadly humanist in nature, follows much the same lines of reasoning. Reportedly intended to defuse racial tensions, this statement urges local citizens to "withdraw support" from the demonstrators (i.e., King); furthermore, the demonstrations are characterized as "unwise and untimely." The ultimate solution to racial tensions, they claim, is a reliance on a racist judicial system and negotiations at a local level. Ultimately, this statement is perceived as well-intentioned, but it also reveals that the clergymen harbored a flawed understanding of the exigencies of a crucial era for black Americans seeking basic civil rights.

—WCM

1   We the undersigned clergymen are among those who, in January, issued "an appeal for law and order and common sense," in dealing with racial problems in Alabama. We expressed understanding that honest convictions in racial matters could properly be pursued in the courts, but urged that decisions of those courts should in the meantime be peacefully obeyed.

2   Since that time there has been some evidence of increased forbearance and a willingness to face facts. Responsible citizens have undertaken to work on various problems which cause racial friction and unrest. In Birmingham, recent public events have given indication that we all have opportunity for a new constructive and realistic approach to racial problems.

3   However, we are now confronted by a series of demonstrations by some of our Negro citizens, directed and led in part by outsiders. We recognize the natural impatience of people who feel that their hopes are slow in being realized. But we are convinced that these demonstrations are unwise and untimely.

4   We agree rather with certain local Negro leadership which has called for honest and open negotiation of racial issues in our area. And we believe this kind of facing of issues can best be accomplished by citizens of our own metropolitan area, white and Negro, meeting with their knowledge and experience of the local situation. All of us need to face that responsibility and find proper channels for its accomplishment.

5   Just as we formerly pointed out that "hatred and violence have no sanction in our religious and political traditions," we also point out that such actions as incite to hatred and violence, however technically peaceful those actions may be, have not contributed to the resolution of our local problems. We do not believe that these days of new hope are days when extreme measures are justified in Birmingham.

6   We commend the community as a whole, and the local news media and law enforcement officials in particular, on the calm manner in which these demonstrations have been handled.

7   We urge the public to continue to show restraint should the demonstrations continue, and the law enforcement officials to remain calm and continue to protect our city from violence.

8   We further strongly urge our own Negro community to withdraw support from these demonstrations, and to unite locally in working peacefully for a better Birmingham. When rights are consistently denied, a cause should be pressed in the courts and in negotiations among local leaders, and not in the streets. We appeal to both our white and Negro citizenry to observe the principles of law and order and common sense.

—Bishop C. C. J. Carpenter, Bishop Joseph A. Durick, Rabbi Milton L. Grafman,
Bishop Paul Hardin, Bishop Nolan B. Harmon, Rev. George M. Murray,
Rev. Edward V. Ramage, Rev. Earl Stallings.
April 12, 1963

Critical Reading Questions:

- **Rhetorical analysis:** Given the clergymen's preference for arguments based on logical appeals, why might the clergy not support the alternative arguments made by African Americans in the form of public demonstration in the streets?

- **Rhetorical analysis:** How does the clergymen's use of "we" throughout this statement enhance their ethos within the text? Why would or wouldn't it be effective for their primary audience(s)?

What Is a Cartoon?

Mort Gerberg

This piece, "What is a Cartoon," is an excerpt from Mort Gerberg's 1983 book titled *The Arbor House Book of Cartooning*. Gerberg is a professional cartoonist whose work has appeared in publications such as *The New Yorker, Playboy, Harvard Business Review,* and *The Huffington Post*. He has also contributed to 43 books on the topic of cartooning during his career. This piece was intended as a guide for aspiring cartoonists to learn the business; however, it functions equally well as a tutorial for students of the rhetoric of cartoons. Gerberg's primary argument here is that cartoons, particularly political and editorial cartoons, are rhetorical constructs which combine images and language to express opinions. During the course of making this argument, Gerberg draws on his own experiences to identify and explain cartoon elements that can enable these seemingly simple texts to engage complex, important, and kairotic issues which are of interest to the public. While Gerberg's intended audience may have been other cartoonists (given the original place of publication), his argument may encourage cartoon consumers' critical engagement with cartoons and their embedded arguments.

—KGR, WCM

1   Cartoons? They're the first thing you read when you open a new issue of *The New Yorker,* or *Playboy*. They pull your eye to print ads and television commercials. You find them Scotch-taped to refrigerators, pinned up on office bulletin boards and sometimes in a letter from a friend, covered with the scrawl, "Oh, Harry, this is so *you!*" Cartoons are the most powerful, the pithiest form of human communication, used everywhere and in many forms. They are an integral part of the American culture and you want to learn to "do" them.

2   A cartoon is totally familiar to you, but do you really know what it is? Webster defines a cartoon as "a drawing, as in a newspaper or magazine, caricaturing or symbolizing, often satirically, some action, situation or person of topical interest." Accurate enough, but if you're looking for guidelines in creating one, ask a cartoonist.

3   Mischa Richter defines a cartoon as "a visual humorous comment about something that's familiar to all of us." Ed Koren sees a cartoon as "a combination of visual and verbal jokes—Buster Keaton and Henny Youngman—a convention of life turned on end, done quickly and succinctly. If you don't get a cartoon right away, you don't hang around to find out why." Arnie Levin thinks of a cartoon as "basically a story—a moment that's been singled out as different from the next one." For Jules Fieffer, "a cartoon is a form of therapy."

4   Henry Martin calls a cartoon a "marriage of a funny idea with a funny drawing." According to Chuck Saxon, "I don't think it's a joke telling thing...a cartoon is primarily a comment or a revelation...that shows some of the foibles and ridiculousness about normal

life." Dana Fradon says it's "something that is first and foremost funny...that illustrates a skeptical attitude...a laugh at the truth, contrasted to the sham that people live by." And in Jack Ziegler's view, "my definition of a cartoon is a drawing that tickles me."

5   As you see, the definitions say the same thing, but differently, varying with the approach of each cartoonist. I'll define a cartoon as *instant communication of a funny idea.* It is designed so that a reader will get its message in a glance, in the flip of a magazine page. It's about a six-second experience for the average reader, but if it's a great cartoon, the experience may echo through a lifetime.

6   A cartoon is a split second in time—the one precise moment in some continuous action that not only perfectly describes that action, but also tells us what immediately preceded it, and perhaps implies what will happen next. We experience a mini-drama, represented by a single picture. The drawing does not move, but it surely is not a still life.

7   It's simple looking, but difficult doing. To be successful, the cartoon must be the *right* freeze frame from the movie. If Modell had drawn a preceding frame when, perhaps, the lawyer was objecting to the judge, it might not have worked. The humor here, as always, depends greatly on timing and tension.

8   In creating a cartoon, the challenge is not only to envision the correct moment, but to reproduce it so readers can see it, too. It's helpful to recognize that within the single-panel cartoon are found familiar elements commonly associated with art and drama. I offer them here only as aids to defining a cartoon and as guidelines for what can go into its creation. The practical approaches will follow.

9   To begin with, there's the *cast,* the people who perform in the cartoon; the actors. Cartoon characters must be of a very specific type. They are people we immediately recognize from life, people we *know,* like Saxon's suburbanites. Cartoon people must *look* the part. Gangsters, professors, salesmen, tycoons must be unmistakably identifiable. To cast the right actor, the cartoonist functions as a casting director and holds "auditions," sketching perhaps thirty faces before he finds the right one. (Sometimes the first is the one that works best, which is why magazines occasionally publish the rough sketch instead of a finished version.) Ed Frascino "auditioned" at least two dozen ladies before he found the two he liked. Want to guess who got the part?

10   Cartoon actors are more than pretty faces, though; they speak *dialogue,* in the form of captions. Here the cartoonist is a dramatist, putting a well-turned phrase into his character's mouth. A cartoon caption is super-disciplined writing—about twelve words painstakingly chosen for their meaning, imagery and sound, then polished and strung together in a rhythm that puts the beat on the funny part. Carl Rose's classic little girl frowning at her plate: "I say it's spinach, and I say the hell with it!" Lee Lorenz's departing churchgoer to the minister: "Just between us, Doctor, how much of that stuff is cast in cement?" Or Donald Reilly's fourteenth-century nobleman looking critically at his portrait and telling the artist, "Give me more angels and make them gladder to see me."

11   Cartoon actors not only look and speak the part, they move in character. This is the element of *gesture,* the facial expressions and body language, the physical acting which helps convey the sense and mood of the cartoon, even before you "get" the situation. A mere glance at Modell's lawyer and judge convinces you they're annoyed. Look at the

postures of Saxon's couple, with arms and legs crossed, chins in hand. You *know* they've been having a quarrel. Their gestures provide a solid frame for the caption.

12   The action of a cartoon is always located in some specific place—the consideration of *setting*. The cartoonist chooses the stage which is most appropriate to his situation, where the idea works funniest and most naturally—a bar, an airport, an office, anyplace in time or space. He not only decides *where* his scene is to be played, he draws only the most characteristic features that make it instantly recognizable to readers. Convincing settings play a major role in Saxon's cartoons. Drawing environments is "my pleasure," he says. And, "certainly, environment tells as much about the people as facial expressions." The same holds true for the chaotic clutter of George Price's rooms, the selected litter on George Booth's lawns or the surreal landscapes of Ziegler and Kliban. Settings may also be minimal.

13   The element of setting includes a consideration of costumes and props. The manner in which characters are dressed and what they carry are visual tipoffs to their profession, their net worth and any number of pertinent things about their personality. In a cartoon, says Saxon, "the reader has to see what you're doing immediately, and you can do that far more than the way people dress..." Clothing distinguishes the panhandler from the passerby. A cartoon doctor has a stethoscope hung around his neck. Professors wear glasses and smoke pipes. Tycoons chew big cigars. Gangsters wear dark shirts and white ties. Stereotypes, of course, but they work.

14   Now in order for a cartoon to communicate instantly, its components must be artfully arranged within the frame so the reader sees them in a particular sequence. The cartoon's *composition* presents elements in proper order and holds them together. It is the cartoonist functioning importantly as director. Imagine that you're telling a joke at a party. You begin, "There was an old man who couldn't sleep..." And you go on to tell what the son said and how the doctor replied, and so on until finally the last thing you utter is the punch line. And everybody laughs. You hope.

15   Composition in a cartoon is the means by which you tell your story to your audience without personally standing in front of them. Composition is remote control....

16   And underneath all of this, one simple principle is operating: *A cartoon violates some cliché in life.* A cliché is anything which is so familiar to us that we automatically accept it, almost without notice. "Patterns of life...natural rhythms," says Arnie Levin.

17   Visual clichés are stop signs, escalators, bicycles, telephones. Clichés are also phrases like "How are you," "Have a nice day," "Glad to meet you," "Thanks for coming." Or situations, like people watching television, sitting in a bar, driving a car, dining in a restaurant. Cartoon clichés are all the clichés of real life, plus those from memory, like well-known fairy tales, history, mythology, literature—and the imagination, which we can thank for the well-worn desert-island situation.

18   The cliché is the vehicle of instant communication. The cartoonist uses it to send his message. And the message is in twisting it, turning the cliché around. Adding a new association. Violating the cliché. Like Sam Gross's amusement park scooter ride, which you recognize, but then a blink later you notice that instead of scooters there are tanks cruising around. Or Bud Handelsman's highway scene, with traffic inching past a group of road

workers standing around a "Men Working" sign. Except that the sign reads, "Men Chatting." Here is my own contemporary variation of a caught-in-the-act cliché.

19   The cliché is the cartoonist's trap. He attracts the reader's interest with the familiar and then fools him by changing it just enough to make it a surprise—and funny. In words as well as pictures. Like my own galley slave in chains at the oars, replying to a slave driver holding a clipboard, "My vacation? How about the first two hours in August?"

20   The cliché is also operative in all the elements of the cartoon. The cartoonist casts the actors who must look as though they belong in a particular situation. In captions the cartoonist uses colloquialisms and catchphrases currently fashionable. He directs his actors in gestures and facial expressions that exactly typify the action. And for his settings he uses backgrounds and props that are immediately identified with the scene. The cliché, in effect, is the cartoonist's shorthand.

21   So much for defining what a cartoon is. Obviously, all cartoons can't be described in these terms, just as cartooning can't be learned easily by following any set of rules; it's too elusive an art form. So don't consider these definitions as chiseled in stone; they're merely points of departure and reference for further study and practice.

Critical Reading Questions:

- **Rhetorical analysis:** In what ways and through what components does Gerberg argue that political and editorial cartoons are inherently rhetorical?

- **Reflection:** After having read and considered Gerberg's argument about the rhetorical nature of cartoons, how will you view this genre of text differently? Why?

The Rhetoric of Advertising

Stuart Hirschberg

Ads are everywhere, and ads are arguments. In this work, Stuart Hirsch-berg, Associate Professor of English at Rutgers University, explores the Aristotelian rhetoric that underlies advertisement. Advertisers deliberately connote connections between their products and happiness, sexual fulfill-ment, glamour, and more—without ever truly promising these attributes. While advertisements imply miracles and wonders, Hirschberg's critical analysis reveals that they actually say nearly nothing. By appealing to our emotions, our reason, and our ethics, advertisers are able to transfer our beliefs and values to their products. However, Hirschberg goes beyond Aristotle to begin exploring how these advertisers create the impression of shared beliefs, values, and needs with their intended audiences. Published in Hirschberg's 1999 collection *Reflections on Language*, the overarching argument of "The Rhetoric of Argument" is that by consuming these adver-tised products, "we are offered the chance to create ourselves, our person-ality, and our relationships through consumption."

—BLS

1   Whether ads are presented as sources of information enabling the consumer to make educated choices between products or aim at offering memorable images or witty, thoughtful, or poetic copy, the underlying intent of all advertising is to persuade specific audiences. Seen in this way, ads appear as mini-arguments whose strategies and tech-niques of persuasion can be analyzed just like a written argument. We can discover which elements are designed to appeal to the audience's emotions (*pathos* according to Aristo-tle), which elements make their appeal in terms of reasons, evidence, or logic (*logos*), and how the advertiser goes about winning credibility for itself or in terms of the spokesperson employed to speak on behalf of the product (the *ethos* dimension). Like arguments, ads can be effective if they appeal to the needs, values, and beliefs of the audience. Although the verbal and visual elements within an ad are designed to work together, we can study these elements separately. We can look at how the composition of the elements within an ad is intended to function. We can look at the role of language and how it is used to persuade. We can study how objects and settings are used to promote the audience's identification with the products being sold. We can judge ads according to the skill with which they deploy all of these resources while at the same time being critically aware of their intended effects on us.

The Techniques of Advertising

2   The claim the ad makes is designed to establish the superiority of the product in the minds of the audience and to create a distinctive image for the product, whether it is a brand of cigarettes, a financial service, or a type of gasoline. The single most impor-

tant technique for creating this image depends on transferring ideas, attributes, or feelings from outside the product onto the product itself. In this way, the product comes to represent an obtainable object or service that embodies, represents, or symbolizes a whole range of meanings. This transfer can be achieved in many ways. For example, when Elizabeth Taylor lends her glamour and beauty to the merchandising of perfume, the consumer is meant to conclude that the perfume must be superior to other perfumes in the way that Elizabeth Taylor embodies beauty, glamour, and sex appeal. The attempt to transfer significance can operate in two ways. It can encourage the audience to discover meanings and to correlate feelings and attributes that the advertiser wishes the product to represent in way s that allow these needs and desires to become attached to specific products. It can also prevent the correlation of thoughts or feelings that might discourage the audience from purchasing a particular product. For example, the first most instinctive response to the thought of smoking a cigarette might be linked with the idea of inhaling hot and dry smoke from what are essentially burning tobacco leaves. Thus, any association the audience might have with burning leaves, coughing, and dry hot smoke must be short-circuited by supplying them with a whole set of other associations to receive and occupy the perceptual "slot" that might have been triggered by their first reactions. Cigarette advertisers do this in a variety of ways:

- By showing active people in outdoorsy settings they put the thought of emphysema, shortness of breath, or lung disease very far away indeed.
- By showing cigarette packs set against the background of grass glistening with morning dew or bubbling streams or cascading waterfalls, they subtly guide the audience's response away from what is dry, hot, congested, or burning toward what is open, airy, moist, cool, and clean.
- In some brands, menthol flavoring and green and blue colors are intended to promote these associations.

3   Thus, ads act as do all other kinds of persuasion to intensify correlations that work to the advertiser's advantage and to suppress associations that would lessen the product's appeal.

4   The kinds of associations audiences are encouraged to perceive reflect a broad range of positive emotional appeals that encourage the audience to find self-esteem through the purchase of a product that by itself offers a way to meet personal and social needs. The particular approach taken in the composition of the ad, the way it is laid out, and the connotations of the advertising copy vary according to the emotional appeal of the ad.

5   The most common manipulative techniques are designed to make consumers want to consume to satisfy deep-seated human drives. Of course, no one consciously believes that purchasing a particular kind of toothpaste, perfume, lipstick, or automobile will meet real psychological and social needs, but that is exactly how products are sold—through the promise of delivering unattainable satisfactions through tangible purchasable objects or services. In purchasing a certain product, we are offered the chance to create ourselves, our personality, and our relationships through consumption.

Emotional Appeals Used in Advertising

6   *The emotional appeals in ads function exactly the way assumptions about value do in written arguments.* They supply the unstated major premise that supplies a rationale to persuade an audience that a particular product will meet one or another of several different kinds of needs. Some ads present the purchase of a product as a means by which consumers can find social acceptance.

7   These ads address the consumer as "you" ("Wouldn't 'you' really rather have a Buick?"). The "you" here is plural but is perceived as being individual and personal by someone who has already formed the connection with the product. Ironically, the price of remaining in good standing with this "group" of fellow consumers requires the consumer to purchase an expensive automobile. In this sense, ads give consumers a chance to belong to social groups that have only one thing in common—the purchase of a particular product.

8   One variation on the emotional need to belong to a designated social group is the appeal to status or "snob appeal." Snob appeal is not new. In 1710, the *Spectator*, a popular newspaper of the time, carried an ad that read:

9   An incomparable Powder for Cleaning Teeth, which has given great
         satisfaction to most of the Nobility Gentry in England. (Quoted in W. Duncan
         Reekie, *Advertising: Its Place in Political and Managerial
         Economics,* 1974.)

10   Ads for scotch, expensive cars, boats, jewelry, and watches, frequently place their products in upper-class settings or depict them in connection with the fine arts (sculpture, ballet, etc.) The *value warrant* in these ads encourages the consumer to imagine that the purchase of the item will confer qualities associated with the background or activities of this upper-class world onto the consumer.

11   In other ads the need to belong takes a more subtle form of offering the product as a way to become part of a time in the past the audience might look back to with nostalgia. Grandmotherly figures wearing aprons and holding products that are advertised as being "like Grandma used to make" offer the consumer an imaginary past, a family tradition, or a simpler time looked back to with warmth and sentimentality. For many years, Smucker's preserves featured ads in which the product was an integral part of a scene emanating security and warmth, which the ad invited us to remember as if it were our own past. Ads of this kind are often photographed through filters that present misty sepia-toned images that carefully recreate old-fashioned kitchens with the accompanying appliances, dishes, clothes, and hairstyles. The ads thus supply us with false memories and invite us to insert ourselves into this imaginary past and to remember it as if it were our own. At the furthest extreme, ads employing the appeal to see ourselves as part of a group may try to evoke patriotic feelings so that the prospective consumer will derive the satisfactions of good citizenship and sense of participation in being part of the collective psyche of an entire nation. The point is that people really do have profound needs that advertisers can exploit, but it would be a rare product indeed that could really fulfill such profound needs.

12   Advertisers use highly sophisticated market research techniques to enable them to define and characterize precisely those people who are most likely to be receptive to ads of particular kinds. The science of demographics is aided and abetted by psychological research that enables advertisers to "target" a precisely designated segment of the general public. For example, manufacturers of various kinds of liquor can rely on studies that inform them that vodka drinkers are most likely to read *Psychology Today* and scotch drinkers the *New Yorker*, while readers of *Time* prefer rum and the audience for *Playboy* has a large number of readers who prefer gin. Once a market segment with defined psychological characteristics has been identified, an individual ad can be crafted for that particular segment and placed in the appropriate publication.

13   Ads, of course, can elicit responses by attempting to manipulate consumers through negative as well as positive emotional appeals. Helen Woodward, the head copywriter for an ad agency, once offered the following advice for ad writers trying to formulate a new ad for baby food: "Give 'em the figures about the baby death rate—but don't say it flatly... if we only had the nerve to put a hearse in the ad, you couldn't keep the women away from the food" (Stuart Ewen, *Captains of Consciousness: Advertising and the Social Roots of Consumer Culture* [1976]). Ads of this kind must first arouse the consumer's anxieties and then offer the product as the solution to the problem that more often than not the ad has created.

14   For example, an advertisement for Polaroid evokes the fear of not having taken pictures of moments that cannot be re-created and then offers the product as a form of insurance that will prevent this calamity from occurring. Nikon does the same in claiming that "a moment is called a moment because it doesn't last forever. Think of sunsets. A child's surprise. A Labrador's licky kiss. This is precisely why the Nikon N50 has the simple 'Simple' switch on top of the camera."

15   Ads for products that promise to guarantee their purchasers sex appeal, youth, health, social acceptance, self-esteem, creativity, enlightenment, a happy family life, loving relationships, escape from boredom, vitality, and many other things frequently employ scare tactics to frighten or worry the consumer into purchasing the product to ease his or her fears. These ads must first make the consumer dissatisfied with the self that exists. In this way, they function exactly as do *policy arguments* that recommend solutions to problems with measurably harmful consequences. The difference is that these kinds of ads actually are designed to arouse and then exploit the anxieties related to these problems.

16   Large industrial conglomerates, whether in oil, chemicals, pharmaceuticals, or agribusiness, frequently use advertising to accomplish different kinds of objectives than simply persuading the consumer to buy a particular product. These companies often seek to persuade the general public that they are not polluting the environment, poisoning the water, or causing environmental havoc in the process of manufacturing their products. The emotional appeal they use is to portray themselves as concerned "corporate citizens," vitally interested in the public good as a whole, and especially in those communities where they conduct their operations. In some cases, the ads present products as if they were directly produced from nature without being subjected to intermediary pro-

cessing, preservatives, and contaminants, thereby lessening concern that they produce harmful byproducts. For example, Mazola might depict a spigot producing corn oil directly inserted into an ear of corn. A Jeep might appear to have materialized out of thin air on a seemingly inaccessible mountain peak. Companies sensitive to accusations that they are polluting the air and water can mount an advertising campaign designed to prove that they are not simply exploiting the local resources (whether timber, oil, fish, coal) for profits but are genuinely interested in putting something back into the community. The folksy good-neighbor tone of these ads is designed to create a benign image of the company.

The Language of Advertising

17   We can see how the creation of a sense of the company's credibility as a concerned citizen corresponds to what Aristotle called the *ethos* dimension. For example, Chevron expresses concern that the light from their oil drilling operations be shielded so that spawning sea turtles won't be unintentionally misdirected and lose their way!

18   The appeals to logic, statements of reasons, and presentations of evidence in ads correspond to the *logos* dimension of argument. The wording of the claims is particularly important, since it determines whether companies are legally responsible for any claims they make.

19   Claims in advertising need to be evaluated to discover whether something is asserted that needs to be proved or is implied without actually being stated.

20   Claims may refer to authoritative-sounding results obtained by supposedly independent laboratories, teams of research scientists, or physicians without ever saying how these surveys were conducted, what statistical methods were used, and who interpreted the results. Ads of this kind may make an impressive-sounding quasi-scientific claim; Ivory Soap used to present itself as "99 and 44/100% pure" without answering "pure" what. Some ads use technical talk and scientific terms to give the impression of a scientific breakthrough. For example, STP claims that it added "an anti-wear agent and viscosity improvers" to your oil. The copy for L.L. Bean claims of one of its jackets that "even in brutal ice winds gusting to 80 knots this remarkable anorak kept team members who wore it warm and comfortable." It would be important to know that the team members referred to are members of the "L.L. Bean test team."

21   Other claims cannot be substantiated, for example, "we're the Dexter Shoe Company. And for nearly four decades we put a lot of Dexter Maine into every pair of shoes we make."

22   In an ad for lipstick, Aveda makes the claim that "it's made of rich, earthy lip colours formulated with pure plant pigment from the Uruku tree. Organically grown by indigenous people in the rain forest."

23   Claims may be deceptive in other ways. Of all the techniques advertisers use to influence what people believe and how they spend their money, none is more basic than the use of so-called *weasel words* that retract the meaning of the words they are next to just as a weasel sucks the meat out of the egg.

24   In modern advertising parlance, a weasel word has come to mean any qualifier or comparative that is used to imply a positive quality that cannot be stated as a fact,

because it cannot be substantiated. For example, if an ad claims a toothpaste will "help" stop cavities it does not obligate the manufacturer to substantiate this claim. So, too, if a product is advertised as "fighting" germs, the equivocal claim hides the fact that the product may fight and lose.

25   A recent ad for STP claimed that "no matter what kind of car you drive, STP gas treatment helps remove the water that leads to gas line freeze. And unlike gas line antifreeze, our unique gas treatment formula works to reduce intake valve deposits and prevent clogged injectors." The key words are "helps" and "works," neither of which obligates STP to be legally accountable to support the claim.

26   The words *virtually* (as in "virtually spotless") and *up to* or *for as long as* (as in "stops coughs up to eight hours") also remove any legal obligation on the part of the manufacturer to justify the claim.

27   Other favorite words in the copywriter's repertoire, such as *free* and *new*, are useful in selling everything from cat food to political candidates.

The Ethical Dimension of Persuasion

28   As we have seen in our examination of the methods advertisers use to influence consumers, ethical questions are implicit in every act of persuasion. For example, what are we to make of a persuader whose objectives in seeking to influence an audience may be praiseworthy but who consciously makes use of distorted facts or seeks to manipulate an audience by playing on their known attitudes, values, and beliefs. Is success in persuasion the only criterion or should we hold would-be persuaders accountable to some ethical standards of responsibility about the means they use to achieve specific ends? Perhaps the most essential quality in determining whether any act of persuasion is an ethical one depends on the writer maintaining an open dialogue with different perspectives that might be advanced on a particular issue. By contrast, any act of persuasion that intentionally seeks to avoid self-criticism or challenges from competing perspectives will come across as insincere, dogmatic, deceptive, and defensive. The desire to shut down debate or control an audience's capacity to respond to the argument might well be considered unethical. The consequence of this attitude may be observed in the arguer's use of fraudulent evidence, illogical reasoning, emotionally laden irrelevant appeals, simplistic representation of the issue, or the pretense of expertise. Standards to apply when judging the ethical dimension in any act of persuasion require us to consider whether any element of coercion, deception, or manipulation is present. This becomes especially true when we look at the relationship between propaganda as a form of mass persuasion and the rhetorical means used to influence large groups of people.

Critical Reading Questions:

- **Analysis:** Using a magazine or newspaper, locate a print advertisement. What are the elements of ethos, logos, and pathos at work in this advertisement? What are the value warrants within your selected advertisement? What are the weasel words within it?

- **Analysis:** While Hirschberg focuses this piece on the pisteis at work within an advertisement, how does the rhetorical element of kairos also factor into advertisement analysis? Hirschberg discusses brands (such as Buick, Smucker's, Polaroid, Mazola, Jeep, Chevron, Ivory Soap, Dexter Shoe company, Aveda, STP, and more), but which of these products remain culturally relevant years after this article was first published? Which have lost their kairotic appeal?

What Is Academic Writing?

L. Lennie Irvin

The following selection, from *Writing Spaces: Readings on Writing*, provides an accessible introduction to what many consider a daunting genre: academic writing. Dr. L. Lennie Irvin, Associate Professor of English at San Antonio College, helps students better understand the nature of college writing and the expectations attached to it. In her article, Irvin begins by debunking some of the commonly held misconceptions about academic writing before she provides insight into its practice. To demystify the process, she discusses the types of assignments students should expect, the analytical skills they will need to succeed in those tasks, and the mentality, or "writer's sense," that is required for a productive academic writing career. Her account is not simply a guide to necessary writing skills; it is also an appeal to students to think about the writing situation and their place within it.

—RT

Introduction: The Academic Writing Task

1   As a new college student, you may have a lot of anxiety and questions about the writing you'll do in college. That word "academic," especially, may turn your stomach or turn your nose. However, with this first year composition class, you begin one of the only classes in your entire college career where you will focus on learning to write. Given the importance of writing as a communication skill, I urge you to consider this class as a gift and make the most of it. But writing is hard, and writing in college may resemble playing a familiar game by completely new rules (that often are unstated). This chapter is designed to introduce you to what academic writing is like, and hopefully ease your transition as you face these daunting writing challenges.

2   So here's the secret. Your success with academic writing depends upon how well you understand what you are doing as you write and then how you approach the writing task. Early research done on college writers discovered that whether students produced a successful piece of writing depended largely upon their representation of the writing task. The writers' mental model for picturing their task made a huge difference. Most people as they start college have wildly strange ideas about what they are doing when they write an essay, or worse—they have no clear idea at all. I freely admit my own past as a clueless freshman writer, and it's out of this sympathy as well as twenty years of teaching college writing that I hope to provide you with something useful. So grab a cup of coffee or a diet coke, find a comfortable chair with good light, and let's explore together this activity of academic writing you'll be asked to do in college. We will start by clearing up some of those wild misconceptions people often arrive at college possessing. Then we will dig more deeply into the components of the academic writing situation and nature of the writing task.

Myths about Writing

3   Though I don't imagine an episode of *MythBusters* will be based on the misconceptions about writing we are about to look at, you'd still be surprised at some of the things people will believe about writing. You may find lurking within you viral elements of these myths—all of these lead to problems in writing.

4   Myth #1: The "Paint by Numbers" myth
Some writers believe they must perform certain steps in a particular order to write "correctly." Rather than being a lock-step linear process, writing is "recursive." That means we cycle through and repeat the various activities of the writing process many times as we write.

5   Myth #2: Writers only start writing when they have everything figured out
Writing is not like sending a fax! Writers figure out much of what they want to write as they write it. Rather than waiting, get some writing on the page—even with gaps or problems. You can come back to patch up rough spots.

6   Myth #3: Perfect first drafts   *— no first are perfect*
We put unrealistic expectations on early drafts, either by focusing too much on the impossible task of making them perfect (which can put a cap on the development of our ideas), or by making too little effort because we don't care or know about their inevitable problems. Nobody writes perfect first drafts; polished writing takes lots of revision.

7   Myth #4: Some got it; I don't—the genius fallacy
When you see your writing ability as something fixed or out of your control (as if it were in your genetic code), then you won't believe you can improve as a writer and are likely not to make any efforts in that direction. With effort and study, though, you can improve as a writer. I promise.

8   Myth #5: Good grammar is good writing
When people say "I can't write," what they often mean is they have problems with grammatical correctness. Writing, however, is about more than just grammatical correctness. Good writing is a matter of achieving your desired effect upon an intended audience. Plus, as we saw in myth #3, no one writes perfect first drafts. *Facts*

9   Myth #6: The Five Paragraph Essay
Some people say to avoid it at all costs, while others believe no other way to write exists. With an introduction, three supporting paragraphs, and a conclusion, the five paragraph essay is a format you should know, but one which you will outgrow. You'll have to gauge the particular writing assignment to see whether and how this format is useful for you.

10   Myth #7: Never use "I"
Adopting this formal stance of objectivity implies a distrust (almost fear) of informality and often leads to artificial, puffed-up prose. Although some writing situations will call on you

to avoid using "I" (for example, a lab report), much college writing can be done in a middle, semi-formal style where it is ok to use "I."

The Academic Writing Situation

11   Now that we've dispelled some of the common myths that many writers have as they enter a college classroom, let's take a moment to think about the academic writing situation. The biggest problem I see in freshman writers is a poor sense of the writing situation in general. To illustrate this problem, let's look at the difference between speaking and writing.

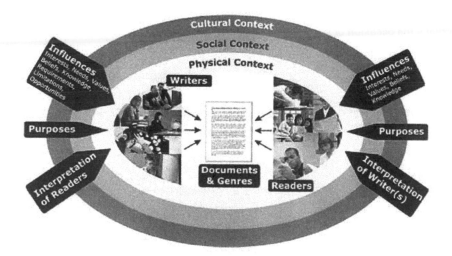

Figure 1. Source: "A Social Model of Writing." Writing@CSU. 2010. Web. 10 March 2010. Used by permission from Mike Palmquist.

12   When we speak, we inhabit the communication situation bodily in three dimensions, but in writing we are confined within the two-dimensional setting of the flat page (though writing for the web—or multimodal writing—is changing all that). Writing resembles having a blindfold over our eyes and our hands tied behind our backs: we can't see exactly whom we're talking to or where we are. Separated from our audience in place and time, we imaginatively have to create this context. Our words on the page are silent, so we must use punctuation and word choice to communicate our tone. We also can't see our audience to gauge how our communication is being received or if there will be some kind of response. It's the same space we share right now as you read this essay. Novice writers often write as if they were mumbling to themselves in the corner with no sense that their writing will be read by a reader or any sense of the context within which their communication will be received.

13   What's the moral here? Developing your "writer's sense" about communicating within the writing situation is the most important thing you should learn in freshman composition. *everyone has a writers sense.*

141

Looking More Closely at the "Academic Writing" Situation

14   Writing in college is a fairly specialized writing situation, and it has developed its own codes and conventions that you need to have a keen awareness of if you are going to write successfully in college. Let's break down the writing situation in college:

Who's your audience?	Primarily the professor and possibly your classmates (though you may be asked to include a secondary outside audience).
What's the occasion or context?	An assignment given by the teacher within a learning context and designed to have you learn and demonstrate your learning.
What's your message?	It will be your learning or the interpretation gained from your study of the subject matter.
What's your purpose?	To show your learning and get a good grade (or to accomplish the goals of the writing assignment).
What documents/genres are used?	The essay is the most frequent type of document used.

15   So far, this list looks like nothing new. You've been writing in school toward teachers for years. What's different in college? Lee Ann Carroll, a professor at Pepperdine University, performed a study of student writing in college and had this description of the kind of writing you will be doing in college:

16   What are usually called 'writing assignments' in college might more accurately be called 'literacy tasks' because they require much more than the ability to construct correct sentences or compose neatly organized paragraphs with topic sentences. . . . Projects calling for high levels of critical literacy in college typically require knowledge of research skills, ability to read complex texts, understanding of key disciplinary concepts, and strategies for synthesizing, analyzing, and responding critically to new information, usually within a limited time frame. (3–4)

17   Academic writing is always a form of evaluation that asks you to demonstrate knowledge and show proficiency with certain disciplinary skills of thinking, interpreting, and pre-

senting. Writing the paper is never "just" the writing part. To be successful in this kind of writing, you must be completely aware of what the professor expects you to do and accomplish with that particular writing task. For a moment, let's explore more deeply the elements of this college writing "literacy task."

Knowledge of Research Skills

18   Perhaps up to now research has meant going straight to Google and Wikipedia, but college will require you to search for and find more in-depth information. You'll need to know how to find information in the library, especially what is available from online databases which contain scholarly articles. Researching is also a process, so you'll need to learn how to focus and direct a research project and how to keep track of all your source information. Realize that researching represents a crucial component of most all college writing assignments, and you will need to devote lots of work to this researching.

The Ability to Read Complex Texts

19   Whereas your previous writing in school might have come generally from your experience, college writing typically asks you to write on unfamiliar topics. Whether you're reading your textbook, a short story, or scholarly articles from research, your ability to write well *that's important* will be based upon the quality of your reading. In addition to the labor of close reading, you'll need to think critically as you read. That means separating fact from opinion, recognizing biases and assumptions, and making inferences. Inferences are how we as readers connect the dots: an inference is a belief (or statement) about something unknown made on the basis of something known. You smell smoke; you infer fire. They are conclusions or interpretations that we arrive at based upon the known factors we discover from our reading. When we, then, write to argue for these interpretations, our job becomes to get our readers to make the same inferences we have made.

The Understanding of Key Disciplinary Concepts

20   Each discipline whether it is English, Psychology, or History has its own key concepts and language for describing these important ways of understanding the world. Don't fool yourself that your professors' writing assignments are asking for your opinion on the topic from just your experience. They want to see you apply and use these concepts in your writing. Though different from a multiple-choice exam, writing similarly requires you to demonstrate your learning. So whatever writing assignment you receive, inspect it closely for what concepts it asks you to bring into your writing.

Strategies for Synthesizing, Analyzing, and Responding Critically to New Information

21   You need to develop the skill of a seasoned traveler who can be dropped in any city around the world and get by. Each writing assignment asks you to navigate through a new terrain of information, so you must develop ways for grasping new subject matter in order, then, to use it in your writing. We have already seen the importance of reading and

research for these literacy tasks, but beyond laying the information out before you, you will need to learn ways of sorting and finding meaningful patterns in this information.

In College, Everything's an Argument: A Guide for Decoding College Writing Assignments

22   Let's restate this complex "literacy task" you'll be asked repeatedly to do in your writing assignments. Typically, you'll be required to write an "essay" based upon your analysis of some reading(s). In this essay you'll need to present an argument where you make a claim (i.e., present a "thesis") and support that claim with good reasons that have adequate and appropriate evidence to back them up. The dynamic of this argumentative task often confuses first-year writers, so let's examine it more closely.

Academic Writing Is an Argument

23   To start, let's focus on argument. What does it mean to present an "argument" in college writing? Rather than a shouting match between two disagreeing sides, argument instead means a carefully arranged and supported presentation of a viewpoint. Its purpose is not so much to win the argument as to earn your audience's consideration (and even approval) of your perspective. It resembles a conversation between two people who may not hold the same opinions, but they both desire a better understanding of the subject matter under discussion. My favorite analogy, however, to describe the nature of this argumentative stance in college writing is the courtroom. In this scenario, you are like a lawyer making a case at trial that the defendant is not guilty, and your readers are like the jury who will decide if the defendant is guilty or not guilty. This jury (your readers) won't just take your word that he's innocent; instead, you must convince them by presenting evidence that proves he is not guilty. Stating your opinion is not enough—you have to back it up too. I like this courtroom analogy for capturing two importance things about academic argument: 1) the value of an organized presentation of your "case," and 2) the crucial element of strong evidence.

Academic Writing Is an Analysis

24   We now turn our attention to the actual writing assignment and that confusing word "analyze." Your first job when you get a writing assignment is to figure out what the professor expects. This assignment may be explicit in its expectations, but often built into the wording of the most defined writing assignments are implicit expectations that you might not recognize. First, we can say that unless your professor specifically asks you to summarize, you won't write a summary. Let me say that again: don't write a summary unless directly asked to. But what, then, does the professor want? We have already picked out a few of these expectations: You can count on the instructor expecting you to read closely, research adequately, and write an argument where you will demonstrate your ability to apply and use important concepts you have been studying. But the writing task also implies that your essay will be the result of an analysis. At times, the writing assignment may even explicitly say to write an analysis, but often this element of the task remains unstated.

25 So what does it mean to analyze? One way to think of an analysis is that it asks you to seek How and Why questions much more than What questions. An analysis involves doing three things:

1. Engage in an open inquiry where the answer is not known at first (and where you leave yourself open to multiple suggestions).
2. Identify meaningful parts of the subject.
3. Examine these separate parts and determine how they relate to each other.

26 An analysis breaks a subject apart to study it closely, and from this inspection, ideas for writing emerge. When writing assignments call on you to analyze, they require you to identify the parts of the subject (parts of an ad, parts of a short story, parts of Hamlet's character), and then show how these parts fit or don't fit together to create some larger effect or meaning. Your interpretation of how these parts fit together constitutes your claim or thesis, and the task of your essay is then to present an argument defending your interpretation as a valid or plausible one to make. My biggest bit of advice about analysis is not to do it all in your head. Analysis works best when you put all the cards on the table, so to speak. Identify and isolate the parts of your analysis, and record important features and characteristics of each one. As patterns emerge, you sort and connect these parts in meaningful ways. For me, I have always had to do this recording and thinking on scratch pieces of paper. Just as critical reading forms a crucial element of the literacy task of a college writing assignment, so too does this analysis process. It's built in.

Three Common Types of College Writing Assignments

27 We have been decoding the expectations of the academic writing task so far, and I want to turn now to examine the types of assignments you might receive. From my experience, you are likely to get three kinds of writing assignments based upon the instructor's degree of direction for the assignment. We'll take a brief look at each kind of academic writing task.

28 *The Closed Writing Assignment*

1. Is Creon a character to admire or condemn?
2. Does your advertisement employ techniques of propaganda, and if so what kind?
3. Was the South justified in seceding from the Union?
4. In your opinion, do you believe Hamlet was truly mad?

29 These kinds of writing assignments present you with two counter claims and ask you to determine from your own analysis the more valid claim. They resemble yes-no questions. These topics define the claim for you, so the major task of the writing assignment then is working out the support for the claim. They resemble a math problem in which the teacher has given you the answer and now wants you to "show your work" in arriving at that answer.

30   Be careful with these writing assignments, however, because often these topics don't have a simple yes/no, either/or answer (despite the nature of the essay question). A close analysis of the subject matter often reveals nuances and ambiguities within the question that your eventual claim should reflect. Perhaps a claim such as, "In my opinion, Hamlet was mad" might work, but I urge you to avoid such a simplistic thesis. This thesis would be better: "I believe Hamlet's unhinged mind borders on insanity but doesn't quite reach it."

31   *The Semi-Open Writing Assignment*
   1.   Discuss the role of law in Antigone.
   2.   Explain the relationship between character and fate in Hamlet.
   3.   Compare and contrast the use of setting in two short stories.
   4.   Show how the Fugitive Slave Act influenced the Abolitionist Movement.

32   Although these topics chart out a subject matter for you to write upon, they don't offer up claims you can easily use in your paper. It would be a misstep to offer up claims such as, "Law plays a role in Antigone" or "In Hamlet we can see a relationship between character and fate." Such statements express the obvious and what the topic takes for granted. The question, for example, is not whether law plays a role in Antigone, but rather what sort of role law plays. What is the nature of this role? What influences does it have on the characters or actions or theme? This kind of writing assignment resembles a kind of archaeological dig. The teacher cordons off an area, hands you a shovel, and says dig here and see what you find.

33   Be sure to avoid summary and mere explanation in this kind of assignment. Despite using key words in the assignment such as "explain," "illustrate," analyze," "discuss," or "show how," these topics still ask you to make an argument. Implicit in the topic is the expectation that you will analyze the reading and arrive at some insights into patterns and relationships about the subject. Your eventual paper, then, needs to present what you found from this analysis—the treasure you found from your digging. Determining your own claim represents the biggest challenge for this type of writing assignment.

34   *The Open Writing Assignment*
   1.   Analyze the role of a character in Dante's *The Inferno*.
   2.   What does it mean to be an "American" in the 21st Century?
   3.   Analyze the influence of slavery upon one cause of the Civil War.
   4.   Compare and contrast two themes within *Pride and Prejudice*.

35   These kinds of writing assignments require you to decide both your writing topic and your claim (or thesis). Which character in *The Inferno* will I pick to analyze? What two themes in *Pride and Prejudice* will I choose to write about? Many students struggle with these types of assignments because they have to understand their subject matter well before they can intelligently choose a topic. For instance, you need a good familiarity with the characters in *The Inferno* before you can pick one. You have to have a solid under-standing defining elements of American identity as well as 21st century culture before you

can begin to connect them. This kind of writing assignment resembles riding a bike without the training wheels on. It says, "You decide what to write about." The biggest decision, then, becomes selecting your topic and limiting it to a manageable size.

Picking and Limiting a Writing Topic

36   Let's talk about both of these challenges: picking a topic and limiting it. Remember how I said these kinds of essay topics expect you to choose what to write about from a solid understanding of your subject? As you read and review your subject matter, look for things that interest you. Look for gaps, puzzling items, things that confuse you, or connections you see. Something in this pile of rocks should stand out as a jewel: as being "do-able" and interesting. (You'll write best when you write from both your head and your heart.) Whatever topic you choose, state it as a clear and interesting question. You may or may not state this essay question explicitly in the introduction of your paper (I actually recommend that you do), but it will provide direction for your paper and a focus for your claim since that claim will be your answer to this essay question. For example, if with the Dante topic you decided to write on Virgil, your essay question might be: "What is the role of Virgil toward the character of Dante in *The Inferno*?" The thesis statement, then, might be this: "Virgil's predominant role as Dante's guide through hell is as the voice of reason." Crafting a solid essay question is well worth your time because it charts the territory of your essay and helps you declare a focused thesis statement.

37   Many students struggle with defining the right size for their writing project. They chart out an essay question that it would take a book to deal with adequately. You'll know you have that kind of topic if you have already written over the required page length but only touched one quarter of the topics you planned to discuss. In this case, carve out one of those topics and make your whole paper about it. For instance, with our Dante example, perhaps you planned to discuss four places where Virgil's role as the voice of reason is evident. Instead of discussing all four, focus your essay on just one place. So your revised thesis statement might be: "Close inspection of Cantos I and II reveal that Virgil serves predominantly as the voice of reason for Dante on his journey through hell." A writing teacher I had in college said it this way: A well tended garden is better than a large one full of weeds. That means to limit your topic to a size you can handle and support well.

Three Characteristics of Academic Writing

38   I want to wrap up this section by sharing in broad terms what the expectations are behind an academic writing assignment. Chris Thaiss and Terry Zawacki conducted research at George Mason University where they asked professors from their university what they thought academic writing was and its standards. They came up with three characteristics:

1. Clear evidence in writing that the writer(s) have been persistent, open-minded, and disciplined in study. (5)
2. The dominance of reason over emotions or sensual perception. (5)
3. An imagined reader who is coolly rational, reading for information, and intending to formulate a reasoned response. (7)

39   Your professor wants to see these three things in your writing when they give you a writing assignment. They want to see in your writing the results of your efforts at the various literacy tasks we have been discussing: critical reading, research, and analysis. Beyond merely stating opinions, they also want to see an argument toward an intelligent audience where you provide good reasons to support your interpretations.

The Format of the Academic Essay

40   Your instructors will also expect you to deliver a paper that contains particular textual features. The following list contains the characteristics of what I have for years called the "critical essay." Although I can't claim they will be useful for all essays in college, I hope that these features will help you shape and accomplish successful college essays. Be aware that these characteristics are flexible and not a formula, and any particular assignment might ask for something different.

Characteristics of the Critical Essay

41   "Critical" here is not used in the sense of "to criticize" as in find fault with. Instead, "critical" is used in the same way "critical thinking" is used. A synonym might be "interpretive" or "analytical."

- It is an argument, persuasion essay that in its broadest sense MAKES A POINT and SUPPORTS IT. (We have already discussed this argumentative nature of academic writing at length.)
- The point ("claim" or "thesis") of a critical essay is interpretive in nature. That means the point is debatable and open to interpretation, not a statement of the obvious. The thesis statement is a clear, declarative sentence that often works best when it comes at the end of the introduction.
- Organization: Like any essay, the critical essay should have a clear introduction, body, and conclusion. As you support your point in the body of the essay, you should "divide up the proof," which means structuring the body around clear primary supports (developed in single paragraphs for short papers or multiple paragraphs for longer papers).
- Support: (a) The primary source for support in the critical essay is from the text (or sources). The text is the authority, so using quotations is required. (b) The continuous movement of logic in a critical essay is "assert then support; assert then support." No assertion (general statement that needs proving) should be left without specific support (often from the text(s)). (c) You need enough support to be convincing. In general, that means for each assertion you need at least three supports. This threshold can vary, but invariably one support is not enough.
- A critical essay will always "document" its sources, distinguishing the use of outside information used inside your text and clarifying where that information came from (following the rules of MLA documentation style or whatever documentation style is required).
- Whenever the author moves from one main point (primary support) to the next, the author needs to clearly signal to the reader that this movement is happening.

This transition sentence works best when it links back to the thesis as it states the topic of that paragraph or section.

- A critical essay is put into an academic essay format such as the MLA or APA document format
- Grammatical correctness: Your essay should have few if any grammatical problems. You'll want to edit your final draft carefully before turning it in.

Conclusion

42   As we leave this discussion, I want to return to what I said was the secret for your success in writing college essays: Your success with academic writing depends upon how well you understand what you are doing as you write and then how you approach the writing task. Hopefully, you now have a better idea about the nature of the academic writing task and the expectations behind it. Knowing what you need to do won't guarantee you an "A" on your paper—that will take a lot of thinking, hard work, and practice—but having the right orientation toward your college writing assignments is a first and important step in your eventual success.

Works Cited

Carroll, Lee Ann. *Rehearsing New Roles: How College Students Develop as Writers*. Carbondale: Southern Illinois UP, 2002. Print.

Thaiss, Chris and Terry Zawacki. *Engaged Writers & Dynamic Disciplines: Research on the Academic Writing Life*. Portsmouth: Boynton/Cook, 2006. Print.

Critical Reading Questions:

- **Summary:** How would Irvin describe a successful academic essay? What are the characteristics or attributes of a strong paper?

- **Summary:** Irvin claims that "[d]eveloping your 'writer's sense' about communicating within the writing situation is the most important thing you should learn in freshman composition." What is the "writer's sense"? How does one go about developing it?

The Declaration of Independence

Thomas Jefferson

Thomas Jefferson's "The Declaration of Independence" is one of the most important documents of American history and an iconic example of American rhetoric. In fact, as Stephen Lucas explains, "The Declaration of Independence is perhaps the most masterfully written state paper of Western civilization." In this declaration, Jefferson enumerates tyrannical abuses by King George III and ultimately concludes that there is no redress for these injustices but independence for the Colonies. Jefferson uses the history of politics in American life to create a new government policy, a logical appeal wherein the government is both deconstructed and being constructed at the same time. Though "The Declaration of Independence" is considered the founding document for American democracy, Jefferson begins the document discussing dissolution of "political bands" to create a separate, but equal state. Jefferson's work here is foundational and is referenced in numerous other works, from decisions of the Supreme Court to The Gettysburg Address.

—BLS

1   When in the Course of human events, it becomes necessary for one people to dissolve the political bands which have connected them with another, and to assume among the powers of the earth, the separate and equal station to which the Laws of Nature and of Nature's God entitle them, a decent respect to the opinions of mankind requires that they should declare the causes which impel them to the separation.

2   We hold these truths to be self-evident, that all men are created equal, that they are endowed by their Creator with certain unalienable Rights, that among these are Life, Liberty and the pursuit of Happiness.—That to secure these rights, Governments are instituted among Men, deriving their just powers from the consent of the governed, —That whenever any Form of Government becomes destructive of these ends, it is the Right of the People to alter or to abolish it, and to institute new Government, laying its foundation on such principles and organizing its powers in such form, as to them shall seem most likely to effect their Safety and Happiness. Prudence, indeed, will dictate that Governments long established should not be changed for light and transient causes; and accordingly all experience hath shewn, that mankind are more disposed to suffer, while evils are sufferable, than to right themselves by abolishing the forms to which they are accustomed. But when a long train of abuses and usurpations, pursuing invariably the same Object evinces a design to reduce them under absolute Despotism, it is their right, it is their duty, to throw off such Government, and to provide new Guards for their future security.—Such has been the patient sufferance of these Colonies; and such is now the necessity which constrains them to alter their former Systems of Government. The history of the present

King of Great Britain is a history of repeated injuries and usurpations, all having in direct object the establishment of an absolute Tyranny over these States. To prove this, let Facts be submitted to a candid world.

3   He has refused his Assent to Laws, the most wholesome
    and necessary for the public good.

4   He has forbidden his Governors to pass Laws of immediate and
    pressing importance, unless suspended in their opera-
    tion till his Assent should be obtained; and when so sus-
    pended, he has utterly neglected to attend to them.

5   He has refused to pass other Laws for the accommodation of large
    districts of people, unless those people would relinquish
    the right of Representation in the Legislature, a right ines-
    timable to them and formidable to tyrants only.

6   He has called together legislative bodies at places unusual,
    uncomfortable, and distant from the depository of their public Records, for
    the sole purpose of fatiguing them into compliance with his measures.

7   He has dissolved Representative Houses repeatedly, for
    opposing with manly firmness his invasions on the rights of the people.

8   He has refused for a long time, after such dissolutions, to cause
    others to be elected; whereby the Legislative powers, incapable
    of Annihilation, have returned to the People at large for their exer-
    cise; the State remaining in the mean time exposed to all the
    dangers of invasion from without, and convulsions within.

9   He has endeavoured to prevent the population of these
     States; for that purpose obstructing the Laws for Naturalization of
    Foreigners; refusing to pass others to encourage their migrations
    hither, and raising the conditions of new Appropriations of Lands.

10 He has obstructed the Administration of Justice, by refusing
    his Assent to Laws for establishing Judiciary powers.

11 He has made Judges dependent on his Will alone, for the tenure
    of their offices, and the amount and payment of their salaries.

12 He has erected a multitude of New Offices, and sent hither
    swarms of Officers to harrass our people, and eat out their substance.

13   He has kept among us, in times of peace, Standing
      Armies without the Consent of our legislatures.

14   He has affected to render the Military independent
      of and superior to the Civil power.

15   He has combined with others to subject us to a jurisdiction
      foreign to our constitution, and unacknowledged by our laws; giv-
      ing his Assent to their Acts of pretended Legislation:

16   For Quartering large bodies of armed troops among us:
17   For protecting them, by a mock Trial, from punishment for any Murders
      which they should commit on the Inhabitants of these States:

18   For cutting off our Trade with all parts of the world:

19   For imposing Taxes on us without our Consent:

20   For depriving us in many cases, of the benefits of Trial by Jury:

21   For transporting us beyond Seas to be tried for pretended offences:

22   For abolishing the free System of English Laws in a neighbouring
      Province, establishing therein an Arbitrary government, and enlarg-
      ing its Boundaries so as to render it at once an example and fit instru-
      ment for introducing the same absolute rule into these Colonies:

23   For taking away our Charters, abolishing our most valuable
      Laws, and altering fundamentally the Forms of our Governments:

24   For suspending our own Legislatures, and declaring themselves
      invested with power to legislate for us in all cases whatsoever.

25   He has abdicated Government here, by declaring
      us out of his Protection and waging War against us.

26   He has plundered our seas, ravaged our Coasts, burnt
      our towns, and destroyed the lives of our people.

27   He is at this time transporting large Armies of foreign Mercenaries
      to compleat the works of death, desolation and tyranny, already begun
      with circumstances of Cruelty & perfidy scarcely paralleled in the most
      barbarous ages, and totally unworthy the Head of a civilized nation.

28   He has constrained our fellow Citizens taken Captive on the
high Seas to bear Arms against their Country, to become the execution-
ers of their friends and Brethren, or to fall themselves by their Hands.

29   He has excited domestic insurrections amongst us, and has endeavoured to
bring on the inhabitants of our frontiers, the merciless Indian
Savages, whose known rule of warfare, is an undistinguished destruction of all ages, sexes and conditions.

30   In every stage of these Oppressions We have Petitioned for Redress in the most humble terms: Our repeated Petitions have been answered only by repeated injury. A Prince
whose character is thus marked by every act which may define a Tyrant, is unfit to be the
ruler of a free people.

31   Nor have We been wanting in attentions to our Brittish brethren. We have warned them
from time to time of attempts by their legislature to extend an unwarrantable jurisdiction over
us. We have reminded them of the circumstances of our emigration and settlement here.
We have appealed to their native justice and magnanimity, and we have conjured them by
the ties of our common kindred to disavow these usurpations, which, would inevitably inter-
rupt our connections and correspondence. They too have been deaf to the voice of justice
and of consanguinity. We must, therefore, acquiesce in the necessity, which denounces
our Separation, and hold them, as we hold the rest of mankind, Enemies in War, in
Peace Friends.

32   We, therefore, the Representatives of the united States of America, in General Congress, Assembled, appealing to the Supreme Judge of the world for the rectitude of our
intentions, do, in the Name, and by Authority of the good People of these Colonies, solemnly
publish and declare, That these United Colonies are, and of Right ought to be Free and
Independent States; that they are Absolved from all Allegiance to the British Crown, and that
all political connection between them and the State of Great Britain, is and ought to be totally
dissolved, and that as Free and Independent States, they have full Power to levy War, conclude Peace, contract Alliances, establish Commerce, and to do all other Acts and Things
which Independent States may of right do. And for the support of this Declaration, with a firm
reliance on the protection of divine Providence, we mutually pledge to each other our Lives,
our Fortunes and our sacred Honor.

Critical Reading Questions:

- **Rhetorical analysis:** This work offers a distinct binary between "the Representatives of the United States of America" and "the present King of Great Britain," but
where does Jefferson place other American or British citizens between these
two extremes? With this in mind, who is Jefferson's intended audience—or audiences? What are some of the ways that Jefferson tries to connect and appeal to
his audience?

- **Rhetorical analysis:** Although there are several words in this document that need to be capitalized, such as "Creator" or "King of Great Britain," there are several other words in this work that are also unexpectedly capitalized—such as "Men," "Cruelty," "We," "Lives," and many more. What is the rhetorical effect of elevating all of these terms to proper noun status?

- **Rhetorical analysis:** Although praised for being a seminal document in the formation of America, how do contemporary American sensibilities deal with Jefferson's critique about "the inhabitants of our frontiers, the merciless Indian Savages, whose known rule of warfare, is an undistinguished destruction of all ages, sexes and conditions"? Should this language be tolerated as an artifact of another era unfairly judged by modern standards, or could it be legitimately be criticized as a racist depiction? Furthermore, how could Jefferson's possible racism be complicated by the fact that his earlier draft of this work called for a cessation of slavery?

Cuban Missile Crisis

John F. Kennedy

1962

The Cuban Missile Crisis (October 14th-October 28th, 1963) has been described by many as "the most dangerous thirteen days in the history of the human race." The crisis marked the height of tensions during the Cold War and led the United States and the Soviet Union to the verge of nuclear war. On October 14th, American spy planes discovered that the Soviet Union had secretly delivered nuclear weapons to their communist allies in Cuba that were being stationed just over 100 miles from the U.S. coastline. The Soviet leader, Nikita Khrushchev, believed the weapons would be ready to launch before they were detected by the U.S. Khrushchev saw Kennedy as a young and inexperienced leader and believed he would be unable to force the Soviets to remove the missiles due to several factors: Kennedy had won his election in 1960 by less than one percent of the popular vote, and the failed U.S. invasion of Cuba at the "Bay of Pigs" in 1961 had hurt his national and international reputation. Additionally, the presence of U.S. nuclear missiles in Turkey (on the border of the Soviet Union) weakened his ability to argue that the Soviet missiles were unacceptably close. After several days of planning and deep consideration, the President used this speech to announce the presence of the missiles and his plan to create a naval blockade around Cuba, separating it from the U.S. and the world.

—PH

Address on the Cuban Crisis October 22, 1962

1   Good evening, my fellow citizens. This Government, as promised, has maintained the closest surveillance of the Soviet military build-up on the island of Cuba. Within the past week unmistakable evidence has established the fact that a series of offensive missile sites is now in preparation on that imprisoned island. The purposes of these bases can be none other than to provide a nuclear strike capability against the Western Hemisphere.

2   Upon receiving the first preliminary hard information of this nature last Tuesday morning (October 16) at 9:00 A.M., I directed that our surveillance be stepped up. And having now confirmed and completed our evaluation of the evidence and our decision on a course of action, this Government feels obliged to report this new crisis to you in fullest detail.

3   The characteristics of these new missile sites indicate two distinct types of installations. Several of them include medium-range ballistic missiles capable of carrying a nuclear warhead for a distance of more than 1,000 nautical miles. Each of these missiles, in short, is capable of striking Washington, D.C., the Panama Canal, Cape Canaveral, Mexico City, or any other city in the southeastern part of the United States, in Central America, or in the Caribbean area.

4   Additional sites not yet completed appear to be designed for intermediate-range ballistic missiles—capable of traveling more than twice as far—and thus capable of striking most of the major cities in the Western Hemisphere, ranging as far north as Hudson Bay, Canada, and as far south as Lima, Peru. In addition, jet bombers, capable of carrying nuclear weapons, are now being uncrated and assembled in Cuba, while the necessary air bases are being prepared.

5   This urgent transformation of Cuba into an important strategic base—by the presence of these large, long-range, and clearly offensive weapons of sudden mass destruction—constitutes an explicit threat to the peace and security of all the Americas, in flagrant and deliberate defiance of the Rio Pact of 1947, the traditions of this nation and Hemisphere, the joint Resolution of the 87th Congress, the Charter of the United Nations, and my own public warnings to the Soviets on September 4 and 13.

6   This action also contradicts the repeated assurances of Soviet spokesmen, both publicly and privately delivered, that the arms build-up in Cuba would retain its original defensive character and that the Soviet Union had no need or desire to station strategic missiles on the territory of any other nation. The size of this undertaking makes clear that it has been planned for some months. Yet only last month, after I had made clear the distinction between any introduction of ground-to-ground missiles and the existence of defensive antiaircraft missiles, the Soviet Government publicly stated on September 11 that, and I quote, "The armaments and military equipment sent to Cuba are designed exclusively for defensive purposes," and I quote the Soviet Government, "There is no need for the Soviet Government to shift its weapons for a retaliatory blow to any other country, for instance Cuba," and that, and I quote their Government, "The Soviet Union has so powerful rockets to carry these nuclear warheads that there is no need to search for sites for them beyond the boundaries of the Soviet Union." That statement was false.

7   Only last Thursday, as evidence of this rapid offensive build-up was already in my hand, Soviet Foreign Minister Gromyko told me in my office that he was instructed to make it clear once again, as he said his Government had already done, that Soviet assistance to Cuba, and I quote, "pursued solely the purpose of contributing to the defense capabilities of Cuba," that, and I quote him, "training by Soviet specialists of Cuban nationals in handling defensive armaments was by no means offensive," and that "if it were otherwise," Mr. Gromyko went on, "the Soviet Government would never become involved in rendering such assistance." That statement also was false.

8   Neither the United States of America nor the world community of nations can tolerate deliberate deception and offensive threats on the part of any nation, large or small. We no longer live in a world where only the actual firing of weapons represents a sufficient challenge to a nation's security to constitute maximum peril. Nuclear weapons are so destructive and ballistic missiles are so swift that any substantially increased possibility of their use or any sudden change in their deployment may well be regarded as a definite threat to peace.

9   For many years both the Soviet Union and the United States, recognizing this fact, have deployed strategic nuclear weapons with great care, never upsetting the precarious status quo which insured that these weapons would not be used in the absence of some

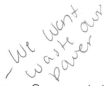

vital challenge. Our own strategic missiles have never been transferred to the territory of any other nation under a cloak of secrecy and deception; and our history, unlike that of the Soviets since the end of World War II, demonstrates that we have no desire to dominate or conquer any other nation or impose our system upon its people. Nevertheless, American citizens have become adjusted to living daily on the bull's eye of Soviet missiles located inside the U.S.S.R. or in submarines.

10   In that sense, missiles in Cuba add to an already clear and present danger—although it should be noted the nations of Latin America have never previously been subjected to a potential nuclear threat. But this secret, swift, and extraordinary build-up of Communist missiles—in an area well known to have a special and historical relationship to the United States and the nations of the Western Hemisphere, in violation of Soviet assurances, and in defiance of American and hemispheric policy—this sudden, clandestine decision to station strategic weapons for the first time outside of Soviet soil—is a deliberately provocative and unjustified change in the status quo which cannot be accepted by this country if our courage and our commitments are ever to be trusted again by either friend or foe.

11   The 1930's taught us a clear lesson: Aggressive conduct, if allowed to grow unchecked and unchallenged, ultimately leads to war. This nation is opposed to war. We are also true to our word. Our unswerving objective, therefore, must be to prevent the use of these missiles against this or any other country and to secure their withdrawal or elimination from the Western Hemisphere.

12   Our policy has been one of patience and restraint, as befits a peaceful and powerful nation, which leads a world-wide alliance. We have been determined not to be diverted from our central concerns by mere irritants and fanatics. But now further action is required, and it is underway; and these actions may only be the beginning. We will not prematurely or unnecessarily risk the costs of worldwide nuclear war in which even the fruits of victory would be ashes in our mouth—but neither will we shrink from that risk at any time it must be faced.

13   Acting, therefore, in the defense of our own security and of the entire Western Hemisphere, and under the authority entrusted to me by the Constitution as endorsed by the resolution of the Congress, I have directed that the following initial steps be taken immediately:

14   First: To halt this offensive build-up, a strict quarantine on all offensive military equipment under shipment to Cuba is being initiated. All ships of any kind bound for Cuba from whatever nation or port will, if found to contain cargoes of offensive weapons, be turned back: This quarantine will be extended, if needed, to other types of cargo and carriers. We are not at this time, however, denying the necessities of life as the Soviets attempted to do in their Berlin blockade of 1948.

15   Second: I have directed the continued and increased close surveillance of Cuba and its military build-up. The Foreign Ministers of the Organization of American States in their communiqué of October 3 rejected secrecy on such matters in this Hemisphere. Should these offensive military preparations continue, thus increasing the threat to the Hemisphere, further action will be justified. I have directed the Armed Forces to prepare for any eventualities; and I trust that in the interests of both the Cuban people and the

Soviet technicians at the sites, the hazards to all concerned of continuing this threat will be recognized.

16   Third: It shall be the policy of this nation to regard any nuclear missile launched from Cuba against any nation in the Western Hemisphere as an attack by the Soviet Union on the United States, requiring a full retaliatory response upon the Soviet Union.

17   Fourth: As a necessary military precaution, I have reinforced our base at Guantanamo, evacuated today the dependents of our personnel there, and ordered additional military units to be on a standby alert basis.

18   Fifth: We are calling tonight for an immediate meeting of the Organ of Consultation, under the Organization of American States, to consider this threat to hemispheric security and to invoke articles six and eight of the Rio Treaty in support of all necessary action. The United Nations Charter allows for regional security arrangements—and the nations of this Hemisphere decided long ago against the military presence of outside powers. Our other allies around the world have also been alerted.

19   Sixth: Under the Charter of the United Nations, we are asking tonight that an emergency meeting of the Security Council be convoked without delay to take action against this latest Soviet threat to world peace. Our resolution will call for the prompt dismantling and withdrawal of all offensive weapons in Cuba, under the supervision of United Nations observers, before the quarantine can be lifted.

20   Seventh and finally: I call upon Chairman Khrushchev to halt and eliminate this clandestine, reckless, and provocative threat to world peace and to stable relations between our two nations. I call upon him further to abandon this course of world domination and to join in an historic effort to end the perilous arms race and transform the history of man. He has an opportunity now to move the world back from the abyss of destruction by returning to his Government's own words that it had no need to station missiles outside its own territory, and withdrawing these weapons from Cuba by refraining from any action which will widen or deepen the present crisis, and then by participating in a search for peaceful and permanent solutions.

21   This nation is prepared to present its case against the Soviet threat to peace, and our own proposals for a peaceful world, at any time and in any forum in the Organization of American States, in the United Nations, or in any other meeting that could be useful—without limiting our freedom of action. We have in the past made strenuous efforts to limit the spread of nuclear weapons. We have proposed the elimination of all arms and military bases in a fair and effective disarmament treaty. We are prepared to discuss new proposals for the removal of tensions on both sides, including the possibilities of a genuinely independent Cuba, free to determine its own destiny. We have no wish to war with the Soviet Union, for we are a peaceful people who desire to live in peace with all other peoples.

22   But it is difficult to settle or even discuss these problems in an atmosphere of intimidation. That is why this latest Soviet threat—or any other threat which is made either independently or in response to our actions this week—must and will be met with determination. Any hostile move anywhere in the world against the safety and freedom of peoples to whom we are committed—including in particular the brave people of West Berlin—will be met by whatever action is needed.

23   Finally, I want to say a few words to the captive people of Cuba, to whom this speech is being directly carried by special radio facilities. I speak to you as a friend, as one who knows of your deep attachment to your fatherland, as one who shares your aspirations for liberty and justice for all. And I have watched and the American people have watched with deep sorrow how your nationalist revolution was betrayed and how your fatherland fell under foreign domination. Now your leaders are no longer Cuban leaders inspired by Cuban ideals. They are puppets and agents of an international conspiracy which has turned Cuba against your friends and neighbors in the Americas—and turned it into the first Latin American country to become a target for nuclear war, the first Latin American country to have these weapons on its soil.

24   These new weapons are not in your interest. They contribute nothing to your peace and well being. They can only undermine it. But this country has no wish to cause you to suffer or to impose any system upon you. We know that your lives and land are being used as pawns by those who deny you freedom. Many times in the past Cuban people have risen to throw out tyrants who destroyed their liberty. And I have no doubt that most Cubans today look forward to the time when they will be truly free—free from foreign domination, free to choose their own leaders, free to select their own system, free to own their own land, free to speak and write and worship without fear or degradation. And then shall Cuba be welcomed back to the society of free nations and to the associations of this Hemisphere.

25   My fellow citizens, let no one doubt that this is a difficult and dangerous effort on which we have set out. No one can foresee precisely what course it will take or what costs or casualties will be incurred. Many months of sacrifice and self-discipline lie ahead—months in which both our patience and our will will be tested, months in which many threats and denunciations will keep us aware of our dangers. But the greatest danger of all would be to do nothing.

26   The path we have chosen for the present is full of hazards, as all paths are; but it is the one most consistent with our character and courage as a nation and our commitments around the world. The cost of freedom is always high—but Americans have always paid it. And one path we shall never choose, and that is the path of surrender or submission.

27   Our goal is not the victory of might but the vindication of right—not peace at the expense of freedom, but both peace and freedom, here in this Hemisphere and, we hope, around the world. God willing, that goal will be achieved.

Critical Reading Questions:

- **Analysis:** In order to avoid war, Kennedy must strike a careful balance between seeming strong enough to risk war while also stressing his genuine desire for peace. He strategically follows statements proposing peace with statements reinforcing his determination to protect American lives. He likewise follows warlike statements with another call for peace. Identify places within the text where Kennedy follows this pattern.

- **Rhetorical analysis:** In 1961, the U.S. invaded Cuba at the "Bay of Pigs." The success of the invasion rested on the belief that the Cuban people were dissatisfied with their leaders and would join with American and rebel forces to overthrow Castro's communist government. How do Kennedy's rhetorical choices throughout the speech encourage the people of Cuba to revolt against their current leadership?

"Two Ways a Woman Can Get Hurt": Advertising and Violence

Jean Kilbourne

Kilbourne is an award-winning author, documentary filmmaker, and scholar whose body of work focuses on interrogating images of women in popular media. In this chapter from her 1999 academic book, *Can't Buy My Love: How Advertising Changes the Way We Think and Feel,* **Kilbourne provides sociopolitical commentary on how advertisements shape cultural beliefs. More specifically, she argues that many ad campaigns play a detrimental role in shaping gender relations in society due to what Kilbourne identifies as dehumanizing representations of young girls and women. Further, she claims that in effect these depictions degrade societal ideals of beauty and intimacy. By correlating an increase in this oppressive rhetoric in ads to an increase of sexual crimes against girls and women, Kilbourne argues that these texts perpetuate a sexist imbalance of power and fuel a normalization of violence against women.**

—CLR

1   Sex in advertising is more about disconnection and distance than connection and closeness. It is also more often about power than passion, about violence than violins. The main goal, as in pornography, is usually power over another, either by the physical dominance or preferred status of men or what is seen as the exploitative power of female beauty and female sexuality. Men conquer and women ensnare, always with the essential aid of a product. The woman is rewarded for her sexuality by the man's wealth, as in an ad for Cigarette boats in which the woman says, while lying in a man's embrace clearly after sex, "Does this mean I get a ride in your Cigarette?"

2   Sex in advertising is pornographic because it dehumanizes and objectifies people, especially women, and because it fetishizes products, imbues them with an erotic charge—which dooms us to disappointment since products never can fulfill our sexual desires or meet our emotional needs. The poses and postures of advertising are often borrowed from pornography, as are many of the themes, such as bondage, sadomasochism, and the sexual exploitation of children. When a beer ad uses the image of a man licking the high-heeled boot of a woman clad in leather, when bondage is used to sell neckties in *The New York Times*, perfume in *The New Yorker*, and watches on city buses, and when a college magazine promotes an S&M Ball, pornography can be considered mainstream.

3   Most of us know all this by now and I suppose some consider it kinky good fun. Pornography is more dangerously mainstream when its glorification of rape and violence shows up in mass media, in films and television shows, in comedy and music videos, and in advertising. Male violence is subtly encouraged by ads that encourage men to be forceful and dominant, and to value sexual intimacy more than emotional intimacy. "Do you want to be the one she tells her deep, dark secret?" asks a three-page ad for

men's cologne. "Or do you want to be her deep, dark secret?" The last page advises men, "Don't be such a good boy." There are two identical women looking adoringly at the man in the ad, but he isn't looking at either one of them. Just what is the deep, dark secret? That he's sleeping with both of them? Clearly the way to get beautiful women is to ignore them, perhaps mistreat them.

4   "Two ways a woman can get hurt," says an ad for shaving gel, featuring a razor and a photo of a handsome man. My first thought is that the man is a batterer or a date rapist, but the ad informs us that he is merely a "heartbreaker." The gel will protect the woman so that "while guys may continue to be a pain, shaving most definitely won't." Desirable men are painful—heartbreakers at best.

5   Wouldn't it be wonderful if, realizing the importance of relationships in all of our lives, we could seek to learn relational skills from women and to help men develop these strengths in themselves? In fact, we so often do the opposite. The popular culture usually trivializes these abilities in women, mocks men who have real intimacy with women (it is almost always married men in ads and cartoons who are jerks), and idealizes a template for relationships between men and women that is a recipe for disaster: a template that views sex as more important than anything else, that ridicules men who are not in control of their women (who are "pussy-whipped"), and that disparages fidelity and commitment (except, of course, to brand names).

6   Indeed the very worst kind of man for a woman to be in an intimate relationship with, often a truly dangerous man, is the one considered most sexy and desirable in the popular culture. And the men capable of real intimacy (the ones we tell our deep, dark secrets to) constantly have their very masculinity impugned. Advertising often encourages women to be attracted to hostile and indifferent men while encouraging boys to become these men. This is especially dangerous for those of us who have suffered from "condemned isolation" in childhood: like heat-seeking missiles, we rush inevitably to mutual destruction.

7   Men are also encouraged to never take no for an answer. Ad after ad implies that girls and women don't really mean "no" when they say it, that women are only teasing when they resist men's advances. "NO" says an ad showing a man leaning over a woman against a wall. Is she screaming or laughing? Oh, it's an ad for deodorant and the second word, in very small print, is "sweat." Sometimes it's "all in good fun," as in the ad for Possession shirts and shorts featuring a man ripping the clothes off a woman who seems to be having a good time.

8   And sometimes it is more sinister. A perfume ad running in several teen magazines features a very young woman, with eyes blackened by makeup or perhaps something else, and the copy, "Apply generously to your neck so he can smell the scent as you shake your head 'no'." In other words, he'll understand that you don't really mean it and he can respond to the scent like any other animal.

9   Sometimes there seems to be no question but that a man should force a woman to have sex. A chilling newspaper ad for a bar in Georgetown features a closeup of a cocktail and the headline, "If your date won't listen to reason, try a Velvet Hammer." A vodka ad pictures a wolf hiding in a flock of sheep, a hideous grin on its face. We all know what wolves do to sheep. A campaign for Bacardi Black rum features shadowy figures almost

obliterated by darkness and captions such as "Some people embrace the night because the rules of the day do not apply." What it doesn't say is that people who are above the rules do enormous harm to other people, as well as to themselves.

10   These ads are particularly troublesome, given that between one third and three-quarters of all cases of sexual assault involve alcohol consumption by the perpetrator, the victim, or both. "Make strangers your friends, and your friends a lot stranger," says one of the ads in a Cuervo campaign that uses colorful cartoon beasts and emphasizes heavy drinking. This ad is especially disturbing when we consider the role of alcohol in date rape, as is another ad in the series that says, "The night began with a bottle of Cuervo and ended with a vow of silence." Over half of all reported rapes on college campuses occur when either the victim or the assailant has been drinking. Alcohol's role has different meaning for men and women, however. If a man is drunk when he commits a rape, he is considered less responsible. If a woman is drunk (or has had a drink or two or simply met the man in a bar), she is considered more responsible.

11   In general, females are still held responsible and hold each other responsible when sex goes wrong—when they become pregnant or are the victims of rape and sexual assault or cause a scandal. Constantly exhorted to be sexy and attractive, they discover when assaulted that that very sexiness is evidence of their guilt, their lack of "innocence." Sometimes the ads play on this by "warning" women of what might happen if they use the product. "Wear it but beware it," says a perfume ad. Beware what exactly? Victoria's Secret tempts young women with blatantly sexual ads promising that their lingerie will make them irresistible. Yet when a young woman accused William Kennedy Smith of raping her, the fact that she wore Victoria's Secret panties was used against her as an indication of her immorality. A jury acquitted Smith, whose alleged history of violence against women was not permitted to be introduced at trial.

12   It is sadly not surprising that the jury was composed mostly of women. Women are especially cruel judges of other women's sexual behavior, mostly because we are so desperate to believe we are in control of what happens to us. It is too frightening to face the fact that male violence against women is irrational and commonplace. It is reassuring to believe that we can avoid it by being good girls, avoiding dark places, staying out of bars, dressing "innocently." An ad featuring two young women talking intimately at a coffee shop says, "Carla and Rachel considered themselves open-minded and non-judgmental people. Although they did agree Brenda was a tramp." These terrible judgments from other women are an important part of what keeps all women in line.

13   If indifference in a man is sexy, then violence is sometimes downright erotic. Not surprisingly, this attitude too shows up in advertising. "Push my buttons," says a young woman, "I'm looking for a man who can totally floor me." Her vulnerability is underscored by the fact that she is in an elevator, often a dangerous place for women. She is young, she is submissive (her eyes are downcast), she is in a dangerous place, and she is dressed provocatively. And she is literally asking for it.

14   "Wear it out and make it scream," says a jeans ad portraying a man sliding his hands under a woman's transparent blouse. This could be a seduction, but it could as easily be an attack. Although the ad that ran in the Czech version of *Elle* portraying three men

attacking a woman seems unambiguous, the terrifying Image is being used to sell jeans *to women*. So someone must think that women would find this image compelling or attractive. Why would we? Perhaps it is simply designed to get our attention, by shocking us and by arousing unconscious anxiety. Or perhaps the intent is more subtle and it is designed to play into the fantasies of domination and even rape that some women use in order to maintain an illusion of being in control (we are the ones having the fantasies, after all, we are the directors).

15   A camera ad features a woman's torso wrapped in plastic, her hands tied behind her back. A smiling woman in a lipstick ad has a padlocked chain around her neck. An ad for MTV shows a vulnerable young woman, her breasts exposed, and the simple copy "Bitch." A perfume ad features a man shadowboxing with what seems to be a woman.

16   Sometimes women are shown dead or in the process of being killed. "Great hair never dies," says an ad featuring a female corpse lying on a bed, her breasts exposed. An ad in the Italian version of *Vogue* shows a man aiming a gun at a nude woman wrapped in plastic, a leather briefcase covering her face. And an ad for Bitch skateboards, for God's sake, shows a cartoon version of a similar scene, this time clearly targeting young people. We believe we are not affected by these images, but most of us experience visceral shock when we pay conscious attention to them. Could they be any less shocking to us on an unconscious level?

17   Most of us become numb to these images, just as we become numb to the daily litany in the news of women being raped, battered, and killed. According to former Surgeon General Antonia Novello, battery is the single greatest cause of injury to women in America, more common than automobile accidents, muggings, and stranger rapes combined, and more than one-third of women slain in this country die at the hands of husbands or boyfriends. Throughout the world, the biggest problem for most women is simply surviving at home. The Global Report on Women's Human Rights concluded that "Domestic violence is a leading cause of female injury in almost every country in the world and is typically ignored by the state or only erratically punished." Although usually numb to these facts on a conscious level, most women live in a state of subliminal terror, a state that, according to Mary Daly, keeps us divided both from each other and from our most passionate, powerful, and creative selves.

18   Ads don't directly cause violence, of course. But the violent images contribute to the state of terror. And objectification and disconnection create a climate in which there is widespread and increasing violence. Turning a human being into a thing, and object, is almost always the first step toward justifying violence against that person. It is very difficult, perhaps impossible, to be violent to someone we think of as an equal, someone we have empathy with, but it is very easy to abuse a thing. We see this with racism, with homophobia. The person becomes an object and violence is inevitable. This step is already taken with women. The violence, the abuse, is partly the chilling but logical result of the objectification.

19   An editorial in *Advertising Age* suggests that even some advertisers are concerned about this: "Clearly it's time to wipe out sexism in beer ads; for the brewers and their agencies to wake up and join the rest of America in realizing that sexism, sexual harassment,

and the cultural portrayal of women in advertising are inextricably linked." Alas, this editorial was written in 1991 and nothing has changed.

20   It is this link with violence that makes the objectification of women a more serious issue than the objectification of men. Our economic system constantly requires the development of new markets. Not surprisingly, men's bodies are the latest territory to be exploited. Although we are growing more used to it, in the beginning the male sex object came as a surprise. In 1994 a "gender bender" television commercial in which a bevy of women office workers gather to watch a construction worker doff his shirt to quaff a Diet Coke led to so much hoopla that you'd have thought women were mugging men on Madison Avenue.

21   There is no question that men are used as sex objects in ads now as never before. We often see nude women with fully clothed men in ads (as in art), but the reverse was unheard of, until recently. These days some ads do feature clothed and often aggressive women with nude men. And women sometimes blatantly objectify men, as in the Metroliner ad that says, "She's reading Nietzsche,' Harris noted to himself as he walked towards the café car for a glass of cabernet. And as he passed her seat, Maureen looked up from her book and thought, 'Nice buns.'"

22   Although these ads are often funny, it is never a good thing for human beings to be objectified. However, there is a world of difference between the objectification of men and that of women. The most important difference is that there is no danger for most men, whereas objectified women are always at risk. In the Diet Coke ad, for instance, the women are physically separated from the shirtless man. He is the one in control. His body is powerful, not passive. Imagine a true reversal of this ad: A group of businessmen gather to leer at a beautiful woman worker on her break, who removes her shirt before drinking her Diet Coke. This scene would be frightening, not funny, as the Diet Coke ad is. And why is the Diet Coke ad funny? Because we know it doesn't describe any truth. However, the ads featuring images of male violence against women do describe a truth, a truth we are all aware of, on one level or another.

23   When power is unequal, when one group is oppressed and discriminated against *as a group*, when there is a context of systemic and historical oppression, stereotypes and prejudice have different weight and meaning. As Anna Quindlen said, writing about "reverse racism": "Hatred by the powerful, the majority, has a different weight—and often very different effects—than hatred by the powerless, the minority." When men objectify women, they do so in a cultural context in which women are constantly objectified and in which there are consequences—from economic discrimination to violence— to that objectification.

24   For men, though, there are no such consequences. Men's bodies are not routinely judged and invaded. Men are not likely to be raped, harassed, or beaten (that is to say, men presumed to be heterosexual are not, and very few men are abused in these ways by women). How many men are frightened to be alone with a woman in an elevator? How many men cross the street when a group of women approach? Jackson Katz, who writes and lectures on male violence, often begins his workshops by asking men to describe the things they do every day to protect themselves from sexual assault. The men are sur-

prised, puzzled, sometimes amused by the question. The women understand the question easily and have no trouble at all coming up with a list of responses. We don't list our full name in the phone directory or on our mailboxes, we try not to be alone after dark, we carry our keys in our hands when we approach our cars, we always look in the back seat before we get in, we are wary of elevators and doorways and bushes, we carry pepper sprays, whistles, Mace.

25   Nonetheless, the rate of sexual assault in the United States is the highest of any industrialized nation in the world. According to a 1998 study by the federal government, one in five of us has been the victim of rape or attempted rape, most often before our seventeenth birthday. And more than half of us have been physically assaulted, most often by the men we live with. In fact, three of four women in the study who responded that they had been raped or assaulted as adults said the perpetrator was a current or former husband, a cohabitating partner or a date. The article reporting the results of this study was buried on page twenty-three of my local newspaper, while the front page dealt with a long story about the New England Patriots football team.

26   A few summers ago, a Diet Pepsi commercial featured Cindy Crawford being ogled by two boys (they seemed to be about twelve years old) as she got out of her car and bought a Pepsi from a machine. The boys made very suggestive comments, which in the end turned out to be about the Pepsi can rather than Ms. Crawford. There was no outcry: The boy's behavior was acceptable and ordinary enough for a soft-drink commercial.

27   Again, let us imagine the reverse: a sexy man gets out of a car in the countryside and two preteen girls make suggestive comments, seemingly about his body, especially his buns. We would fear for them and rightly so. But the boys already have the right to ogle, to view women's bodies as property to be looked at, commented on, touched, perhaps eventually hit and raped. The boys have also learned that men ogle primarily to impress other men (and to affirm their heterosexuality). If anyone is in potential danger in this ad, it is the woman (regardless of the age of the boys). Men are not seen as *property* in this way by woman. Indeed if a woman does whistle at a man or touches his body or even makes direct eye contact, it is still *she* who is at risk and the man who has the power.

28   "I always lower my eyes to see if a man is worth following," says the woman in an ad for men's pants. Although the ad is offensive to everyone, the woman is endangering only herself.

29   "Where women are women and men are roadkill," says an ad for motorcycle clothing featuring an angry-looking African-American woman. Women are sometimes hostile and angry in ads these days, especially women of color who are often seen as angrier and more threatening than white women. But, regardless of color, we all know that women are far more likely than men to end up as roadkill—and, when it happens, they are blamed for being on the road in the first place.

30   Even little girls are sometimes held responsible for the violence against them. In 1990 a male Canadian judge accused a three-year-old girl of being "sexually aggressive" and suspended the sentence of her molester, who was then free to return to his job of babysitter. The deeply held belief that all women, regardless of age, are really temptresses in

disguise, nymphets, sexually insatiable and seductive, conveniently transfers all blame and responsibility onto women.

31 All women are vulnerable in a culture in which there is such widespread objectification of women's bodies, such glorification of disconnection, so much violence against women, and such blaming of the victim. When everything and everyone is sexualized, it is the powerless who are most at risk. Young girls, of course, are especially vulnerable. In the past twenty years or so, there have been several trends in fashion and advertising that could be seen as cultural reactions to the women's movement, as perhaps unconscious fear of female power. One has been the obsession with thinness. Another has been an increase in images of violence against women. Most disturbing has been the increasing sexualization of children, especially girls. Sometimes the little girl is made up and seductively posed. Sometimes the language is suggestive. "Very cherry," says the ad featuring a sexy little African-American girl who is wearing a dress with cherries all over it. A shocking ad in a gun magazine features a smiling little girl, a toddler, in a bathing suit that is tugged up suggestively in the rear. The copy beneath the photo says, "short BUTTS from FLEMING FIREARMS." Other times girls are juxtaposed with grown women, as in the ad for underpants that says "You already know the feeling."

32 This is not only an American phenomenon. A growing national obsession in Japan with schoolgirls dressed in uniforms is called "Loli-con," after Lolita. In Tokyo hundreds of "image clubs" allow Japanese men to act out their fantasies with make-believe schoolgirls. A magazine called *V-Club* featuring pictures of naked elementary-school girls competes with another called *Anatomical Illustrations of Junior High School Girls*. Masao Miyamoto, a male psychiatrist, suggests that Japanese men are turning to girls because they feel threatened by the growing sophistication of older women.

33 In recent years, this sexualization of little girls has become even more disturbing as hints of violence enter the picture. A three-page ad for Prada clothing features a girl or very young woman with a barely pubescent body, clothed in what seem to be cotton panties and perhaps a training bra, viewed through a partially opened door. She seems surprised, startled, worried, as if she's heard a strange sound or glimpsed someone watching her. I suppose this could be a woman awaiting her lover, but it could as easily be a girl being preyed upon.

34 The 1996 murder of six-year-old JonBenet Ramsey was a gold mine for the media, combining as it did child pornography and violence. In November of 1997 *Advertising Age* reported in an article entitled "JonBenet keeps hold on magazines" that the child had been on five magazine covers in October, "Enough to capture the Cover Story lead for the month. The pre-adolescent beauty queen, found slain in her home last Christmas, garnered 6.5 points. The case earned a *triple play* [italics mine] on the *National Enquirer*, and one-time appearances on *People* and *Star*." Imagine describing a six-year-old child as "pre-adolescent."

35 Sometimes the models in ads are children, other times they just look like children. Kate Moss was twenty when she said of herself, "I look twelve." She epitomized the vacant, hollow-cheeked look known as "heroin chic" that was popular in the mid-nineties.

She also often looked vulnerable, abused, and exploited. In one ad she is nude in the corner of a huge sofa, cringing as if braced for an impending sexual assault. In another, she is lying nude on her stomach, pliant, available, androgynous enough to appeal to all kinds of pedophiles. In a music video she is dead and bound to a chair while Johnny Cash sings "Delia's Gone."

36   It is not surprising that Kate Moss models for Calvin Klein, the fashion designer who specializes in breaking taboos and thereby getting himself public outrage, media coverage, and more bang for his buck. In 1995 he brought the federal government down on himself by running a campaign that may have crossed the line into child pornography. Very young models (and others who just seemed young) were featured in lascivious print ads and in television commercials designed to mimic child porn. The models were awkward, self-conscious. In one commercial, a boy stands in what seems to be a finished basement. A male voiceover tells him he has a great body and asks him to take off his shirt. The boy seems embarrassed but he complies. There was a great deal of protest, which brought the issue into national consciousness but which also gave Klein the publicity and free media coverage he was looking for. He pulled the ads but, at the same time, projected that his jean sales would almost double from $115 million to $220 million that year, partly because of the free publicity but also because the controversy made his critics seem like prudes and thus positioned Klein as the daring rebel, a very appealing image to the majority of his customers.

37   Having learned from this, in 1999 Klein launched a very brief advertising campaign featuring very little children frolicking in their underpants, which included a controversial billboard in Times Square. Although in some ways this campaign was less offensive than the earlier one and might have gone unnoticed had the ads come from a department store catalog rather than from Calvin Klein, there was the expected protest and Klein quickly withdrew the ads, again getting a windfall of media coverage. In my opinion, the real obscenity of this campaign is the whole idea of people buying designer underwear for their little ones, especially in a country in which at least one in five children doesn't have enough to eat.

38   Although boys are sometimes sexualized in an overt way, they are more often portrayed as sexually precocious, as in the Pepsi commercial featuring the young boys ogling Cindy Crawford or the jeans ad portraying a very little boy looking up a woman's skirt. It may seem that I am reading too much into this ad, but imagine if the genders were reversed. We would fear for a little girl who was unzipping a man's fly in an ad (and we would be shocked, I would hope). Boys are vulnerable to sexual abuse too, but cultural attitudes make it difficult to take this seriously. As a result, boys are less likely to report abuse and to get treatment.

39   Many boys grow up feeling that they are unmanly if they are not always "ready for action," capable of and interested in sex with any woman who is available. Advertising doesn't cause this attitude, of course, but it contributes to it. A Levi Strauss commercial that ran in Asia features the shock of a schoolboy who discovers that the seductive young woman who has slipped a note into the jeans of an older student is his teacher. And an ad for BIC pens pictures a young boy wearing X-ray glasses while ogling the derriere of an

older woman. Again, these ads would be unthinkable if the genders were reversed. It is increasingly difficult in such a toxic environment to see children, boys or girls, as *children*.
40   In the past few years there had been a proliferation of sexually grotesque toys for boys, such as a Spider Man female action figure whose exaggerated breasts have antennae coming out of them and a female Spawn figure with carved skulls for breasts. Meantime even children have easy access to pornography in video games and on the World Wide Web, which includes explicit photographs of women having intercourse with groups of men, with dogs, donkeys, horses, and snakes; photographs of women being raped and tortured; some of these women made up to look like little girls.
41   It is hard for girls not to learn self-hatred in an environment in which there is such widespread and open contempt for women and girls. In 1997 a company called Senate distributed clothing with the inside labels that included, in addition to the usual cleaning instructions, the line "Destroy all girls." A Senate staffer explained that he thought it was "kind of cool." Given all this, it's not surprising that when boys and girls were asked in a recent study to write an essay on what it would be like to be the other gender, many boys wrote they would rather be dead. Girls had no trouble writing essays about activities, power, freedom, but boys were often stuck, could think of nothing.
42   It is also not surprising that, in such an environment, sexual harassment is considered normal and ordinary. According to an article in the journal *Eating Disorders:*
43   In our work with young women, we have heard countless accounts of this contempt being expressed by their male peers: the girls who do not want to walk down a certain hallway in their high school because they are afraid of being publicly rated on a scale of one to ten; the girls who are subjected to barking, grunting and mooing calls and labels of "dogs, cows or pigs" when they pass by groups of male students; those who are teased about not measuring up to buxom, bikiniclad [models]; and the girls who are grabbed, pinched, groped and fondled as they try to make their way through the school corridors.

44   Harassing words do not slide harmlessly away as the taunting sounds dissipate...They are slowly absorbed into the child's identity and developing sense of self, becoming an essential part of whom she sees herself to be. Harassment involves the use of words as weapons to inflict pain and assert power. Harassing words are meant to instill fear, heighten bodily discomfort, and diminish the sense of self.

45   It is probably difficult for those of us who are older to understand how devastating and cruel and pervasive this harassment is, how different from the "teasing" some of us might remember from our own childhoods (not that that didn't hurt and do damage as well). A 1993 report by the American Association of University Women found that 76 percent of female students in grades eight to eleven and 56 percent of male students said they had been sexually harassed in school. One high-school junior described a year of torment at her vocational school: "The boys called me slut, bitch. They call me a 10-timer, because

they say I go with 10 guys at the same time. I put up with it because I have no choice. The teachers say it's because the boys think I'm pretty."

46   High school and junior high school have always been hell for those who were different in any way (gay teens have no doubt suffered the most, although "overweight" girls are a close second), but the harassment is more extreme and more physical these days. Many young men feel thy have the right to judge and touch young women and the women often feel they have no choice but to submit. One young woman recalled that "the guys at school routinely swiped their hands across girls' legs to patrol their shaving prowess and then taunt them if they were slacking off. If I were running late, I'd protect myself by faux shaving—just doing the strip between the bottom of my jeans and the top of my cotton socks."

47   Sexual battery, as well as inappropriate sexual gesturing, touching, and fondling, is increasing not only in high schools but in elementary and middle schools as well. There are reports of sexual assaults by students on other students as young as eight. A fifth-grade boy in Georgia repeatedly touched the breasts and genitals of one of his fellow students while saying, "I want to get in bed with you" and "I want to feel your boobs." Authorities did nothing, although the girl complained and her grades fell. When her parents found a suicide note she had written, they took the board of education to court.

48   A high-school senior in an affluent suburban school in the Boston area said she has been dragged by her arms so boys could look up her skirt and that boys have rested their heads on her chest while making lewd comments. Another student in the same school was pinned down on a lunch table while a boy simulated sex on top of her. Neither student reported any of the incidents, for fear of being ostracized by their peers. In another school in the Boston area, a sixteen-year-old girl, who had been digitally raped by a classmate, committed suicide.

49   According to Nan Stein, a researcher at Wellesley College:

50   Schools may in fact be training grounds for the insidious cycle of
        domestic violence….The school's hidden curriculum teaches young women
        to suffer abuse privately, that resistance is futile. When they witness harass-
        ment of others and fail to respond, they absorb a different kind of powerless-
        ness—that they are incapable of standing up to injustice or acting in soli-
        darity with their peers. Similarly, in schools boys receive permission, even
        training, to become batterers through the practice of sexual harassment.

51   This pervasive harassment of and contempt for girls and women constitute a kind of abuse. We know that addictions for women are rooted in trauma, that girls who are sexually abused are far more likely to become addicted to one substance or another. I contend that all girls growing up in this culture are sexually abused—abused by the pornographic images of female sexuality that surround them from birth, abused by all the violence against women and girls, and abused by the constant harassment and threat of violence. Abuse is a continuum, of course, and I am by no means implying that cultural abuse is as terrible as literally being raped and assaulted. However, it hurts, it does damage, and it

sets girls up for addictions and self-destructive behavior. Many girls turn to food, alcohol, cigarettes, and other drugs in a misguided attempt to cope.

52   As Marian Sandmaier said in *The Invisible Alcoholics: Women and Alcohol Abuse in America*, "In a culture that cuts off women from many of their own possibilities before they barely have had a chance to sense them, that pain belongs to all women. Outlets for coping may vary widely, and may be more or less addictive, more or less self-destructive. But at some level, all women know what it is to lack access to their own power, to live with a piece of themselves unclaimed.

53   Today, every girl is endangered, not just those who have been physically and sexually abused. If girls from supportive homes with positive role models are at risk, imagine then how vulnerable are the girls who have been violated. No wonder they so often go under for good—ending up in abusive marriages, in prison, on the streets. And those who do are almost always in the grip of one addiction or another. More than half of women in prison are addicts and most are there for crimes directly related to their addiction. Many who are there for murder killed men who had been battering them for years. Almost all of the women who are homeless or in prisons and mental institutions are the victims of male violence.

54   Male violence exists within the same cultural and sociopolitical context that contributes to addiction. Both can be fully understood only within this context, way beyond individual psychology and family dynamics. It is a context of systemic violence and oppression, including racism, classism, heterosexism, weightism, and ageism, as well as sexism, all of which are traumatizing in and of themselves. Advertising is only one part of this cultural context, but it is an important part and thus is part of what traumatizes.

55   All right, you might think, these ads are shocking. They are probably not good for us. But just what is the relationship of all these sexist and violent ads to addiction? Am I blaming advertisers for everything now? No. But I do contend that ads that contribute to a climate of disconnection also contribute to addiction. Ads that objectify women and sexualize children also play a role in the victimization of women and girls that often leads to addiction. When women are shown in positions of powerlessness, submission, and subjugation, the message to men is clear: Women are always available as the targets of aggression and violence, women are inferior to men and thus deserve to be dominated, and women exist to fulfill the needs of men.

56   There is a further connection between the images that legitimize male domination of females and addiction. In his classic essay "The Cybernetics of Self" Gregory Bateson describes the fundamental belief of Western culture that we can dominate, control, and have power over almost every aspect of our experience. We can get rid of pain, we can dominate people who threaten us, we can win in any interaction, we can be invulnerable. Bateson theorizes that his belief is fundamentally erroneous and leads to addiction, which he sees as a distorted attempt to get to a more "correct" state of mind, one in which we permit dependency, vulnerability, and mutuality. Bateson argues that we have no culturally sanctioned, nonaddictive way to achieve this state.

57   Claudia Bepko takes Bateson's theory further by arguing that the stage is set for addiction by the overriding belief system maintaining that men have power and women are the objects of that power. This assumption is as erroneous as is the assumption that we can control our emotions. But our entire culture is predicated on this illusion of male dominance, and our institutions are set up in ways that perpetuate it. According to Bepko, being socialized in an erroneous belief system leads to addiction because incongruity may arise between what one believes and how one actually feels. A man who feels he must be dominant but who actually feels vulnerable might use an addictive substance to lessen his feeling of vulnerability or to enhance his sense of dominance. A woman forced to show dependence who really feels powerful might use a drug or other substance either to enhance or disqualify the impulse to be powerful (as the old Jefferson Airplane song says, "One pill makes you larger and one pill makes you small"). Thus gender-role socialization both shapes and is continually challenged by addictive behavior.

58   Bepko describes what she calls "the yin and yang of addiction." Both men and women become addicted and suffer, but their individual addictions arise from their different positions in the world and have different effects. Men operate within a context in which both autonomy and entitlement to be taken care of are assumed; women within a context in which both dependency on a man and emotional and physical nurturing and caretaking are assumed. The contradictions in these prescriptions obviously create a bind: The male is independent but taken care of and the woman is dependent but the caretaker. Addiction is one response to the pain created by these contradictions.

59   Although the critical issues are dependency and control, these have radically different meanings and outcomes for women and men. Since money, sexuality, size, strength, and competitive work convey power and status for men, gambling, sexual addictions, and work addiction tend to be predominantly male forms of compulsive behavior (although women are catching up as gender roles change). Women are still socialized to be physically and emotionally nurturing, so eating disorders, obsessive shopping or cleaning, self-mutilation, and compulsive behavior, as is prescription drug abuse, which reflects the cultural belief that women's emotions need to be subdued and controlled. A man is more likely to engage in addictive behavior that involves having power over others, whereas a woman's attempt at control is often focused on her own body.

60   It would be foolish to suggest that advertising is *the cause* of violence against women—or of alcoholism or eating disorders or any other major problem. These problems are complex and have many contributing factors. There is no doubt that flagrant sexism and sex role stereotyping abound in all forms of the media. There is abundant information about this. It is far more difficult to document the effects of these stereotypes and images on the individuals and institutions exposed to them because, as I've said, it is difficult to separate media effects from other aspects of the socialization process and almost impossible to find a comparison group (just about everyone in America has been exposed to massive doses of advertising).

61   But, at the very least, advertising helps to create a climate in which certain attitudes and values flourish, such as the attitude that women are valuable only as objects of men's desire, that real men are always sexually aggressive, that violence is erotic, and that

women who are the victims of sexual assault "asked for it." These attitudes have especially terrible consequences for women abused as children, most of whom grow up feeling like objects and believing they are responsible for their own abuse. These are the very women who are likely to mutilate and starve themselves, to smoke, to become addicted to alcohol and other drugs. As Judith Herman wrote in her classic book *Father-Daughter Incest*:

62   These women alone suffered the consequences of their psychological
        impairment. Almost always, their anger and disappointment were expressed
        in self-destructive action: in unwanted pregnancies, in submission to rape
        and beatings, in addiction to alcohol and drugs, in attempted suicide.

63   ...Consumed with rage, they nevertheless rarely caused trouble
        to anyone but themselves. In their own flesh, they bore repeated pun-
        ishment for the crimes committed against them in their childhood.

64   Addictions are not incidental in the lives of women. Most often they are caused by (or at least related to) disturbances in relationships in childhood, often violent disturbances. They are fueled by a culture that sexualizes children, objectifies, trivializes, and silences women, disparages our interest in and skill at relating, and constantly threatens us with violence. Feeling isolated and disconnected, a girl or a woman reaches out to a sub-stance to numb her pain, to be sure, but also to end her isolation, to relate, to connect. She reaches for alcohol or other drugs, she reaches for cigarettes, she reaches for men who don't love her, or she reaches for food. The advertisers are ready for her.

Critical Reading Questions:

- **Interpretation:** What is Kilbourne's overarching purpose in this chapter of her book? In other words, what is Kilbourne trying to get her intended audience to think, feel, and/or do? Her overarching claim is evaluative. What does she evaluate and how?

- **Analysis:** Select at least two excerpts that exemplify appeals to pathos. Based on what you know about the audience, what specific emotions are evoked and why? Which claims evoke emotion from her audience? Do you think this rhetori-cal strategy is effective considering her audience?

- **Reflection:** To what degree did Kilbourne convince you that interrogating popular texts might be important to you as a member of society? Did she con-vince you that these texts might reveal societal issues that are exigent? Why or why not?

Letter from Birmingham Jail

Martin Luther King, Jr.

Arrested on Good Friday in the city that many African-Americans called "Bombingham," Dr. Martin Luther King, Jr., was placed in solitary confinement in the Birmingham jail. On April 12, 1963, King's attorney passed him a copy of the *Birmingham News* which had published a letter from eight clergymen who called King's actions "unwise and untimely." In the margins of that newspaper and later on sheets of toilet paper and legal pads, King wrote his response. "Letter from Birmingham Jail" is an epistolary essay and an example of prison literature. King makes a case for civil disobedience and eloquently opposes the murderous status quo. At turns prophetic and diplomatic, King's argument is consistently theological. King calls on the church to follow Jesus, whom he defines as "an extremist for love, truth, and goodness." King's letter was finished on April 16, 1963. *The New York Times* refused to print it; it was first published in the June 1963 issue of *Liberation* and later that same month in *The Christian Century*.

—MA

April 16, 1963

1   My Dear Fellow Clergymen:

2   While confined here in the Birmingham city jail, I came across your recent statement calling my present activities "unwise and untimely." Seldom do I pause to answer criticism of my work and ideas. If I sought to answer all the criticisms that cross my desk, my secretaries would have little time for anything other than such correspondence in the course of the day, and I would have no time for constructive work. But since I feel that you are men of genuine good will and that your criticisms are sincerely set forth, I want to try to answer your statements in what I hope will be patient and reasonable terms.

3   I think I should indicate why I am here In Birmingham, since you have been influenced by the view which argues against "outsiders coming in." I have the honor of serving as president of the Southern Christian Leadership Conference, an organization operating in every southern state, with headquarters in Atlanta, Georgia. We have some eighty-five affiliated organizations across the South, and one of them is the Alabama Christian Movement for Human Rights. Frequently we share staff, educational and financial resources with our affiliates. Several months ago the affiliate here in Birmingham asked us to be on call to engage in a nonviolent direct-action program if such were deemed necessary. We readily consented, and when the hour came we lived up to our promise. So I, along with several members of my staff, am here because I was invited here. I am here because I have organizational ties here.

4   But more basically, I am in Birmingham because injustice is here. Just as the prophets of the eighth century B.C. left their villages and carried their "thus saith the Lord" far beyond the boundaries of their home towns, and just as the Apostle Paul left his village of Tarsus and carried the gospel of Jesus Christ to the far corners of the Greco Roman world, so am I. compelled to carry the gospel of freedom beyond my own home town. Like Paul, I must constantly respond to the Macedonian call for aid.

5   Moreover, I am cognizant of the interrelatedness of all communities and states. I cannot sit idly by in Atlanta and not be concerned about what happens in Birmingham. Injustice anywhere is a threat to justice everywhere. We are caught in an inescapable network of mutuality, tied in a single garment of destiny. Whatever affects one directly, affects all indirectly. Never again can we afford to live with the narrow, provincial "outside agitator" idea. Anyone who lives inside the United States can never be considered an outsider anywhere within its bounds.

6   You deplore the demonstrations taking place In Birmingham. But your statement, I am sorry to say, fails to express a similar concern for the conditions that brought about the demonstrations. I am sure that none of you would want to rest content with the superficial kind of social analysis that deals merely with effects and does not grapple with underlying causes. It is unfortunate that demonstrations are taking place in Birmingham, but it is even more unfortunate that the city's white power structure left the Negro community with no alternative.

7   In any nonviolent campaign there are four basic steps: collection of the facts to determine whether injustices exist; negotiation; self-purification; and direct action. We have gone through all these steps in Birmingham. There can be no gainsaying the fact that racial injustice engulfs this community. Birmingham is probably the most thoroughly segregated city in the United States. Its ugly record of brutality is widely known. Negroes have experienced grossly unjust treatment in the courts. There have been more unsolved bombings of Negro homes and churches in Birmingham than in any other city in the nation. These are the hard, brutal facts of the case. On the basis of these conditions, Negro leaders sought to negotiate with the city fathers. But the latter consistently refused to engage in good-faith negotiation.

8   Then, last September, came the opportunity to talk with leaders of Birmingham's economic community. In the course of the negotiations, certain promises were made by the merchants—for example, to remove the stores' humiliating racial signs. On the basis of these promises, the Reverend Fred Shuttlesworth and the leaders of the Alabama Christian Movement for Human Rights agreed to a moratorium on all demonstrations. As the weeks and months went by, we realized that we were the victims of a broken promise. A few signs, briefly removed, returned; the others remained.

9   As in so many past experiences, our hopes bad been blasted, and the shadow of deep disappointment settled upon us. We had no alternative except to prepare for direct action, whereby we would present our very bodies as a means of laying our case before the conscience of the local and the national community. Mindful of the difficulties involved, we decided to undertake a process of self-purification. We began a series of workshops on nonviolence, and we repeatedly asked ourselves: "Are you able to accept blows without retaliating?" "Are you able to endure the ordeal of jail?" We decided to schedule our

direct-action program for the Easter season, realizing that except for Christmas, this is the main shopping period of the year. Knowing that a strong economic withdrawal program would be the by-product of direct action, we felt that this would be the best time to bring pressure to bear on the merchants for the needed change.

10   Then it occurred to us that Birmingham's mayoralty election was coming up in March, and we speedily decided to postpone action until after election day. When we discovered that the Commissioner of Public Safety, Eugene "Bull" Connor, had piled up enough votes to be in the run-off we decided again to postpone action until the day after the run-off so that the demonstrations could not be used to cloud the issues. Like many others, we waited to see Mr. Connor defeated, and to this end we endured postponement after postponement. Having aided in this community need, we felt that our direct-action program could be delayed no longer.

11   You may well ask: "Why direct action? Why sit-ins, marches and so forth? Isn't negotiation a better path?" You are quite right in calling for negotiation. Indeed, this is the very purpose of direct action. Nonviolent direct action seeks to create such a crisis and foster such a tension that a community which has constantly refused to negotiate is forced to confront the issue. It seeks so to dramatize the issue that it can no longer be ignored. My citing the creation of tension as part of the work of the nonviolent resister may sound rather shocking. But I must confess that I am not afraid of the word "tension." I have earnestly opposed violent tension, but there is a type of constructive, nonviolent tension which is necessary for growth. Just as Socrates felt that it was necessary to create a tension in the mind so that individuals could rise from the bondage of myths and half-truths to the unfettered realm of creative analysis and objective appraisal, we must we see the need for nonviolent gadflies to create the kind of tension in society that will help men rise from the dark depths of prejudice and racism to the majestic heights of understanding and brotherhood. The purpose of our direct-action program is to create a situation so crisis-packed that it will inevitably open the door to negotiation. I therefore concur with you in your call for negotiation. Too long has our beloved Southland been bogged down in a tragic effort to live in monologue rather than dialogue.

12   One of the basic points in your statement is that the action that I and my associates have taken in Birmingham is untimely. Some have asked: "Why didn't you give the new city administration time to act?" The only answer that I can give to this query is that the new Birmingham administration must be prodded about as much as the outgoing one, before it will act. We are sadly mistaken if we feel that the election of Albert Boutwell as mayor will bring the millennium to Birmingham. While Mr. Boutwell is a much more gentle person than Mr. Connor, they are both segregationists, dedicated to maintenance of the status quo. I have hope that Mr. Boutwell will be reasonable enough to see the futility of massive resistance to desegregation. But he will not see this without pressure from devotees of civil rights. My friends, I must say to you that we have not made a single gain in civil rights without determined legal and nonviolent pressure. Lamentably, it is an historical fact that privileged groups seldom give up their privileges voluntarily. Individuals may see the moral light and voluntarily give up their unjust posture; but, as Reinhold Niebuhr has reminded us, groups tend to be more immoral than individuals.

13   We know through painful experience that freedom is never voluntarily given by the oppressor; it must be demanded by the oppressed. Frankly, I have yet to engage in a direct-action campaign that was "well timed" in the view of those who have not suffered unduly from the disease of segregation For years now I have heard tho word "Wait!" It rings in the ear of every Negro with piercing familiarity. This "Wait" has almost always meant "Never." We must come to see, with one of our distinguished jurists, that "justice too long delayed is justice denied."

14   We have waited for more than 340 years for our constitutional and God-given rights. The nations of Asia and Africa are moving with jetlike speed toward gaining political independence, but we still creep at horse-and-buggy pace toward gaining a cup of coffee at a lunch counter. Perhaps it is easy for those who have never felt the stinging dark of segregation to say, "Wait." But when you have seen vicious mobs lynch your mothers and fathers at will and drown your sisters and brothers at whim; when you have seen hate-filled policemen curse, kick and even kill your black brothers and sisters; when you see the vast majority of your twenty million Negro brothers smothering in an airtight cage of poverty in the midst of an affluent society; when you suddenly find your tongue twisted and your speech stammering as you seek to explain to your six-year-old daughter why she can't go to the public amusement park that has just been advertised on television, and see tears welling up in her eyes when she is told that Funtown is closed to colored children, and see ominous clouds of inferiority beginning to form in her little mental sky, and see her beginning to distort her personality by developing an unconscious bitterness toward white people; when you have to concoct an answer for a five-year-old son who is asking: "Daddy, why do white people treat colored people so mean?"; when you take a cross-county drive and find it necessary to sleep night after night in the uncomfortable corners of your automobile because no motel will accept you; when you are humiliated day in and day out by nagging signs reading "white" and "colored"; when your first name becomes "nigger," your middle name becomes "boy" (however old you are) and your last name becomes "John," and your wife and mother are never given the respected title "Mrs,"; when you are harried by day and haunted by night by the fact that you are a Negro, living constantly at tiptoe stance, never quite knowing what to expect next, and are plagued with inner fears and outer resentments; when you are forever fighting a degenerating sense of "nobodiness"—then you will understand why we find it difficult to wait. There comes a time when the cup of endurance runs over, and men are no longer willing to be plunged into the abyss of despair. I hope, sirs, you can understand our legitimate and unavoidable impatience.

15   You express a great deal of anxiety over our willingness to break laws. This is certainly a legitimate concern. Since we so diligently urge people to obey the Supreme Court's decision of 1954 outlawing segregation in the public schools, at first glance it may seem rather paradoxical for us consciously to break laws. One may well ask: "How can you advocate breaking some laws and obeying others?" The answer lies in the fact that there are two types of laws: just and unjust. I would be the first to advocate obeying just laws. One has not only a legal but a moral responsibility to obey just laws. Conversely, one has a moral responsibility to disobey unjust laws. I would agree with St. Augustine that "an unjust law is no law at all."

16   Now, what is the difference between the two? How does one determine whether a law is just or unjust? A just law is a man-made code that squares with the moral law or the law of God. An unjust law is a code that is out of harmony with the moral law. To put it in the terms of St. Thomas Aquinas: An unjust law is a human law that is not rooted in eternal law and natural law. Any law that uplifts human personality is just. Any law that degrades human personality is unjust. All segregation statutes are unjust because segregation distorts the soul and damages the personality. It gives the segregator a false sense of superiority and the segregated a false sense of inferiority. Segregation, to use the terminology of the Jewish philosopher Martin Buber, substitutes an "I-it" relationship for an "I-thou" relationship and ends up relegating persons to the status of things. Hence segregation is not only politically, economically and sociologically unsound, it is morally wrong and awful. Paul Tillich said that sin is separation. Is not segregation an existential expression of man's tragic separation, his awful estrangement, his terrible sinfulness? Thus it is that I can urge men to obey the 1954 decision of the Supreme Court, for it is morally right; and I can urge them to disobey segregation ordinances, for they are morally wrong.

17   Let us consider a more concrete example of just and unjust laws. An unjust law is a code that a numerical or power majority group compels a minority group to obey but does not make binding on itself. This is difference made legal. By the same token, a just law is a code that a majority compels a minority to follow and that it is willing to follow itself. This is sameness made legal. Let me give another explanation. A law is unjust if it is inflicted on a minority that, as a result of being denied the right to vote, had no part in enacting or devising the law. Who can say that the legislature of Alabama which set up that state's segregation laws was democratically elected? Throughout Alabama all sorts of devious methods are used to prevent Negroes from becoming registered voters, and there are some counties in which, even though Negroes constitute a majority of the population, not a single Negro is registered. Can any law enacted under such circumstances be considered democratically structured?

18   Sometimes a law is just on its face and unjust in its application. For instance, I have been arrested on a charge of parading without a permit. Now, there is nothing wrong in having an ordinance which requires a permit for a parade. But such an ordinance becomes unjust when it is used to maintain segregation and to deny citizens the First Amendment privilege of peaceful assembly and protest.

19   I hope you are able to see the distinction I am trying to point out. In no sense do I advocate evading or defying the law, as would the rabid segregationist. That would lead to anarchy. One who breaks an unjust law must do so openly, lovingly, and with a willingness to accept the penalty. I submit that an individual who breaks a law that conscience tells him is unjust and who willingly accepts the penalty of imprisonment in order to arouse the conscience of the community over its injustice, is in reality expressing the highest respect for law.

20   Of course, there is nothing new about this kind of civil disobedience. It was evidenced sublimely in the refusal of Shadrach, Meshach and Abednego to obey the laws of Nebuchadnezzar, on the ground that a higher moral law was at stake. It was practiced superbly by the early Christians, who were willing to face hungry lions and the excru-

ciating pain of chopping blocks rather than submit to certain unjust laws of the Roman Empire. To a degree, academic freedom is a reality today because Socrates practiced civil disobedience. In our own nation, the Boston Tea Party represented a massive act of civil disobedience.

21   We should never forget that everything Adolf Hitler did in Germany was "legal" and everything the Hungarian freedom fighters did in Hungary was "illegal." It was "illegal" to aid and comfort a Jew in Hitler's Germany. Even so, I am sure that, had I lived in Germany at the time, I would have aided and comforted my Jewish brothers. If today I lived in a Communist country where certain principles dear to the Christian faith are suppressed, I would openly advocate disobeying that country's antireligious laws.

22   I must make two honest confessions to you, my Christian and Jewish brothers. First, I must confess that over the past few years I have been gravely disappointed with the white moderate. I have almost reached the regrettable conclusion that the Negro's great stumbling block in his stride toward freedom is not the White Citizen's Counciler or the Ku Klux Klanner, but the white moderate, who is more devoted to "order" than to justice; who prefers a negative peace which is the absence of tension to a positive peace which is the presence of justice; who constantly says: "I agree with you in the goal you seek, but I cannot agree with your methods of direct action"; who paternalistically believes he can set the timetable for another man's freedom; who lives by a mythical concept of time and who constantly advises the Negro to wait for a "more convenient season." Shallow understanding from people of good will is more frustrating than absolute misunderstanding from people of ill will. Lukewarm acceptance is much more bewildering than outright rejection.

23   I had hoped that the white moderate would understand that law and order exist for the purpose of establishing justice and that when they fan in this purpose they become the dangerously structured dams that block the flow of social progress. I had hoped that the white moderate would understand that the present tension in the South is a necessary phase of the transition from an obnoxious negative peace, in which the Negro passively accepted his unjust plight, to a substantive and positive peace, in which all men will respect the dignity and worth of human personality. Actually, we who engage in nonviolent direct action are not the creators of tension. We merely bring to the surface the hidden tension that is already alive. We bring it out in the open, where it can be seen and dealt with. Like a boil that can never be cured so long as it is covered up but must be opened with an its ugliness to the natural medicines of air and light, injustice must be exposed, with all the tension its exposure creates, to the light of human conscience and the air of national opinion before it can be cured.

24   In your statement you assert that our actions, even though peaceful, must be condemned because they precipitate violence. But is this a logical assertion? Isn't this like condemning a robbed man because his possession of money precipitated the evil act of robbery? Isn't this like condemning Socrates because his unswerving commitment to truth and his philosophical inquiries precipitated the act by the misguided populace in which they made him drink hemlock? Isn't this like condemning Jesus because his unique God-consciousness and never-ceasing devotion to God's will precipitated the evil act of crucifixion? We must come to see that, as the federal courts have consistently affirmed,

it is wrong to urge an individual to cease his efforts to gain his basic constitutional rights because the quest may precipitate violence. Society must protect the robbed and punish the robber.

25   I had also hoped that the white moderate would reject the myth concerning time in relation to the struggle for freedom. I have just received a letter from a white brother in Texas. He writes: "An Christians know that the colored people will receive equal rights eventually, but it is possible that you are in too great a religious hurry. It has taken Christianity almost two thousand years to accomplish what it has. The teachings of Christ take time to come to earth." Such an attitude stems from a tragic misconception of time, from the strangely rational notion that there is something in the very flow of time that will inevitably cure all ills. Actually, time itself is neutral; it can be used either destructively or constructively. More and more I feel that the people of ill will have used time much more effectively than have the people of good will. We will have to repent in this generation not merely for the hateful words and actions of the bad people but for the appalling silence of the good people. Human progress never rolls in on wheels of inevitability; it comes through the tireless efforts of men willing to be co-workers with God, and without this 'hard work, time itself becomes an ally of the forces of social stagnation. We must use time creatively, in the knowledge that the time is always ripe to do right. Now is the time to make real the promise of democracy and transform our pending national elegy into a creative psalm of brotherhood. Now is the time to lift our national policy from the quicksand of racial injustice to the solid rock of human dignity.

26   You speak of our activity in Birmingham as extreme. At first I was rather disappointed that fellow clergymen would see my nonviolent efforts as those of an extremist. I began thinking about the fact that I stand in the middle of two opposing forces in the Negro community. One is a force of complacency, made up in part of Negroes who, as a result of long years of oppression, are so drained of self respect and a sense of "somebodiness" that they have adjusted to segregation; and in part of a few middle-class Negroes who, because of a degree of academic and economic security and because in some ways they profit by segregation, have become insensitive to the problems of the masses. The other force is one of bitterness and hatred, and it comes perilously close to advocating violence. It is expressed in the various black nationalist groups that are springing up across the nation, the largest and best known being Elijah Muhammad's Muslim movement. Nourished by the Negro's frustration over the continued existence of racial discrimination, this movement is made up of people who have lost faith in America, who have absolutely repudiated Christianity, and who have concluded that the white man is an incorrigible "devil."

27   I have tried to stand between these two forces, saying that we need emulate neither the "do-nothingism" of the complacent nor the hatred and despair of the black nationalist. For there is the more excellent way of love and nonviolent protest. I am grateful to God that, through the influence of the Negro church, the way of nonviolence became an integral part of our struggle.

28   If this philosophy had not emerged, by now many streets of the South would, I am convinced, be flowing with blood. And I am further convinced that if our white brothers dismiss as "rabble rousers" and "outside agitators" those of us who employ nonviolent

direct action, and if they refuse to support our nonviolent efforts, millions of Negroes will, out of frustration and despair, seek solace and security in black nationalist ideologies—a development that would inevitably lead to a frightening racial nightmare.

29   Oppressed people cannot remain oppressed forever. The yearning for freedom eventually manifests itself, and that is what has happened to the American Negro. Something within has reminded him of his birthright of freedom, and something without has reminded him that it can be gained. Consciously or unconsciously, he has been caught up by the Zeitgeist, and with his black brothers of Africa and his brown and yellow brothers of Asia, South America and the Caribbean, the United States Negro is moving with a sense of great urgency toward the promised land of racial justice. If one recognizes this vital urge that has engulfed the Negro community, one should readily understand why public demonstrations are taking place. The Negro has many pent-up resentments and latent frustrations, and he must release them. So let him march; let him make prayer pilgrimages to the city hall; let him go on freedom rides and try to understand why he must do so. If his repressed emotions are not released in nonviolent ways, they will seek expression through violence; this is not a threat but a fact of history. So I have not said to my people: "Get rid of your discontent." Rather, I have tried to say that this normal and healthy discontent can be channeled into the creative outlet of nonviolent direct action. And now this approach is being termed extremist.

30   But though I was initially disappointed at being categorized as an extremist, as I continued to think about the matter I gradually gained a measure of satisfaction from the label. Was not Jesus an extremist for love: "Love your enemies, bless them that curse you, do good to them that hate you, and pray for them which despitefully use you, and persecute you." Was not Amos an extremist for justice: "Let justice roll down like waters and righteousness like an ever-flowing stream." Was not Paul an extremist for the Christian gospel: "I bear in my body the marks of the Lord Jesus." Was not Martin Luther an extremist: "Here I stand; I cannot do otherwise, so help me God." And John Bunyan: "I will stay in jail to the end of my days before I make a butchery of my conscience." And Abraham Lincoln: "This nation cannot survive half slave and half free." And Thomas Jefferson: "We hold these truths to be self-evident, that an men are created equal ..." So the question is not whether we will be extremists, but what kind of extremists we will be. Will we be extremists for hate or for love? Will we be extremists for the preservation of injustice or for the extension of justice? In that dramatic scene on Calvary's hill three men were crucified. We must never forget that all three were crucified for the same crime—the crime of extremism. Two were extremists for immorality, and thus fell below their environment. The other, Jeans Christ, was an extremist for love, truth and goodness, and thereby rose above his environment. Perhaps the South, the nation and the world are in dire need of creative extremists.

31   I had hoped that the white moderate would see this need. Perhaps I was too optimistic; perhaps I expected too much. I suppose I should have realized that few members of the oppressor race can understand the deep groans and passionate yearnings of the oppressed race, and still fewer have the vision to see that injustice must be rooted out by strong, persistent and determined action. I am thankful, however, that some of our white brothers in the South have grasped the meaning of this social revolution and committed

themselves to it. They are still too few in quantity, but they are big in quality. Some—such as Ralph McGill, Lillian Smith, Harry Golden, James McBride Dabbs, Ann Braden and Sarah Patton Boyle—have written about our struggle in eloquent and prophetic terms. Others have marched with us down nameless streets of the South. They have languished in filthy, roach-infested jails, suffering the abuse and brutality of policemen who view them as "dirty nigger-lovers." Unlike so many of their moderate brothers and sisters, they have recognized the urgency of the moment and sensed the need for powerful "action" antidotes to combat the disease of segregation.

32   Let me take note of my other major disappointment. I have been so greatly disappointed with the white church and its leadership. Of course, there are some notable exceptions. I am not unmindful of the fact that each of you has taken some significant stands on this issue. I commend you, Reverend Stallings, for your Christian stand on this past Sunday, in welcoming Negroes to your worship service on a non-segregated basis. I commend the Catholic leaders of this state for integrating Spring Hill College several years ago.

33   But despite these notable exceptions, I must honestly reiterate that I have been disappointed with the church. I do not say this as one of those negative critics who can always find something wrong with the church. I say this as a minister of the gospel, who loves the church; who was nurtured in its bosom; who has been sustained by its spiritual blessings and who will remain true to it as long as the cord of life shall lengthen.

34   When I was suddenly catapulted into the leadership of the bus protest in Montgomery, Alabama, a few years ago, I felt we would be supported by the white church. I felt that the white ministers, priests and rabbis of the South would be among our strongest allies. Instead, some have been outright opponents, refusing to understand the freedom movement and misrepresenting its leaders all; an too many others have been more cautious than courageous and have remained silent behind the anesthetizing security of stained-glass windows.

35   In spite of my shattered dreams, I came to Birmingham with the hope that the white religious leadership of this community would see the justice of our cause and, with deep moral concern, would serve as the channel through which our just grievances could reach the power structure. I had hoped that each of you would understand. But again I have been disappointed.

36   I have heard numerous southern religious leaders admonish their worshipers to comply with a desegregation decision because it is the law, but I have longed to hear white ministers declare: "Follow this decree because integration is morally right and because the Negro is your brother." In the midst of blatant injustices inflicted upon the Negro, I have watched white churchmen stand on the sideline and mouth pious irrelevancies and sanctimonious trivialities. In the midst of a mighty struggle to rid our nation of racial and economic injustice, I have heard many ministers say: "Those are social issues, with which the gospel has no real concern." And I have watched many churches commit themselves to a completely other worldly religion which makes a strange, on Biblical distinction between body and soul, between the sacred and the secular.

37   I have traveled the length and breadth of Alabama, Mississippi and all the other southern states. On sweltering summer days and crisp autumn mornings I have looked at the South's beautiful churches with their lofty spires pointing heavenward. I have beheld the impressive outlines of her massive religious-education buildings. Over and over I have found myself asking: "What kind of people worship here? Who is their God? Where were their voices when the lips of Governor Barnett dripped with words of interposition and nullification? Where were they when Governor Wallace gave a clarion call for defiance and hatred? Where were their voices of support when bruised and weary Negro men and women decided to rise from the dark dungeons of complacency to the bright hills of creative protest?"

38   Yes, these questions are still in my mind. In deep disappointment I have wept over the laxity of the church. But be assured that my tears have been tears of love. There can be no deep disappointment where there is not deep love. Yes, I love the church. How could I do otherwise? I am in the rather unique position of being the son, the grandson and the great-grandson of preachers. Yes, I see the church as the body of Christ. But, oh! How we have blemished and scarred that body through social neglect and through fear of being nonconformists.

39   There was a time when the church was very powerful in the time when the early Christians rejoiced at being deemed worthy to suffer for what they believed. In those days the church was not merely a thermometer that recorded the ideas and principles of popular opinion; it was a thermostat that transformed the mores of society. Whenever the early Christians entered a town, the people in power became disturbed and immediately sought to convict the Christians for being "disturbers of the peace" and "outside agitators'" But the Christians pressed on, in the conviction that they were "a colony of heaven," called to obey God rather than man. Small in number, they were big in commitment. They were too God- intoxicated to be "astronomically intimidated." By their effort and example they brought an end to such ancient evils as infanticide. and gladiatorial contests.

40   Things are different now. So often the contemporary church is a weak, ineffectual voice with an uncertain sound. So often it is an archdefender of the status quo. Far from being disturbed by the presence of the church, the power structure of the average community is consoled by the church's silent—and often even vocal—sanction of things as they are.

41   But the judgment of God is upon the church as never before. If today's church does not recapture the sacrificial spirit of the early church, it will lose its authenticity, forfeit the loyalty of millions, and be dismissed as an irrelevant social club with no meaning for the twentieth century. Every day I meet young people whose disappointment with the church has turned into outright disgust.

42   Perhaps I have once again been too optimistic. Is organized religion too inextricably bound to the status quo to save our nation and the world? Perhaps I must turn my faith to the inner spiritual church, the church within the church, as the true ekklesia and the hope of the world. But again I am thankful to God that some noble souls from the ranks of organized religion have broken loose from the paralyzing chains of conformity

and joined us as active partners in the struggle for freedom, They have left their secure congregations and walked the streets of Albany, Georgia, with us. They have gone down the highways of the South on tortuous rides for freedom. Yes, they have gone to jail with us. Some have been dismissed from their churches, have lost the support of their bishops and fellow ministers. But they have acted in the faith that right defeated is stronger than evil triumphant. Their witness has been the spiritual salt that has preserved the true meaning of the gospel in these troubled times. They have carved a tunnel of hope through the dark mountain of disappointment.

43   I hope the church as a whole will meet the challenge of this decisive hour. But even if the church does not come to the aid of justice, I have no despair about the future. I have no fear about the outcome of our struggle in Birmingham, even if our motives are at present misunderstood. We will reach the goal of freedom in Birmingham and all over the nation, because the goal of America is freedom. Abused and scorned though we may be, our destiny is tied up with America's destiny. Before the pilgrims landed at Plymouth, we were here. Before the pen of Jefferson etched the majestic words of the Declaration of Independence across the pages of history, we were here. For more than two centuries our forebears labored in this country without wages; they made cotton king; they built the homes of their masters while suffering gross injustice and shameful humiliation—and yet out of a bottomless vitality they continued to thrive and develop. If the inexpressible cruelties of slavery could not stop us, the opposition we now face will surely fail. We will win our freedom because the sacred heritage of our nation and the eternal will of God are embodied in our echoing demands.

44   Before closing I feel impelled to mention one other point in your statement that has troubled me profoundly. You warmly commended the Birmingham police force for keeping "order" and "preventing violence." I doubt that you would have so warmly commended the police force if you had seen its dogs sinking their teeth into unarmed, nonviolent Negroes. I doubt that you would so quickly commend the policemen if you were to observe their ugly and inhumane treatment of Negroes here in the city jail; if you were to watch them push and curse old Negro women and young Negro girls; if you were to see them slap and kick old Negro men and young boys; if you were to observe them, as they did on two occasions, refuse to give us food because we wanted to sing our grace together. I cannot join you in your praise of the Birmingham police department.

45   It is true that the police have exercised a degree of discipline in handing the demonstrators. In this sense they have conducted themselves rather "nonviolently" in pubic. But for what purpose? To preserve the evil system of segregation. Over the past few years I have consistently preached that nonviolence demands that the means we use must be as pure as the ends we seek. I have tried to make clear that it is wrong to use immoral means to attain moral ends. But now I must affirm that it is just as wrong, or perhaps even more so, to use moral means to preserve immoral ends. Perhaps Mr. Connor and his policemen have been rather nonviolent in public, as was Chief Pritchett in Albany, Georgia but they have used the moral means of nonviolence to maintain the immoral end of racial injustice. As T. S. Eliot has said: "The last temptation is the greatest treason: To do the right deed for the wrong reason."

46   I wish you had commended the Negro sit-inners and demonstrators of Birmingham for their sublime courage, their willingness to suffer and their amazing discipline in the midst of great provocation. One day the South will recognize its real heroes. They will be the James Merediths, with the noble sense of purpose that enables them to face jeering and hostile mobs, and with the agonizing loneliness that characterizes the life of the pioneer. They will be old, oppressed, battered Negro women, symbolized in a seventy-two-year-old woman in Montgomery, Alabama, who rose up with a sense of dignity and with her people decided not to ride segregated buses, and who responded with ungrammatical profundity to one who inquired about her weariness: "My feets is tired, but my soul is at rest." They will be the young high school and college students, the young ministers of the gospel and a host of their elders, courageously and nonviolently sitting in at lunch counters and willingly going to jail for conscience' sake. One day the South will know that when these disinherited children of God sat down at lunch counters, they were in reality standing up for what is best in the American dream and for the most sacred values in our Judaeo-Christian heritage, thereby bringing our nation back to those great wells of democracy which were dug deep by the founding fathers in their formulation of the Constitution and the Declaration of Independence.

47   Never before have I written so long a letter. I'm afraid it is much too long to take your precious time. I can assure you that it would have been much is shorter if I had been writing from a comfortable desk, but what else can one do when he k alone in a narrow jail cell, other than write long letters, think long thoughts and pray long prayers?

48   If I have said anything in this letter that overstates the truth and indicates an unreasonable impatience, I beg you to forgive me. If I have said anything that understates the truth and indicates my having a patience that allows me to settle for anything less than brotherhood, I beg God to forgive me.

49   I hope this letter finds you strong in the faith. I also hope that circumstances will soon make it possible for me to meet each of you, not as an integrationist or a civil rights leader but as a fellow clergyman and a Christian brother. Let us all hope that the dark clouds of racial prejudice will soon pass away and the deep fog of misunderstanding will be lifted from our fear-drenched communities, and in some not too distant tomorrow the radiant stars of love and brotherhood will shine over our great nation with all their scintillating beauty.

Yours for the cause of Peace and Brotherhood,
MARTIN LUTHER KING, JR.

Critical Reading Questions:

- **Rhetorical analysis:** Write down the passages where King notes time, appeals to urgency, or questions the case for waiting? What pattern do you see? How does this appeal to *kairos* shape and inform his argument?

- **Summary:** What are the steps in a "nonviolent campaign," and how has King arrived at "direct action"?

- **Rhetorical analysis:** King writes as a clergyman to clergymen. Why? How does that change his appeal? What theological and Biblical evidence does he use?

What Writing Is

Stephen King

Ernest Hemingway famously wrote standing at a desk in his bedroom. Annie Dillard slides her writing chair "out into the middle of the air," so that "the desk and chair float thirty feet from the ground, between the crowns of maple trees." Stephen King writes "in a basement place where there are lots of bright lights and clear images." His is a "far-seeing place" where he can practice the "real telepathy" that is writing. In this article, an excerpt from *On Writing*, his 2000 memoir of craft, King makes an argument of definition and an argument of analogy. Like all of the best writers, he insists on precision (a cloth is "turkey red") and meets the reader in images. In June of 1999, King was walking on the shoulder of Route 5 in Lovell, Maine, when he was hit by a distracted driver. To repair his many injuries, he had five surgeries over the next ten days. The link between writing and living became all the more urgent when King returned to this book, and though his tone is informal, he makes a serious plea.

—MA

1   Telepathy, of course. It's amusing when you stop to think about it—for years people have argued about whether or not such a thing exists, folks like J. B. Rhine have busted their brains trying to create a valid testing process to isolate it, and all the time it's been right there, lying out in the open like Mr. Poe's Purloined Letter. All the arts depend upon telepathy to some degree, but I believe that writing offers the purest distillation. Perhaps I'm prejudiced, but even if I am we may as well stick with writing, since it's what we came here to think and talk about.

2   My name is Stephen King. I'm writing the first draft of this part at my desk (the one under the eave) on a snowy morning in December of 1997. There are things on my mind. Some are worries (bad eyes, Christmas shopping not even started, wife under the weather with a virus), some are good things (our younger son made a surprise visit home from college, I got to play Vince Taylor's "Brand New Cadillac" with The Wallflowers at a concert), but right now all that stuff is up top. I'm in another place, a basement place where there are lots of bright lights and clear images. This is a place I've built for myself over the years. It's a far-seeing place. I know it's a little strange, a little bit of a contradiction, that a far-seeing place should also be a basement place, but that's how it is with me. If you construct your own far-seeing place, you might put it in a treetop or on the roof of the World Trade Center or on the edge of the Grand Canyon. That's your little red wagon, as Robert McCammon says in one of his novels.

3   This book is scheduled to be published in the late summer or early fall of 2000. If that's how things work out, then you are somewhere downstream on the timeline from me ... but you're quite likely in your own far-seeing place, the one where you go to receive telepathic messages. Not that you *have* to be there; books are a uniquely portable

magic. I usually listen to one in the car (always unabridged; I think abridged audio-books are the pits), and carry another wherever I go. You just never know when you'll want an escape hatch: mile-long lines at tollbooth plazas, the fifteen minutes you have to spend in the hall of some boring college building waiting for your advisor (who's got some yank-off in there threatening to commit suicide because he/she is flunking Custom Kurmfurling 101) to come out so you can get his signature on a drop-card, airport boarding lounges, laundromats on rainy afternoons, and the absolute worst, which is the doctor's office when the guy is running late and you have to wait half an hour in order to have something sensitive mauled. At such times I find a book vital. If I have to spend time in purgatory before going to one place or the other, I guess I'll be all right as long as there's a lending library (if there is it's probably stocked with nothing but novels by Danielle Steel and *Chicken Soup* books, ha-ha, joke's on you, Steve).

4   So I read where I can, but I have a favorite place and probably you do, too—a place where the light is good and the vibe is unusually strong. For me it's the blue chair in my study. For you it might be the couch on the sunporch, the rocket in the kitchen, or maybe it's propped up in your bed—reading in bed can be heaven, assuming you can get just the right amount of light on the page and aren't prone to spilling your coffee or cognac on the sheets.

5   So let's assume that you're in your favorite receiving place just as I am in the place where I do my best transmitting. We'll have to perform our mentalist routine not just over distance but over time as well, yet that presents no real problem; if we can still read Dickens, Shakespeare, and (with the help of a footnote or two) Herodotus, I think we can manage the gap between 1997 and 2000. And here we go—actual telepathy in action. You'll notice I have nothing up my sleeves and that my lips never move. Neither, most likely, do yours.

6   Look—here's a table covered with a red cloth. On it is a cage the size of a small fish aquarium. In the cage is a white rabbit with a pink nose and pink-rimmed eyes. In its front paws is a carrot-stub upon which it is contentedly munching. On its back, clearly marked in blue ink, is the numeral 8.

7   Do we see the same thing? We'd have to get together and compare notes to make absolutely sure, but I think we do. There will be necessary variations, of course: some receivers will see a cloth which is turkey red, some will see one that's scarlet, while others may see still other shades. (To colorblind receivers, the red tablecloth is the dark gray of cigar ashes.) Some may see scalloped edges, some may see straight ones. Decorative souls may add a little lace, and welcome—my tablecloth is your tablecloth, knock yourself out.

8   Likewise, the matter of the cage leaves quite a lot of room for individual interpretation. For one thing, it is described in terms of *rough comparison*, which is useful only if you and I see the world and measure the things in it with similar eyes. It's easy to become careless when making rough comparisons, but the alternative is a prissy attention to detail that takes all the fun out of writing. What am I going to say, "on the table is a cage three feet, six inches in length, two feet in width, and fourteen inches high"? That's not prose, that's

an instruction manual. The paragraph also doesn't tell us what sort of material the cage is made of—wire mesh? steel rods? glass?—but does it really matter? We all understand the cage is a see-through medium; beyond that, we don't care. The most interesting thing here isn't even the carrot-munching rabbit in the cage, but the number on its back. Not a six, not a four, not nineteen-point-five. It's an eight. This is what were looking at, and we all see it. I didn't tell you. You didn't ask me. I never opened my mouth and you never opened yours. We're not even in the same year together, let alone the same room . . . except we *are* together. We're close.

9   We're having a meeting of the minds.

10   I sent you a table with a red cloth on it, a cage, a rabbit, and the number eight in blue ink. You got them all, especially that blue eight. We've engaged in an act of telepathy. No mythy-mountain shit; real telepathy. I'm not going to belabor the point, but before we go any further you have to understand that I'm not trying to be cute; there is a point to be made.

11   You can approach the act of writing with nervousness, excitement, hopefulness, or even despair—the sense that you can never completely put on the page what's in your mind and heart. You can come to the act with your fists clenched and your eyes narrowed, ready to kick ass and take down names. You can come to it because you want a girl to marry you or because you want to change the world. Come to it any way but lightly. Let me say it again: *you must not come lightly to the blank page.*

12   I'm not asking you to come reverently or unquestioningly; I'm not asking you to be politically correct or cast aside your sense of humor (please God you have one). This isn't a popularity contest, it's not the moral Olympics, and it's not church. But it's *writing*, damn it, not washing the car or putting on eyeliner. If you can take it seriously, we can do business. If you can't or won't, it's time for you to close the book and do something else.

13   Wash the car, maybe.

Critical Reading Questions:

- **Analysis:** King asks the reader to think of writing as work that is set apart. If you want to write, you must take it seriously, he argues. Where in the text do you find evidence of his own serious commitment to writing and reading?

- **Rhetorical analysis:** "Look—here's a table covered with a red cloth," King writes; then he sharpens and complicates that image. How is this passage different from the rest of the essay? What do images do? In what way are they real? Why does writing become more vivid when an author appeals to a reader's senses?

- **Interpretation:** Where does King make an appeal to the timelessness of writing and the way that it creates a communion between strangers? How is this sort of writing different from an "instruction manual"?

Shitty First Drafts

Anne Lamott

In this piece, Anne Lamott reflects on the writing process while emphasizing the importance of revision. She has published both novels and non-fiction—on such diverse subjects as alcoholism, single-motherhood, depression, and Christianity. Lamott uses wit and humor to drive "Shitty First Drafts," while informing readers about her writing process and the multi-draft processes of other writers that she knows (except for that one writer, "but we do not like her very much"). Lamott says while working as a food critic, she would agonize over her reviews and her experiences while writing her initial drafts. She uses personal narrative to examine her revision process and writing frustrations. Lamott acknowledges roadblocks in the writing process, while also discussing ways to address those obstacles. Her tongue-in-cheek approach makes her multiple-draft argument palatable to writers who just wish they could write the perfect draft the first time.

—BLS

[handwritten: It doesn't have to be perfect the first time.]

1   Now, practically even better news than that of short assignments is the idea of shitty first drafts. All good writers write them. This is how they end up with good second drafts and terrific third drafts. People tend to look at successful writers, writers who are getting their books published and maybe even doing well financially, and think that they sit down at their desks every morning feeling like a million dollars, feeling great about who they are and how much talent they have and what a great story they have to tell; that they take in a few deep breaths, push back their sleeves, roll their necks a few times to get all the cricks out, and dive in, typing fully formed passages as fast as a court reporter. But this is just the fantasy of the uninitiated. I know some very great writers, writers you love who write beautifully and have made a great deal of money, and not one of them sits down routinely feeling wildly enthusiastic and confident. Not one of them writes elegant first drafts. All right, one of them does, but we do not like her very much. We do not think that she has a rich inner life or that God likes her or can even stand her. (Although when I mentioned this to my priest friend Tom, he said you can safely assume you've created God in your own image when it turns out that God hates all the same people you do.)

2   Very few writers really know what they are doing until they've done it. Nor do they go about their business feeling dewy and thrilled. They do not type a few stiff warm-up sentences and then find themselves bounding along like huskies across the snow. One writer I know tells me that he sits down every morning and says to himself nicely, "It's not like you don't have a choice, because you do—you can either type or kill yourself." We all often feel like we are pulling teeth, even those writers whose prose ends up being the most natural and fluid. The right words and sentences just do not come pouring out like ticker tape most of the time. Now, Muriel Spark is said to have felt that she was taking dictation from God every morning—sitting there, one supposes, plugged into a Dictaphone, typing

away, humming. But this is a very hostile and aggressive position. One might hope for bad things to rain down on a person like this.

3   For me and most of the other writers I know, writing is not rapturous. In fact, the only way I can get anything written at all is to write really, really shitty first drafts. The first draft is the child's draft, where you let it all pour out and then let it romp all over the place, knowing that no one is going to see it and that you can shape it later. You just let this childlike part of you channel whatever voices and visions come through and onto the page. If one of the characters wants to say, "Well, so what, Mr. Poopy Pants?," you let her. No one is going to see it. If the kid wants to get into really sentimental, weepy, emotional territory, you let him. Just get it all down on paper, because there may be something great in those six crazy pages that you would never have gotten to by more rational, grown-up means. There may be something in the very last line of the very last paragraph on page six that you just love, that is so beautiful or wild that you now know what you're supposed to be writing about, more or less, or in what direction you might go—but there was no way to get to this without first getting through the first five and a half pages.

4   I used to write food reviews for *California* magazine before it folded. (My writing food reviews had nothing to do with the magazine folding, although every single review did cause a couple of canceled subscriptions. Some readers took umbrage at my comparing mounds of vegetable puree with various ex-presidents' brains.) These reviews always took two days to write. First I'd go to a restaurant several times with a few opinionated, articulate friends in tow. I'd sit there writing down everything anyone said that was at all interesting or funny. Then on the following Monday I'd sit down at my desk with my notes, and try to write the review. Even after I'd been doing this for years, panic would set in. I'd try to write a lead, but instead I'd write a couple of dreadful sentences, xx them out, try again, xx everything out, and then feel despair and worry settle on my chest like an x-ray apron. It's over, I'd think, calmly. I'm not going to be able to get the magic to work this time. I'm ruined. I'm through. I'm toast. Maybe, I'd think, I can get my old job back as a clerk-typist. But probably not. I'd get up and study my teeth in the mirror for a while. Then I'd stop, remember to breathe, make a few phone calls, hit the kitchen and chow down. Eventually I'd go back and sit down at my desk, and sigh for the next ten minutes.

5   Finally I would pick up my one-inch picture frame, stare into it as if for the answer, and every time the answer would come: all I had to do was to write a really shitty first draft of, say, the opening paragraph. And no one was going to see it. So I'd start writing without reining myself in. It was almost just typing, just making my fingers move. And the writing would be terrible. I'd write a lead paragraph that was a whole page, even though the entire review could only be three pages long, and then I'd start writing up descriptions of the food, one dish at a time, bird by bird, and the critics would be sitting on my shoulders, commenting like cartoon characters. They'd be pretending to snore, or rolling their eyes at my overwrought descriptions, no matter how hard I tried to tone those descriptions down, no matter how conscious I was of what a friend said to me gently in my early days of restaurant reviewing. "Annie," she said, "it is just a piece of chicken. It is just a bit of cake."

6   But because by then I had been writing for so long, I would eventually let myself trust the process—sort of, more or less. I'd write a first draft that was maybe twice as long

even pros get writers block

as it should be, with a self-indulgent and boring beginning, stupefying descriptions of the meal, lots of quotes from my black-humored friends that made them sound more like the Manson girls than food lovers, and no ending to speak of. The whole thing would be so long and incoherent and hideous that for the rest of the day I'd obsess about getting creamed by a car before I could write a decent second draft. I'd worry that people would read what I'd written and believe that the accident had really been a suicide, that I had panicked because my talent was waning and my mind was shot.

7 The next day, though, I'd sit down, go through it all with a colored pen, take out everything I possibly could, find a new lead somewhere on the second page, figure out a kicky place to end it, and then write a second draft. It always turned out fine, sometimes even funny and weird and helpful. I'd go over it one more time and mail it in. Then, a month later, when it was time for another review, the whole process would start again, complete with the fears that people would find my first draft before I could rewrite it.

8 Almost all good writing begins with terrible first efforts. You need to start somewhere. Start by getting something—anything—down on paper. A friend of mine says that the first draft is the down draft—you just get it down. The second draft is the up draft—you fix it up. You try to say what you have to say more accurately. And the third draft is the dental draft, where you check every tooth, to see if it's loose or cramped or decayed, or even, God help us, healthy.

9 What I've learned to do when I sit down to work on a shitty first draft is to quiet the voices in my head. First there's the vinegar-lipped Reader Lady, who says primly, "Well, that's not very interesting, is it?" And there's the emaciated German male who writes these Orwellian memos detailing your thought crimes. And there are your parents, agonizing over your lack of loyalty and discretion; and there's William Burroughs, dozing off or shooting up because he finds you as bold and articulate as a houseplant; and so on. And there are also the dogs; let's not forget the dogs, the dogs in their pen who will surely hurtle and snarl their way out if you ever stop writing, because writing is, for some of us, the latch that keeps the door of the pen closed, keeps those crazy ravenous dogs contained.

10 Quieting those voices is at least half the battle I fight daily. But this is better than it used to be. It used to be 87 percent. Left to its own devices, my mind spends much of its time having conversations with people who aren't there. I walk along defending myself to people, or exchanging repartee with them, or rationalizing my behavior, or seducing them with gossip, or pretending I'm on their TV talk show or whatever. I speed or run an aging yellow light or don't come to a full stop, and one nanosecond later am explaining to imaginary cops exactly why I had to do what I did, or insisting that I did not in fact do it.

11 I happened to mention this to a hypnotist I saw many years ago, and he looked at me very nicely. At first I thought he was feeling around on the floor for the silent alarm button, but then he gave me the following exercise, which I still use to this day. Close your eyes and get quiet for a minute, until the chatter starts up. Then isolate one of the voices and imagine the person speaking as a mouse. Pick it up by the tail and drop it into a mason jar. Then isolate another voice, pick it up by the tail, drop it in the jar. And so on. Drop in any high-maintenance parental units, drop in any contractors, lawyers, colleagues, children, anyone who is whining in your head. Then put the lid on, and watch all these mouse

people clawing at the glass, jabbering away, trying to make you feel like shit because you won't do what they want—won't give them more money, won't be more successful, won't see them more often. Then imagine that there is a volume-control button on the bottle. Turn it all the way up for a moment, and listen to the stream of angry, neglected, guilt-mongering voices. Then turn it all the way down and watch the frantic mice lunge at the glass, trying to get to you. Leave it down, and get back to your shitty first draft.

12   A writer friend of mine suggests opening the jar and shooting them all in the head. But I think he's a little angry, and I'm sure nothing like this would ever occur to you.

Igit frustrated writing too.

Critical Reading Questions:

- **Rhetorical analysis:** Several times in the article Lamott uses profanity. What is the rhetorical effect of using this language? Is this an emotional appeal? Does this make her ethos more approachable, or does it undermine her authority?

- **Analysis:** Lamott shifts from first person to second person to third person. What is the effect of these shifts? Who, specifically, is the "you" that she is constructing as her intended audience?

- **Reflection:** What are your thoughts about Lamott's writing process? How do you feel about writing a draft that "maybe twice as long as it should be" yet treating this initial writing as merely a "shitty first draft"?

The Gettysburg Address

Abraham Lincoln

Abraham Lincoln was a humble man born in a log cabin in Kentucky and self-educated, yet he was one of our greatest presidents. His combination of intelligence and common sense are clearly evident in his rhetoric, especially in "The Gettysburg Address," the speech he delivered four months after the battle of Gettysburg, Pennsylvania, at the battlefield graveyard where 51,000 soldiers had been killed or wounded. The Union troops had managed a victory that became the turning point of the Civil War. In this speech, delivered on November 19th, 1863, Lincoln calls upon the American principle of human equality articulated in the Declaration of Independence and reframes the Civil War as a struggle for that principle, constructing his arguments around the themes of life, death, and rebirth. In spite of his assertion that the "world will little note nor long remember" this speech, the speech is one of the iconic American texts.

—SF

Gettysburg, Pennsylvania
November 19, 1863

1   Four score and seven years ago our fathers brought forth on this continent, a new nation, conceived in Liberty, and dedicated to the proposition that all men are created equal.

2   Now we are engaged in a great civil war, testing whether that nation, or any nation so conceived and so dedicated, can long endure. We are met on a great battle-field of that war. We have come to dedicate a portion of that field, as a final resting place for those who here gave their lives that that nation might live. It is altogether fitting and proper that we should do this.

3   But, in a larger sense, we can not dedicate—we can not consecrate—we can not hallow—this ground. The brave men, living and dead, who struggled here, have consecrated it, far above our poor power to add or detract. The world will little note, nor long remember what we say here, but it can never forget what they did here. It is for us the living, rather, to be dedicated here to the unfinished work which they who fought here have thus far so nobly advanced. It is rather for us to be here dedicated to the great task remaining before us—that from these honored dead we take increased devotion to that cause for which they gave the last full measure of devotion—that we here highly resolve that these dead shall not have died in vain—that this nation, under God, shall have a new birth of freedom and that government of the people, by the people, for the people, shall not perish from the earth.

Critical Reading Questions:

- **Rhetorical analysis:** How do Lincoln's connections of the past and future to the present function as rhetorical appeals?

- **Rhetorical analysis:** What words does Lincoln repeat, and what is the persuasive effect of doing so?

- **Rhetorical analysis:** Where do you see parallel structure? How might this structure serve to underscore Lincoln's rhetorical purpose?

With These Words, I Can Sell You Anything

William Lutz

In "With These Words, I Can Sell You Anything," an excerpt from William Lutz's book *Doublespeak*, the author explains the many tactics advertisers use when trying to sell their products. Lutz is a retired English professor; his primary purpose in this text is to uncover and lay bare the rhetorical strategies of advertisers that often conceal the true product or embellish its effectiveness. This analysis of advertising techniques focuses on "weasel words," a term coined by Theodore Roosevelt in 1916 to characterize empty governmental rhetoric. Lutz elaborates the various forms of discursive deception related to this broad concept, including unfinished words, rhetorical questions, and action weasel words, as well as suspect appeals involving technology and pseudoscience claims. His essay functions as a consumer-friendly guide to detecting and deflecting language that is carefully designed to "push our buttons" psychologically speaking.

—KH, WCM

1   One problem advertisers have when they try to convince you that the product they are pushing is really different from other, similar products is that their claims are subject to some laws. Not a lot of laws, but there are some designed to prevent fraudulent or untruthful claims in advertising. Even during the happy years of nonregulation under President Ronald Reagan, the FTC did crack down on the more blatant abuses in advertising claims. Generally speaking, advertisers have to be careful in what they say in their ads, in the claims they make for the products they advertise. Parity claims are safe because they are legal and supported by a number of court decisions. But beyond parity claims there are weasel words.

2   Advertisers use weasel words to appear to be making a claim for a product when in fact they are making no claim at all. Weasel words get their name from the way weasels eat the eggs they find in the nests of other animals. A weasel will make a small hole in the egg, suck out the insides, then place the egg back in the nest. Only when the egg is examined closely is it found to be hollow. That's the way it is with weasel words in advertising: Examine weasel words closely and you'll find that they're as hollow as any egg sucked by a weasel. Weasel words appear to say one thing when in fact they say the opposite, or nothing at all.

"Help"—The Number One Weasel Word

3   The biggest weasel word used in advertising doublespeak is "help." Now "help" only means to aid or assist, nothing more. It does not mean to conquer, stop, eliminate, end, solve, heal, cure, or anything else. But once the ad says "help," it can say just about anything after that because "help" qualifies everything coming after it. The trick is that the claim that comes after the weasel word is usually so strong and so dramatic that you

forget the word "help" and concentrate only on the dramatic claim. You read into the ad a message that the ad does not contain. More importantly, the advertiser is not responsible for the claim that you read into the ad, even though the advertiser wrote the ad so you would read that claim into it.

4   The next time you see an ad for a cold medicine that promises that it "helps relieve cold symptoms fast," don't rush out to buy it. Ask yourself what this claim is really saying. Remember, "helps" means only that the medicine will aid or assist. What will it aid or assist in doing? Why, "relieve your cold symptoms." "Relieve" only means to ease, alleviate, or mitigate, not to stop, end, or cure. Nor does the claim say how much relieving this medicine will do. Nowhere does this ad claim it will cure anything. In fact, the ad doesn't even claim it will do anything at all. The ad only claims that it will aid in relieving (not curing) your cold symptoms, which are probably a runny nose, watery eyes, and a headache. In other words, this medicine probably contains a standard decongestant and some aspirin. By the way, what does "fast" mean? Ten minutes, one hour, one day? What is fast to one person can be very slow to another. Fast is another weasel word.

5   Ad claims using "help" are among the most popular ads. One says, "Helps keep you young looking," but then a lot of things will help keep you young looking, including exercise, rest, good nutrition, and a facelift. More importantly, this ad doesn't say the product will keep you young, only "young looking." Someone may look young to one person and old to another.

6   A toothpaste ad says, "Helps prevent cavities," but it doesn't say it will actually prevent cavities. Brushing your teeth regularly, avoiding sugars in food, and flossing daily will also help prevent cavities. A liquid cleaner ad says, "Helps keep your home germ free," but it doesn't say it actually kills germs, nor does it even specify which germs it might kill.

7   "Help" is such a useful weasel word that it is often combined with other action-verb weasel words such as "fight" and "control." Consider the claim, "Helps control dandruff symptoms with regular use." What does it really say? It will assist in controlling (not eliminating, stopping, ending, or curing) the symptoms of dandruff, not the cause of dandruff nor the dandruff itself. What are the symptoms of dandruff? The ad deliberately leaves that undefined, but assume that the symptoms referred to in the ad are the flaking and itching commonly associated with dandruff. But just shampooing with any shampoo will temporarily eliminate these symptoms, so this shampoo isn't any different from any other. Finally, in order to benefit from this product, you must use it regularly. What is "regular use"—daily, weekly, hourly? Using another shampoo "regularly" will have the same effect. Nowhere does this advertising claim say this particular shampoo stops, eliminates, or cures dandruff. In fact, this claim says nothing at all, thanks to all the weasel words.

8   Look at ads in magazines and newspapers, listen to ads on radio and television, and you'll find the word "help" in ads for all kinds of products. How often do you read or hear such phrases as "helps stop," "helps overcome," "helps eliminate ...," "helps you feel ...," or "helps you look ..."? If you start looking for this weasel word in advertising, you'll be amazed at how often it occurs. Analyze the claims in the ads using "help," and you will discover that these ads are really saying nothing.

9   There are plenty of other weasel words used in advertising. In fact, there are so many that to list them all would fill the rest of this book. But in order to identify the doublespeak of advertising and understand the real meaning of an ad, you have to be aware of the most popular weasel words in advertising today

Virtually Spotless

10   One of the most powerful weasel words is "virtually," a word so innocent that most people don't pay any attention to it when it is used in an advertising claim. But watch out. "Virtually" is used in advertising claims that appear to make specific, definite promises when there is no promise. After all, what does "virtually" mean? It means "in essence or effect, although not in fact." Look at that definition again. "Virtually" means not in fact. It does not mean "almost" or "just about the same as," or anything else. And before you dismiss all this concern over such a small word, remember that small words can have big consequences.

11   In 1971 a federal court rendered its decision on a case brought by a woman who became pregnant while taking birth control pills. She sued the manufacturer, Eli Lilly and Company, for breach of warranty. The woman lost her case. Basing its ruling on a statement in the pamphlet accompanying the pills, which stated that, "When taken as directed, the tablets offer virtually 100% protection," the court ruled that there was no warranty, expressed or implied, that the pills were absolutely effective. In its ruling, the court pointed out that, according to Webster's Third New International Dictionary, "virtually" means "almost entirely" and clearly does not mean "absolute" (Whittington v. Eli Lilly and Company 333 F. Supp. 9S). In other words, the Eli Lilly company was really saying that its birth control pill, even when taken as directed, did not in fact provide 100 percent protection against pregnancy. But Eli Lilly didn't want to put it that way because then many women might not have bought Lilly's birth control pills.

12   The next time you see the ad that says that this dishwasher detergent "leaves dishes virtually spotless," just remember how advertisers twist the meaning of the weasel word "virtually." You can have lots of spots on your dishes after using this detergent and the ad claim will still be true, because what this claim really means is that this detergent does not in fact leave your dishes spotless. Whenever you see or hear an ad claim that uses the word "virtually," just translate that claim into its real meaning. So the television set that is "virtually trouble free" becomes the television set that is not in fact trouble free, the "virtually foolproof operation" of any appliance becomes an operation that is in fact not foolproof, and the product that "virtually never needs service" becomes the product that is not in fact service free.

New and Improved

13   If "new" is the most frequently used word on a product package, "improved" is the second most frequent. In fact, the two words are almost always used together. It seems just about everything sold these days is "new and improved." The next time you're in the supermarket, try counting the number of times you see these words on products. But

you'd better do it while you're walking down just one aisle, otherwise you'll need a calcula-tor to keep track of your counting.

14   Just what do these words mean? The use of the word "new" is restricted by regula-tions, so an advertiser can't just use the word on a product or in an ad without meeting certain requirements. For example, a product is considered new for about six months dur-ing a national advertising campaign. If the product is being advertised only in a limited test market area, the word can be used longer, and in some instances has been used for as long as two years.

15   What makes a product "new"? Some products have been around for a long time, yet every once in a while you discover that they are being advertised as "new." Well, an advertiser can call a product new if there has been "a material functional change" in the product. What is "a material functional change," you ask? Good question. In fact it's such a good question it's being asked all the time. It's up to the manufacturer to prove that the product has undergone such a change. And if the manufacturer isn't challenged on the claim, then there's no one to stop it. Moreover, the change does not have to be an improvement in the product. One manufacturer added an artificial lemon scent to a clean-ing product and called it "new and improved," even though the product did not clean any better than without the lemon scent. The manufacturer defended the use of the word "new" on the grounds that the artificial scent changed the chemical formula of the prod-uct and therefore constituted "a material functional change."

16   Which brings up the word "improved." When used in advertising, "improved" does not mean "made better." It only means "changed" or "different from before." So, if the detergent maker puts a plastic pour spout on the box of detergent, the product has been "improved," and away we go with a whole new advertising campaign. Or, if the cereal maker adds more fruit or a different kind of fruit to the cereal, there's an improved product. Now you know why manufacturers are constantly making little changes in their products. Whole new advertising campaigns, designed to convince you that the product has been changed for the better, are based on small changes in superficial aspects of a product. The next time you see an ad for an "improved" product, ask yourself what was wrong with the old one. Ask yourself just how "improved" the product is. Finally, you might check to see whether the "improved" version costs more than the unimproved one. After all, some-one has to pay for all the millions of dollars spent advertising the improved product.

17   Of course, advertisers really like to run ads that claim a product is "new and improved." While what constitutes a "new" product may be subject to some regulation, "improved" is a subjective judgment. A manufacturer changes the shape of its stick deodorant, but the shape doesn't improve the function of the deodorant. That is, changing the shape doesn't affect the deodorizing ability of the deodorant, so the manufacturer calls it "improved." Another manufacturer adds ammonia to its liquid cleaner and calls it "new and improved." Since adding ammonia does affect the cleaning ability of the product, there has been a "material functional change" in the product and the manufacturer can now call its cleaner "new," and "improved" as well. Now the weasel words "new and improved" are plastered all over the package and are the basis for a multimillion-dollar ad campaign. But after six months the word "new" will have to go, until someone can dream up another change in the

product. Perhaps it will be adding color to the liquid, or changing the shape of the package, or maybe adding a new dripless pour spout, or perhaps—the "improvements" are endless and so are the new advertising claims and campaigns.

18   "New" is just too useful and powerful a word in advertising for advertisers to pass it up easily. So they use weasel words that say "new" without really saying it. One of their favorites is "Introducing," as in, "Introducing improved Tide," or "Introducing the stain remover." The first is simply saying here's our improved soap; the second here's our new advertising campaign for our detergent. Another favorite is "now," as in "Now there's Sinex," which simply means that Sinex is available. Then there are phrases like "Today's Chevrolet" and "Presenting Dristan," and "A fresh way to start the day." The list is really endless because advertisers are always finding new ways to say "new" without really saying it. If there is a second edition of this book I'll call it the "new and improved" edition. Wouldn't you really rather have a "new and improved" edition of this book rather than a "second edition"?

Acts Fast

19   "Acts" and "works" are two popular weasel words in advertising because they bring action to the product and to the advertising claim. When you see the ad for the cough syrup that "Acts on the cough control center," ask yourself what this cough syrup is claiming to do. Well, it's just claiming to "act," to do something, to perform an action. What is it that the cough syrup does? The ad doesn't say. It only claims to perform an action or do something on your "cough control center." By the way, what and where is your "cough control center"? I don't remember learning about that part of the body in human biology class.

20   Ads that use such phrases as "acts fast," "acts against," "acts to prevent," and the like are saying essentially nothing because "act" is a word empty of any specific meaning. The ads are always careful not to specify exactly what "act" the product performs. Just because a brand of aspirin claims to "act fast" for headache relief doesn't mean this aspirin is any better than any other aspirin. What is the "act" that this aspirin performs? You're never told. Maybe it just dissolves quickly. Since aspirin is a parity product all aspirin is the same and therefore functions the same.

Works Like Anything Else

21   If you don't find the word "acts" in an ad, you will probably find the weasel word "works." In fact, the two words are almost interchangeable in advertising. Watch out for ads that say a product "works against," "works like," "works for," or "works longer."

22   As with "acts," "works" is the same meaningless verb used to make you think that this product really does something, and maybe even something special or unique. But "works," like "acts," is basically a word empty of any specific meaning.

Like Magic

23   Whenever advertisers want you to stop thinking about the product and to start thinking about something bigger, better, or more attractive than the product they use that very popular weasel word, "like." The word "like" is the advertiser's equivalent of a magician's use of misdirection. "Like" gets you to ignore the product and concentrate on the claim the

advertiser is making about it. "For skin like peaches and cream" claims the ad for a skin cream. What is this ad really claiming? It doesn't say this cream will give you peaches-and-cream skin. There is no verb in this claim, so it doesn't even mention using the product. How is skin ever like "peaches and cream"? Remember, ads must be read literally and exactly, according to the dictionary definition of words. (Remember "virtually" in the Eli Lilly case.) The ad is making absolutely no promise or claim whatsoever for this skin cream. If you think this cream will give you soft, smooth, youthful-looking skin, you are the one who has read that meaning into the ad.

24   The wine that claims "It's like taking a trip to France" wants you to think about a romantic evening in Paris as you walk along the boulevard after a wonderful meal in an intimate little bistro. Of course, you don't really believe that a wine can take you to France, but the goal of the ad is to get you to think pleasant romantic thoughts about France and not about how the wine tastes or how expensive it may be. That little word "like" has taken you away from crushed grapes into a world of your own imaginative making. Who knows, maybe the next time you buy wine, you'll think those pleasant thoughts when you see this brand of wine, and you'll buy it. Or, maybe you weren't even thinking about buying wine at all, but now you just might pick up a bottle the next time you're shopping. Ah, the power of "like" in advertising.

25   How about the most famous "like" claim of all, "Winston tastes good like a cigarette should"? Ignoring the grammatical error here, you might want to know what this claim is saying. Whether a cigarette tastes good or bad is a subjective judgment because what tastes good to one person may well taste horrible to another. Not everyone likes fried snails, even if they are called escargot. (*De gustibus non est disputandum*, which was probably the Roman rule for advertising as well as for defending the games in the Colosseum.) There are many people who say all cigarettes taste terrible, other people who say only some cigarettes taste all right, and still others who say all cigarettes taste good. Who's right? Everyone, because taste is a matter of personal judgment.

26   Moreover, note the use of the conditional, "should." The complete claim is "Winston tastes good like a cigarette should taste." But should cigarettes taste "good"? Again, this is a matter of personal judgment and probably depends most on one's experiences with smoking. So, the Winston ad is simply saying that Winston cigarettes are just like any other cigarette: Some people like them and some people don't. On that statement R. J. Reynolds conducted a very successful multimillion-dollar advertising campaign that helped keep Winston the number-two-selling cigarette in the United States, close behind number one, Marlboro.

Can It Be Up to the Claim?

27   Analyzing ads for doublespeak requires that you pay attention to every word in the ad and determine what each word really means. Advertisers try to wrap their claims in language that sounds concrete, specific, and objective, when in fact the language of advertising is anything but. Your job is to read carefully and listen critically so that when the announcer says that Crest "can be" of "significant value" you know immediately that this claim says absolutely nothing. Where is the doublespeak in this ad? Start with the second word.

28   Once again, you have to look at what words really mean, not what you think they mean or what the advertiser wants you to think they mean. The ad for Crest only says that using Crest "can be" of "significant value." What really throws you off in this ad is the brilliant use of "significant." It draws your attention to the word "value" and makes you forget that the ad only claims that Crest "can be." The ad doesn't say that Crest is of value, only that it is "able" or "possible" to be of value, because that's all that "can" means.

29   It's so easy to miss the importance of those little words "can be." Almost as easy as missing the importance of the words "up to" in an ad. These words are very popular in sale ads. You know, the ones that say, "Up to 50% off!" Now, what does that claim mean? Not much, because the store or manufacturer has to reduce the price of only a few items by 50 percent. Everything else can be reduced a lot less, or not even reduced. Moreover, don't you want to know, 50 percent off of what? Is it 50 percent off the "manufacturer's suggested list price," which is the highest possible price? Was the price artificially inflated and then reduced? In other ads, "up to" expresses an ideal situation. The medicine that works "up to ten times faster," the battery that lasts "up to twice as long," and the soap that gets you "up to twice as clean" all are based on ideal situations for using those products, situations in which you can be sure you will never find yourself.

Unfinished Words

30   Unfinished words are a kind of "up to" claim in advertising. The claim that a battery lasts "up to twice as long" usually doesn't finish the comparison twice as long as what? A birthday candle? A tank of gas? A cheap battery made in a country not noted for its technological achievements? The implication is that the battery lasts twice as long as batteries made by other battery makers, or twice as long as earlier model batteries made by the advertiser, but the ad doesn't really make these claims. You read these claims into the ad, aided by the visual images the advertiser so carefully provides.

31   Unfinished words depend on you to finish them, to provide the words the advertisers so thoughtfully left out of the ad. Pall Mall cigarettes were once advertised as "A longer finer and milder smoke. The question is, longer, finer, and milder than what? The aspirin that claims it contains "twice as much of the pain reliever doctors recommend most" doesn't tell you what pain reliever it contains twice as much of. (By the way, it's aspirin. That's right; it just contains twice the amount of aspirin. And how much is twice the amount? Twice of what amount?) Panadol boasts that "nobody reduces fever faster," but, since Panadol is a parity product, this claim simply means that Panadol isn't any better than any other product in its parity class. "You can be sure if it's Westinghouse," you're told, but just exactly what it is you can be sure of is never mentioned. "Magnavox gives you more" doesn't tell you what you get more of. More value? More television? More than they gave you before? It sounds nice, but it means nothing, until you fill in the claim with your own words, the words the advertiser didn't use. Since each of us fills in the claim differently, the ad and the product can become all things to all people, and not promise a single thing.

32   Unfinished words abound in advertising because they appear to promise so much. More importantly, they can be joined with powerful visual images on television to appear

to be making significant promises about a product's effectiveness without really making any promises. In a television ad, the aspirin product that claims fast relief can show a person with a headache taking the product and then, in what appears to be a matter of minutes, claiming complete relief. This visual image is far more powerful than any claim made in unfinished words. Indeed, the visual image completes the unfinished words for you, filling in with pictures what the words leave out. And you thought the ads didn't affect you. What brand of aspirin do you use?

33   Some years ago, Ford's advertisements proclaimed "Ford LTD—700% quieter." Now, what do you think Ford was claiming with these unfinished words? What was the Ford LTD quieter than? A Cadillac? A Mercedes Benz? BMW? Well, when the FTC asked Ford to substantiate this unfinished claim, Ford replied that it meant that the inside of the LTD was 700% quieter than its outside. How did you finish those unfinished words when you first read them? Did you even come close to Ford's meaning?

Combining Weasel Words

34   A lot of ads don't fall neatly into one category or another because they use a variety of different devices and words. Different weasel words are often combined to make an ad claim. The claim, "Coffee-Mate gives coffee more body, more flavor," uses Unfinished Words ("more" than what?) and also uses words that have no specific meaning ("body" and "flavor"). Along with "taste" (remember the Winston ad and its claim to taste good), "body" and "flavor" mean nothing because their meaning is entirely subjective. To you, "body" in coffee might mean thick, black, almost bitter coffee, while I might take it to mean a light brown, delicate coffee. Now, if you think you understood that last sentence, read it again because it said nothing of objective value; it was filled with weasel words of no specific meaning: "thick," "black," "bitter," "light brown," and "delicate." Each of those words has no specific objective meaning, because each of us can interpret them differently.

35   Try this slogan: "Looks, smells, tastes like ground-roast coffee." So are you now going to buy Taster's Choice instant coffee because of this ad? "Looks," "smells," and "tastes" are all words with no specific meaning and depend on your interpretation of them for any meaning. Then there's that great weasel word "like," which simply suggests a comparison but does not make the actual connection between the product and the quality. Besides, do you know what "ground-roast" coffee is? I don't, but it sure sounds good. So, out of seven words in this ad, four are definite weasel words, two are quite meaningless, and only one has any clear meaning.

36   Remember the Anacin ad—"twice as much of the pain reliever doctors recommend most"? There's a whole lot of weaseling going on in this ad. First what's the pain reliever they're talking about in this ad? Aspirin, of course. In fact, any time you see or hear an ad using those words "pain reliever" you can automatically substitute the word "aspirin" for them. (Makers of acetaminophen and ibuprofen pain relievers are careful in their advertising to identify their products as nonaspirin products.) So, now we know that Anacin has aspirin in it. Moreover, we know that Anacin has twice as much aspirin in it but we don't know twice as much as what. Does it have twice as much aspirin as an ordinary aspirin tablet? If so, what is an ordinary aspirin tablet, and how much aspirin does it con-

tain? Twice as much as Excedrin or Bufferin? Twice as much as a chocolate chip cookie? Remember those Unfinished Words and how they lead you on without saying anything.

37   Finally, what about those doctors who are doing all that recommending? Who are they? How many of them are there? What kind of doctors are they? What are their qualifications? Who asked them about recommending pain relievers? What other pain relievers did they recommend? And there are a whole lot more questions about this "poll" of doctors to which I'd like to know the answers, but you get the point. Sometimes, when I call my doctor, she tells me to take two aspirin and call her office in the morning. Is that where Anacin got this ad?

Read the Label, or the Brochure

38   Words aren't just found on television, on the radio, or in newspaper and magazine ads. Just about any language associated with a product will contain the doublespeak of advertising. Remember the Eli Lilly case and the doublespeak on the information sheet that came with the birth control pills. Here's another example.

39   In 1983, the Estee Lauder cosmetics company announced a new product called "Night Repair." A small brochure distributed with the product stated that "Night Repair" was scientifically formulated in Estee Lauder's U.S. laboratories as part of the Swiss Age-Controlling Skincare Program: "Although only nature controls the aging process, this program helps control the signs of aging and encourages skin to look and feel younger." You might want to read these two sentences again, because they sound great but say nothing.

40   First, note that the product was "scientifically formulated" in the company's laboratories. What does that mean? What constitutes a scientific formulation? You wouldn't expect the company to say that the product was casually, mechanically, or carelessly formulated, or just thrown together one day when the people in the white coats didn't have anything better to do. But the word "scientifically" lends an air of precision and promise that just isn't there.

41   It is the second sentence, however, that's really weasely, both syntactically and semantically. The only factual part of this sentence is the introductory dependent clause "only nature controls the aging process." Thus, the only fact in the ad is relegated to a dependent clause, a clause dependent on the main clause, which contains no factual or definite information at all and indeed purports to contradict the independent clause. The new "skincare program" (notice it's not a skin cream but a "program") does not claim to stop or even retard the aging process. What, then, does Night Repair, at a price of over $35 (in 1983 dollars) for a .87-ounce bottle do? According to this brochure, nothing. It only "helps," and the brochure does not say how much it helps. Moreover, it only "helps control," and then it only helps control the "signs of aging," not the aging itself. Also, it "encourages" skin not to be younger but only to "look and feel" younger. The brochure does not say younger than what. Of the sixteen words in the main clause of this second sentence, nine are weasel words. So, before you spend all that money for Night Repair, or any other cosmetic product, read the words carefully, and then decide if you're getting what you think you're paying for.

Other Tricks of the Trade

42   Advertisers' use of doublespeak is endless. Remember the explanation of adver- tis- ing's function given by Rosser Reeves earlier in this chapter: to make something out of nothing. The best way advertisers can make something out of nothing is through words. Although there are a lot of visual images used on television and in magazines and newspapers, every advertiser wants to create that memorable line that will stick in the public consciousness. I am sure pure joy reigned in one advertising agency when a study found that children who were asked to spell the word "relief" promptly and proudly responded "r-o-l-a-i-d-s."

43   The variations, combinations, and permutations of doublespeak used in adver- tising go on and on, running from the use of rhetorical questions ("Wouldn't you really rather have a Buick?" "If you can't trust Prestone, who can you trust?") to flattering you with compliments ("The lady has taste." "We think a cigar smoker is someone special." "You've come a long way baby."). You know, of course, how you're supposed to answer those questions, and you know that those compliments are just leading up to the sales pitches for the products. Before you dismiss such tricks of the trade as obvious, however, just remember that all of these statements and questions were part of very successful advertising campaigns.

44   A more subtle approach is the ad that proclaims a supposedly unique quality for a product, a quality that really isn't unique. "If it doesn't say Goodyear, It can't be polyglas." Sounds good, doesn't it? Polyglas is available only from Goodyear because Goodyear copyrighted that trade name. Any other tire manufacturer could make exactly the same tire but could not call it "polyglas," because that would be copyright infringement. "Polyglas" is simply Goodyear's name for its fiberglass-reinforced tire.

45   Since we like to think of ourselves as living in a technologically advanced country, sci- ence and technology have a great appeal in selling products. Advertisers are quick to use scientific doublespeak to push their products. There are all kinds of elixirs, additives, sci- entific potions, and mysterious mixtures added to all kinds of products. Gasoline contains "HTA," "F310," "Platformate," and other chemical-sounding additives, but nowhere does an advertisement give any real information about the additive.

46   Shampoo, deodorant, mouthwash, cold medicine, sleeping pills, and any number of other products all seem to contain some special chemical ingredient that allows them to work wonders. "Certs contains a sparkling drop of Retsyn." So what? What's "retsyn"? What's it do? What's so special about it?

47   When they don't have a secret ingredient in their product, advertisers still find a way to claim scientific validity. There's "Sinarest. Created by a research scientist who actually gets sinus headaches." Sounds nice, but what kind of research does this scientist do? How do you know if she is any kind of expert on sinus medicine? Besides, this ad doesn't tell you a thing about the medicine itself and what it does.

Advertising Doublespeak Quick Quiz

48 Now it's time to test your awareness of advertising doublespeak. (You didn't think I would just let you read this and forget it, did you?) The following is a list of statements from some recent ads. Your job is to figure out what each of these ads really says.

Domino's Pizza:	"Because nobody delivers better."
Sinutab:	"It can stop the pain."
Tums:	"The stronger acid neutralizer."
Maximum Strength Dristan:	"Strong medicine for tough sinus colds."
Listermint:	"Making your mouth a cleaner place."
Cascade:	"For virtually spotless dishes nothing beats Cascade."
Nuprin:	"Little. Yellow. Different. Better."
Anacin:	"Better relief."
Sudafed:	"Fast sinus relief that won't put you fast asleep."
Advil:	"Advanced medicine for pain."

Critical Reading Questions:

- **Interpretation:** How do advertisers employ rhetorical strategies to deceive consumers? How does this give rhetoric a bad name?

- **Reflection:** How does the use of doublespeak affect the ethos of a product? Of a brand?

- **Reflection:** Do you think Lutz thinks consumers are naïve? Discuss what you believe the consumer realizes vs. how much they are misled.

Discovering the Power of Language

Malcolm X

In this excerpt from his autobiography, published in 1964, Malcolm X provides a detailed narrative of his time spent in prison for burglary, writing letters to people he had once known in the world of hustling. After repeated attempts to communicate with friends and receiving no reply, he soon realized that they were too uneducated to write a letter in response. He was thus forced to reflect upon his own access to words and language. Recognizing that others, including opponents to racial equality, would never accept the validity of his beliefs or arguments for equality while he delivered them in "common prose," he began a journey of self-education in order to better learn how to read and write. In doing this, he discovered the true power of rhetoric and how language can lead to freedom.

—OM

1   I've never been one for inaction. Everything I've ever felt strongly about, I've done something about. I guess that's why, unable to do anything else, I soon began writing to people I had known in the hustling world, such as Sammy the Pimp, John Hughes, the gambling house owner, the thief Jumpsteady, and several dope peddlers. I wrote them all about Allah and Islam and Mr. Elijah Muhammad. I had no idea where most of them lived. I addressed their letters in care of the Harlem or Roxbury bars and clubs where I'd known them.

2   I never got a single reply. The average hustler and criminal was too uneducated to write a letter. I have known many slick sharp-looking hustlers, who would have you think they had an interest in Wall Street; privately, they would get someone else to read a letter if they received one. Besides, neither would I have replied to anyone writing me something as wild as "the white man is the devil."

3   What certainly went on the Harlem and Roxbury wires was that Detroit Red was going crazy in stir, or else he was trying some hype to shake up the warden's office.

4   During the years that I stayed in the Norfolk Prison Colony, never did any official directly say anything to me about those letters, although, of course, they all passed through the prison censorship. I'm sure, however they monitored what I wrote to add to the files which every state and federal prison keeps on the conversion of Negro inmates by the teachings of Mr. Elijah Muhammad.

5   But at that time, I felt that the real reason was that the white man knew that he was the devil.

6   Later on, I even wrote to the Mayor of Boston, to the Governor of Massachusetts, and to Harry S. Truman. They never answered; they probably never even saw my letters. I handscratched to them how the white man's society was responsible for the black man's condition in this wilderness of North America.

7   It was because of my letters that I happened to stumble upon starting to acquire some kind of homemade education.

8   I became increasingly frustrated at not being able to express what I wanted to convey in letters that I wrote, especially to Mr. Elijah Muhammad. In the street, I had been the most articulate hustler out there—I had commanded attention when I said something. But now, trying to write simple English, I not only wasn't articulate, I wasn't even functional. How would I sound writing in slang, the way I would *say* it, something such as, "Look, daddy, let me pull your coat about a cat, Elijah Muhammad—"

9   Many who today hear me somewhere in person, or on television, or those who read something I've said, will think I went to school far beyond the eighth grade. This impression is due entirely to my prison studies.

10   It had really begun back in the Charlestown Prison, when Bimbi first made me feel envy of his stock of knowledge. Bimbi had always taken charge of any conversation he was in, and I had tried to emulate him. But every book I picked up had few sentences which didn't contain anywhere from one to nearly all of the words that might as well have been in Chinese. When I just skipped those words, of course, I really ended up with little idea of what the book said. So I had come to the Norfolk Prison Colony still going through only book-reading motions. Pretty soon, I would have quit even these motions, unless I had received the motivation that I did.

11   I saw that the best thing I could do was get hold of a dictionary—to study, to learn some words. I was lucky enough to reason also that I should try to improve my penmanship. It was sad. I couldn't even write in a straight line. It was both ideas together that moved me to request a dictionary along with some tablets and pencils from the Norfolk Prison Colony school.

12   I spent two days just rifling uncertainly through the dictionary's pages. I'd never realized so many words existed! I didn't know *which* words I needed to learn. Finally, just to start some kind of action, I began copying.

13   In my slow, painstaking, ragged handwriting, I copied into my tablet everything printed on that first page, down to the punctuation marks.

14   I believe it took me a day. Then, aloud, I read back to myself, everything I'd written on the tablet. Over and over, aloud, to myself, I read my own handwriting.

15   I woke up the next morning, thinking about those words—immensely proud to realize that not only had I written so much at one time, but I'd written words, that I never knew were in the world. Moreover, with a little effort, I also could remember what many of these words meant. I reviewed the words whose meanings I didn't remember. Funny thing, from the dictionary first page right now, that "aardvark" springs to my mind. The dictionary had a picture of it, a long-tallied, long-eared, burrowing African mammal, which lives off termites caught by sticking out its tongue as an anteater does for ants.

16   I was so fascinated that I went on—I copied the dictionary's next page. And the same experience came when I studied that. With every succeeding page, I also learned of people and places and events from history. Actually the dictionary is like a miniature encyclopedia. Finally the dictionary's A section had filled a whole tablet—and I went on into the B's. That was the way I started copying what eventually became the entire dictionary. I

went a lot faster after so much practice helped me to pick up handwriting speed. Between what I wrote in my tablet, and writing letters, during the rest of my time in prison I would guess I wrote a million words.

17   I suppose it was inevitable that as my word-base broadened, I could for the first time pick up a book and read and now begin to understand what the book was saying. Anyone who has read a great deal can imagine the new world that opened. Let me tell you something, from then until I left that prison, in every free moment I had, if I was not reading in the library, I was reading on my bunk. You couldn't have gotten me out of books with a wedge. Between Mr. Muhammad's teachings, my correspondence, my visitors…and my reading of books, months passed without my even thinking about being imprisoned. In fact, up to then, I never had been so truly free in my life.

Critical Reading Questions:

- **Rhetorical analysis:** What are some rhetorical devices that Malcolm X uses to reinforce his claim that developing language ability leads to true power and freedom?

- **Rhetorical analysis:** What contextual elements provided by Malcolm X serve as indicators of his rhetorical situation and his desire for literacy?

The Ballot or the Bullet

Malcolm X

"The Ballot or the Bullet" is a public speech given by Malcolm X on April 12, 1964, at Cory Methodist Church in Detroit, Michigan. In the speech, Malcolm X attempts to persuade African Americans that they need to exercise their right to vote; however, he also warns the U.S. government that it needs to stop blocking minorities from attaining equality, or they might turn to violence. In this speech, delivered at a time when racial inequality was rampant in the U.S., Malcolm X argues against the rhetoric used by fellow civil rights leaders that recommended nonviolence in an attempt to persuade his audience that the fight for equal rights is no longer merely a civil rights issue, but a human rights issue as well.

—OM

1   Mr. Moderator, Reverend Cleage, Brother Lomax, brothers and sisters, and friends—and I see some enemies. In fact, I think we'd be fooling ourselves if we had an audience this large and didn't realize that there were some enemies present.

2   This afternoon we want to talk about "The ballot or the bullet." The ballot or the bullet explains itself. But before we get into it, since this is the year of the ballot or the bullet, I would like to clarify some things that refer to me personally—concerning my own personal position.

3   I'm still a Muslim. That is, my religion is still Islam. My religion is still Islam. I still credit Mr. Mohammed for what I know and what I am. He's the one who opened my eyes. At present, I'm the minister of the newly founded Muslim Mosque Incorporated, which has its offices in the Teresa Hotel, right in the heart of Harlem—that's the black belt in New York City. And when we realize that Adam Clayton Powell is a Christian minister, he's the—he heads Abyssinian Baptist Church, but at the same time, he's more famous for his political struggling.

4   And Dr. King is a Christian minister, in Atlanta—from Atlanta, Georgia—or in Atlanta, Georgia, but he's become more famous for being involved in the civil rights struggle. There's another in New York, Reverend Galamison—I don't know if you've heard of him out here—he's a Christian minister from Brooklyn, but has become famous for his fight against a segregated school system in Brooklyn. Reverend Clee, right here, is a Christian minister, here in Detroit. He's the head of the "Freedom Now Party." All of these are Christian ministers—All of these are Christian ministers, but they don't come to us as Christian ministers. They come to us as fighters in some other category.

5   I'm a Muslim minister. The same as they are Christian ministers, I'm a Muslim minister. And I don't believe in fighting today in any one front, but on all fronts. In fact, I'm a "Black Nationalist Freedom Fighter." Islam is my religion, but I believe my religion is my personal business. It governs my personal life, my personal morals. And my religious philosophy is personal between me and the God in whom I believe; just as the religious philosophy of these others is between them and the God in whom they believe.

6   And this is best this way. Were we to come out here discussing religion, we'd have too many differences from the outstart and we could never get together. So today, though Islam is my religious philosophy, my political, economic, and social philosophy is Black Nationalism. You and I—as I say, if we bring up religion we'll have differences; we'll have arguments; and we'll never be able to get together. But if we keep our religion at home, keep our religion in the closet, keep our religion between ourselves and our God, but when we come out here, we have a fight that's common to all of us against a [sic] enemy who is common to all of us.

7   The political philosophy of Black Nationalism only means that the black man should control the politics and the politicians in his own community. The—The time—The time when white people can come in our community and get us to vote for them so that they can be our political leaders and tell us what to do and what not to do is long gone. By the same token, the time when that same white man, knowing that your eyes are too far open, can send another Negro into the community and get you and me to support him so he can use him to lead us astray—those days are long gone too.

8   The political philosophy of Black Nationalism only means that if you and I are going to live in a Black community—and that's where we're going to live, 'cause as soon as you move into one of their—soon as you move out of the Black community into their community, it's mixed for a period of time, but they're gone and you're right there all by yourself again. We must—We must understand the politics of our community and we must know what politics is supposed to produce. We must know what part politics plays in our lives. And until we become politically mature we will always be misled, led astray, or deceived or maneuvered into supporting someone politically who doesn't have the good of our community at heart. So the political philosophy of Black Nationalism only means that we will have to carry on a program, a political program, of reeducation to open our people's eyes, make us become more politically conscious, politically mature, and then we will—whenever we get ready to cast our ballot, that ballot will be—will be cast for a man of the community who has the good of the community of heart.

9   The economic philosophy of Black Nationalism only means that we should own and operate and control the economy of our community. You would never—You can't open up a black store in a white community. White men won't even patronize you. And he's not wrong. He's got sense enough to look out for himself. You the one who don't have sense enough to look out for yourself. The white man—The white man is too intelligent to let someone else come and gain control of the economy of his community. But you will let anybody come in and take control of the economy of your community, control the housing, control the education, control the jobs, control the businesses, under the pretext that you want to integrate. No, you're out of your mind.

10   The political—The economic philosophy of Black Nationalism only means that we have to become involved in a program of reeducation to educate our people into the importance of knowing that when you spend your dollar out of the community in which you live, the community in which you spend your money becomes richer and richer; the community out of which you take your money becomes poorer and poorer. And because these Negroes, who have been misled, misguided, are breaking their necks to take their

money and spend it with The Man, The Man is becoming richer and richer, and you're becoming poorer and poorer. And then what happens? The community in which you live becomes a slum. It becomes a ghetto. The conditions become run down. And then you have the audacity to—to complain about poor housing in a run down community. Why, you run it down yourself when you take your dollar out.

11   And you and I are in a double-track, because not only do we lose by taking our money someplace else and spending it, when we try and spend it in our own community we're trapped because we haven't had sense enough to set up stores and control the businesses of our community. The man who's controlling the stores in our community is a man who doesn't look like we do. He's a man who doesn't even live in the community. So you and I, even when we try and spend our money in the block where we live or the area where we live, we're spending it with a man who, when the sun goes down, takes that basket full of money in another part of the town.

12   So we're trapped, trapped, double-trapped, triple-trapped. Anywhere we go we find that we're trapped. And every kind of solution that someone comes up with is just another trap. But the political and economic philosophy of Black Nationalism—the economic philosophy of Black Nationalism shows our people the importance of setting up these little stores and developing them and expanding them into larger operations. Woolworth didn't start out big like they are today. They started out with a dime store and expanded and expanded and then expanded until today, they are all over the country and all over the world, and they get to some of everybody's money. Now this is what you and I—General Motors [is] the same way. They didn't start out like it is. It started out just a little rat race type operation. And it expanded and it expanded until today it's where it is right now. And you and I have to make a start and the best place to start is right in the community where we live.

13   So our people not only have to be reeducated to the importance of supporting black business, but the black man himself has to be made aware of the importance of going into business. And once you and I go into business, we own and operate at least the businesses in our community. What we will be doing is developing a situation wherein we will actually be able to create employment for the people in the community. And once you can create some—some employment in the community where you live it will eliminate the necessity of you and me having to act ignorantly and disgracefully, boycotting and picketing some practice some place else trying to beg him for a job.

14   Anytime you have to rely upon your enemy for a job, you're in bad shape. When you have—He is your enemy. Let me tell you, you wouldn't be in this country if some enemy hadn't kidnapped you and brought you here. On the other hand, some of you think you came here on the Mayflower.

15   So as you can see brothers and sisters, today—this afternoon, it's not our intention to discuss religion. We're going to forget religion. If we bring up religion, we'll be in an argument, and the best way to keep away from arguments and differences, as I said earlier, put your religion at home—in the closet. Keep it between you and your God. Because if it hasn't done anything more for you than it has, you need to forget it anyway.

16   Whether you are—Whether you are a Christian, or a Muslim, or a Nationalist, we all have the same problem. They don't hang you because you're a Baptist; they hang you 'cause you're black. They don't attack me because I'm a Muslim; they attack me 'cause I'm black. They attack all of us for the same reason; all of us catch hell from the same enemy. We're all in the same bag, in the same boat. We suffer political oppression, economic exploitation, and social degradation—all of them from the same enemy. The government has failed us; you can't deny that. Anytime you live in the twentieth century, 1964, and you walkin' around here singing "We Shall Overcome," the government has failed us.

17   This is part of what's wrong with you—you do too much singing. Today it's time to stop singing and start swinging. You can't sing up on freedom, but you can swing up on some freedom. Cassius Clay can sing, but singing didn't help him to become the heavyweight champion of the world; swinging helped him become the heavyweight champion. This government has failed us; the government itself has failed us, and the white liberals who have been posing as our friends have failed us.

18   And once we see that all these other sources to which we've turned have failed, we stop turning to them and turn to ourselves. We need a self-help program, a do-it—a do-it-yourself philosophy, a do-it-right-now philosophy, a it's-already-too-late philosophy. This is what you and I need to get with, and the only time—the only way we're going to solve our problem is with a self-help program. Before we can get a self-help program started we have to have a self-help philosophy.

19   Black Nationalism is a self-help philosophy. What's so good about it? You can stay right in the church where you are and still take Black Nationalism as your philosophy. You can stay in any kind of civic organization that you belong to and still take Black Nationalism as your philosophy. You can be an atheist and still take Black Nationalism as your philosophy. This is a philosophy that eliminates the necessity for division and argument. 'Cause if you're black you should be thinking black, and if you are black and you not thinking black at this late date, well I'm sorry for you.

20   Once you change your philosophy, you change your thought pattern. Once you change your thought pattern, you change your—your attitude. Once you change your attitude, it changes your behavior pattern and then you go on into some action. As long as you gotta sit-down philosophy, you'll have a sit-down thought pattern, and as long as you think that old sit-down thought you'll be in some kind of sit-down action. They'll have you sitting in everywhere. It's not so good to refer to what you're going to do as a "sit-in." That right there castrates you. Right there it brings you down. What—What goes with it? What—Think of the image of a someone sitting. An old woman can sit. An old man can sit. A chump can sit. A coward can sit. Anything can sit. Well you and I been sitting long enough, and it's time today for us to start doing some standing, and some fighting to back that up.

21   When we look like—at other parts of this earth upon which we live, we find that black, brown, red, and yellow people in Africa and Asia are getting their independence. They're not getting it by singing "We Shall Overcome." No, they're getting it through nationalism. It is nationalism that brought about the independence of the people in Asia. Every nation in

Asia gained its independence through the philosophy of nationalism. Every nation on the African continent that has gotten its independence brought it about through the philosophy of nationalism. And it will take Black Nationalism—that to bring about the freedom of 22 million Afro-Americans here in this country where we have suffered colonialism for the past 400 years.

22   America is just as much a colonial power as England ever was. America is just as much a colonial power as France ever was. In fact, America is more so a colonial power than they because she's a hypocritical colonial power behind it.

23   What is 20th—What do you call second-class citizenship? Why, that's colonization. Second-class citizenship is nothing but 20th-century slavery. How you gonna tell me you're a second-class citizen? They don't have second-class citizenship in any other government on this earth. They just have slaves and people who are free. Well this country is a hypocrite. They try and make you think they set you free by calling you a second-class citizen. No, you're nothing but a 20th-century slave.

24   Just as it took nationalism to move—to remove colonialism from Asia and Africa, it'll take Black Nationalism today to remove colonialism from the backs and the minds of 22 million Afro-Americans here in this country.

25   And 1964 looks like it might be the year of the ballot or the bullet.

26   Why does it look like it might be the year of the ballot or the bullet? Because Negroes have listened to the trickery, and the lies, and the false promises of the white man now for too long. And they're fed up. They've become disenchanted. They've become disillusioned. They've become dissatisfied, and all of this has built up frustrations in the black community that makes the black community throughout America today more explosive than all of the atomic bombs the Russians can ever invent. Whenever you got a racial powder keg sitting in your lap, you're in more trouble than if you had an atomic powder keg sitting in your lap. When a racial powder keg goes off, it doesn't care who it knocks out the way. Understand this, it's dangerous.

27   And in 1964 this seems to be the year, because what can the white man use now to fool us after he put down that march on Washington? And you see all through that now. He tricked you, had you marching down to Washington. Yes, had you marching back and forth between the feet of a dead man named Lincoln and another dead man named George Washington singing "We Shall Overcome." He made a chump out of you. He made a fool out of you. He made you think you were going somewhere and you end up going nowhere but between Lincoln and Washington.

28   So today, our people are disillusioned. They've become disenchanted. They've become dissatisfied, and in their frustrations they want action.

29   And in 1964 you'll see this young black man, this new generation asking for the ballot or the bullet. That old Uncle Tom action is outdated. The young generation don't want to hear anything about the odds are against us. What do we care about odds?

30   When this country here was first being founded there were 13 colonies. The—The whites were colonized. They were fed up with this taxation without representation, so some of them stood up and said "liberty or death." Though I went to a white school over

here in Mason, Michigan, the white man made the mistake of letting me read his history books. He made the mistake of teaching me that Patrick Henry was a patriot, and George Washington, wasn't nothing non-violent about old Pat or George Washington.

31   Liberty or death was what brought about the freedom of whites in this country from the English. They didn't care about the odds. Why, they faced the wrath of the entire British Empire. And in those days they used to say that the British Empire was so vast and so powerful that the sun—the sun would never set on it. This is how big it was, yet these 13 little scrawny states, tired of taxation without representation, tired of being exploited and oppressed and degraded, told that big British Empire "liberty or death."

32   And here you have 22 million Afro-American black people today catching more hell than Patrick Henry ever saw. And I'm—I'm here to tell you in case you don't know it—that you got a new—you got a new generation of black people in this country who don't care anything whatsoever about odds. They don't want to hear you old Uncle Tom handkerchief heads talking about the odds. No. This is a new generation. If they're gonna draft these young black men and send them over to Korea or South Vietnam to face 800 million Chinese—if you're not afraid of those odds, you shouldn't be afraid of these odds.

33   Why is—Why does this loom to be such an explosive political year? Because this is the year of politics. This is the year when all of the white politicians are going to come into the Negro community. You never see them until election time. You can't find them until election time. They're going to come in with false promises, and as they make these false promises they're gonna feed our frustrations and this will only serve to make matters worse.

34   I'm no politician. I'm not even a student of politics. I'm not a Republican, nor a Democrat, nor an American, and got sense enough to know it. I'm one of the 22 million black victims of the Democrats, one of the 22 million black victims of the Republicans, and one of the 22 million black victims of Americanism. And when I speak, I don't speak as a Democrat, or a Republican, *nor an American.* I speak as a victim of America's so-called democracy. You and I have never seen democracy; all we've seen is hypocrisy. When we open our eyes today and look around America, we see America not through the eyes of someone who have—who has enjoyed the fruits of Americanism, we see America through the eyes of someone who has been the victim of Americanism. We don't see any American dream; we've experienced only the American nightmare. We haven't benefited from America's democracy; we've only suffered from America's hypocrisy. And the generation that's coming up now can see it and are not afraid to say it.

35   If you—If you go to jail, so what? If you black, you were born in jail. If you black, you were born in jail, in the North as well as the South. Stop talking about the South. Long as you south of the—Long as you south of the Canadian border, you're south. Don't call Governor Wallace a Dixie governor; Romney is a Dixie governor.

36   Twenty-two million black victims of Americanism are waking up and they're gaining a new political consciousness, becoming politically mature. And as they become—develop this political maturity, they're able to see the recent trends in these political elections. They see that the whites are so evenly divided that every time they vote the race is so close they have to go back and count the votes all over again. And that . . . which means that

any block, any minority that has a block of votes that stick together is in a strategic position. Either way you go, that's who gets it. You're—You're in a position to determine who will go to the White House and who will stay in the dog house. You're the one who has that power. You can keep Johnson in Washington D.C., or you can send him back to his Texas cotton patch. You're the one who sent Kennedy to Washington. You're the one who put the present Democratic Administration in Washington D.C. The whites were evenly divided. It was the fact that you threw 80 percent of your votes behind the Democrats that put the Democrats in the White House.

37 When you see this, you can see that the Negro vote is the key factor. And despite the fact that you are in a position to—to be the determining factor, what do you get out of it? The Democrats have been in Washington D.C. only because of the Negro vote. They've been down there four years, and they're—all other legislation they wanted to bring up they brought it up and gotten it out of the way, and now they bring up you. And now, they bring up you. You put them first, and they put you last, 'cause you're a chump, a political chump.

38 In Washington D.C., in the House of Representatives, there are 257 who are Democrats; only 177 are Republican. In the Senate there are 67 Democrats; only 33 are Republicans. The Party that you backed controls two-thirds of the House of Representatives and the Senate, and still they can't keep their promise to you, 'cause you're a chump. Anytime you throw your weight behind a political party that controls two-thirds of the government, and that party can't keep the promise that it made to you during election time, and you're dumb enough to walk around continuing to identify yourself with that party, you're not only a chump, but you're a traitor to your race.

39 And what kind of alibi do they come up with? They try and pass the buck to the Dixiecrats. Now back during the days when you were blind, deaf, and dumb, ignorant, politically immature, naturally you went along with that. But today as your eyes come open, and you develop political maturity, you're able to see and think for yourself, and you can see that a Dixiecrat is nothing but a Democrat in disguise.

40 You look at the structure of the government that controls this country; it's controlled by 16 senatorial committees and 20 congressional committees. Of the 16 senatorial committees that run the government, 10 of them are in the hands of Southern segregationists. Of the 20 congressional committees that run the government, 12 of them in the—are in the hands of Southern segregationists. And they're going to tell you and me that the South lost the war.

41 You, today, have—are in the hands of a government of segregationists, racists, white supremacists who belong to the Democratic party, but disguise themselves as Dixiecrats. A Dixiecrat is nothing but a Democrat. Whoever runs the Democrats is also the father of the Dixiecrats, and the father of all of them is sitting in the White House. I say and I say it again: You got a President who's nothing but a Southern segregationist from the state of Texas. They'll lynch you in Texas as quick as they'll lynch you in Mississippi. Only in—in Texas they lynch you with a Texas accent; in Mississippi they lynch you with a Mississippi accent.

42 And the first thing the cracker does when he comes in power, he takes all the Negro leaders and invites them for coffee to show that he's alright. And those Uncle Toms can't

pass up the coffee. They come away from the coffee table telling you and me that this man is alright 'cause he's from the South, and since he's from the South he can deal with the South. Look at the logic that they're using. What about Eastland? He's from the South. Make him the President. He can—If Johnson is a good man 'cause he's from Texas, and being from Texas will enable him to deal with the South, Eastland can deal with the South better than Johnson. Oh, I say you been misled. You been had. You been took.

43   I was in Washington a couple weeks ago while the Senators were filibustering, and I noticed in the back of the Senate a huge map, and on this map it showed the distribution of Negroes in America, and surprisingly the same Senators that were involved in the filibuster were from the states where there were the most Negroes. Why were they filibustering the civil rights legislation? Because the civil rights legislation is supposed to guarantee voting rights to Negroes in those states, and those senators from those states know that if the Negroes in those states can vote, those senators are down the drain. The Representatives of those states go down the drain. And in the Constitution of this country it has a stipulation wherein whenever the rights, the voting rights, of people in a certain district are violated, then the Representative who—who's from that particular district, according to the Constitution, is supposed to be expelled from the Congress. Now, if this particular aspect of the Constitution was enforced, why you wouldn't have a cracker in Washington D.C. But what would happen when you expel the Dixiecrat, you're expelling the Democrat. When you destroy the power of the Dixiecrat, you're destroying the power—power of the Democratic Party. So how in the world can the Democratic Party in the South actually side with you in sincerity, when all of its power is based in the—in the South?

44   These Northern Democrats are in cahoots with the Southern Democrats. They're playing a giant con game, a political con game. You know how it goes. One of them—One of them comes to you and makes believe he's for you, and he's in cahoots with the other one that's not for you. Why? Because neither one of them is for you, but they got to make you go with one of them or the other. So this is a con game. And this is what they've been doing with you and me all these years.

45   First thing Johnson got off the plane when he become President, he asked "Where's Dicky?" You know who "Dicky" is? Dicky is old Southern cracker Richard—Richard Russell. Look here, yes. Lyndon B. Johnson's best friend is the one who is the head, who's heading the forces that are filibustering civil rights legislation. You tell me how in the hell is he going to be Johnson's best friend? How can Johnson be his friend and your friend too? No, that man is too tricky. Especially if his friend is still old Dicky.

46   Whenever the Negroes keep the Democrats in power, they're keeping the Dixiecrats in power. Is this true? A vote for a Democrat is nothing but a vote for a Dixiecrat. I know you don't like me saying that, but I . . . I'm not the kind of person who come here to say what you like. I'm going to tell you the truth whether you like it or not.

47   Up here, in the North you have the same thing. The Democratic Party don't—don't do it—they don't do it that way. They got a thing that they call gerrymandering. They—They maneuver you out of power. Even though you can vote, they fix it so you're voting for nobody; they got you going and coming. In the South, they're outright political wolves. In the North, they're political foxes. A fox and a wolf are both canine, both belong to the dog

family. Now you take your choice. You going to choose a Northern dog or a Southern dog? Because either dog you choose I guarantee you you'll still be in the dog house.

48   This is why I say it's the ballot or the bullet. It's liberty or it's death. It's freedom for everybody or freedom for nobody. America today finds herself in a unique situation. Historically, revolutions are bloody. Oh, yes, they are. They haven't never had a bloodless revolution, or a nonviolent revolution. That don't happen even in Hollywood. You don't have a revolution in which you love your enemy, and you don't have a revolution in which you are begging the system of exploitation to integrate you into it. Revolutions overturn systems. Revolutions destroy systems.

49   A revolution is bloody, but America is in a unique position. She's the only country in history in a position actually to become involved in a bloodless revolution. The—The Russian revolution was bloody; Chinese revolution was bloody; French revolution was bloody; Cuban revolution was bloody; and there was nothing more bloody then the American Revolution. But today this country can become involved in a revolution that won't take bloodshed. All she's got to do is give the black man in this country everything that's due him—everything.

50   I hope that the white man can see this, 'cause if he don't see it you're finished. If you don't see it you're going to be coming—you're going to become involved in some action in which you don't have a chance. And we don't care anything about your atomic bomb; it's—it's useless because other countries have atomic bombs. When two or three different countries have atomic bombs, nobody can use them, so it means that the white man today is without a weapon. If you're gonna—If you want some action, you gotta come on down to Earth. And there's more black people on Earth than there are white people on Earth.

51   I only got a couple more minutes. The white man can never win another war on the ground. His days of war, victory, his great—his days of that ground victory are over. Can I prove it? Yes. Take all the action that's going on on this earth right now that he's involved in. Tell me where he's winning. Nowhere.

52   Why some rice farmers—some rice farmers—some rice eaters ran him out of Korea. Yes, they ran him out of Korea. Rice eaters with nothing but gym shoes and a rifle and a bowl of rice took him and his tanks and his napalm and all that other action he's supposed to have and ran him across the Yalu. Why? 'Cause the day that he can win on the ground has passed.

53   Up in French Indochina those little peasants, rice growers, took on the might of the French army and ran all the Frenchmen—you remember Dien Bien Phu. No.

54   The same thing happened in Algeria, in Africa. They didn't have anything but a rifle. The French had all these highly mechanized instruments of warfare, but they put some guerila action on, and a—and a—and a white man can't fight a guerila warfare. Guerila action takes heart, takes nerve, and he doesn't have that. He's brave when he's got tanks. He's brave when he's got planes. He's brave when he's got bombs. He's brave when he got a whole lot of company along with him, but you take that little man from Africa and Asia, turn him loose in the woods with a blade, with a blade—that's all he needs, all he needs is a blade—and when the sun comes down—goes down and it's dark, it's even-steven.

55   So it's the—it's the ballot or the bullet. Today our people can see that we're faced with a government conspiracy. This government has failed us. The senators who are filibustering concerning your and my rights, that's the government. Don't say it's Southern senators. This is the government; this is a government filibuster. It's not a segregationist filibuster. It's a government filibuster. Any kind of activity that takes place on the floor of the Congress or the Senate, that's the government. Any kind of dilly-dallying, that's the government. Any kind of pussy-footing, that's the government. Any kind of act that's designed to delay or deprive you and me right now of getting full rights, that's the government that's responsible. And any time you find the government involved in a conspiracy to violate the citizenship or the civil rights of a people, then you are wasting your time going to that government expecting redress. Instead, you have to take that government to the World Court and accuse it of genocide and all of the other crimes that it is guilty of today.

56   So those of us whose political, and economic, and social philosophy is Black Nationalism have become involved in the civil rights struggle. We have injected ourselves into the civil rights struggle, and we intend to expand it from the level of civil rights to the level of human rights. As long as you're—As long as you're fighting on the level of civil rights, you're under Uncle Sam's jurisdiction. You're going to his court expecting him to correct the problem. He created the problem. He's the criminal. You don't take your case to the criminal; you take your criminal to court. When the government of South Africa began to trample upon the human rights of the people of South Africa, they were taken to the U.N. When the government of Portugal began to trample upon the—the rights of our brothers and sisters in Angola, it was taken before the U.N. Why even the white man took the Hungarian question to the U.N. And just this week Chief Justice Goldberg was crying over three million Jews in Russia about their human rights, charging Russia with violating the U.N. charter because of its mistreatment of the human rights of Jews in Russia.

57   Now you tell me how can the plight of everybody on this earth reach the halls of the United Nations, and you have 22 million Afro-Americans whose churches are being bombed, whose little girls are being murdered, whose—whose leaders are being shot down in broad daylight. Now you tell me why the leaders of this struggle have never taken it before the United Nations.

58   So our next move is to take the entire civil rights struggle problem into the United Nations and let the world see that Uncle Sam is guilty of violating the human rights of 22 million Afro-Americans. . . .

59   [short audio gap, content uncertain]

60   [Uncle Sam . . .] and still has the audacity or the nerve to stand up and represent himself as the leader of the free world. Not only is he a crook, he's a hypocrite. There he is standing up in front of other people, Uncle Sam, with the blood of your and my mothers and fathers on his hands, with the blood dripping down his jaws like a bloody-jawed wolf, and still got the nerve to point his finger at other countries. You can't even get civil rights legislation. And this man has got the nerve to stand up and talk about South Africa, or talk about Nazi Germany, or talk about [unclear]. Nah, no more days like those.

61   So, I say in my conclusion the only way we're going to solve it—we gotta unite in unity and harmony, and Black Nationalism is the key. How we gonna overcome the tendency

to be at each other's throats that always exists in our neighborhoods? And the reason this tendency exists, the strategy of the white man has always been divide and conquer. He keeps us divided in order to conquer us. He tells you I'm for separation and you're for integration to keep us fighting with each other. No, I'm not for separation and you're not for integration. What you and I are for is freedom. Only you think that integration will get you freedom, I think separation will get me freedom. We both got the same objective. We just got different ways of getting at it.

62   So I . . . studied this man, Billy Graham, who preaches White Nationalism. That's what he preaches. I say that's what he preaches. The whole church structure in this country is White Nationalism. You go inside a white church—that's what they preaching: White Nationalism. They got Jesus white, Mary white, God white, everybody white—that's White Nationalism. So what he does—the way he—the way he—the way he circumvents the—the jealousy and envy that he ordinarily would incur among the heads of the church, wherever he goes into an area where the church already is you going into trouble, 'cause they got that thing—what you call it—syndicate, they got a syndicate just like the Racketeers have. I'm going to say what's on my mind 'cause the churches are, the preachers already proved to you that they got a syndicate.

63   And when you're out in the rackets, whenever you're getting in another man's territory, you know, they gang up on you. And that's the same way with you—you ran into the same thing. So how Billy Graham gets around that, instead of going into somebody else's territory, like he going to start up a new church, he don't—he doesn't try to start a church. He just goes in preaching Christ. And he says everybody who believe in Him, you go wherever—you go wherever you find him. So this helps all the churches and so since it helps all the churches they don't fight him.

64   Well, we gonna do the same thing, only our gospel is Black Nationalism. His gospel is White Nationalism; our gospel is Black Nationalism. And the gospel of Black Nationalism, as I told you, means you should control your own—the politics of your community, the economy of your community, and all of the society in which you live should be under your control. And . . . once you . . . feel that this philosophy will solve your problem, go join any church where that's preached. Don't join a church where White Nationalism is preached. Now you can go to a negro church and be exposed to White Nationalism, 'cause you are—when you walk in a negro church and a white Mary and some white angels—that Negro church is preaching White Nationalism.

65   But when you go to a church and you see the pastor of that church with a philosophy and a program that's designed to bring black people together and elevate black people—join that church. Join that church. If you see where the NAACP is preaching and practicing that which is designed to make Black Nationalism materialize—join the NAACP. Join any kind of organization—civic, religious, fraternal, political, or otherwise that's based on lifting the black man up and making him master of his own community.

66   It'll be—It'll be the—the ballot or it'll be the bullet. It'll be liberty or it'll be death. And if you're not ready to pay that price don't use the word freedom in your vocabulary.

67   One more thing: I was on a program in Illinois recently with Senator Paul Douglas, a so-called liberal, so-called Democrat, so-called white man, at . . . which time he told me

that our African brothers were not interested in us in Africa. He said the Africans are not interested in the American Negro. I knew he was lying, but during the next two or three weeks it's my intention and plan to make a tour of our African homeland. And I hope that when I come back, I'll be able to come back and let you know how our African brothers and sisters feel toward us. And I know before I go there that they love us. We're one; we're the same; the same man who has colonized them all these years, colonized you and me too all these years. And all we have to do now is wake up and work in unity and harmony and the battle will be over.

68   I want to thank the Freedom Now Party and the [unclear]. I want to thank Milton and Richard Henley for inviting me here this afternoon, and also Reverend Cleage. And I want them to know that anything that I can ever do, at any time, to work with anybody in any kind of program that is sincerely designed to eliminate the political, the economic, and the social evils that confront all of our people, in Detroit and elsewhere, all they got to do is give me a telephone call and I'll be on the next jet right on into the city.

Critical Reading Questions:

- **Rhetorical analysis:** Select excerpts that provide a direct counterclaim to the more common and traditional civil rights rhetoric of the era (recommending non-violence), and indicate how they work to illuminate the exigency of Malcolm X's claims?

- **Rhetorical analysis:** First, determine how Malcolm X establishes ethos in his speech. Then consider some ways in which the credibility of Malcolm X's claims might be undermined by detractors?

Why Bother?

Michael Pollan

A University of California Berkeley professor of journalism, Michael Pollan is among the most recognized voices in current, ongoing public discourse about food and its production. In his articles and several books, Pollan investigates and contemplates the origins of food, revealing troubling practices in our food industry and acting as a voice for the eater. His work has received much critical and popular acclaim, and Pollan has gained recognition as a person of significant cultural influence. In this April 2008 article published in *The New York Times Magazine*, Pollan advances a contemplative argument for personal lifestyle changes that initially seem insignificant to address monumental problems associated with climate change. He urges readers to grow at least a little of their own food. Citing Wendell Berry and the Victory Garden movement, Pollan invokes deep historical and ethical context for a range of readers, those versed in conversations about environmental concerns and those moved by acts of engaged citizenship and service to country. Pollan's exploration of our multiple identities— as producers, as consumers, as citizens—provides stable logical ground upon which to articulate the ethical, emotional, and material benefits of his proposal and demonstrate its practical applicability as a powerful, if partial, solution to complex environmental issues.

—AMW

1   Why bother? That really is the big question facing us as individuals hoping to do something about climate change, and it's not an easy one to answer. I don't know about you, but for me the most upsetting moment in "An Inconvenient Truth" came long after Al Gore scared the hell out of me, constructing an utterly convincing case that the very survival of life on earth as we know it is threatened by climate change. No, the really dark moment came during the closing credits, when we are asked to . . . change our light bulbs. That's when it got really depressing. The immense disproportion between the magnitude of the problem Gore had described and the puniness of what he was asking us to do about it was enough to sink your heart.

2   But the drop-in-the-bucket issue is not the only problem lurking behind the "why bother" question. Let's say I do bother, big time. I turn my life upside-down, start biking to work, plant a big garden, turn down the thermostat so low I need the Jimmy Carter signature cardigan, forsake the clothes dryer for a laundry line across the yard, trade in the station wagon for a hybrid, get off the beef, go completely local. I could theoretically do all that, but what would be the point when I know full well that halfway around the world there lives my evil twin, some carbon-footprint doppelgänger in Shanghai or Chongqing who has just bought his first car (Chinese car ownership is where ours was back in 1918), is

eager to swallow every bite of meat I forswear and who's positively itching to replace every last pound of CO_2 I'm struggling no longer to emit. So what exactly would I have to show for all my trouble?

3   A sense of personal virtue, you might suggest, somewhat sheepishly. But what good is that when virtue itself is quickly becoming a term of derision? And not just on the editorial pages of *The Wall Street Journal* or on the lips of the vice president, who famously dismissed energy conservation as a "sign of personal virtue." No, even in the pages of *The New York Times* and *The New Yorker*, it seems the epithet "virtuous," when applied to an act of personal environmental responsibility, may be used only ironically. Tell me: How did it come to pass that virtue—a quality that for most of history has generally been deemed, well, a virtue—became a mark of liberal softheadedness? How peculiar, that doing the right thing by the environment—buying the hybrid, eating like a locavore—should now set you up for the Ed Begley Jr. treatment.

4   And even if in the face of this derision I decide I am going to bother, there arises the whole vexed question of getting it right. Is eating local or walking to work really going to reduce my carbon footprint? According to one analysis, if walking to work increases your appetite and you consume more meat or milk as a result, walking might actually emit more carbon than driving. A handful of studies have recently suggested that in certain cases under certain conditions, produce from places as far away as New Zealand might account for less carbon than comparable domestic products. True, at least one of these studies was co-written by a representative of agribusiness interests in (surprise!) New Zealand, but even so, they make you wonder. If determining the carbon footprint of food is really this complicated, and I've got to consider not only "food miles" but also whether the food came by ship or truck and how lushly the grass grows in New Zealand, then maybe on second thought I'll just buy the imported chops at Costco, at least until the experts get their footprints sorted out.

5   There are so many stories we can tell ourselves to justify doing nothing, but perhaps the most insidious is that, whatever we do manage to do, it will be too little too late. Climate change is upon us, and it has arrived well ahead of schedule. Scientists' projections that seemed dire a decade ago turn out to have been unduly optimistic: the warming and the melting is occurring much faster than the models predicted. Now truly terrifying feedback loops threaten to boost the rate of change exponentially, as the shift from white ice to blue water in the Arctic absorbs more sunlight and warming soils everywhere become more biologically active, causing them to release their vast stores of carbon into the air. Have you looked into the eyes of a climate scientist recently? They look really scared.

6   So do you still want to talk about planting gardens?

7   I do.

8   Whatever we can do as individuals to change the way we live at this suddenly very late date does seem utterly inadequate to the challenge. It's hard to argue with Michael Specter, in a recent *New Yorker* piece on carbon footprints, when he says: "Personal choices, no matter how virtuous [N.B.!], cannot do enough. It will also take laws and money." So it will. Yet it is no less accurate or hardheaded to say that laws and money cannot do enough, either; that it will also take profound changes in the way we live. Why? Because

the climate-change crisis is at its very bottom a crisis of lifestyle—of character, even. The Big Problem is nothing more or less than the sum total of countless little everyday choices, most of them made by us (consumer spending represents 70 percent of our economy), and most of the rest of them made in the name of our needs and desires and preferences.

9   For us to wait for legislation or technology to solve the problem of how we're living our lives suggests we're not really serious about changing—something our politicians cannot fail to notice. They will not move until we do. Indeed, to look to leaders and experts, to laws and money and grand schemes, to save us from our predicament represents precisely the sort of thinking—passive, delegated, dependent for solutions on specialists—that helped get us into this mess in the first place. It's hard to believe that the same sort of thinking could now get us out of it.

10   Thirty years ago, Wendell Berry, the Kentucky farmer and writer, put forward a blunt analysis of precisely this mentality. He argued that the environmental crisis of the 1970s—an era innocent of climate change; what we would give to have back that environmental crisis!—was at its heart a crisis of character and would have to be addressed first at that level: at home, as it were. He was impatient with people who wrote checks to environmental organizations while thoughtlessly squandering fossil fuel in their everyday lives—the 1970s equivalent of people buying carbon offsets to atone for their Tahoes and Durangos. Nothing was likely to change until we healed the "split between what we think and what we do." For Berry, the "why bother" question came down to a moral imperative: "Once our personal connection to what is wrong becomes clear, then we have to choose: we can go on as before, recognizing our dishonesty and living with it the best we can, or we can begin the effort to change the way we think and live."

11   For Berry, the deep problem standing behind all the other problems of industrial civilization is "specialization," which he regards as the "disease of the modern character." Our society assigns us a tiny number of roles: we're producers (of one thing) at work, consumers of a great many other things the rest of the time, and then once a year or so we vote as citizens. Virtually all of our needs and desires we delegate to specialists of one kind or another—our meals to agribusiness, health to the doctor, education to the teacher, entertainment to the media, care for the environment to the environmentalist, political action to the politician.

12   As Adam Smith and many others have pointed out, this division of labor has given us many of the blessings of civilization. Specialization is what allows me to sit at a computer thinking about climate change. Yet this same division of labor obscures the lines of connection—and responsibility—linking our everyday acts to their real-world consequences, making it easy for me to overlook the coal-fired power plant that is lighting my screen, or the mountaintop in Kentucky that had to be destroyed to provide the coal to that plant, or the streams running crimson with heavy metals as a result.

13   Of course, what made this sort of specialization possible in the first place was cheap energy. Cheap fossil fuel allows us to pay distant others to process our food for us, to entertain us and to (try to) solve our problems, with the result that there is very little we know how to accomplish for ourselves. Think for a moment of all the things you suddenly need to do for yourself when the power goes out—up to and including entertaining your-

self. Think, too, about how a power failure causes your neighbors—your community—to suddenly loom so much larger in your life. Cheap energy allowed us to leapfrog community by making it possible to sell our specialty over great distances as well as summon into our lives the specialties of countless distant others.

14   Here's the point: Cheap energy, which gives us climate change, fosters precisely the mentality that makes dealing with climate change in our own lives seem impossibly difficult. Specialists ourselves, we can no longer imagine anyone but an expert, or anything but a new technology or law, solving our problems. Al Gore asks us to change the light bulbs because he probably can't imagine us doing anything much more challenging, like, say, growing some portion of our own food. We can't imagine it, either, which is probably why we prefer to cross our fingers and talk about the promise of ethanol and nuclear power—new liquids and electrons to power the same old cars and houses and lives.

15   The "cheap-energy mind," as Wendell Berry called it, is the mind that asks, "Why bother?" because it is helpless to imagine—much less attempt—a different sort of life, one less divided, less reliant. Since the cheap-energy mind translates everything into money, its proxy, it prefers to put its faith in market-based solutions—carbon taxes and pollution-trading schemes. If we could just get the incentives right, it believes, the economy will properly value everything that matters and nudge our self-interest down the proper channels. The best we can hope for is a greener version of the old invisible hand. Visible hands it has no use for.

16   But while some such grand scheme may well be necessary, it's doubtful that it will be sufficient or that it will be politically sustainable before we've demonstrated to ourselves that change is possible. Merely to give, to spend, even to vote, is not to do, and there is so much that needs to be done—without further delay. In the judgment of James Hansen, the NASA climate scientist who began sounding the alarm on global warming 20 years ago, we have only 10 years left to start cutting—not just slowing—the amount of carbon we're emitting or face a "different planet." Hansen said this more than two years ago, however; two years have gone by, and nothing of consequence has been done. So: eight years left to go and a great deal left to do.

17   Which brings us back to the "why bother" question and how we might better answer it. The reasons not to bother are many and compelling, at least to the cheap-energy mind. But let me offer a few admittedly tentative reasons that we might put on the other side of the scale:

18   If you do bother, you will set an example for other people. If enough other people bother, each one influencing yet another in a chain reaction of behavioral change, markets for all manner of green products and alternative technologies will prosper and expand. (Just look at the market for hybrid cars.) Consciousness will be raised, perhaps even changed: new moral imperatives and new taboos might take root in the culture. Driving an S.U.V. or eating a 24-ounce steak or illuminating your McMansion like an airport runway at night might come to be regarded as outrages to human conscience. Not having things might become cooler than having them. And those who did change the way they live would acquire the moral standing to demand changes in behavior from others–from other people, other corporations, even other countries.

19   All of this could, theoretically, happen. What I'm describing (imagining would prob-ably be more accurate) is a process of viral social change, and change of this kind, which is nonlinear, is never something anyone can plan or predict or count on. Who knows, maybe the virus will reach all the way to Chongqing and infoot my Chinese evil twin. Or not. Maybe going green will prove a passing fad and will lose steam after a few years, just as it did in the 1980s, when Ronald Reagan took down Jimmy Carter's solar panels from the roof of the White House.

20   Going personally green is a bet, nothing more or less, though it's one we probably all should make, even if the odds of it paying off aren't great. Sometimes you have to act as if acting will make a difference, even when you can't prove that it will. That, after all, was pre-cisely what happened in Communist Czechoslovakia and Poland, when a handful of indi-viduals like Vaclav Havel and Adam Michnik resolved that they would simply conduct their lives "as if" they lived in a free society. That improbable bet created a tiny space of liberty that, in time, expanded to take in, and then help take down, the whole of the Eastern bloc.

21   So what would be a comparable bet that the individual might make in the case of the environmental crisis? Havel himself has suggested that people begin to "conduct them-selves as if they were to live on this earth forever and be answerable for its condition one day." Fair enough, but let me propose a slightly less abstract and daunting wager. The idea is to find one thing to do in your life that doesn't involve spending or voting, that may or may not virally rock the world but is real and particular (as well as symbolic) and that, come what may, will offer its own rewards. Maybe you decide to give up meat, an act that would reduce your carbon footprint by as much as a quarter. Or you could try this: deter-mine to observe the Sabbath. For one day a week, abstain completely from economic activity: no shopping, no driving, no electronics.

22   But the act I want to talk about is growing some—even just a little—of your own food. Rip out your lawn, if you have one, and if you don't—if you live in a high-rise, or have a yard shrouded in shade—look into getting a plot in a community garden. Measured against the Problem We Face, planting a garden sounds pretty benign, I know, but in fact it's one of the most powerful things an individual can do—to reduce your carbon foot-print, sure, but more important, to reduce your sense of dependence and dividedness: to change the cheap-energy mind.

23   A great many things happen when you plant a vegetable garden, some of them directly related to climate change, others indirect but related nevertheless. Growing food, we forget, comprises the original solar technology: calories produced by means of pho-tosynthesis. Years ago the cheap-energy mind discovered that more food could be pro-duced with less effort by replacing sunlight with fossil-fuel fertilizers and pesticides, with a result that the typical calorie of food energy in your diet now requires about 10 calories of fossil-fuel energy to produce. It's estimated that the way we feed ourselves (or rather, allow ourselves to be fed) accounts for about a fifth of the greenhouse gas for which each of us is responsible.

24   Yet the sun still shines down on your yard, and photosynthesis still works so abun-dantly that in a thoughtfully organized vegetable garden (one planted from seed, nour-ished by compost from the kitchen and involving not too many drives to the garden cen-

ter), you can grow the proverbial free lunch—CO_2-free and dollar-free. This Is the most-local food you can possibly eat (not to mention the freshest, tastiest and most nutritious), with a carbon footprint so faint that even the New Zealand lamb council dares not challenge it. And while we're counting carbon, consider too your compost pile, which shrinks the heap of garbage your household needs trucked away even as it feeds your vegetables and sequesters carbon in your soil. What else? Well, you will probably notice that you're getting a pretty good workout there in your garden, burning calories without having to get into the car to drive to the gym. (It is one of the absurdities of the modern division of labor that, having replaced physical labor with fossil fuel, we now have to burn even more fossil fuel to keep our unemployed bodies in shape.) Also, by engaging both body and mind, time spent in the garden is time (and energy) subtracted from electronic forms of entertainment.

25   You begin to see that growing even a little of your own food is, as Wendell Berry pointed out 30 years ago, one of those solutions that, instead of begetting a new set of problems–the way "solutions" like ethanol or nuclear power inevitably do—actually beget other solutions, and not only of the kind that save carbon. Still more valuable are the habits of mind that growing a little of your own food can yield. You quickly learn that you need not be dependent on specialists to provide for yourself—that your body is still good for something and may actually be enlisted in its own support. If the experts are right, if both oil and time are running out, these are skills and habits of mind we're all very soon going to need. We may also need the food. Could gardens provide it? Well, during World War II, victory gardens supplied as much as 40 percent of the produce Americans ate.

26   But there are sweeter reasons to plant that garden, to bother. At least in this one corner of your yard and life, you will have begun to heal the split between what you think and what you do, to commingle your identities as consumer and producer and citizen. Chances are, your garden will re-engage you with your neighbors, for you will have produce to give away and the need to borrow their tools. You will have reduced the power of the cheap-energy mind by personally overcoming its most debilitating weakness: its helplessness and the fact that it can't do much of anything that doesn't involve division or subtraction. The garden's season-long transit from seed to ripe fruit—will you get a load of that zucchini?!—suggests that the operations of addition and multiplication still obtain, that the abundance of nature is not exhausted. The single greatest lesson the garden teaches is that our relationship to the planet need not be zero-sum, and that as long as the sun still shines and people still can plan and plant, think and do, we can, if we bother to try, find ways to provide for ourselves without diminishing the world.

Critical Reading Questions:

- **Interpretation:** Track Pollan's invocations of audience. How does Pollan explicitly define his readers for the purpose of this text? Note his deliberate shifts in person and consider any pattern or design in such choices. What are the persuasive effects of his speaking sometimes in first person, sometimes in third, and finally in second person?

- **Interpretation:** In what role does Pollan position himself in this discussion? What virtues does he enact? How does this enactment serve to facilitate his readers' developing a sense of identification with him and his argument?

Address at Brandenburg Gate

Ronald Reagan

On June 12th, 1987, U.S. President Ronald Reagan traveled to West Berlin. He stood before the Berlin Wall and called on Soviet leader Mikhail Gorbachev to open the Brandenburg Gate and allow free movement between East and West Berlin. Following the defeat of the Nazi regime at the end of WW II, Berlin, Germany, and the whole of Europe had been divided along political lines between the largely democratic and capitalist Western countries (led by the U.S. and its British and French allies) and the communist states in Eastern Europe which were centrally controlled by the Soviet Communist Party. The Wall itself had been erected in 1961 to prevent citizens from fleeing communist East Berlin and escaping to the West. Reagan explicitly asks Gorbachev to remove the physical wall and allow free movement across the city. However, he also implicitly encourages Gorbachev to continue with his current liberal policies of *glasnost* (political and economic openness) and *perestroika* (governmental reform and self-determination for other nations).

—PH

1   Thank you. Thank you, very much.

2   Chancellor Kohl, Governing Mayor Diepgen, ladies and gentlemen: Twenty-four years ago, President John F. Kennedy visited Berlin, and speaking to the people of this city and the world at the city hall. Well, since then two other presidents have come, each in his turn, to Berlin. And today I, myself, make my second visit to your city.

3   We come to Berlin, we American Presidents, because it's our duty to speak in this place of freedom. But I must confess, we're drawn here by other things as well; by the feeling of history in this city—more than 500 years older than our own nation; by the beauty of the Grunewald and the Tiergarten; most of all, by your courage and determination. Perhaps the composer, Paul Linke, understood something about American presidents. You see, like so many presidents before me, I come here today because wherever I go, whatever I do: "Ich hab noch einen koffer in Berlin". [I still have a suitcase in Berlin.]

4   Our gathering today is being broadcast throughout Western Europe and North America. I understand that it is being seen and heard as well in the East. To those listening throughout Eastern Europe, I extend my warmest greetings and the good will of the American people. To those listening in East Berlin, a special word: Although I cannot be with you, I address my remarks to you just as surely as to those standing here before me. For I join you, as I join your fellow countrymen in the West, in this firm, this unalterable belief: Es gibt nur ein Berlin. [There is only one Berlin.]

5   Behind me stands a wall that encircles the free sectors of this city, part of a vast system of barriers that divides the entire continent of Europe. From the Baltic South, those barriers cut across Germany in a gash of barbed wire, concrete, dog runs, and guard

towers. Farther south, there may be no visible, no obvious wall. But there remain armed guards and checkpoints all the same—still a restriction on the right to travel, still an instrument to impose upon ordinary men and women the will of a totalitarian state.

6   Yet, it is here in Berlin where the wall emerges most clearly, here, cutting across your city, where the news photo and the television screen have imprinted this brutal division of a continent upon the mind of the world.

7   Standing before the Brandenburg Gate, every man is a German separated from his fellow men.

8   Every man is a Berliner, forced to look upon a scar.

9   President Von Weizsäcker has said, "The German question is open as long as the Brandenburg Gate is closed." Well today—today I say: As long as this gate is closed, as long as this scar of a wall is permitted to stand, it is not the German question alone that remains open, but the question of freedom for all mankind.

10   Yet, I do not come here to lament. For I find in Berlin a message of hope, even in the shadow of this wall, a message of triumph.

11   In this season of spring in 1945, the people of Berlin emerged from their air-raid shelters to find devastation. Thousands of miles away, the people of the United States reached out to help. And in 1947 Secretary of State—as you've been told—George Marshall announced the creation of what would become known as the Marshall Plan. Speaking precisely 40 years ago this month, he said: "Our policy is directed not against any country or doctrine, but against hunger, poverty, desperation, and chaos."

12   In the Reichstag a few moments ago, I saw a display commemorating this 40th anniversary of the Marshall Plan. I was struck by a sign—the sign on a burnt-out, gutted structure that was being rebuilt. I understand that Berliners of my own generation can remember seeing signs like it dotted throughout the western sectors of the city. The sign read simply: "The Marshall Plan is helping here to strengthen the free world." A strong, free world in the West—that dream became real. Japan rose from ruin to become an economic giant. Italy, France, Belgium—virtually every nation in Western Europe saw political and economic rebirth; the European Community was founded.

13   In West Germany and here in Berlin, there took place an economic miracle, the Wirtschaftswunder. Adenauer, Erhard, Reuter, and other leaders understood the practical importance of liberty—that just as truth can flourish only when the journalist is given freedom of speech, so prosperity can come about only when the farmer and businessman enjoy economic freedom. The German leaders—the German leaders reduced tariffs, expanded free trade, lowered taxes. From 1950 to 1960 alone, the standard of living in West Germany and Berlin doubled.

14   Where four decades ago there was rubble, today in West Berlin there is the greatest industrial output of any city in Germany: busy office blocks, fine homes and apartments, proud avenues, and the spreading lawns of parkland. Where a city's culture seemed to have been destroyed, today there are two great universities, orchestras and an opera, countless theaters, and museums. Where there was want, today there's abundance— food, clothing, automobiles—the wonderful goods of the Kudamm. From devastation, from utter ruin, you Berliners have, in freedom, rebuilt a city that once again ranks as one

of the greatest on earth. Now the Soviets may have had other plans. But my friends, there were a few things the Soviets didn't count on: Berliner Herz, Berliner Humor, ja, und Berliner Schnauze. [Berliner heart, Berliner humor, yes, and a Berliner Schnauze.]

15   In the 1950s—In the 1950s Khrushchev predicted: "We will bury you." But in the West today, we see a free world that has achieved a level of prosperity and well-being unprecedented in all human history. In the Communist world, we see failure, technological backwardness, declining standards of health, even want of the most basic kind—too little food. Even today, the Soviet Union still cannot feed itself. After these four decades, then, there stands before the entire world one great and inescapable conclusion: Freedom leads to prosperity. Freedom replaces the ancient hatreds among the nations with comity and peace. Freedom is the victor.

16   And now—now the Soviets themselves may, in a limited way, be coming to understand the importance of freedom. We hear much from Moscow about a new policy of reform and openness. Some political prisoners have been released. Certain foreign news broadcasts are no longer being jammed. Some economic enterprises have been permitted to operate with greater freedom from state control.

17   Are these the beginnings of profound changes in the Soviet state? Or are they token gestures intended to raise false hopes in the West, or to strengthen the Soviet system without changing it? We welcome change and openness; for we believe that freedom and security go together, that the advance of human liberty—the advance of human liberty can only strengthen the cause of world peace.

18   There is one sign the Soviets can make that would be unmistakable, that would advance dramatically the cause of freedom and peace.

19   General Secretary Gorbachev, if you seek peace, if you seek prosperity for the Soviet Union and Eastern Europe, if you seek liberalization: Come here to this gate.

20   Mr. Gorbachev, open this gate.

21   Mr. Gorbachev—Mr. Gorbachev, tear down this wall!

22   I understand the fear of war and the pain of division that afflict this continent, and I pledge to you my country's efforts to help overcome these burdens. To be sure, we in the West must resist Soviet expansion. So, we must maintain defenses of unassailable strength. Yet we seek peace; so we must strive to reduce arms on both sides.

23   Beginning 10 years ago, the Soviets challenged the Western alliance with a grave new threat, hundreds of new and more deadly SS-20 nuclear missiles capable of striking every capital in Europe. The Western alliance responded by committing itself to a counter-deployment (unless the Soviets agreed to negotiate a better solution)—namely, the elimination of such weapons on both sides. For many months, the Soviets refused to bargain in earnestness. As the alliance, in turn, prepared to go forward with its counter-deployment, there were difficult days, days of protests like those during my 1982 visit to this city; and the Soviets later walked away from the table.

24   But through it all, the alliance held firm. And I invite those who protested then—I invite those who protest today—to mark this fact: Because we remained strong, the Soviets came back to the table. Because we remained strong, today we have within reach the possibility, not merely of limiting the growth of arms, but of eliminating, for the first time, an entire class of nuclear weapons from the face of the earth.

25   As I speak, NATO ministers are meeting in Iceland to review the progress of our proposals for eliminating these weapons. At the talks in Geneva, we have also proposed
deep cuts in strategic offensive weapons. And the Western allies have likewise made far-
reaching proposals to reduce the danger of conventional war and to place a total ban on
chemical weapons.

26   While we pursue these arms reductions, I pledge to you that we will maintain the
capacity to deter Soviet aggression at any level at which it might occur. And in cooperation with many of our allies, the United States is pursuing the Strategic Defense Initiative—
research to base deterrence not on the threat of offensive retaliation, but on defenses that
truly defend; on systems, in short, that will not target populations, but shield them. By these
means we seek to increase the safety of Europe and all the world. But we must remember
a crucial fact: East and West do not mistrust each other because we are armed; we are
armed because we mistrust each other. And our differences are not about weapons but
about liberty. When President Kennedy spoke at the City Hall those 24 years ago, freedom
was encircled; Berlin was under siege. And today, despite all the pressures upon this city,
Berlin stands secure in its liberty. And freedom itself is transforming the globe.

27   In the Philippines, in South and Central America, democracy has been given a
rebirth. Throughout the Pacific, free markets are working miracle after miracle of economic
growth. In the industrialized nations, a technological revolution is taking place, a revolution
marked by rapid, dramatic advances in computers and telecommunications.

28   In Europe, only one nation and those it controls refuse to join the community of freedom. Yet in this age of redoubled economic growth, of information and innovation, the Soviet
Union faces a choice: It must make fundamental changes, or it will become obsolete.

29   Today, thus, represents a moment of hope. We in the West stand ready to cooperate
with the East to promote true openness, to break down barriers that separate people, to
create a safer, freer world. And surely there is no better place than Berlin, the meeting
place of East and West, to make a start.

30   Free people of Berlin: Today, as in the past, the United States stands for the strict
observance and full implementation of all parts of the Four Power Agreement of 1971. Let
us use this occasion, the 750th anniversary of this city, to usher in a new era, to seek a still
fuller, richer life for the Berlin of the future. Together, let us maintain and develop the ties
between the Federal Republic and the Western sectors of Berlin, which is permitted by the
1971 agreement.

31   And I invite Mr. Gorbachev: Let us work to bring the Eastern and Western parts of the
city closer together, so that all the inhabitants of all Berlin can enjoy the benefits that come
with life in one of the great cities of the world.

32   To open Berlin still further to all Europe, East and West, let us expand the vital air
access to this city, finding ways of making commercial air service to Berlin more convenient, more comfortable, and more economical. We look to the day when West Berlin can
become one of the chief aviation hubs in all central Europe.

33   With—With our French—With our French and British partners, the United States is
prepared to help bring international meetings to Berlin. It would be only fitting for Berlin to
serve as the site of United Nations meetings, or world conferences on human rights and
arms control, or other issues that call for international cooperation.

34   There is no better way to establish hope for the future than to enlighten young minds, and we would be honored to sponsor summer youth exchanges, cultural events, and other programs for young Berliners from the East. Our French and British friends, I'm certain, will do the same. And it's my hope that an authority can be found in East Berlin to sponsor visits from young people of the Western sectors.

35   One final proposal, one close to my heart: Sport represents a source of enjoyment and ennoblement, and you may have noted that the Republic of Korea—South Korea— has offered to permit certain events of the 1988 Olympics to take place in the North. International sports competitions of all kinds could take place in both parts of this city. And what better way to demonstrate to the world the openness of this city than to offer in some future year to hold the Olympic games here in Berlin, East and West.

36   In these four decades, as I have said, you Berliners have built a great city. You've done so in spite of threats—the Soviet attempts to impose the East-mark, the blockade. Today the city thrives in spite of the challenges implicit in the very presence of this wall. What keeps you here? Certainly there's a great deal to be said for your fortitude, for your defiant courage. But I believe there's something deeper, something that involves Berlin's whole look and feel and way of life—not mere sentiment. No one could live long in Berlin without being completely disabused of illusions. Something instead, that has seen the difficulties of life in Berlin but chose to accept them, that continues to build this good and proud city in contrast to a surrounding totalitarian presence, that refuses to release human energies or aspirations, something that speaks with a powerful voice of affirmation, that says "yes" to this city, yes to the future, yes to freedom. In a word, I would submit that what keeps you in Berlin—is "love."

37   Love both profound and abiding.

38   Perhaps this gets to the root of the matter, to the most fundamental distinction of all between East and West. The totalitarian world produces backwardness because it does such violence to the spirit, thwarting the human impulse to create, to enjoy, to worship. The totalitarian world finds even symbols of love and of worship an affront.

39   Years ago, before the East Germans began rebuilding their churches, they erected a secular structure: the television tower at Alexander Platz. Virtually ever since, the authorities have been working to correct what they view as the tower's one major flaw: treating the glass sphere at the top with paints and chemicals of every kind. Yet even today when the sun strikes that sphere, that sphere that towers over all Berlin, the light makes the sign of the cross. There in Berlin, like the city itself, symbols of love, symbols of worship, cannot be suppressed.

40   As I looked out a moment ago from the Reichstag, that embodiment of German unity, I noticed words crudely spray-painted upon the wall, perhaps by a young Berliner (quote):

41   "This wall will fall. Beliefs become reality."

42   Yes, across Europe, this wall will fall, for it cannot withstand faith; it cannot withstand truth. The wall cannot withstand freedom.

43   And I would like, before I close, to say one word. I have read, and I have been questioned since I've been here about certain demonstrations against my coming. And I would

like to say just one thing, and to those who demonstrate so. I wonder if they have ever asked themselves that if they should have the kind of government they apparently seek, no one would ever be able to do what they're doing again.

44 Thank you and God bless you all. Thank you.

Critical Reading Questions:

- **Analysis:** Reagan has often been called the "great communicator" and has been widely praised for his use of simple language, specific examples, and narrative form to replace the use of political jargon, complex logical argument, and elaborate rephrasing of main ideas. How does this speech reflect these principles of communication?

- **Rhetorical Analysis:** Reagan delivers the speech on television in front of a live crowd of German citizens and uses the physical Brandenburg Gate (part of the actual wall) as the backdrop for his speech. How does Reagan make use of his live crowd and his physical setting to strengthen the persuasive appeal of his speech?

D.C = discourse community

Aria: A Memoir of a Bilingual Childhood

Richard Rodriguez

Richard Rodriguez's article appeared in *The American Scholar* magazine at a critical time in the debate over bilingual education models. Many support these models out of concern for identity politics due to the integral connection between one's native tongue and identity. Here, Rodriguez examines the merits of this concern, as he narrates his experience entering an American school as a non-native English-speaking child of Mexican immigrants. He expresses the "loss" of his "intimate" language (Spanish) and the effects of this loss on him and his family. Also embedded in his poignant argument are claims that further complicate the issue and seemingly support English-only initiatives because they reveal a crucial paradox: the "gains" of his "Americanization." Of these gains, Rodriguez passionately emphasizes access to the "power" or "public" language (Standard English)—access he argues is the key to "rights and opportunities" afforded to members of a society.

—CLR

Starting new d.c (english) speak'n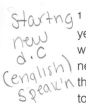

1   I remember, to start with, that day in Sacramento, in a California now nearly thirty years past, when I first entered a classroom—able to understand about fifty stray English words. The third of four children, I had been preceded by my older brother and sister to a neighborhood Roman Catholic school. But neither of them had revealed very much about their classroom experiences. They left each morning and returned each afternoon, always together, speaking Spanish as they climbed the five steps to the porch. And their mysterious books, wrapped in brown shopping-bag paper, remained on the table next to the door, closed firmly behind them.

2   An accident of geography sent me to a school where all my classmates were white and many were the children of doctors and lawyers and business executives. On that first day of school, my classmates must certainly have been uneasy to find themselves apart from their families, in the first institution of their lives. But I was astonished. I was fated to be the "problem student" in class.

3   The nun said, in a friendly but oddly impersonal voice: "Boys and girls, this is Richard Rodriguez." (I heard her sound it out: *Rich-heard Road-ree-guess.*) It was the first time I had heard anyone say my name in English. "Richard," the nun repeated more slowly, writing my name down in her book. Quickly I turned to see my mother's face dissolve in a watery blur behind the pebbled-glass door.

4   Now, many years later, I hear of something called "bilingual education"—a scheme proposed in the late 1960s by Hispanic-American social activists, later endorsed by a congressional vote. It is a program that seeks to permit non-English-speaking children (many from lower class homes) to use their "family language" as the language of school.

Such, at least, is the aim its supporters announce. I hear them, and am forced to say no: It is not possible for a child, any child, ever to use his family's language in school. Not to understand this is to misunderstand the public uses of schooling and to trivialize the nature of intimate life.

5   Memory teaches me what I know of these matters. The boy reminds the adult. I was a bilingual child, but of a certain kind: "socially disadvantaged," the son of working-class parents, both Mexican immigrants.

6   In the early years of my boyhood, my parents coped very well in America. My father had steady work. My mother managed at home. They were nobody's victims. When we moved to a house many blocks from the Mexican-American section of town, they were not intimidated by those two or three neighbors who initially tried to make us unwelcome. ("Keep your brats away from my sidewalk!") But despite all they achieved, or perhaps because they had so much to achieve, they lacked any deep feeling of ease, of belonging in public. They regarded the people at work or in crowds as being very distant from us. Those were the others, *los gringos*. That term was interchangeable in their speech with another, even more telling: *los americanos*.

7   I grew up in a house where the only regular guests were my relations. On a certain day, enormous families of relatives would visit us, and there would be so many people that the noise and the bodies would spill out to the backyard and onto the front porch. Then for weeks no one would come. (If the doorbell rang, it was usually a salesman.) Our house stood apart—gaudy yellow in a row of white bungalows. We were the people with the noisy dog, the people who raised chickens. We were the foreigners on the block. A few neighbors would smile and wave at us. We waved back. But until I was seven years old, I did not know the name of the old couple living next door or the names of the kids living across the street.

8   In public, my father and mother spoke a hesitant, accented, and not always grammatical English. And then they would have to strain, their bodies tense, to catch the sense of what was rapidly said by *los gringos*. At home, they returned to Spanish. The language of their Mexican past sounded in counterpoint to English spoken in public. The words would come quickly, with ease. Conveyed through those sounds was the pleasing, soothing, consoling reminder that one was at home.

9   During those years when I was first learning to speak, my mother and father addressed me only in Spanish; in Spanish I learned to reply. By contrast, English (*inglés*) was the language I came to associate with gringos, rarely heard in the house. I learned my first words of English overhearing my parents speaking to strangers. At six years of age, I knew just enough words for my mother to trust me on errands to stores one block away—but no more.

10   I was then a listening child, careful to hear the very different sounds of Spanish and English. Wide-eyed with hearing, I'd listen to sounds more than to words. First, there were English (gringo) sounds. So many words still were unknown to me that when the butcher or the lady at the drugstore said something, exotic polysyllabic sounds would bloom in the midst of their sentences. Often the speech of people in public seemed to me very loud, booming with confidence. The man behind the counter would literally ask, "What

can I do for you?" But by being so firm and clear, the sound of his voice said that he was a gringo; he belonged in public society. There were also the high, nasal notes of middle-class American speech—which I rarely am conscious of hearing today because I hear them so often, but could not stop hearing when I was a boy. Crowds at Safeway or at bus stops were noisy with the birdlike sounds of *los gringos*. I'd move away from them all—all the chirping chatter above me.

11   My own sounds I was unable to hear, but I knew that I spoke English poorly. My words could not extend to form complete thoughts. And the words I did speak I didn't know well enough to make distinct sounds. (Listeners would usually lower their heads to hear better what I was trying to say.) But it was one thing for me to speak English with difficulty; it was more troubling to hear my parents speaking in public: their high-whining vowels and guttural consonants; their sentences that got stuck with "eh" and "ah" sounds; the confused syntax; the hesitant rhythm of sounds so different from the way gringos spoke. I'd notice, moreover, that my parents' voices were softer than those of gringos we would meet.

12   I am tempted to say now that none of this mattered. (In adulthood I am embarrassed by childhood fears.) And, in a way, it didn't matter very much that my parents could not speak English with ease. Their linguistic difficulties had no serious consequences. My mother and father made themselves understood at the county hospital clinic and at government offices. And yet, in another way, it mattered very much. It was unsettling to hear my parents struggle with English. Hearing them, I'd grow nervous, and my clutching trust in their protection and power would be weakened.

13   There were many times like the night at a brightly lit gasoline station (a blaring white memory) when I stood uneasily hearing my father talk to the teenage attendant. I do not recall what they were saying, but I cannot forget the sounds my father made as he spoke. At one point his words slid together to form one long word—sounds as confused as the threads of blue and green oil in the puddle next to my shoes. His voice rushed through what he had left to say. Toward the end, he reached falsetto notes, appealing to his listener's understanding. I looked away at the lights of passing automobiles. I tried not to hear any more. But I heard only too well the attendant's reply, his calm, easy tones. Shortly afterward, headed for home, I shivered when my father put his hand on my shoulder. The very first chance that I got, I evaded his grasp and ran on ahead into the dark, skipping with feigned boyish exuberance.

14   But then there was Spanish: *español*, the language rarely heard away from the house; *español*, the language which seemed to me therefore a private language, my family's language. To hear its sounds was to feel myself specially recognized as one of the family, apart from *los otros*. A simple remark, an inconsequential comment could convey that assurance. My parents would say something to me and I would feel embraced by the sounds of their words. Those sounds said: I am speaking with ease in Spanish. I am addressing you in words I never use with los gringos. *I recognize you as someone special, close, like no one outside. You belong with us. In the family. Ricardo.*

15   At the age of six, well past the time when most middle-class children no longer notice the difference between sounds uttered at home and words spoken in public, I had a different experience. I lived in a world compounded of sounds. I was a child longer than most.

I lived in a magical world, surrounded by sounds both pleasing and fearful. I shared with my family a language enchantingly private—different from that used in the city around us.
16   Just opening or closing the screen door behind me was an important experience. I'd rarely leave home all alone or without feeling reluctance. Walking down the sidewalk, under the canopy of tall trees, I'd warily notice the (suddenly) silent neighborhood kids who stood warily watching me. Nervously, I'd arrive at the grocery store to hear there the sounds of the gringo, reminding me that in this so-big world I was a foreigner. But if leaving home was never routine, neither was the coming back. Walking toward our house, climbing the steps from the sidewalk, in summer when the front door was open, I'd hear voices beyond the screen door talking in Spanish. For a second or two I'd stay, linger there listening. Smiling, I'd hear my mother call out, saying in Spanish, "Is that you, Richard?" Those were her words, but all the while her sounds would assure me: You are home now. *Come close inside. With us. "Sí,"* I'd reply.
17   Once more inside the house, I would resume my place in the family. The sounds would grow harder to hear. Once more at home, I would grow less conscious of them. It required, however, no more than the blurt of the doorbell to alert me all over again to listen to sounds. The house would turn instantly quiet while my mother went to the door. I'd hear her hard English sounds. I'd wait to hear her voice turn to soft-sounding Spanish, which assured me, as surely as did the clicking tongue of the lock on the door, that the stranger was gone.
18   Plainly it is not healthy to hear such sounds so often. It is not healthy to distinguish public from private sounds so easily. I remained cloistered by sounds, timid and shy in public, too dependent on the voices at home. I remember many nights when my father would come back from work, and I'd hear him call out to my mother in Spanish, sounding relieved. In Spanish, his voice would sound the light and free notes that he never could manage in English. Some nights I'd jump up just hearing his voice. My brother and I would come running into the room where he was with our mother. Our laughing (so deep was the pleasure!) became screaming. Like others who feel the pain of public alienation, we transformed the knowledge of our public separateness into a consoling reminder of our intimacy. Excited, our voices joined in a celebration of sounds. *We are speaking now the way we never speak out in public—we are together,* the sounds told me. Some nights no one seemed willing to loosen the hold that sounds had on us. At dinner we invented new words that sounded Spanish, but made sense only to us. We pieced together new words by taking, say, an English verb and giving it Spanish endings. My mother's instructions at bedtime would be lacquered with mock-urgent tones. Or a word like *sí,* sounded in several notes, would convey added measures of feeling. Tongues lingered around the edges of words, especially fat vowels, and we happily sounded that military drum roll, the twirling roar of the Spanish *r.* Family language, my family's sounds: the voices of my parents and sisters and brother. Their voices insisting: *You belong here. We are family members. Related. Special to one another. Listen!* Voices singing and sighing, rising and straining, then surging, teeming with pleasure which burst syllables into fragments of laughter. At times it seemed there was steady quiet only when, from another room, the rustling whispers of my parents faded and I edged closer to sleep.

19   Supporters of bilingual education today imply that students like me miss a great deal by not being taught in their family's language. What they seem not to recognize is that, as a socially disadvantaged child, I considered Spanish to be a private language. It was a ghetto language that deepened and strengthened my feeling of separateness. What I needed to learn in school was that I had the right, and the obligation, to speak the public language. The odd truth is that my first-grade classmates could have become bilingual, in the conventional sense of that word, more easily than I. Had they been taught early (as upper-middle-class children often are taught) a "second language" like Spanish or French, they could have regarded it simply as another public language. In my case, such bilingualism could not have been so quickly achieved. What I did not believe was that I could speak a single public language.

20   Without question, it would have pleased me to have heard my teachers address me in Spanish when I entered the classroom. I would have felt much less afraid. I would have imagined that my instructors were somehow "related" to me; I would indeed have heard their Spanish as my family's language. I would have trusted them and responded with ease. But I would have delayed—postponed for how long?—having to learn the language of public society. I would have evaded—and for how long?—learning the great lesson of school: that I had a public identity.

21   Fortunately, my teachers were unsentimental about their responsibility. What they understood was that I needed to speak a public English. So their voices would search me out, asking me questions. Each time I heard them I'd look up in surprise to see a nun's face frowning at me. I'd mumble, not really meaning to answer. The nun would persist, "Richard, stand up. Don't look at the floor. Speak up. Speak to the entire class, not just to me!" But I couldn't believe English could be my language to use. (In part, I did not want to believe it.) I continued to mumble. I resisted the teacher's demands. (Did I somehow suspect that once I learned public language my family life would be changed?) Silent, waiting for the bell to sound, I remained dazed, different, afraid.

22   Because I wrongly imagined that English was intrinsically a public language and Spanish was intrinsically private, I easily noted the difference between classroom language and the language at home. At school, words were directed to a general audience of listeners. ("Boys and girls...") Words were meaningfully ordered. And the point was not self-expression alone, but to make oneself understood by many others. The teacher quizzed: "Boys and girls, why do we use that word in this sentence? Could we think of a better word to use there? Would the sentence change its meaning if the words were differently arranged? Isn't there a better way of saying much the same thing?" (I couldn't say. I wouldn't try to say.)

23   Three months passed. Five. A half year. Unsmiling, ever watchful, my teachers noted my silence. They began to connect my behavior with the slow progress my brother and sisters were making. Until, one Saturday morning, three nuns arrived at the house to talk to our parents. Stiffly they sat on the blue living-room sofa. From the doorway of another room, spying on the visitors, I noted the incongruity, the clash of two worlds, the faces and voices of school intruding upon the familiar setting of home. I overheard one voice

gently wondering, "Do your children speak only Spanish at home, Mrs. Rodriguez?" While another voice added, "That Richard especially seems so timid and shy."

24   That *Rich-heard*!

25   With great tact, the visitors continued, "Is it possible for you and your husband to encourage your children to practice their English when they are home?" Of course my parents complied. What would they not do for their children's well-being? And how could they question the Church's authority which those women represented? In an instant they agreed to give up the language (the sounds) which had revealed and accentuated our family's closeness. The moment after the visitors left, the change was observed. "*Ahora*, speak to us only *en inglés*," my father and mother told us.

26   At first, it seemed a kind of game. After dinner each night, the family gathered to practice "our" English. It was still then *inglés*, a language foreign to us, so we felt drawn to it as strangers. Laughing, we would try to define words we could not pronounce. We played with strange English sounds, often over-anglicizing our pronunciations. And we filled the smiling gaps of our sentences with familiar Spanish sounds. But that was cheating, somebody shouted, and everyone laughed.

27   In school, meanwhile, like my brother and sisters, I was required to attend a daily tutoring session. I needed a full year of this special work. I also needed my teachers to keep my attention from straying in class by calling out, "*Rich-heard*"—their English voices slowly loosening the ties to my other name, with its three notes, *Ri-car-do*. Most of all, I needed to hear my mother and father speak to me in a moment of seriousness in "broken"—suddenly heartbreaking—English. This scene was inevitable. One Saturday morning I entered the kitchen where my parents were talking, but I did not realize that they were talking in Spanish until, the moment they saw me, their voices changed and they began speaking English. The gringo sounds they uttered startled me. Pushed me away. In that moment of trivial misunderstanding and profound insight, I felt my throat twisted by unsounded grief. I simply turned and left the room. But I had no place to escape to where I could grieve in Spanish. My brother and sisters were speaking English in another part of the house.

28   Again and again in the days following, as I grew increasingly angry, I was obliged to hear my mother and father encouraging me: "Speak to us en *inglés*." Only then did I determine to learn classroom English. Thus, sometime afterward it happened: One day in school, I raised my hand to volunteer an answer to a question. I spoke out in a loud voice and I did not think it remarkable when the entire class understood. That day I moved very far from being the disadvantaged child I had been only days earlier. Taken hold at last was the belief, the calming assurance, that I *belonged* in public.

29   Shortly after, I stopped hearing the high, troubling sounds of *los gringos*. A more and more confident speaker of English, I didn't listen to how strangers sounded when they talked to me. With so many English-speaking people around me, I no longer heard American accents. Conversations quickened. Listening to persons whose voices sounded eccentrically pitched, I might note their sounds for a few seconds, but then I'd concentrate on what they were saying. Now when I heard someone's tone of voice—angry or question-

ing or sarcastic or happy or sad—I didn't distinguish it from the words it expressed. Sound and word were thus tightly wedded. At the end of a day, I was often bemused, and always relieved, to realize how "soundless," though crowded with words, my day in public had been. An eight-year-old boy, I finally came to accept what had been technically true since my birth: I was an American citizen.

30   But diminished by then was the special feeling of closeness at home. Gone was the desperate, urgent, intense feeling of being at home among those with whom I felt intimate. Our family remained a loving family, but one greatly changed. We were no longer so close, no longer bound tightly together by the knowledge of our separateness from *los gringos*. Neither my older brother nor my sisters rushed home after school anymore. Nor did I. When I arrived home, often there would be neighborhood kids in the house. Or the house would be empty of sounds.

31   Following the dramatic Americanization of their children, even my parents grew more publicly confident—especially my mother. First she learned the names of all the people on the block. Then she decided we needed to have a telephone in our house. My father, for his part, continued to use the word gringo, but it was no longer charged with the bitterness or distrust. Stripped of any emotional content, the word simply became a name for those Americans not of Hispanic descent. Hearing him, sometimes, I wasn't sure if he was pronouncing the Spanish word *gringo* or saying gringo in English.

32   There was a new silence at home. As we children learned more and more English, we shared fewer and fewer words with our parents. Sentences needed to be spoken slowly when one of us addressed our mother or father. Often the parent wouldn't understand. The child would need to repeat himself. Still the parent misunderstood. The young voice, frustrated, would end up saying, "Never mind"—the subject was closed. Dinners would be noisy with the clinking of knives and forks against dishes. My mother would smile softly between her remarks; my father, at the other end of the table, would chew and chew his food, while he stared over the heads of his children.

33   My mother! My father! After English became my primary language, I no longer knew what words to use in addressing my parents. The old Spanish words (those tender accents of sound) I had earlier used—*mamá* and *papá*—I couldn't use anymore. They would have been all-too-painful reminders of how much had changed in my life. On the other hand, the words I heard neighborhood kids call their parents seemed equally unsatisfactory. "Mother" and "father," "ma," "pa," "dad," "pop" (how I hated the all-American sound of that last word)—all these terms I felt were unsuitable terms of address for my parents. As a result, I never used them at home. Whenever I'd speak to my parents, I would try to get their attention by looking at them. In public conversations, I'd refer to them as my "parents" or my "mother" and "father."

34   My mother and father, for their part, responded differently, as their children spoke to them less. My mother grew restless, seemed troubled and anxious at the scarceness of words exchanged in the house. She would question me about my day when I came home from school. She smiled at my small talk. She pried at the edges of my sentences to get me to say something more. ("What...?") She'd join conversations that she overheard, but

[handwritten marginal note: he didn't know what to call his parents]

her intrusions often stopped her children's talking. By contrast, my father seemed to grow reconciled to the new quiet. Though his English somewhat improved, he tended more and more to retire into silence. At dinner he spoke very little. One night his children and even his wife helplessly giggled at his garbled English pronunciation of the Catholic "Grace Before Meals." Thereafter he made his wife recite the prayer at the start of each meal, even on formal occasions when there were guests in the house.

35   Hers became the public voice of the family. On official business it was she, not my father, who would usually talk to strangers on the phone or in the stores. We children grew so accustomed to his silence that years later we would routinely refer to his "shyness." (My mother often tried to explain: Both of his parents died when he was eight. He was raised by an uncle who treated him as little more than a menial servant. He was never encouraged to speak. He grew up alone—a man of few words.) But I realized my father was not shy whenever I'd watch him speaking Spanish with relatives. Using Spanish, he was quickly effusive. Especially when talking with other men, his voice would spark, flicker, flare alive with varied sounds. In Spanish, he expressed ideas and feelings he rarely revealed when speaking English. With firm Spanish sounds he conveyed confidence and authority that English would never allow him.

36   The silence at home, however, was not simply the result of fewer words passed between parents and children. More profound for me was the silence created by my inattention to sounds. At about the time I no longer bothered to listen with care to the sounds of English in public, I grew careless about listening to the sounds made by my family when they spoke. Most of the time I would hear someone speaking at home and didn't distinguish his sounds from the words people uttered in public. I didn't even pay much attention to my parents' accented and ungrammatical speech—at least not at home. Only when I was with them in public would I become alert to their accents. But even then their sounds caused me less and less concern. For I was increasingly confident of my own public identity.

37   I would have been happier about my public success had I not recalled, sometimes, what it had been like earlier, when my family conveyed its intimacy through a set of con-veniently private sounds. Sometimes in public, hearing a stranger, I'd hark back to my lost past. A Mexican farm worker approached me downtown. He wanted directions to some place. "*Hijito,…*" he said. And his voice stirred old longings. Another time I was standing beside my mother in the visiting room of a Carmelite convent, before the dense screen which rendered the nuns shadowy figures. I heard several of them speaking Spanish in their busy, singsong, overlapping voices, assuring my mother that yes, yes, we were remembered, in their prayers. Those voices echoed faraway family sounds. Another day, a dark-faced old woman touched my shoulder lightly to steady herself as she boarded a bus. She murmured something to me I couldn't quite comprehend. Her Spanish voice came near, like the face of a never-before-seen relative in the instant before I was kissed. That voice, like so many of the Spanish voices I'd hear in public, recalled the golden age of my childhood.

38   Bilingual educators say today that children lose a degree of "Individuality" by becoming assimilated into public society. (Bilingual schooling is a program popularized in the seventies, that decade when middle-class "ethnics" began to resist the process of assimilation—the "American melting pot.") But the bilingualists oversimplify when they scorn the value and necessity of assimilation. They do not seem to realize that a person is individualized in two ways. So they do not realize that, while one suffers a diminished sense of *private* individuality by being assimilated into public society, such assimilation makes possible the achievement of *public* individuality.

39   Simplistically again, the bilingualists insist that a student should be reminded of his difference from others in mass society, of his "heritage." But they equate mere separateness with individuality. The fact is that only in private—with intimates—is separateness from the crowd a prerequisite for individuality; an intimate "tells" me that I am unique, unlike all others, apart from the crowd. In public, by contrast, full individuality is achieved, paradoxically, by those who are able to consider themselves members of the crowd. Thus it happened for me. Only when I was able to think of myself as an American, no longer an alien in gringo society, could I seek the rights and opportunities necessary for full public individuality. The social and political advantages I enjoy as a man began on the day I came to believe that my name is indeed *Rich-heard Road-ree-guess*. It is true that my public society today is often impersonal; in fact, my public society is usually mass society. But despite the anonymity of the crowd, and despite the fact that the individuality I achieve in public is often tenuous—because it depends on my being one in a crowd—I celebrate the day I acquired my new name. Those middle-class ethnics who scorn assimilation seem to me filled with decadent self-pity, obsessed by the burden of public life. Dangerously, they romanticize public separateness and trivialize the dilemma of those who are truly socially disadvantaged.

40   If I rehearse here the changes in my private life after my Americanization, it is finally to emphasize a public gain. The loss implies the gain. The house I returned to each afternoon was quiet. Intimate sounds no longer greeted me at the door. Inside there were other noises. The telephone rang. Neighborhood kids ran past the door of the bedroom where I was reading my schoolbooks—covered with brown shopping-bag paper. Once I learned the public language, it would never again be easy for me to hear intimate family voices. More and more of my day was spent hearing words, not sounds. But that may only be a way of saying that on the day I raised my hand in class and spoke loudly to an entire roomful of faces, my childhood started to end.

Critical Reading Questions:

- **Rhetorical analysis:** Rodriguez frames his argument in a personal narrative. Considering audience members and their values (presuppositions), do you think this rhetorical choice is effective? Why or why not? How might this choice build ethos with the audience? For instance, do certain passages demonstrate Rodriguez might be an authority on the issue? If so, will this way of building ethos be effective with the audience?

- **Rhetorical analysis:** Select passages in the article that make emotional appeals to the audience. Do these appeals to pathos support Rodriguez's claim effectively? By referring to the values of the audience, explain why or why not.

The Great Arsenal of Democracy

Franklin Delano Roosevelt

President Franklin Delano Roosevelt delivered this speech as a "fireside chat" with the American people on December 29, 1940. While this characterization might indicate a casual tone, these "fireside chats" were normally about significant issues. In this instance, the speech was about the Nazis taking over Europe. FDR had to appeal to the American public to give Europe more support, but to do so, he had to address the competing values of two ideals: isolationism and globalization, between which, the United States has struggled since the time of the Whigs and Tories. These two ideals are fully articulated here. The United States at the time was exhausted by the last Great War, yet the country wanted to support Great Britain and the other free countries. FDR appeals to the globalists by calling on the U.S. to manufacture arms and become the "arsenal of democracy," aiding and equipping the other "free countries" of the world. FDR appeals to the isolationists by saying that the purpose of being this arsenal is to "keep [the Nazis] away from our country and people."

—JT

1   My friends:

2   This is not a fireside chat on war. It is a talk on national security; because the nub of the whole purpose of your President is to keep you now, and your children later, and your grandchildren much later, out of a last-ditch war for the preservation of American independence, and all of the things that American independence means to you and to me and to ours.

3   Tonight, in the presence of a world crisis, my mind goes back eight years to a night in the midst of a domestic crisis. It was a time when the wheels of American industry were grinding to a full stop, when the whole banking system of our country had ceased to function. I well remember that while I sat in my study in the White House, preparing to talk with the people of the United States, I had before my eyes the picture of all those Americans with whom I was talking. I saw the workmen in the mills, the mines, the factories, the girl behind the counter, the small shopkeeper, the farmer doing his Spring plowing, the widows and the old men wondering about their life's savings. I tried to convey to the great mass of American people what the banking crisis meant to them in their daily lives.

4   Tonight, I want to do the same thing, with the same people, in this new crisis which faces America. We met the issue of 1933 with courage and realism. We face this new crisis, this new threat to the security of our nation, with the same courage and realism. Never before since Jamestown and Plymouth Rock has our American civilization been in such danger as now. For on September 27th, 1940—this year—by an agreement signed in Berlin, three powerful nations, two in Europe and one in Asia, joined themselves together

in the threat that if the United States of America interfered with or blocked the expansion program of these three nations—a program aimed at world control—they would unite in ultimate action against the United States.

5   The Nazi masters of Germany have made it clear that they intend not only to dominate all life and thought in their own country, but also to enslave the whole of Europe, and then to use the resources of Europe to dominate the rest of the world. It was only three weeks ago that their leader stated this: "There are two worlds that stand opposed to each other." And then in defiant reply to his opponents he said this: "Others are correct when they say: 'With this world we cannot ever reconcile ourselves.' I can beat any other power in the world." So said the leader of the Nazis.

6   In other words, the Axis not merely admits but the Axis proclaims that there can be no ultimate peace between their philosophy—their philosophy of government—and our philosophy of government. In view of the nature of this undeniable threat, it can be asserted, properly and categorically, that the United States has no right or reason to encourage talk of peace until the day shall come when there is a clear intention on the part of the aggressor nations to abandon all thought of dominating or conquering the world.

7   At this moment the forces of the States that are leagued against all peoples who live in freedom are being held away from our shores. The Germans and the Italians are being blocked on the other side of the Atlantic by the British and by the Greeks, and by thousands of soldiers and sailors who were able to escape from subjugated countries. In Asia the Japanese are being engaged by the Chinese nation in another great defense. In the Pacific Ocean is our fleet.

8   Some of our people like to believe that wars in Europe and in Asia are of no concern to us. But it is a matter of most vital concern to us that European and Asiatic war-makers should not gain control of the oceans which lead to this hemisphere. One hundred and seventeen years ago the Monroe Doctrine was conceived by our government as a measure of defense in the face of a threat against this hemisphere by an alliance in Continental Europe. Thereafter, we stood guard in the Atlantic, with the British as neighbors. There was no treaty. There was no "unwritten agreement." And yet there was the feeling, proven correct by history, that we as neighbors could settle any disputes in peaceful fashion. And the fact is that during the whole of this time the Western Hemisphere has remained free from aggression from Europe or from Asia.

9   Does anyone seriously believe that we need to fear attack anywhere in the Americas while a free Britain remains our most powerful naval neighbor in the Atlantic? And does anyone seriously believe, on the other hand, that we could rest easy if the Axis powers were our neighbors there? If Great Britain goes down, the Axis powers will control the Continents of Europe, Asia, Africa, Austral-Asia, and the high seas. And they will be in a position to bring enormous military and naval resources against this hemisphere. It is no exaggeration to say that all of us in all the Americas would be living at the point of a gun—a gun loaded with explosive bullets, economic as well as military. We should enter upon a new and terrible era in which the whole world, our hemisphere included, would be run by threats of brute force. And to survive in such a world, we would have to convert ourselves permanently into a militaristic power on the basis of war economy.

10   Some of us like to believe that even if Britain falls, we are still safe, because of the broad expanse of the Atlantic and of the Pacific. But the width of those oceans is not what it was in the days of clipper ships. At one point between Africa and Brazil the distance is less than it is from Washington to Denver, Colorado, five hours for the latest type of bomber. And at the north end of the Pacific Ocean, America and Asia almost touch each other. Why, even today we have planes that could fly from the British Isles to New England and back again without refueling. And remember that the range of the modern bomber is ever being increased.

11   During the past week many people in all parts of the nation have told me what they wanted me to say tonight. Almost all of them expressed a courageous desire to hear the plain truth about the gravity of the situation. One telegram, however, expressed the attitude of the small minority who want to see no evil and hear no evil, even though they know in their hearts that evil exists. That telegram begged me not to tell again of the ease with which our American cities could be bombed by any hostile power which had gained bases in this Western Hemisphere. The gist of that telegram was: "Please, Mr. President, don't frighten us by telling us the facts." Frankly and definitely there is danger ahead— danger against which we must prepare. But we well know that we cannot escape danger, or the fear of danger, by crawling into bed and pulling the covers over our heads.

12   Some nations of Europe were bound by solemn nonintervention pacts with Germany. Other nations were assured by Germany that they need never fear invasion. Nonintervention pact or not, the fact remains that they were attacked, overrun, thrown into modern slavery at an hour's notice—or even without any notice at all. As an exiled leader of one of these nations said to me the other day, "The notice was a minus quantity. It was given to my government two hours after German troops had poured into my country in a hundred places." The fate of these nations tells us what it means to live at the point of a Nazi gun.

13   The Nazis have justified such actions by various pious frauds. One of these frauds is the claim that they are occupying a nation for the purpose of "restoring order." Another is that they are occupying or controlling a nation on the excuse that they are "protecting it" against the aggression of somebody else. For example, Germany has said that she was occupying Belgium to save the Belgians from the British. Would she then hesitate to say to any South American country: "We are occupying you to protect you from aggression by the United States"? Belgium today is being used as an invasion base against Britain, now fighting for its life. And any South American country, in Nazi hands, would always constitute a jumping off place for German attack on any one of the other republics of this hemisphere.

14   Analyze for yourselves the future of two other places even nearer to Germany if the Nazis won. Could Ireland hold out? Would Irish freedom be permitted as an amazing pet exception in an unfree world? Or the islands of the Azores, which still fly the flag of Portugal after five centuries? You and I think of Hawaii as an outpost of defense in the Pacific. And yet the Azores are closer to our shores in the Atlantic than Hawaii is on the other side.

15   There are those who say that the Axis powers would never have any desire to attack the Western Hemisphere. That is the same dangerous form of wishful thinking which has destroyed the powers of resistance of so many conquered peoples. The plain facts are

that the Nazis have proclaimed, time and again, that all other races are their inferiors and therefore subject to their orders. And most important of all, the vast resources and wealth of this American hemisphere constitute the most tempting loot in all of the round world.

16   Let us no longer blind ourselves to the undeniable fact that the evil forces which have crushed and undermined and corrupted so many others are already within our own gates. Your government knows much about them and every day is ferreting them out. Their secret emissaries are active in our own and in neighboring countries. They seek to stir up suspicion and dissension, to cause internal strife. They try to turn capital against labor, and vice versa. They try to reawaken long slumbering racial and religious enmities which should have no place in this country. They are active in every group that promotes intolerance. They exploit for their own ends our own natural abhorrence of war. These trouble-breeders have but one purpose. It is to divide our people, to divide them into hostile groups and to destroy our unity and shatter our will to defend ourselves.

17   There are also American citizens, many of them in high places, who, unwittingly in most cases, are aiding and abetting the work of these agents. I do not charge these American citizens with being foreign agents. But I do charge them with doing exactly the kind of work that the dictators want done in the United States. These people not only believe that we can save our own skins by shutting our eyes to the fate of other nations. Some of them go much further than that. They say that we can and should become the friends and even the partners of the Axis powers. Some of them even suggest that we should imitate the methods of the dictatorships. But Americans never can and never will do that.

18   The experience of the past two years has proven beyond doubt that no nation can appease the Nazis. No man can tame a tiger into a kitten by stroking it. There can be no appeasement with ruthlessness. There can be no reasoning with an incendiary bomb. We know now that a nation can have peace with the Nazis only at the price of total surrender. Even the people of Italy have been forced to become accomplices of the Nazis; but at this moment they do not know how soon they will be embraced to death by their allies.

19   The American appeasers ignore the warning to be found in the fate of Austria, Czechoslovakia, Poland, Norway, Belgium, the Netherlands, Denmark, and France. They tell you that the Axis powers are going to win anyway; that all of this bloodshed in the world could be saved, that the United States might just as well throw its influence into the scale of a dictated peace and get the best out of it that we can. They call it a "negotiated peace." Nonsense! Is it a negotiated peace if a gang of outlaws surrounds your community and on threat of extermination makes you pay tribute to save your own skins? For such a dictated peace would be no peace at all. It would be only another armistice, leading to the most gigantic armament race and the most devastating trade wars in all history. And in these contests the Americas would offer the only real resistance to the Axis power. With all their vaunted efficiency, with all their parade of pious purpose in this war, there are still in their background the concentration camp and the servants of God in chains.

20   The history of recent years proves that the shootings and the chains and the concentration camps are not simply the transient tools but the very altars of modern dictatorships. They may talk of a "new order" in the world, but what they have in mind is only a revival of the oldest and the worst tyranny. In that there is no liberty, no religion, no hope. The

proposed "new order" is the very opposite of a United States of Europe or a United States of Asia. It is not a government based upon the consent of the governed. It is not a union of ordinary, self-respecting men and women to protect themselves and their freedom and their dignity from oppression. It is an unholy alliance of power and pelf to dominate and to enslave the human race.

21   The British people and their allies today are conducting an active war against this unholy alliance. Our own future security is greatly dependent on the outcome of that fight. Our ability to "keep out of war" is going to be affected by that outcome. Thinking in terms of today and tomorrow, I make the direct statement to the American people that there is far less chance of the United States getting into war if we do all we can now to support the nations defending themselves against attack by the Axis than if we acquiesce in their defeat, submit tamely to an Axis victory, and wait our turn to be the object of attack in another war later on.

22   If we are to be completely honest with ourselves, we must admit that there is risk in any course we may take. But I deeply believe that the great majority of our people agree that the course that I advocate involves the least risk now and the greatest hope for world peace in the future.

23   The people of Europe who are defending themselves do not ask us to do their fighting. They ask us for the implements of war, the planes, the tanks, the guns, the freighters which will enable them to fight for their liberty and for our security. Emphatically, we must get these weapons to them, get them to them in sufficient volume and quickly enough so that we and our children will be saved the agony and suffering of war which others have had to endure.

24   Let not the defeatists tell us that it is too late. It will never be earlier. Tomorrow will be later than today.

25   Certain facts are self-evident.

26   In a military sense Great Britain and the British Empire are today the spearhead of resistance to world conquest. And they are putting up a fight which will live forever in the story of human gallantry. There is no demand for sending an American expeditionary force outside our own borders. There is no intention by any member of your government to send such a force. You can therefore, nail, nail any talk about sending armies to Europe as deliberate untruth. Our national policy is not directed toward war. Its sole purpose is to keep war away from our country and away from our people.

27   Democracy's fight against world conquest is being greatly aided, and must be more greatly aided, by the rearmament of the United States and by sending every ounce and every ton of munitions and supplies that we can possibly spare to help the defenders who are in the front lines. And it is no more un-neutral for us to do that than it is for Sweden, Russia, and other nations near Germany to send steel and ore and oil and other war materials into Germany every day in the week.

28   We are planning our own defense with the utmost urgency, and in its vast scale we must integrate the war needs of Britain and the other free nations which are resisting aggression. This is not a matter of sentiment or of controversial personal opinion. It is a

matter of realistic, practical military policy, based on the advice of our military experts who are in close touch with existing warfare. These military and naval experts and the members of the Congress and the Administration have a single-minded purpose: the defense of the United States.

29   This nation is making a great effort to produce everything that is necessary in this emergency, and with all possible speed. And this great effort requires great sacrifice. I would ask no one to defend a democracy which in turn would not defend everyone in the nation against want and privation. The strength of this nation shall not be diluted by the failure of the government to protect the economic well-being of its citizens. If our capacity to produce is limited by machines, it must ever be remembered that these machines are operated by the skill and the stamina of the workers.

30   As the government is determined to protect the rights of the workers, so the nation has a right to expect that the men who man the machines will discharge their full responsibilities to the urgent needs of defense. The worker possesses the same human dignity and is entitled to the same security of position as the engineer or the manager or the owner. For the workers provide the human power that turns out the destroyers, and the planes, and the tanks. The nation expects our defense industries to continue operation without interruption by strikes or lockouts. It expects and insists that management and workers will reconcile their differences by voluntary or legal means, to continue to produce the supplies that are so sorely needed. And on the economic side of our great defense program, we are, as you know, bending every effort to maintain stability of prices and with that the stability of the cost of living.

31   Nine days ago I announced the setting up of a more effective organization to direct our gigantic efforts to increase the production of munitions. The appropriation of vast sums of money and a well-coordinated executive direction of our defense efforts are not in themselves enough. Guns, planes, ships and many other things have to be built in the factories and the arsenals of America. They have to be produced by workers and managers and engineers with the aid of machines which in turn have to be built by hundreds of thousands of workers throughout the land. In this great work there has been splendid cooperation between the government and industry and labor. And I am very thankful.

32   American industrial genius, unmatched throughout all the world in the solution of production problems, has been called upon to bring its resources and its talents into action. Manufacturers of watches, of farm implements, of Linotypes and cash registers and automobiles, and sewing machines and lawn mowers and locomotives, are now making fuses and bomb packing crates and telescope mounts and shells and pistols and tanks.

33   But all of our present efforts are not enough. We must have more ships, more guns, more planes—more of everything. And this can be accomplished only if we discard the notion of "business as usual." This job cannot be done merely by superimposing on the existing productive facilities the added requirements of the nation for defense. Our defense efforts must not be blocked by those who fear the future consequences of surplus plant capacity. The possible consequences of failure of our defense efforts now are much more to be feared. And after the present needs of our defense are past, a proper handling of the

country's peacetime needs will require all of the new productive capaclty, If not still more. No pessimistic policy about the future of America shall delay the immediate expansion of those industries essential to defense. We need them.

34   I want to make it clear that it is the purpose of the nation to build now with all possible speed every machine, every arsenal, every factory that we need to manufacture our defense material. We have the men, the skill, the wealth, and above all, the wlll. I am confident that if and when production of consumer or luxury goods in certain industries requires the use of machines and raw materials that are essential for defense purposes, then such production must yield, and will gladly yield, to our primary and compelling purpose.

35   So I appeal to the owners of plants, to the managers, to the workers, to our own government employees to put every ounce of effort into producing these munitions swiftly and without stint. With this appeal I give you the pledge that all of us who are officers of your government will devote ourselves to the same whole-hearted extent to the great task that lies ahead.

36   As planes and ships and guns and shells are produced, your government, with its defense experts, can then determine how best to use them to defend this hemisphere. The decision as to how much shall be sent abroad and how much shall remain at home must be made on the basis of our overall military necessities.

37   We must be the great arsenal of democracy.

38   For us this is an emergency as serious as war itself. We must apply ourselves to our task with the same resolution, the same sense of urgency, the same spirit of patriotism and sacrifice as we would show were we at war.

39   We have furnished the British great material support and we will furnish far more in the future. There will be no "bottlenecks" in our determination to aid Great Britain. No dictator, no combination of dictators, will weaken that determination by threats of how they will construe that determination. The British have received invaluable military support from the heroic Greek Army and from the forces of all the governments in exile. Their strength is growing. It is the strength of men and women who value their freedom more highly than they value their lives.

40   I believe that the Axis powers are not going to win this war. I base that belief on the latest and best of information.

41   We have no excuse for defeatism. We have every good reason for hope—hope for peace, yes, and hope for the defense of our civilization and for the building of a better civilization in the future. I have the profound conviction that the American people are now determined to put forth a mightier effort than they have ever yet made to increase our production of all the implements of defense, to meet the threat to our democratic faith.

42   As President of the United States, I call for that national effort. I call for it in the name of this nation which we love and honor and which we are privileged and proud to serve. I call upon our people with absolute confidence that our common cause will greatly succeed.

Critical Reading Questions:

- **Rhetorical analysis:** Often, when rhetors are faced with particularly challenging persuasive aims, they will carefully blend pathos with logos and/or ethos. Where do we see FDR doing this? Why is he doing it?

- **Rhetorical analysis:** Consider the *kairos* happening here. FDR is not advocating for the U.S. to send troops to the war just yet. Why is this speech not advocating that? What is the impetus here? What will be the impetus for going to war? How are those two moments different? How are they similar?

Reading Games: Strategies for Reading Scholarly Sources

Karen Rosenberg

Serving as the Director of the Writing and Communication Center at the University of Washington-Bothell, Karen Rosenberg has a unique understanding of some of the most common obstacles facing students in the academic world. In the following essay, she explains the art of "wrestling with academic journal articles" by offering students guidance to help them "read smarter, not harder." For instance, Rosenberg advises students to understand and examine the anatomy of the article; sections such as titles, abstracts, section headings, and introductions become useful guides for locating an author's main ideas and argument. But reading academic articles is more than employing a strategic reading agenda. Deep understanding and appreciation of academic articles, Rosenberg suggests, depend on "joining the conversation." She explains a process called "rhetorical reading," in which students must actively engage with their readings and recognize how authors present their arguments within a broader context. By carrying on a dialogue with the author and classmates and professors, students are ultimately invited to join the conversation.

—RT

1   If at First You Fall Asleep . . .

2   During my first year in college, I feared many things: calculus, cafeteria food, the stained, sweet smelling mattress in the basement of my dorm. But I did not fear reading. I didn't really think about reading at all, that automatic making of meaning from symbols in books, newspapers, on cereal boxes. And, indeed, some of my coziest memories of that bewildering first year involved reading. I adopted an overstuffed red chair in the library that enveloped me like the lap of a department store Santa. I curled up many evenings during that first, brilliant autumn with my English homework: Toni Morrison's *The Bluest Eye*, Gloria Naylor's *Mama Day*, Sandra Cisneros' *The House on Mango Street*. I'd read a gorgeous passage, snuggle deeper into my chair, and glance out to the sunset and fall leaves outside of the library window. This felt deeply, unmistakably collegiate.

3   But English was a requirement—I planned to major in political science. I took an intro course my first semester and brought my readings to that same chair. I curled up, opened a book on the Chinese Revolution, started reading, and fell asleep. I woke up a little drooly, surprised at the harsh fluorescent light, the sudden pitch outside. Not to be deterred, I bit my lip and started over. I'd hold on for a paragraph or two, and then suddenly I'd be thinking about my classmate Joel's elbows, the casual way he'd put them on the desk when our professor lectured, sometimes resting his chin in his hands. He was a long limbed runner and smelled scrubbed—a mixture of laundry detergent and shampoo. He had black hair and startling blue eyes. Did I find him sexy?

4   Crap! How many paragraphs had my eyes grazed over while I was thinking about Joel's stupid elbows? By the end of that first semester, I abandoned ideas of majoring in political science. I vacillated between intense irritation with my assigned readings and a sneaking suspicion that perhaps the problem was me—I was too dumb to read academic texts. Whichever it was—a problem with the readings or with me—I carefully chose my classes so that I could read novels, poetry, and plays for credit. But even in my English classes, I discovered, I had to read dense scholarly articles. By my Junior year, I trained myself to spend days from dawn until dusk hunkered over a carrel in the library's basement armed with a dictionary and a rainbow of highlighters. Enjoying my reading seemed hopelessly naïve—an indulgence best reserved for beach blankets and bathtubs. A combination of obstinacy, butt-numbingly hard chairs, and caffeine helped me survive my scholarly reading assignments. But it wasn't fun.

5   Seven years later I entered graduate school. I was also working and living on my own, cooking for myself instead of eating off cafeteria trays. In short, I had a life. My days were not the blank canvas they had been when I was an undergraduate and could sequester myself in the dungeon of the library basement. And so, I finally learned how to read smarter, not harder. Perhaps the strangest part of my reading transformation was that I came to *like* reading those dense scholarly articles; I came to crave the process of sucking the marrow from the texts. If you can relate to this, if you also love wrestling with academic journal articles, take joy in arguing with authors in the margins of the page, I am not writing for you.

6   However, if your reading assignments confound you, if they send you into slumber, or you avoid them, or they seem to take you *way* too long, then pay attention. Based on my experience as a frustrated student and now as a teacher of reading strategies, I have some insights to share with you designed to make the reading process more productive, more interesting, and more enjoyable.

Joining the Conversation[1]

7   Even though it may seem like a solitary, isolated activity, when you read a scholarly work, you are participating in a conversation. Academic writers do not make up their arguments off the top of their heads (or solely from creative inspiration). Rather, they look at how others have approached similar issues and problems. Your job—and one for which you'll get plenty of help from your professors and your peers—is to locate the writer and yourself in this larger conversation. Reading academic texts is a deeply social activity; talking with your professors and peers about texts can not only help you understand your readings better, but it can push your thinking and clarify your own stances on issues that really matter to you.

8   In your college courses, you may have come across the term "rhetorical reading."[2] Rhetoric in this context refers to how texts work to persuade readers—a bit different from the common connotation of empty, misleading, or puffed up speech. Rhetorical reading refers to a set of practices designed to help us understand how texts work and to engage more deeply and fully in a conversation that extends beyond the boundaries of any particular reading. Rhetorical reading practices ask us to think deliberately about the role and relationship between the writer, reader, and text.

9   When thinking about the writer, we are particularly interested in clues about the writer's motivation and agenda. If we know something about what the writer cares about and is trying to accomplish, it can help orient us to the reading and understand some of the choices the writer makes in his or her work.

10   As readers, our role is quite active. We pay attention to our own motivation and agenda for each reading. On one level, our motivation may be as simple as wanting to do well in a class, and our agenda may involve wanting to understand as much as necessary in order to complete our assignments. In order to meet these goals, we need to go deeper, asking, "Why is my professor asking me to read this piece?" You may find clues in your course syllabus, comments your professor makes in class, or comments from your classmates. If you aren't sure why you are being asked to read something, ask! Most professors will be more than happy to discuss in general terms what "work" they want a reading to do—for example, to introduce you to a set of debates, to provide information on a specific topic, or to challenge conventional thinking on an issue.

11   Finally, there is the text—the thing that the writer wrote and that you are reading. In addition to figuring out *what* the text says, rhetorical reading strategies ask us to focus on *how* the text delivers its message. In this way of thinking about texts, there is not one right and perfect meaning for the diligent reader to uncover; rather, interpretations of the reading will differ depending on the questions and contexts readers bring to the text.

Strategies for Rhetorical Reading

12   Here are some ways to approach your reading that better equip you for the larger conversation. First, consider the **audience**. When the writer sat down to write your assigned reading, to whom was he or she implicitly talking? Textbooks, for the most part, have students like you in mind. They may be boring, but you've probably learned what to do with them: pay attention to the goals of the chapter, check out the summary at the end, ignore the text in the boxes because it's usually more of a "fun fact" than something that will be on the test, and so on. Magazines in the checkout line at the supermarket also have you in mind: you can't help but notice headlines about who is cheating or fat or anorexic or suicidal. Writers of scholarly sources, on the other hand, likely don't think much about you at all when they sit down to write. Often, academics write primarily for other academics. But just because it's people with PhDs writing for other people with PhDs doesn't mean that you should throw in the towel. There's a formula for these types of texts, just like there's a formula for all the *Cosmo* articles that beckon with titles that involve the words "hot," "sex tips," "your man," and "naughty" in different configurations.

13   It's just that the formula is a little more complicated.

14   The formula also changes depending on the flavor of study (physics, management, sociology, English, etc.) and the venue. However, if you determine that the audience for your reading is other academics, recognize that you are in foreign territory. You won't understand all of the chatter you hear on street corners, you may not be able to read the menus in the restaurants, but, with a little practice, you will be able to find and understand the major road signs, go in the right direction, and find your way.

15   How can you figure out the primary audience? First, look at the publication venue. (Here, to some extent, you can judge a book by its cover). If the reading comes from an academic journal, then chances are good that the primary audience is other academics. Clues that a journal is academic (as opposed to popular, like *Time* or *Newsweek*) include a citation format that refers to a volume number and an issue number, and often this information appears at the top or bottom of every page. Sometimes you can tell if a reading comes from an academic journal based on the title—e.g., do the *Journal for Research in Mathematics Education* or *Qualitative Research in Psychology* sound like they are written for a popular audience? What if you're still not sure? Ask your reference librarians, classmates, your instructor, or friends and family who have more experience with these types of readings than you do.

16   There are two implications that you should be aware of if you are not the primary audience for a text. First, the author will assume prior knowledge that you likely don't have. You can expect sentences like "as Durkheim has so famously argued . . ." or "much ink has been spilled on the implications of the modernization hypothesis" where you have no idea who Durkheim is or what the modernization hypothesis says. That's OK. It might even be OK to not look these things up at all and still get what you need from the reading (but you won't know that yet). In the first reading of an article, it's smart to hold off on looking too many things up. Just be prepared to face a wall of references that don't mean a whole lot to you.

17   Second, if you're not the primary audience, don't be surprised if you find that the writing isn't appealing to you. Whereas a novelist or a magazine writer works hard to draw us in as readers, many academic authors don't use strategies to keep us hooked. In fact, many of these strategies (use of sensory language, suspense, etc.) would never get published in academic venues. By the same token, you'll use very different strategies to read these scholarly texts.

18   You may be wondering, if you're not the intended audience for the text, why do you have to read it in the first place? This is an excellent question, and one that you need to answer before you do your reading. As I mentioned earlier in the discussion of the role of the reader, you may need to do a little sleuthing to figure this out. In addition to the suggestions I provided earlier, look to your course notes and syllabus for answers. Often professors will tell you why they assign specific readings. Pay attention—they will likely offer insights on the context of the reading and the most important points. If after all of this, you still have no idea why you're supposed to read six articles on the history of Newtonian physics, then ask your professor. Use the answers to help you focus on the really important aspects of the texts and to gloss over the parts that are less relevant to your coursework. If you remain confused, continue to ask for clarification. Ask questions in class (your classmates will be grateful). Go to office hours. Most faculty love the opportunity to talk about readings that they have chosen with care.

19   Once you have an idea who the intended audience is for the article and why you are assigned to read it, don't sit down and read the article from start to finish, like a good mystery. Get a lay of the land before you go too deep. One way to do this is to study the architecture of the article. Here are some key components to look for:

20   **The title**. As obvious as it sounds, pay attention to the title because it can convey a lot of information that can help you figure out how to read the rest of the article more efficiently. Let's say that I know my reading will be about the Russian Revolution. Let's say I even know that it will be about the role of music in the Russian Revolution. Let's say the title is "'Like the beating of my heart': A discourse analysis of Muscovite musicians' letters during the Russian Revolution." This tells me not only the subject matter of the article (something about letters Russian musicians wrote during the Revolution) but it also tells me something about the methodology, or the way that the author approaches the subject matter. I might not know exactly what discourse analysis is, but I can guess that you can do it to letters and that I should pay particular attention to it when the author mentions it in the article. On the other hand, if the title of the article were "Garbage cans and metal pipes: Bolshevik music and the politics of proletariat propaganda" I would know to look out for very different words and concepts. Note, also, that the convention within some academic disciplines to have a pretty long title separated by a colon usually follows a predictable pattern. The text to the left of the colon serves as a teaser, or as something to grab a reader's attention (remember that the author is likely not trying to grab your attention, so you may not find these teasers particularly effective—though it is probably packed with phrases that would entice someone who already studies the topic). The information to the right of the colon typically is a more straightforward explanation of what the article is about.

21   **The abstract.** Not all of your readings will come with abstracts, but when they do, pay close attention. An abstract is like an executive summary. Usually one paragraph at the beginning of an article, the abstract serves to encapsulate the main points of the article. It's generally a pretty specialized summary that seeks to answer specific questions. These include: the main problem or question, the approach (how did the author(s) do the work they write about in the article?), the shiny new thing that this article does (more on this later, but to be published in an academic journal you often need to argue that you are doing something that has not been done before), and why people who are already invested in this field should care (in other words, you should be able to figure out why another academic should find the article important). The abstract often appears in database searches, and helps scholars decide if they want to seek out the full article.

22   That's a whole lot to accomplish in one paragraph.

23   As a result, authors often use specialized jargon to convey complex ideas in few words, make assumptions of prior knowledge, and don't worry much about general readability. Abstracts, thus, are generally dense, and it's not uncommon to read through an abstract and not have a clue about what you just read. This is a good place to re-read, highlight, underline, look up what you don't know. You still may not have a firm grasp on everything in the abstract, but treat the key terms in the abstract like parts of a map when you see them in the main text, leading you to treasure: understanding the main argument.

24   **The introduction**. The introduction serves some of the same functions as the abstract, but there is a lot more breathing room here. When I started reading academic texts, I'd breeze through the introduction to get to the "meat" of the text. This was exactly the wrong thing to do. I can't remember how many times I'd find myself in the middle of

some dense reading, perhaps understanding the content of a particular paragraph, but completely unable to connect that paragraph with the overall structure of the article. I'd jump from the lily pad of one paragraph to the next, continually fearful that I'd slip off and lose myself in a sea of total confusion (and I often did slip)

25   If the author is doing her/his job well, the introduction will not only summarize the whole piece, present the main idea, and tell us why we should care, but it will also often offer a road map for the rest of the article. Sometimes, the introduction will be called "intro-duction," which makes things easy. Sometimes, it's not. Generally, treat the first section of an article as the introduction, regardless if it's explicitly called that or not.

26   There are times where your reading will have the introduction chopped off. This makes your work harder. The two most common instances of introduction-less readings are assigned excerpts of articles and lone book chapters. In the first case, you only have a portion of an article so you cannot take advantage of many of the context clues the writer set out for readers. You will need to rely more heavily on the context of your course in general and your assignment in particular to find your bearings here. If the reading is high stakes (e.g., if you have to write a paper or take an exam on it), you may want to ask your professor how you can get the whole article. In the second case, your professor assigns a chapter or two from the middle of an academic book. The chapter will hopefully contain some introductory material (and generally will include much more than the middle of a journal article), but you will likely be missing some context clues that the author included in the introduction to the whole book. If you have trouble finding your footing here, and it's important that you grasp the meaning and significance of the chapter, seek out the book itself and skim the introductory chapter to ground you in the larger questions that the author is addressing. Oddly, even though you'll be doing more reading, it may save you time because you can read your assigned chapter(s) more efficiently.

27   Roadmaps included in the introduction are often surprisingly straightforward. They often are as simple as "in the first section, we examine . . . in the second section we argue . . ." etc. Search for these maps. Underline them. Highlight them. Go back to them when you find your comprehension slipping.

28   **Section headings.** A section heading serves as a title for a particular part of an article. Read all of these to get a sense of the trajectory of the text before delving into the content in each section (with the exception of the introduction and the conclusion which you should read in detail). Get a passing familiarity with the meanings of the words in the section headings—they are likely important to understanding the main argument of the text.

29   **Conclusion.** When writing papers, you've likely heard the cliché "in the introduction, write what you will say, then say it, then write what you just said." With this formula, it would seem logical to gloss over the conclusion, because, essentially, you've already read it already. However, this is not the case. Instead, pay close attention to the conclusion. It can help you make sure you understood the introduction. Sometimes a slight re-phrasing can help you understand the author's arguments in an important, new way. In addition, the conclusion is often where authors indicate the limitations of their work, the unanswered questions, the horizons left unexplored. And this is often the land of exam and essay questions . . . asking you to extend the author's analysis beyond its own shores.

30   At this point, you have pored over the title, the introduction, the section headings, and the conclusion. You haven't really read the body of the article yet. Your next step is to see if you can answer the question: what is the **main argument or idea** in this text?

31   Figuring out the main argument is *the* key to reading the text effectively and efficiently. Once you can identify the main argument, you can determine how much energy to spend on various parts of the reading. For example, if I am drowning in details about the temperance movement in the United States in the 19th Century, I need to know the main argument of the text to know if I need to slow down or if a swift skim will do. If the main argument is that women's organizing has taken different forms in different times, it will probably be enough for me to understand that women organized against the sale and consumption of alcohol. That might involve me looking up "temperance" and getting the gist of women's organizing. However, if the main argument were that scholars have misunderstood the role of upper class white women in temperance organizing in Boston from 1840–1865, then I would probably need to slow down and pay closer attention.

32   Unless the reading is billed as a review or a synthesis, the only way that an academic text can even get published is if it claims to argue something new or different. However, unlike laundry detergent or soft drinks, academic articles don't advertise what makes them new and different in block letters inside cartoon bubbles. In fact, finding the main argument can sometimes be tricky. Mostly, though, it's just a matter of knowing where to look. The abstract and the introduction are the best places to look first. With complicated texts, do this work with your classmates, visit your campus writing center (many of them help with reading assignments), or drag a friend into it.

33   Once you understand the different parts of the text and the writer's main argument, use this information to see how and where you can enter the conversation. In addition, keep your own agenda as a reader in mind as you do this work.

Putting It All Together

34   Collectively, these suggestions and guidelines will help you read and understand academic texts. They ask you to bring a great deal of awareness and preparation to your reading—for example, figuring out who the primary audience is for the text and, if you are not that audience, why your professor is asking you to read it anyway. Then, instead of passively reading the text from start to finish, my suggestions encourage you to pull the reading into its constituent parts—the abstract, the introduction, the section headings, conclusion, etc.—and read them unevenly and out of order to look for the holy grail of the main argument. Once you have the main argument you can make wise decisions about which parts of the text you need to pore over and which you can blithely skim. The final key to reading smarter, not harder is to make it social. When you have questions, ask. Start conversations with your professors about the reading. Ask your classmates to work with you to find the main arguments. Offer a hand to your peers who are drowning in dense details. Academics write to join scholarly conversations. Your professors assign you their texts so that you can join them too.

Notes

1. In this discussion I draw on Norgaard's excellent discussion of reading as joining a conversation (1–28). By letting you, the reader, know this in a footnote, I am not only citing my source (I'd be plagiarizing if I didn't mention this somewhere), but I'm also showing how I enter this conversation and give you a trail to follow if you want to learn more about the metaphor of the conversation. Following standard academic convention, I put the full reference to Norgaard's text at the end of this article, in the references.
2. I draw on—and recommend—Rounsaville et al.'s discussion of rhetorical sensitivity, critical reading and rhetorical reading (1–35).

Works Cited

Norgaard, Rolf. *Composing Knowledge: Readings for College Writers.* Boston: Bedford/St. Martin's, 2007. Print.

Rounsaville, Angela, Rachel Goldberg, Keith Feldman, Cathryn Cabral, and Anis Bawarshi, eds. *Situating Inquiry: An Introduction to Reading, Research, and Writing at the University of Washington.* Boston: Bedford/St. Martin's, 2008. Print.

Critical Reading Questions:

- **Analysis:** One of Rosenberg's suggestions for reading a dense academic text is not to "read the article from start to finish." Why might this prove to be a useful strategy? What advantages does reading strategically offer?

- **Summary:** Rosenberg asserts that productive reading is active. What is active reading? Describe its characteristics and attributes.

Generation Why?

Zadie Smith

Shortly after the release of the 2010 film, *The Social Network*, Zadie Smith, a Harvard grad educated alongside the film's focal point, Mark Zuckerberg, wrote this quippy response to the film, its icon, and to their generation 2.0 and was published in *The New York Times Book Review*. She initially analyzes scenes in the film which portray Zuckerberg as a nerdy programmer. However, she soon claims the film is a lie—just as Zuckerberg did not create Facebook to impress a girl, the real Zuckerberg is not reflected in the film character. This idea should inform young, interested viewers that perhaps Facebook itself is not a construct that should be trusted. In fact, the film should act as a warning against using Facebook. Smith suggests that such software is severely limited; it focuses on quantity of connections rather than quality of relationships. Smith herself leaves Facebook and proposes that users should do the same or demand something different. Her hope is that the demand will entice change, but she believes it is more likely Facebook will soon be something laughable, regrettable. Smith is a noted British novelist, essayist, and short story writer.

—KH

1   How long is a generation these days? I must be in Mark Zuckerberg's generation—there are only nine years between us—but somehow it doesn't feel that way. This despite the fact that I can say (like everyone else on Harvard's campus in the fall of 2003) that "I was there" at Facebook's inception, and remember Facemash and the fuss it caused; also that tiny, exquisite movie star trailed by fan-boys through the snow wherever she went, and the awful snow itself, turning your toes gray, destroying your spirit, bringing a bloodless end to a squirrel on my block: frozen, inanimate, perfect—like the Blaschka glass flowers. Doubtless years from now I will misremember my closeness to Zuckerberg, in the same spirit that everyone in '60s Liverpool met John Lennon.

2   At the time, though, I felt distant from Zuckerberg and all the kids at Harvard. I still feel distant from them now, ever more so, as I increasingly opt out (by choice, by default) of the things they have embraced. We have different ideas about things. Specifically we have different ideas about what a person is, or should be. I often worry that my idea of personhood is nostalgic, irrational, inaccurate. Perhaps Generation Facebook have built their virtual mansions in good faith, in order to house the People 2.0 they genuinely are, and if I feel uncomfortable within them it is because I am stuck at Person 1.0. Then again, the more time I spend with the tail end of Generation Facebook (in the shape of my students) the more convinced I become that some of the software currently shaping their generation is unworthy of them. They are more interesting than it is. They deserve better.

3   In *The Social Network* Generation Facebook gets a movie almost worthy of them, and this fact, being so unexpected, makes the film feel more delightful than it probably, objec-

tively, is. From the opening scene it's clear that this is a movie about 2.0 people made by 1.0 people (Aaron Sorkin and David Fincher, forty-nine and forty-eight respectively). It's a *talkie*, for goodness' sake, with as many words per minute as *His Girl Friday*. A boy, Mark, and his girl, Erica, sit at a little table in a Harvard bar, zinging each other, in that relentless Sorkin style made famous by *The West Wing* (though at no point does either party say "Walk with me"—for this we should be grateful).

4   But something is not right with this young man: his eye contact is patchy; he doesn't seem to understand common turns of phrase or ambiguities of language; he is literal to the point of offense, pedantic to the point of aggression. ("Final clubs," says Mark, correcting Erica, as they discuss those exclusive Harvard entities, "*Not* Finals clubs.") He doesn't understand what's happening as she tries to break up with him. ("Wait, wait, this is real?") Nor does he understand *why*. He doesn't get that what he may consider a statement of fact might yet have, for this other person, some personal, painful import:

5   ERICA: I have to go study.

6   MARK: You don't have to study.

7   ERICA: *How do you know I don't have to study?!*

8   MARK: *Because you go to B.U.!*

9   Simply put, he is a computer nerd, a social "autistic": a type as recognizable to Fincher's audience as the cynical newshound was to Howard Hawks's. To create this Zuckerberg, Sorkin barely need brush his pen against the page. We came to the cinema expecting to meet this guy and it's a pleasure to watch Sorkin color in what we had already confidently sketched in our minds. For sometimes the culture surmises an individual personality, collectively. Or thinks it does. Don't we all know why nerds do what they do? To get money, which leads to popularity, which leads to girls. Sorkin, confident of his foundation myth, spins an exhilarating tale of double rejection—spurned by Erica and the Porcellian, the Finaliest of the Final Clubs, Zuckerberg begins his spite-fueled rise to the top. Cue a lot of betrayal. A lot of scenes of lawyers' offices and miserable, character-damning depositions. ("Your best friend is suing you!") Sorkin has swapped the military types of *A Few Good Men* for a different kind of all-male community in a different uniform: GAP hoodies, North Face sweats.

10   At my screening, blocks from NYU, the audience thrilled with intimate identification. But if the hipsters and nerds are hoping for Fincher's usual pyrotechnics they will be disappointed: in a lawyer's office there's not a lot for Fincher to *do*. He has to content himself with excellent and rapid cutting between Harvard and the later court cases, and after that, the discreet pleasures of another, less-remarked-upon Fincher skill: great casting. It'll be a long time before a cinema geek comes along to push Jesse Eisenberg, the actor who plays Zuckerberg, off the top of our nerd typologies. The passive-aggressive, flat-line voice. The shifty boredom when anyone, other than himself, is speaking. The barely suppressed smirk. Eisenberg even chooses the correct nerd walk: not the sideways corridor shuffle (the *Don't Hit Me!*), but the puffed chest vertical march (the *I'm not 5'8", I'm 5'9"!*).

11   With rucksack, naturally. An extended four-minute shot has him doing exactly this all the way through the Harvard campus, before he lands finally where he belongs, the only place he's truly comfortable, in front of his laptop, with his blog:

12   Erica Albright's a bitch. You think that's because her family changed their name from Albrecht or do you think it's because all B.U. girls are bitches?

13   Oh, yeah. We know this guy. Overprogrammed, furious, lonely. Around him Fincher arranges a convincing bunch of 1.0 humans, by turns betrayed and humiliated by him, and as the movie progresses they line up to sue him. If it's a three-act movie it's because Zuckerberg screws over more people than a two-act movie can comfortably hold: the Winklevoss twins and Divya Navendra (from whom Zuckerberg allegedly stole the Facebook concept), and then his best friend, Eduardo Saverin (the CFO he edged out of the company), and finally Sean Parker, the boy king of Napster, the music-sharing program, although he, to be fair, pretty much screws himself. It's in Eduardo—in the actor Andrew Garfield's animate, beautiful face—that all these betrayals seem to converge, and become personal, painful. The arbitration scenes—that should be dull, being so terribly static—get their power from the eerie opposition between Eisenberg's unmoving countenance (his eyebrows hardly ever move; the real Zuckerberg's eyebrows *never* move) and Garfield's imploring disbelief, almost the way Spencer Tracy got all worked up opposite Frederic March's rigidity in another courtroom epic, *Inherit the Wind*.

14   Still, Fincher allows himself one sequence of (literal) showboating. Halfway through the film, he inserts a ravishing but quite unnecessary scene of the pretty Winklevoss twins (for a story of nerds, all the men are surprisingly comely) at the Henley Regatta. These two blond titans row like champs. (One actor, Armie Hammer, has been digitally doubled. I'm so utterly 1.0 that I spent an hour of the movie trying to detect any difference between the twins.) Their arms move suspiciously fast, faster than real human arms, their muscles seem outlined by a fine pen, the water splashes up in individual droplets as if painted by Caravaggio, and the music! Trent Reznor, of Nine Inch Nails, commits exquisite brutality upon Edward Grieg's already pretty brutal "In the Hall of the Mountain King." All synths and white noise. It's music video stuff—the art form in which my not-quite generation truly excels—and it demonstrates the knack for hyperreality that made Fincher's *Fight Club* so compelling while rendering the real world, for so many of his fans, always something of a disappointment. Anyway, the twins lose the regatta, too, by a nose, which allows Fincher to justify the scene by thematic reiteration: sometimes very close is simply not close enough. Or as Mark pleasantly puts it across a conference table: "If you guys were the inventors of Facebook you'd have invented Facebook."

15   All that's left for Zuckerberg is to meet the devil at the crossroads: naturally he's an Internet music entrepreneur. It's a Generation Facebook instinct to expect (hope?) that a pop star will fall on his face in the cinema, but Justin Timberlake, as Sean Parker, neatly steps over that expectation: whether or not you think he's a shmuck, he sure plays a great shmuck. Manicured eyebrows, sweaty forehead, and that coked-up, wafer-thin self-confidence, always threatening to collapse into paranoia. Timberlake shimmies into view in the third act to offer the audience, and Zuckerberg, the very same thing, essentially, that he's been offering us for the past decade in his videos: a vision of the good life.

16   This vision is also wafer-thin, and Fincher satirizes it mercilessly. Again, we know its basic outline: a velvet rope, a cocktail waitress who treats you like a king, the best of every-

thing on tap, a special booth of your own, fussy tiny expensive food ("Could you bring out some things? The lacquered pork with that ginger confit? I don't know, tuna tartar, some lobster claws, the foie gras and the shrimp dumplings, that'll get us started"), appletinis, a Victoria's Secret model date, wild house parties, fancy cars, slick suits, cocaine, and a "sky's the limit" objective: "A million dollars isn't cool. You know what's cool?... A *billion* dollars." Over cocktails in a glamorous nightclub, Parker dazzles Zuckerberg with tales of the life that awaits him on the other side of a billion. Fincher keeps the thumping Euro house music turned up to exactly the level it would be in real life: the actors have to practically scream to be heard above it. Like many a nerd before him, Zuckerberg is too hyped on the idea that he's in heaven to notice he's in hell.

17   Generation Facebook's obsession with this type of "celebrity lifestyle" is more than familiar. It's pitiful, it pains us, and we recognize it. But would Zuckerberg recognize it, the real Zuckerberg? Are these really *his* motivations, *his* obsessions? No—and the movie knows it. Several times the script tries to square the real Zuckerberg's apparent indifference to money with the plot arc of *The Social Network*—and never quite succeeds. In a scene in which Mark argues with a lawyer, Sorkin attempts a sleight of hand, swapping an interest in money for an interest in power:

18   Ma'am, I know you've done your homework and so you know that money
          isn't a big part of my life, but at the moment I could buy Harvard Uni-
          versity, take the Phoenix Club and turn it into my ping pong room.

19   But that doesn't explain why the teenage Zuckerberg gave away his free app for an MP3 player (similar to the very popular Pandora, as it recognized your taste in music), rather than selling it to Microsoft. What power was he hoping to accrue to himself in high school, at seventeen? Girls, was it? Except the girl motivation is patently phony—with a brief interruption Zuckerberg has been dating the same Chinese-American, now a medical student, since 2003, a fact the movie omits entirely. At the end of the film, when all the suing has come to an end ("Pay them. In the scheme of things it's a parking ticket"), we're offered a Zuckerberg slumped before his laptop, still obsessed with the long-lost Erica, sending a "Friend request" to her on Facebook, and then refreshing the page, over and over, in expectation of her reply.... Fincher's contemporary window-dressing is so convincing that it wasn't until this very last scene that I realized the obvious progenitor of this wildly enjoyable, wildly inaccurate biopic. Hollywood still believes that behind every mogul there's an idée fixe: Rosebud—meet Erica.

20   If it's not for money and it's not for girls—what is it for? With Zuckerberg we have a real American mystery. Maybe it's not mysterious and he's just playing the long game, holding out: not a billion dollars but a hundred billion dollars. Or is it possible *he just loves programming*? No doubt the filmmakers considered this option, but you can see their dilemma: how to convey the pleasure of programming—if such a pleasure exists—in a way that is both cinematic and comprehensible? Movies are notoriously bad at showing the pleasures and rigors of art-making, even when the medium is familiar.

21   Programming is a whole new kind of problem. Fincher makes a brave stab at showing the intensity of programming in action ("He's wired in," people say to other people to

stop them disturbing a third person who sits before a laptop wearing noise-reducing ear-phones) and there's a "vodka-shots-and-programming" party in Zuckerberg's dorm room that gives us some clue of the pleasures. But even if we spent half the film looking at those busy screens (and we do get glimpses), most of us would be none the wiser. Watching this movie, even though you know Sorkin wants your disapproval, you can't help feel a little swell of pride in this 2.0 generation. They've spent a decade being berated for not making the right sorts of paintings or novels or music or politics. Turns out the brightest 2.0 kids have been doing something else extraordinary. They've been making a world.

22   World makers, social network makers, ask one question first: How can I do it? Zuck-erberg solved that one in about three weeks. The other question, the ethical question, he came to later: Why? Why Facebook? Why this format? Why do it like that? Why not do it another way? The striking thing about the real Zuckerberg, in video and in print, is the relative banality of his ideas concerning the "Why" of Facebook. He uses the word "con-nect" as believers use the word "Jesus," as if it were sacred in and of itself: "So the idea is really that, um, the site helps everyone connect with people and share information with the people they want to stay connected with...." Connection is the goal. The quality of that connection, the quality of the information that passes through it, the quality of the relation-ship that connection permits—none of this is important. That a lot of social networking software explicitly encourages people to make weak, superficial connections with each other (as Malcolm Gladwell has recently argued[1]), and that this might not be an entirely positive thing, seem to never have occurred to him.

23   He is, to say the least, dispassionate about the philosophical questions concerning privacy—and sociality itself—raised by his ingenious program. Watching him interviewed I found myself waiting for the verbal wit, the controlled and articulate sarcasm of that famous Zuckerberg kid—then remembered that was only Sorkin. The real Zuckerberg is much more like his website, on each page of which, once upon a time (2004), he embla-zoned the legend: *A Mark Zuckerberg Production.* Controlled but dull, bright and clean but uniformly plain, nonideological, affectless.

24   In Zuckerberg's *New Yorker* profile it is revealed that his own Facebook page lists, among his interests, Minimalism, revolutions, and "eliminating desire."[2] We also learn of his affection for the culture and writings of ancient Greece. Perhaps this is the disjunct between real Zuckerberg and fake Zuckerberg: the movie places him in the Roman world of betrayal and excess, but the real Zuckerberg may belong in the Greek, perhaps with the Stoics ("eliminating desire"?). There's a clue in the two Zuckerbergs' relative physi-ognomies: real Zuckerberg (especially in profile) is Greek sculpture, noble, featureless, a little like the Doryphorus (only facially, mind—his torso is definitely not seven times his head). Fake Mark looks Roman, with all the precise facial detail filled in. Zuckerberg, with his steady relationship and his rented house and his refusal to get angry on television even when people are being very rude to him (he sweats instead), has something of the teenage Stoic about him. And of course if you've eliminated desire you've got nothing to hide, right?

25   It's *that* kind of kid we're dealing with, the kind who would never screw a groupie in a bar toilet—as happens in the movie—or leave his doctor girlfriend for a Victoria's Secret

model. It's this type of kid who would think that giving people *less* privacy was a good idea. What's striking about Zuckerberg's vision of an open Internet is the very blandness it requires to function, as Facebook members discovered when the site changed their privacy settings, allowing more things to become more public, with the (unintended?) consequence that your Aunt Dora could suddenly find out you joined the group Queer Nation last Tuesday. Gay kids became un-gay, partiers took down their party photos, political firebrands put out their fires. In real life we can be all these people on our own terms, in our own way, with whom we choose. For a revealing moment Facebook forgot that. Or else got bored of waiting for us to change in the ways it's betting we will. On the question of privacy, Zuckerberg informed the world: "That social norm is just something that has evolved over time." On this occasion, the world protested, loudly, and so Facebook has responded with "Groups," a site revamp that will allow people to divide their friends into "cliques," some who see more of our profile and some who see less.

26   How "Groups" will work alongside "Facebook Connect" remains to be seen. Facebook Connect is the "next iteration of Facebook Platform," in which users are "allowed" to "'connect' their Facebook identity, friends and privacy to any site." In this new, open Internet, we will take our real identities with us as we travel through the Internet. This concept seems to have some immediate Stoical advantages: no more faceless bile, no more inflammatory trolling: if your name and social network track you around the virtual world beyond Facebook, you'll have to restrain yourself and so will everyone else. On the other hand, you'll also take your likes and dislikes with you, your tastes, your preferences, all connected to your name, through which people will try to sell you things.

27   Maybe it will be like an intensified version of the Internet I already live in, where ads for dental services stalk me from pillar to post and I am continually urged to buy my own books. Or maybe the whole Internet will simply become like Facebook: falsely jolly, fake-friendly, self-promoting, slickly disingenuous. For all these reasons I quit Facebook about two months after I'd joined it. As with all seriously addictive things, giving up proved to be immeasurably harder than starting. I kept changing my mind: Facebook remains the greatest distraction from work I've ever had, and I loved it for that. I think a lot of people love it for that. Some work-avoidance techniques are onerous in themselves and don't make time move especially quickly: smoking, eating, calling people up on the phone. With Facebook hours, afternoons, entire days went by without my noticing.

28   When I finally decided to put a stop to it, once and for all, I was left with the question bothering everybody: Are you ever truly removed, once and for all? In an interview on *The Today Show*, Matt Lauer asked Zuckerberg the same question, but because Matt Lauer doesn't listen to people when they talk, he accepted the following answer and moved on to the next question: "Yeah, so what'll happen is that none of that information will be shared with anyone going forward."

29   You want to be optimistic about your own generation. You want to keep pace with them and not to fear what you don't understand. To put it another way, if you feel discomfort at the world they're making, you want to have a good reason for it. Master programmer and virtual reality pioneer Jaron Lanier (b. 1960) is not of my generation, but he knows and understands us well, and has written a short and frightening book, *You Are Not a Gadget*,

which chimes with my own discomfort, while coming from a position of real knowledge and insight, both practical and philosophical. Lanier is interested in the ways in which people "reduce themselves" in order to make a computer's description of them appear more accurate. "Information systems," he writes, "need to have information in order to run, but information *underrepresents reality*" (my italics). In Lanier's view, there is no perfect computer analogue for what we call a "person." In life, we all profess to know this, but when we get online it becomes easy to forget. In Facebook, as it is with other online social networks, life is turned into a database, and this is a degradation, Lanier argues, which is

30   based on [a] philosophical mistake…the belief that computers can presently
        represent human thought or human relationships. These
        are things computers cannot currently do.

31   We know the consequences of this instinctively; we feel them. We know that having two thousand Facebook friends is not what it looks like. We know that we are using the software to behave in a certain, superficial way toward others. We know what we are doing "in" the software. But do we know, are we alert to, what the software is doing to us? Is it possible that what is communicated between people online "eventually becomes their truth"? What Lanier, a software expert, reveals to me, a software idiot, is what must be obvious (to software experts): software is not neutral. Different software embeds different philosophies, and these philosophies, as they become ubiquitous, become invisible.

32   Lanier asks us to consider, for example, the humble file, or rather, to consider a world without "files." (The first iteration of the Macintosh, which never shipped, didn't have files.) I confess this thought experiment stumped me about as much as if I'd been asked to consider persisting in a world without "time." And then consider further that these designs, so often taken up in a slap-dash, last-minute fashion, become "locked in," and, because they are software, used by millions, too often become impossible to adapt, or change. MIDI, an inflexible, early-1980s digital music protocol for connecting different musical components, such as a keyboard and a computer, takes no account of, say, the fluid line of a soprano's coloratura; it is still the basis of most of the tinny music we hear every day—in our phones, in the charts, in elevators—simply because it became, in software terms, too big to fail, too big to change.

33   Lanier wants us to be attentive to the software into which we are "locked in." Is it really fulfilling our needs? Or are we reducing the needs we feel in order to convince ourselves that the software isn't limited? As Lanier argues:

34   Different media designs stimulate different potentials in human nature. We
        shouldn't seek to make the pack mentality as efficient as possible. We
        should instead seek to inspire the phenomenon of individual intelligence.

35   But the pack mentality is precisely what Open Graph, a Facebook innovation of 2008, is designed to encourage. Open Graph allows you to see everything your friends are reading, watching, eating, so that you might read and watch and eat as they do. In his *New Yorker* profile, Zuckerberg made his personal "philosophy" clear:

36   Most of the information that we care about is things that are in our heads,
right? And that's not out there to be indexed, right?... It's
like hardwired into us in a deeper way: you really want to
know what's going on with the people around you.

37   Is that really the best we can do online? In the film, Sean Parker, during one of his
coke-fueled "Sean-athon monologues," delivers what is intended as a generation-defining
line: "We lived on farms, then we lived in cities and now we're gonna live on the internet."
To this idea Lanier, one of the Internet's original visionaries, can have no profound objection. But his skeptical interrogation of the "Nerd reductionism" of Web 2.0 prompts us to
ask a question: What kind of life?[3] Surely not this one, where 500 million connected people
all decide to watch the reality-TV show *Bride Wars* because their friends are? "You have to
be somebody," Lanier writes, "before you can share yourself." But to Zuckerberg sharing
your choices with everybody (and doing what they do) *is* being somebody.

38   Personally I don't think Final Clubs were ever the point; I don't think exclusivity was
ever the point; nor even money. E Pluribus Unum—that's the point. Here's my guess: he
wants to be like everybody else. He wants to be liked. Those 1.0 people who couldn't
understand Zuckerberg's apparently ham-fisted PR move of giving the school system of
Newark $100 million on the very day the movie came out—they just don't get it. For our
self-conscious generation (and in this, I and Zuckerberg, and everyone raised on TV in the
Eighties and Nineties, share a single soul), *not being liked* is as bad as it gets. Intolerable
to be thought of badly for a minute, even for a moment. He didn't need to just get out "in
front" of the story. He had to get right on top of it and try to stop it breathing. Two weeks
later, he went to a screening. Why? Because everybody liked the movie.

39   When a human being becomes a set of data on a website like Facebook, he or she
is reduced. Everything shrinks. Individual character. Friendships. Language. Sensibil-
ity. In a way it's a transcendent experience: we lose our bodies, our messy feelings, our
desires, our fears. It reminds me that those of us who turn in disgust from what we consider an overinflated liberal-bourgeois sense of self should be careful what we wish for:
our denuded networked selves don't look more free, they just look more owned.

40   With Facebook, Zuckerberg seems to be trying to create something like a Noosphere,
an Internet with one mind, a uniform environment in which it genuinely doesn't matter who
you are, as long as you make "choices" (which means, finally, purchases). If the aim is to
be liked by more and more people, whatever is unusual about a person gets flattened out.
One nation under a format. To ourselves, we are special people, documented in wonderful
photos, and it also happens that we sometimes buy things. This latter fact is an incidental
matter, to us. However, the advertising money that will rain down on Facebook—if and
when Zuckerberg succeeds in encouraging 500 million people to take their Facebook
identities onto the Internet at large—this money thinks of us the other way around. To the
advertisers, we are our capacity to buy, attached to a few personal, irrelevant photos.

41   Is it possible that we have begun to think of ourselves that way? It seemed significant
to me that on the way to the movie theater, while doing a small mental calculation (how
old I was when at Harvard; how old I am now), I had a Person 1.0 panic attack. Soon I

will be forty, then fifty, then soon after dead; I broke out in a Zuckerberg sweat, my heart went crazy, I had to stop and lean against a trashcan. Can you have that feeling, on Facebook? I've noticed—and been ashamed of noticing—that when a teenager is murdered, at least in Britain, her Facebook wall will often fill with messages that seem to not quite comprehend the gravity of what has occurred. You know the type of thing: *Sorry babes! Missin' you!!! Hopin' u iz with the Angles. I remember the jokes we used to have LUL! PEACE XXXXX*

42   When I read something like that, I have a little argument with myself: "It's only poor education. They feel the same way as anyone would, they just don't have the language to express it." But another part of me has a darker, more frightening thought. Do they genuinely believe, because the girl's wall is still up, that she is still, in some sense, alive? What's the difference, after all, if all your contact was virtual?[4]

43   Software may reduce humans, but there are degrees. Fiction reduces humans, too, but bad fiction does it more than good fiction, and we have the option to read good fiction. Jaron Lanier's point is that Web 2.0 "lock-in" happens soon; is happening; has to some degree already happened. And what has been "locked in"? It feels important to remind ourselves, at this point, that Facebook, our new beloved interface with reality, was designed by a Harvard sophomore with a Harvard sophomore's preoccupations. What is your relationship status? (Choose one. There can be only one answer. People need to know.) Do you have a "life"? (Prove it. Post pictures.) Do you like the right sort of things? (Make a list. Things to like will include: movies, music, books and television, but not architecture, ideas, or plants.)

44   But here I fear I am becoming nostalgic. I am dreaming of a Web that caters to a kind of person who no longer exists. A private person, a person who is a mystery, to the world and—which is more important—to herself. Person as mystery: this idea of personhood is certainly changing, perhaps has already changed. Because I find I agree with Zuckerberg: selves evolve.

45   Of course, Zuckerberg insists selves simply do this by themselves and the technology he and others have created has no influence upon the process. That is for techies and philosophers to debate (ideally techie-philosophers, like Jaron Lanier). Whichever direction the change is coming from, though, it's absolutely clear to me that the students I teach now are not like the student I once was or even the students I taught seven short years ago at Harvard. Right now I am teaching my students a book called *The Bathroom* by the Belgian experimentalist Jean-Philippe Toussaint—at least I used to *think* he was an experimentalist. It's a book about a man who decides to pass most of his time in his bathroom, yet to my students this novel feels perfectly realistic; an accurate portrait of their own denuded selfhood, or, to put it neutrally, a close analogue of the undeniable boredom of urban twenty-first-century existence.

46   In the most famous scene, the unnamed protagonist, in one of the few moments of "action," throws a dart into his girlfriend's forehead. Later, in the hospital they reunite with a kiss and no explanation. "It's just between them," said one student, and looked happy. To a reader of my generation, Toussaint's characters seemed, at first glance, to have no interiority—in fact theirs is not an absence but a refusal, and an ethical one. *What's inside of me is none of your business*. To my students, *The Bathroom* is a true romance.

47   Toussaint was writing in 1985, in France. In France philosophy seems to come before technology; here in the Anglo-American world we race ahead with technology and hope the ideas will look after themselves. Finally, it's the *idea* of Facebook that disappoints. If it were a genuinely interesting interface, built for these genuinely different 2.0 kids to live in, well, that would be something. It's not that. It's the wild west of the Internet tamed to fit the suburban fantasies of a suburban soul. Lanier:

48   These designs came together very recently, and there's a haphazard,
         accidental quality to them. Resist the easy grooves they
         guide you into. If you love a medium made of software,
         there's a danger that you will become entrapped in some-
         one else's recent careless thoughts. Struggle against that!

49   Shouldn't we struggle against Facebook? Everything in it is reduced to the size of its founder. Blue, because it turns out Zuckerberg is red-green color-blind. "Blue is the richest color for me—I can see all of blue." Poking, because that's what shy boys do to girls they are scared to talk to. Preoccupied with personal trivia, because Mark Zuckerberg thinks the exchange of personal trivia is what "friendship" *is*. A Mark Zuckerberg Production indeed! We were going to live online. It was going to be extraordinary. Yet what kind of living is this? Step back from your Facebook Wall for a moment: Doesn't it, suddenly, look a little ridiculous? *Your* life in *this* format?

50   The last defense of every Facebook addict is: *but it helps me keep in contact with people who are far away!* Well, e-mail and Skype do that, too, and they have the added advantage of not forcing you to interface with the mind of Mark Zuckerberg—but, well, you know. We all know. If we *really* wanted to write to these faraway people, or see them, we would. What we actually want to do is the bare minimum, just like any nineteen-year-old college boy who'd rather be doing something else, or nothing.

51   At my screening, when a character in the film mentioned the early blog platform Live-Journal (still popular in Russia), the audience laughed. I can't imagine life without files but I can just about imagine a time when Facebook will seem as comically obsolete as Live-Journal. In this sense, *The Social Network* is not a cruel portrait of any particular real-world person called "Mark Zuckerberg." It's a cruel portrait of us: 500 million sentient people entrapped in the recent careless thoughts of a Harvard sophomore.

Notes

1.   See "Small Change: Why the Revolution Will Not Be Tweeted," *The New Yorker*, October 4, 2010.
2.   See Jose Antonio Vargas, "The Face of Facebook: Mark Zuckerberg Opens Up," *The New Yorker*, September 20, 2010.
3.   Lanier: "Individual web pages as they first appeared in the early 1990s had the flavor of personhood. MySpace preserved some of that flavor, though a process of regularized formatting had begun. Facebook went further, organizing people into multiple-choice identities, while Wikipedia seeks to erase point of view entirely."

4. Perhaps the reason why there has not been more resistance to social network-ing among older people is because 1.0 people do not use Web 2.0 software in the way 2.0 people do. An analogous situation can be found in the way the two generations use cell phones. For me, text messaging is simply a new medium for an old form of communication: I write to my friends in heavily punctuated, fully expressive, standard English sentences—and they write back to me in the same way. Text-speak is unknown between us. Our relationship with the English language predates our relationships with our phones.

Critical Reading Questions:

- **Interpretation:** What is a "person" in this generation? How has this idea changed over time? Why is this important to understanding a generation? According to Smith, how is technology ruining personalities?

- **Reflection:** Smith claims that users "reduce" themselves in online communica-tion. Do you believe this to be true? Provide examples.

What the Indian Means to America

Luther Standing Bear

Luther Standing Bear, a Lakota Sioux from the Pine Ridge Reservation, uses "What the Indian Means to America" to argue that Native America *is* America. To support this argument, Standing Bear relies on the freedom of an indigenous approach to life, as illustrated by his own memories and experiences. The reading is the final chapter of a larger work titled *Land of the Spotted Eagle* which chronicles both the day-to-day lives of Native Americans and their deep spiritual foundations. Standing Bear is a passionate voice for a marginalized minority in the American population. His primary claim in this text is clear when he articulates the stark tension between "white" and "native" cultures: " The attempted transformation of the Indian by the white man and the chaos that resulted are but the fruits of the white man's disobedience of a fundamental spiritual law."

—KGR, WCM

1   The feathered and blanketed figure of the American Indian has come to symbolize the American continent. He is the man who through centuries has been moulded and sculpted by the same hand that shaped its mountains, forests, and plains, and marked the course of its rivers.

2   The American Indian is of the soil, whether it be the region of forests, plains, pueblos, or mesas. He fits into the landscape, for the hand that fashioned the continent also fashioned the man for his surroundings. He once grew as naturally as the wild sunflowers; he belongs just as the buffalo belonged.

3   With a physique that fitted, the man developed fitting skills—crafts which today are called American. And the body had a soul, also formed and moulded by the same master hand of harmony. Out of the Indian approach to existence there came a great freedom— an intense and absorbing love for nature; a respect for life; enriching faith in a Supreme Power; and principles of truth, honesty, generosity, equity, and brotherhood as a guide to mundane relations.

4   Becoming possessed of a fitting philosophy and art, it was by them that native man perpetuated his identity; stamped it into the history and soul of this country—made land and man one.

5   By living—struggling, losing, meditating, imbibing, aspiring, achieving—he wrote himself into ineraceable evidence—an evidence that can be and often has been ignored, but never totally destroyed. Living—and all the intangible forces that constitute that phenomenon—are brought into being by Spirit, that which no man can alter. Only the hand of the Supreme Power can transform man; only Wakan Tanka can transform the Indian. But of such deep and infinite graces finite man has little comprehension. He has, therefore, no weapons with which to slay the unassailable. He can only foolishly trample.

6   The white man does not understand the Indian for the reason that he does not understand America. He is too far removed from its formative processes. The roots of the tree of his life have not yet grasped the rock and soil. The white man is still troubled with primitive fears; he still has in his consciousness the perils of this frontier continent, some of its vastnesses not yet having yielded to his questing footsteps and inquiring eyes. He shudders still with the memory of the loss of his forefathers upon its scorching deserts and forbidding mountain-tops. The man from Europe is still a foreigner and an alien. And he still hates the man who questioned his path across the continent.

7   But in the Indian the spirit of the land is still vested; it will be until other men are able to divine and meet its rhythm. Men must be born and reborn to belong. Their bodies must be formed of the dust of their forefathers' bones.

8   The attempted transformation of the Indian by the white man and the chaos that has resulted are but the fruits of the white man's disobedience of a fundamental and spiritual law. The pressure that has been brought to bear upon the native people, since the cessation of armed conflict, in the attempt to force conformity of custom and habit has caused a reaction more destructive than war, and the injury has not only affected the Indian, but has extended to the white population as well. Tyranny, stupidity, and lack of vision have brought about the situation now alluded to as the "Indian Problem."

9   There is, I insist, no Indian problem as created by the Indian himself. Every problem that exists today in regard to the native population is due to the white man's cast of mind, which is unable, at least reluctant, to seek understanding and achieve adjustment in a new and a significant environment into which it has so recently come.

10   The white man excused his presence here by saying that he had been guided by the will of his God; and in so saying absolved himself of all responsibility for his appearance in a land occupied by other men.

11   Then, too, his law was a written law; his divine Decalogue reposed in a book. And what better proof that his advent into this country and his subsequent acts were the result of divine will! He brought the Word! There ensued a blind worship of written history, of books, of the written word, that has denuded the spoken word of its power and sacredness. The written word became established as a criterion of the superior man—a symbol of emotional fineness. The man who could write his name on a piece of paper, whether or not he possessed the spiritual fineness to honor those words in speech, was by some miraculous formula a more highly developed and sensitized person than the one who had never had a pen in hand, but whose spoken word was inviolable and whose sense of honor and truth was paramount. With false reasoning was the quality of human character measured by man's ability to make with an implement a mark upon paper. But granting this mode of reasoning be correct and just, then where are to be placed the thousands of illiterate whites who are unable to read and write? Are they, too, "savages"? Is not humanness a matter of heart and mind, and is it not evident in the form of relationship with men? Is not kindness more powerful than arrogance; and truth more powerful than the sword?

12   True, the white man brought great change. But the varied fruits of his civilization, though highly colored and inviting, are sickening and deadening. And if it be the part of civilization to maim, rob, and thwart, then what is progress?

13   I am going to venture that the man who sat on the ground in his tipi meditating on life and its meaning, accepting the kinship of all creatures, and acknowledging unity with the universe of things was infusing into his being the true essence of civilization. And when native man left off this form of development, his humanization was retarded in growth

14   Another most powerful agent that gave native man promise of developing into a true human was the responsibility accepted by parenthood. Mating among Lakotas was motivated, of course, by the same laws of attraction that motivate all beings; however, considerable thought was given by parents of both boy and girl to the choosing of mates. And a still greater advantage accrued to the race by the law of self-mastery which the young couple voluntarily placed upon themselves as soon as they discovered they were to become parents. Immediately, and for some time after, the sole thought of the parents was in preparing the child for life. And true civilization lies in the dominance of self and not in the dominance of other men.

15   How far this idea would have gone in carrying my people upward and toward a better plane of existence, or how much of an influence it was in the development of their spiritual being, it is not possible to say. But it had its promises. And it cannot be gainsaid that the man who is rising to a higher estate is the man who is putting into his being the essence of humanism. It is self-effort that develops, and by this token the greatest factor today in dehumanizing races is the manner in which the machine is used—the product of one man's brain doing the work for another. The hand is the tool that has built man's mind; it, too, can refine it.

The Savage

16   After subjugation, after dispossession, there was cast the last abuse upon the people who so entirely resented their wrongs and punishments, and that was the stamping and the labeling of them as savages. To make this label stick has been the task of the white race and the greatest salve that it has been able to apply to its sore and troubled conscience now hardened through the habitual practice of injustice.

17   But all the years of calling the Indian a savage has never made him one; all the denial of his virtues has never taken them from him; and the very resistance he has made to save the things inalienably his has been his saving strength—that which will stand him in need when justice does make its belated appearance and he undertakes rehabilitation.

18   All sorts of feeble excuses are heard for the continued subjection of the Indian. One of the most common is that he is not yet ready to mingle as a social entity.

19   This, I maintain, is beside the question. The matter is not one of making-over the external Indian into the likeness of the white race—a process detrimental to both races. Who can say that the white man's way is better for the Indian? Where resides the human judgment with the competence to weigh and value Indian ideals and spiritual concepts; or substitute for them other values?

20   Then, has the white man's social order been so harmonious and ideal as to merit the respect of the Indian, and for that matter the thinking class of the white race? Is it wise to urge upon the Indian a foreign social form? Let none but the Indian answer!

21   Rather, let the white brother face about and cast his mental eye upon a new angle of vision. Let him look upon the Indian world as a human world; then let him see to it that human rights be accorded to the Indians. And this for the purpose of retaining for his own order of society a measure of humanity.

The Indian School of Thought

22   I say again that Indians should teach Indians; that Indians should serve Indians, especially on reservations where the older people remain. There is a definite need of the old for the care and sympathy of the young and they are today perishing for the joys that naturally belong to the old Indian people. Old Indians are very close to their progeny. It was their delightful duty to care for and instruct the very young, while in turn they looked forward to being cared for by sons and daughters. These were the privileges and blessings of old age.

23   Many of the grievances of the old Indian, and his disagreements with the young, find root in the far-removed boarding-school which sometimes takes the little ones at a very tender age. More than one tragedy has resulted when a young boy or girl has returned home again almost an utter stranger. I have seen these happenings with my own eyes and I know they can cause naught but suffering. The old Indian cannot, even if he wished, reconcile himself to an institution that alienates his young. And there is something evil in a system that brings about an unnatural reaction to life; when it makes young hearts callous and unheedful of the needs and joys of the old.

24   The old people do not speak English and they never will be English-speaking. To place upon such people the burden of understanding and functioning through an office bound up with the routine and red tape of the usual Government office is silly and futile, and every week or so I receive letters from the reservation evidencing this fact. The Indian's natural method of settling questions is by council and conference. From time immemorial, for every project affecting their material, social, and spiritual lives, the people have met together to 'talk things over.'

25   To the end that young Indians will be able to appreciate both their traditional life and modern life they should be doubly educated. Without forsaking reverence for their ancestral teachings, they can be trained to take up modern duties that relate to tribal and reservation life. And there is no problem of reservation importance but can be solved by the joint efforts of the old and the young Indians.

26   There certainly can be no doubt in the public mind today as to the capacity of the younger Indians in taking on white modes and manners. For many years, and particularly since the days of General Pratt, the young Indian has been proving his efficiency when entering the fields of white man's endeavor and has done well in copying and acquiring the ways of the white man.

27   The Indian liked the white man's horse and straightway became an expert horseman; he threw away his age-old weapons, the bow and arrow, and matched the white man's skill with gun and pistol; in the field of sports—games of strength and skill—the Indian enters with no shame in comparison; the white man's beads the Indian woman took, developed a technique and an art distinctly her own with no competitor in design; and in the white

man's technique of song and dance the Indian has made himself a creditable exponent.

28   However, despite the fact that Indian schools have been established over several generations, there is a dearth of Indians in the professions. It is most noticeable on the reservation where the numerous positions of consequence are held by white employees instead of trained Indians. For instance, why are not the stores, post-offices, and Government office jobs on the Sioux Reservation held by trained Indians? Why cannot Sioux be reservation nurses and doctors; and road-builders too? Much road work goes on every summer, but the complaint is constant that it is always done by white workmen, and in such a manner as to necessitate its being done again in a short time. Were these numerous positions turned over to trained Indians, the white population would soon find reservation life less attractive and less lucrative.

29   With school facilities already fairly well established and the capability of the Indian unquestioned, every reservation could well be supplied with Indian doctors, nurses, engineers, road- and bridge-builders, draughtsmen, architects, dentists, lawyers, teachers, and instructors in tribal lore, legends, orations, song, dance, and ceremonial ritual. The Indian, by the very sense of duty, should become his own historian, giving his account of the race—fairer and fewer accounts of the wars and more of statecraft, legends, languages, oratory, and philosophical conceptions. No longer should the Indian be dehumanized in order to make material for lurid and cheap fiction to embellish street-stands. Rather, a fair and correct history of the native American should be incorporated in the curriculum of the public school.

30   Caucasian youth is fed, and rightly so, on the feats and exploits of their old-world heroes, their revolutionary forefathers, their adventurous pioneer trail-blazers, and in our Southwest through pageants, fiestas, and holidays the days of the Spanish *conquistador* are kept alive.

31   But Indian youth! They, too, have fine pages in their past history; they, too, have patriots and heroes. And it is not fair to rob Indian youth of their history, the stories of their patriots, which, if impartially written, would fill them with pride and dignity. Therefore, give back to the Indian youth all, everything in their heritage that belongs to them and augment it with the best in the modern schools. I repeat, doubly educate the Indian boy and girl.

32   What a contrast this would make in comparison with the present unhealthy, demoralized place the reservation is today, where the old are poorly fed, shabbily clothed, divested of pride and incentive; and where the young are unfitted for tribal life and untrained for the world of white man's affairs except to hold an occasional job!

33   Why not a school of Indian thought, built on the Indian pattern and conducted by Indian instructors? Why not a school of tribal art?

34   Why should not America be cognizant of itself; aware of its identity? In short, why should not America be preserved?

35   There were ideals and practices in the life of my ancestors that have not been improved upon by the elements of benefit; and there were influences that would broaden any life. But that almost an entire public needs to be enlightened as to this fact need not be discouraging. For many centuries the human mind labored under the delusion that the world was flat; and thousands of men have believed that the heavens were supported by

the strength of an Atlas. The human mind is not yet free from fallacious reasoning; it is not yet an open mind and its deepest recesses are not yet swept free of errors.

36   But it is now time for a destructive order to be reversed, and it is well to inform other races that the aboriginal culture of America was not devoid of beauty. Furthermore, in denying the Indian his ancestral rights and heritages the white race is but robbing itself. But America can be revived, rejuvenated, by recognizing a native school of thought. The Indian can save America.

The Living Spirit of the Indian—His Art

37   The spiritual health and existence of the Indian was maintained by song, magic, ritual, dance, symbolism, oratory (or council), design, handicraft, and folk-story.

38   Manifestly, to check or thwart this expression is to bring about spiritual decline. And it is in this condition of decline that the Indian people are today. There is but a feeble effort among the Sioux to keep alive their traditional songs and dances, while among other tribes there is but a half-hearted attempt to offset the influence of the Government school and at the same time recover from the crushing and stifling régime of the Indian Bureau.

39   One has but to speak of Indian verse to receive uncomprehending and unbelieving glances. Yet the Indian loved verse and into this mode of expression went his deepest feelings. Only a few ardent and advanced students seem interested; nevertheless, they have given in book form enough Indian translations to set forth the character and quality of Indian verse.

40   Oratory receives a little better understanding on the part of the white public, owing to the fact that oratorical compilations include those of Indian orators.

41   Hard as it seemingly is for the white man's ear to sense the differences, Indian songs are as varied as the many emotions which inspire them, for no two of them are alike. For instance, the Song of Victory is spirited and the notes high and remindful of an unrestrained hunter or warrior riding exultantly over the prairies. On the other hand, the song of the *Cano unye* is solemn and full of urge, for it is meant to inspire the young men to deeds of valor. Then there are the songs of death and the spiritual songs which are connected with the ceremony of initiation. These are full of the spirit of praise and worship, and so strong are some of these invocations that the very air seems as if surcharged with the presence of the Big Holy.

42   The Indian loved to worship. From birth to death he revered his surroundings. He considered himself born in the luxurious lap of Mother Earth and no place was to him humble. There was nothing between him and the Big Holy. The contact was immediate and personal, and the blessings of Wakan Tanka flowed over the Indian like rain showered from the sky. Wakan Tanka was not aloof, apart, and ever seeking to quell evil forces. He did not punish the animals and the birds, and likewise He did not punish man. He was not a punishing God. For there was never a question as to the supremacy of an evil power over and above the power of Good. There was but one ruling power, and that was *Good*.

43   Of course, none but an adoring one could dance for days with his face to the sacred sun, and that time is all but done. We cannot have back the days of the buffalo and beaver; we cannot win back our clean blood-stream and superb health, and we can never

again expect that beautiful *rapport* we once had with Nature. The springs and lakes have dried and the mountains are bare of forests. The plow has changed the face of the world. Wi-wila is dead! No more may we heal our sick and comfort our dying with a strength founded on faith, for even the animals now fear us, and fear supplants faith.

44   And the Indian wants to dance! It is his way of expressing devotion, of communing with unseen power, and in keeping his tribal identity. When the Lakota heart was filled with high emotion, he danced. When he felt the benediction of the warming rays of the sun, he danced. When his blood ran hot with success of the hunt or chase, he danced. When his heart was filled with pity for the orphan, the lonely father, or bereaved mother, he danced. All the joys and exaltations of life, all his gratefulness and thankfulness, all his acknowledgements of the mysterious power that guided life, and all his aspirations for a better life, culminated in one great dance—the Sun Dance.

45   Today we see our young people dancing together the silly jazz-dances that add nothing to the beauty and fineness of our lives and certainly nothing to our history, while the dances that record the life annals of a people die. It is the American Indian who contributes to this country its true folk-dancing, growing, as we did, out of the soil. The dance is far older than his legends, songs, or philosophy.

46   Did dancing mean much to the white people they would better understand ours. Yet at the same time there is no attraction that brings people from such distances as a certain tribal dance, for the reason that the white mind senses its mystery, for even the white man's inmost feelings are unconsciously stirred by the beat of the tomtom. They are heartbeats, and once all men danced to its rhythm.

47   When the Indian has forgotten the music of his forefathers, when the sound of the tomtom is no more, when noisy jazz has drowned the melody of the flute, he will be a dead Indian. When the memory of his heroes are no longer told in story, and he forsakes the beautiful white buckskin for factory shoddy, he will be dead. When from him has been taken all that is his, all that he has visioned in nature, all that has come to him from infinite sources, he then, truly, will be a dead Indian. His spirit will be gone, and though we will walk crowded streets, he will, in truth, be—*dead!*

48   But all this must not perish; it must live, to the end that America shall be educated no longer to regard native production of whatever tribe—folk-story, basketry, pottery, dance, song, poetry—as curios, and native artists as curiosities. For who but the man indigenous to the soil could produce its song, story, and folk-tale; who but the man who loved the dust beneath his feet could shape it and put it into undying, ceramic form; who but he who loved the reeds that grew beside still waters, and the damp roots of shrub and tree, could save it from seasonal death, and with almost superhuman patience weave it into enduring objects of beauty—into timeless art!

49   Regarding the 'civilization' that has been thrust upon me since the days of reservation, it has not added one whit to my sense of justice; to my reverence for the rights of life; to my love for truth, honesty, and generosity; nor to my faith in Wakan Tanka—God of the Lakotas. For after all the great religions have been preached and expounded, or have been revealed by brilliant scholars, or have been written in books and embellished in fine language with finer covers, man—all man—is still confronted with the Great Mystery.

50   So if today I had a young mind to direct, to start on the journey of life, and I was faced with the duty of choosing between the natural way of my forefathers and that of the white man's present way of civilization, I would, for its welfare, unhesitatingly set that child's feet in the part of my forefathers. I would raise him to be an Indian!

Critical Reading Questions:

- **Rhetorical analysis:** Examine Standing Bear's claims about spiritual principles and practices to determine their appeal/effectiveness for his audience.

- **Interpretation:** Use Standing Bear's explanation of the American Indian's natural relationship with Native America to describe how he defines the Indian as essentially American.

Seneca Falls Declaration

Elizabeth Cady Stanton

For 50 years, Elizabeth Cady Stanton was a tireless leader and primary force in the Women's Rights Movement, one of history's largest agents of social change. It was a revolution of language in action, a bloodless revolution. An accomplished writer, Stanton designed and articulated the movement's most important strategies and documents—including many speeches for delivery by Susan B. Anthony. The movement was initiated at the First Women's Rights Convention held in Seneca Falls, NY, on July 19, 1848, where Stanton presented this declaration. Her very deliberate rhetorical choice to model the document on the "Declaration of Independence" invokes the fundamental values that define the American ethos and code of law and thus underscores the document's message—the demand that the rights of women be acknowledged and respected by law and society. The Declaration and the Conference constitute and symbolize acts of language with profound and far-reaching global influence. The document was signed by sixty-eight women and thirty-two men, a third of the 300 women and men in attendance at the convention. Stanton died in 1902, eighteen years before Congress ratified the 19th Amendment granting women the right to vote.

—AMW

1. Declaration of Sentiments

1   When, in the course of human events, it becomes necessary for one portion of the family of man to assume among the people of the earth a position different from that which they have hitherto occupied, but one to which the laws of nature and of nature's God entitle them, a decent respect to the opinions of mankind requires that they should declare the causes that impel them to such a course.

2   We hold these truths to be self-evident: that all men and women are created equal; that they are endowed by their Creator with certain inalienable rights; that among these are life, liberty, and the pursuit of happiness; that to secure these rights governments are instituted, deriving their just powers from the consent of the governed. Whenever any form of government becomes destructive of these ends, it is the right of those who suffer from it to refuse allegiance to it, and to insist upon the institution of a new government, laying its foundation on such principles, and organizing its powers in such form, as to them shall seem most likely to effect their safety and happiness. Prudence, indeed, will dictate that governments long established should not be changed for light and transient causes; and accordingly all experience hath shown that mankind are more disposed to suffer while evils are sufferable, than to right themselves by abolishing the forms to which they are accustomed. But when a long train of abuses and usurpations, pursuing invariably the

same object, evinces a design to reduce them under absolute despotism, it is their duty to throw off such government, and to provide new guards for their future security. Such has been the patient sufferance of the women under this government, and such is now the necessity which constrains them to demand the equal station to which they are entitled. The history of mankind is a history of repeated injuries and usurpations on the part of man toward woman, having in direct object the establishment of an absolute tyranny over her. To prove this, let facts be submitted to a candid world.

3   He has never permitted her to exercise her inalienable right to the
         elective franchise.

4   He has compelled her to submit to laws, in the formation of which she
         had no voice.

5   He has withheld from her rights which are given to the most ignorant
         and degraded men both natives and foreigners.

6   Having deprived her of this first right of a citizen, the elective franchise.
         thereby leaving her without representation in the halls of leg-
         islation, he has oppressed her on all sides.

7   He has made her, if married, in the eye of the law, civilly dead. He has
         taken from her all right in property, even to the wages she earns.

8   He has made her, morally, an irresponsible being, as she can commit
         many crimes with impunity, provided they be
         done in the presence of her husband.

9   In the covenant of marriage, she is compelled to promise obedience to
         her husband, he becoming, to all intents and pur-
         poses, her master the law giving him power to deprive
         her of her liberty, and to administer chastisement.

10   He has so framed the laws of divorce, as to what shall be the proper causes,
         and in case of separation, to whom the guardianship of the chil-
         dren shall be given, as to be wholly regardless of the happiness
         of women—the law, in all cases, going upon a false supposition
         of the supremacy of man, and giving all power into his hands.

11   After depriving her of all rights as a married woman, if single, and the owner
         of property, he has taxed her to support a government which rec-
         ognizes her only when her property can be made profitable to it.

12   He has monopolized nearly all the profitable employments, and from those
she is permitted to follow, she receives but a scanty remunera-
tion. He closes against her all the avenues to wealth and distinction which he considers most honorable to himself. As a
teacher of theology, medicine, or law, she is not known.

13   He has denied her the facilities for obtaining a thorough education, all
colleges being closed against her.

14   He allows her in Church, as well as State, but a subordinate position,
claiming Apostolic authority for her exclusion from the ministry, and, with
some exceptions, from any public participation in the affairs of the Church.

15   He has created a false public sentiment by giving to the world a different
code of morals for men and women, by which moral delin-
quencies which exclude women from society, are not only
tolerated, but deemed of little account in man.

16   He has usurped the prerogative of Jehovah himself, claiming it as his right
to assign for her a sphere of action, when that
belongs to her conscience and to her God.

17   He has endeavored, in every way that he could, to destroy her confidence in
her own powers, to lessen her self-respect and to make
her willing to lead a dependent and abject life.

18   Now, in view of this entire disfranchisement of one-half the people of this country, their
social and religious degradation in view of the unjust laws above mentioned, and because
women do feel themselves aggrieved, oppressed, and fraudulently deprived of their most
sacred rights, we insist that they have immediate admission to all the rights and privileges
which belong to them as citizens of the United States.

19   In entering upon the great work before us, we anticipate no small amount of misconception, misrepresentation, and ridicule; but we shall use every instrumentality within our
power to effect our object. We shall employ agents, circulate tracts, petition the State and
National legislatures, and endeavor to enlist the pulpit and the press in our behalf. We
hope this Convention will be followed by a series of Conventions embracing every part of
the country.

2. Resolutions

20   Whereas, the great precept of nature is conceded to be, "that man shall pursue his
own true and substantial happiness." Blackstone in his Commentaries remarks, that this
law of Nature being coeval with mankind, and dictated by God himself, is of course superior in obligation to any other. It is binding over all the globe, in all countries and at all

times; no human laws are of any validity if contrary to this, and such of them as are valid, derive all their force, and all their validity, and all their authority, mediately and immediately, from this original; Therefore,

21   Resolved, That such laws as conflict, in any way with the true and substantial happiness of woman, are contrary to the great precept of nature and of no validity, for this is "superior in obligation to any other."

22   Resolved, That all laws which prevent woman from occupying such a station in society as her conscience shall dictate, or which place her in a position inferior to that of man, are contrary to the great precept of nature, and therefore of no force or authority.

23   Resolved, That woman is man's equal was intended to be so by the Creator, and the highest good of the race demands that she should be recognized as such.

24   Resolved, That the women of this country ought to be enlightened in regard to the laws under which they live, that they may no longer publish their degradation by declaring themselves satisfied with their present position, nor their ignorance, by asserting that they have all the rights they want.

25   Resolved, That inasmuch as man, while claiming for himself intellectual superiority, does accord to woman moral superiority, it is pre-eminently his duty to encourage her to speak and teach, as she has an opportunity, in all religious assemblies.

26   Resolved, That the same amount of virtue, delicacy, and refinement of behavior that is required of woman in the social state, should also be required of man, and the same transgressions should be visited with equal severity on both man and woman.

27   Resolved, That the objection of indelicacy and impropriety, which is so often brought against woman when she addresses a public audience, comes with a very ill-grace from those who encourage, by their attendance, her appearance on the stage, in the concert, or in feats of the circus.

28   Resolved, That woman has too long rested satisfied in the circumscribed limits which corrupt customs and a perverted application of the Scriptures have marked out for her, and that it is time she should move in the enlarged sphere which her great Creator has assigned her.

29   Resolved, That it is the duty of the women of this country to secure to themselves their sacred right to the elective franchise.

30   Resolved, That the equality of human rights results necessarily from the fact of the identity of the race in capabilities and responsibilities.

31   Resolved, Therefore, That, being invested by the creator with the same capabilities, and the same consciousness of responsibility for their exercise, it is demonstrably the right and duty of woman, equally with man, to promote every righteous cause by every righteous means; and especially in regard to the great subjects of morals and religion, it is self-evidently her right to participate with her brother in teaching them, both in private and in public, by writing and by speaking, by any instrumentalities proper to be used, and in any assemblies proper to be held; and this being a self evident truth growing out of the divinely implanted principles of human nature, any custom or authority adverse to it, whether modern or wearing the hoary sanction of antiquity, is to be regarded as a self-evident falsehood, and at war with mankind.

32   Resolved, That the speedy success of our cause depends upon the zealous and untiring efforts of both men and women, for the overthrow of the monopoly of the pulpit, and for the securing to women an equal participation with men in the various trades, professions, and commerce.

Critical Reading Questions:

- **Rhetorical analysis:** Explore the means by which Stanton authorizes herself to advance criticisms and demands, given the cultural and legal contexts which denied women authority. In modeling her declaration upon "The Declaration of Independence," what authority and what values does Stanton invoke? In what other ways does she construct an authoritative ethos?

- **Rhetorical analysis:** Stanton delivered the "Declaration" in the midst of ongoing and impassioned debates about the freedom and equality of slaves. Track Stanton's use of language and ideas that might function as symbols associated with slavery. What specific emotions might they invoke, and what is the persuasive value of doing so in the context of this document?

Responding—Really Responding— to Other Students' Writing

Richard Straub

Associate Professor of English at Florida State University, Richard Straub made a name for himself by highlighting best practices for responding to student writing. To this end, Straub edited four books on the subject including *Key Works on Teacher Response*, *The Practice of Response*, *A Sourcebook for Responding to Student Writing*, and *Twelve Readers Reading*, in addition to the following article "Responding—Really Responding—to Other Students' Writing." In this work, Straub connects with his audience by writing directly to the reader by using the second person (you) and offers direct instruction on what the reader, is to do when responding to other students: "Consider yourself a friendly reader," "Sound like you normally sound," and "Challenge yourself to write as many praise comments as criticisms." In the last section of this piece, Straub shifts from the second person to the third in order to illustrate how feedback should be executed. He offers a sample student paper—complete with feedback—and explains its purpose and how it is effective.

—BLS

1   Okay. You've got a student paper you have to read and make comments on for Thursday. It's not something you're looking forward to. But that's alright, you think. There isn't really all that much to it. Just keep it simple. Read it quickly and mark whatever you see. Say something about the introduction. Something about details and examples. Ideas you can say you like. Mark any typos and spelling errors. Make your comments brief. Abbreviate where possible: *awk, good intro, give ex, frag.* Try to imitate the teacher. Mark what he'd mark and sound like he'd sound. But be cool about it. Don't praise anything really, but no need to get harsh or cut throat either. Get in and get out. You're okay, I'm okay. Everybody's happy. What's the problem?

2   This is, no doubt, a way of getting through the assignment. Satisfy the teacher and no surprises for the writer. It might just do the trick. But say you want to do a *good* job. Say you're willing to put in the time and effort—though time is tight and you know it's not going to be easy—and help the writer look back on the paper and revise it. And maybe in the process learn something more yourself about writing. What do you look for? How do you sound? How much do you take up? What exactly are you trying to accomplish? Here are some ideas.

How Should You Look at Yourself as a Responder?

3   Consider yourself a friendly reader. A test pilot. A roommate who's been asked to look over the paper and tell the writer what you think. Except you don't just take on the role of The Nice Roommate or The Ever-faithful Friend and tell her what she wants to hear.

This all looks good. I wouldn't change a thing. There are a couple places that I think he might not like, but I can see what you're doing there. I'd go with it. Good stuff. You're supportive. You give her the benefit of the doubt and look to see the good in her writing. But friends don't let friends think their writing is the best thing since *The Great Gatsby* and they don't lead them to think that all is fine and well when it's not. Look to help this friend, this roommate writer—okay, this person in your class—to get a better piece of writing. Point to problems and areas for improvement but do it in a constructive way. See what you can do to push her to do even more than she's done and stretch herself as a writer.

What Are Your Goals?

4   First, don't set out to seek and destroy all errors and problems in the writing. You're not an editor. You're not a teacher. You're not a cruise missile. And don't rewrite any parts of the paper. You're not the writer; you're a reader. One of many. The paper is not yours; it's the writer's. She writes. You read. She is in charge of what she does to her writing. That doesn't mean you can't make suggestions. It doesn't mean you can't offer a few sample rewrites here and there, as models. But make it clear they're samples, models. Not rewrites. Not edits. Not corrections. Be reluctant at first even to say what you would do if the paper were yours. It's not yours. Again: Writers write, readers read and show what they're understanding and maybe make suggestions. What to do instead: Look at your task as a simple one. You're there to play back to the writer how you read the paper: what you got from it; what you found interesting; where you were confused; where you wanted more. With this done, you can go on to point out problems, ask questions, offer advice, and wonder out loud with the writer about her ideas. Look to help her improve the writing or encourage her to work on some things as a writer.

How Do You Get Started?

5   Before you up and start reading the paper, take a minute (alright, thirty seconds) to make a mental checklist about the circumstances of the writing, the context. You're not going to just read a text. You're going to read a text within a certain context, a set of circumstances that accompany the writing and that you bring to your reading. It's one kind of writing or another, designed for one audience and purpose or another. It's a rough draft or a final draft. The writer is trying to be serious or casual, straight or ironic. Ideally, you'll read the paper with an eye to the circumstances that it was written in and the situation it is looking to create. That means looking at the writing in terms of the assignment, the writer's particular interests and aims, the work you've been doing in class, and the stage of drafting.

- *The assignment*: What kind of writing does the assignment call (or allow) for? Is the paper supposed to be a personal essay? A report? An analysis? An argument? Consider how well the paper before you meets the demands of the kind of writing the writer is taking up.
- *The writer's interests and aims*: What does the writer want to accomplish? If she's writing a personal narrative, say, is she trying to simply recount a past experience? Is she trying to recount a past experience and at the same time amuse her readers? Is

she trying to show a pleasant experience on the surface, yet suggest underneath that everything was not as pleasant as it seems? Hone in on the writer's particular aims in the writing.

- *The work of the class*: Try to tie your comments to the concepts and strategies you've been studying in class. If you've been doing a lot of work on using detail, be sure to point to places in the writing where the writer uses detail effectively or where she might provide richer detail. If you've been working on developing arguments through examples and sample cases, indicate where the writer might use such methods to strengthen her arguments. If you've been considering various ways to sharpen the style of your sentences, offer places where the writer can clarify her sentence structure or arrange a sentence for maximum impact. The best comments will ring familiar even as they lead the writer to try to do something she hasn't quite done before, or done in quite the same way. They'll be comforting and understandable even as they create some need to do more, a need to figure out some better way.

Organization is great

- *The stage of drafting*: Is it an early draft? A full but incomplete draft? A nearly final draft? Pay attention to the stage of drafting. Don't try to deal with everything all at once if it's a first, rough draft. Concentrate on the large picture: the paper's focus; the content; the writer's voice. Don't worry about errors and punctuation problems yet. There'll be time for them later. If it's closer to a full draft, go ahead and talk, in addition to the overall content, about arrangement, pacing, and sentence style. Wait till the final draft to give much attention to fine-tuning sentences and dealing in detail with proofreading. Remember: You're not an editor. Leave these sentence revisions and corrections for the writer. It's her paper. And she's going to learn best by detecting problems and making her own changes.

What to Address in Your Comments?

6   Try to focus your comments on a couple of areas of writing. Glance through the paper quickly first. Get an idea whether you'll deal mostly with the overall content and purpose of the writing, its shape and flow, or (if these are more or less in order) with local matters of paragraph structure, sentence style, and correctness. Don't try to cover everything that comes up or even all instances of a given problem. Address issues that are most important to address in this paper, at this time.

Where to Put Your Comments?

Nice idea

7   Some teachers like to have students write comments in the margins right next to the passage. Some like to have students write out their comments in an end note or in a separate letter to the writer. I like to recommend using both marginal comments and a note or letter at the end. The best of both worlds. Marginal comments allow you to give a quick moment-by-moment reading of the paper. They make it easy to give immediate and specific feedback. You still have to make sure you specify what you're talking about and what you have to say, but they save you some work telling the writer what you're addressing and allow you to focus your end note on things that are most important. Comments at the end allow you to provide some perspective on your response. This doesn't mean that

you have to size up the paper and give it a thumbs up or a thumbs down. You can use the end comment to emphasize the key points of your response, explain and elaborate on issues you want to deal with more fully, and mention additional points that you don't want to address in detail. One thing to avoid: plastering comments all over the writing: in between and over the lines of the other person's writing—up, down, and across the page. Write in your space, and let the writer keep hers.

How to Sound?

8   Not like a teacher. Not like a judge. Not like an editor or critic or shotgun. (Wouldn't you want someone who was giving you comments not to sound like a teacher's red pen, a judge's ruling, an editor's impatience, a critic's wrath, a shotgun's blast?) Sound like you normally sound when you're speaking with a friend or acquaintance. Talk to the writer. You're not just marking up a text: you're responding to the writer. You're a reader, a helper, a colleague. Try to sound like someone who's a reader, who's helpful, and who's collegial. Supportive. And remember: Even when you're tough and demanding you can still be supportive.

How Much to Comment?

9   Don't be stingy. Write most of your comments out in full statements. Instead of writing two or three words, write seven or eight. Instead of making only one brief comment and moving on, say what you have to say and then go back over the statement and explain what you mean or why you said it or note other alternatives. Let the writer know again and again how you are understanding her paper, what you take her to be saying. And elaborate on your key comments. Explain your interpretations, problems, questions, and advice.

Is It Okay to Be Short and Sweet?

10   No. At least not most of the time. Get specific. Don't rely on general statements alone. How much have generic comments helped you as a writer? "Add detail." "Needs better structure." "Unclear." Try to let the writer know what exactly the problem is. Refer specifically to the writer's words and make them a part of your comments. "Add some detail on what it was like working at the beach." "I think we'll need to know more about your high school crowd before we can understand the way you've changed." "This sentence is not clear. Were *you* disappointed or were *they* disappointed?" This way the writer will see what you're talking about, and she'll have a better idea what to work on.

Do You Praise or Criticize or What?

11   Be always of two (or three) minds about your response to the paper. You like the paper, but it could use some more interesting detail. You found this statement interesting, but these ideas in the second paragraph are not so hot. It's an alright paper, but it could be outstanding if the writer said what was really bothering her. Always be ready to praise. But always look to point to places that are not working well or that are not yet working as well as they might. Always be ready to expect more from the writer.

How to Present Your Comments?

12   Don't steer away from being critical. Feel free—in fact, feel obliged—to tell the writer what you like and don't like, what is and is not working, and where you think it can be made to work better. But use some other strategies, too. Try to engage the writer in considering her choices and thinking about possible ways to improve the paper. Make it a goal to write two or three comments that look to summarize or paraphrase what the writer is saying. Instead of *telling* the reader what to do, *suggest* what she might do. Identify the questions that are raised for you as you read:

- Play back your way of understanding the writing:
  This seems to be the real focus of the paper, the issue you seem most interested in.
  So you're saying that you really weren't interested in her romantically?
- Temper your criticisms:
  This sentence is a bit hard to follow.
  I'm not sure this paragraph is necessary.
- Offer advice:
  It might help to add an example here.
  Maybe save this sentence for the end of the paper.
- Ask questions, especially real questions:
  What else were you feeling at the time?
  What kind of friend? Would it help to say?
  Do you need this opening sentence?
  In what ways were you "a daddy's little girl"?
- Explain and follow up on your initial comments:
  You might present this episode first. This way we can see what you mean when
    you say that he was always too busy.
  How did you react? Did you cry or yell? Did you walk away?
  This makes her sound cold and calculating. Is that what you want?
- Offer some praise, and then explain to the writer why the writing works:
  Good opening paragraph. You've got my attention.
  Good detail. It tells me a lot about the place.
  I like the descriptions you provide—for instance, about your grand
    mother cooking, at the bottom of page 1; about her house, in the
    middle of the page 2; and about how she said her rosary at night:
  "quick but almost pleading, like crying without tears."

How Much Criticism? How Much Praise?

13   Challenge yourself to write as many praise comments as criticisms. When you praise, praise well. Think about it. Sincerity and specificity are everything when it comes to a compliment.

How Much Should You Be Influenced by What You Know About the Writer?

14   Consider the person behind the writer when you make your comments. If she's not done so well in class lately, maybe you can give her a pick-me-up in your comments. If she's shy and seems reluctant to go into the kind of personal detail the paper seems to need, encourage her. Make some suggestions or tell her what you would do. If she's confident and going on arrogant, see what you can do to challenge her with the ideas she presents in the paper. Look for other views she may not have thought about, and find ways to lead her to consider them. Always be ready to look at the text in terms of the writer behind the text.

15   Good comments, this listing shows, require a lot from a reader. But you don't have to make a checklist out of these suggestions and go through each one methodically as you read. It's amazing how they all start coming together when you look at your response as a way of talking with the writer seriously about the writing, recording how you experience the words on the page and giving the writer something to think about for revision. The more you see examples of thoughtful commentary and the more you try to do it yourself, the more you'll get a feel for how it's done.

16   Here's a set of student comments on a student paper. They were done in the last third of a course that focused on the personal essay and concentrated on helping students develop the content and thought of their writing. The class had been working on finding ways to develop and extend the key statements of their essays (by using short, representative details, full-blown examples, dialogue, and multiple perspectives) and getting more careful about selecting and shaping parts of their writing. The assignment called on students to write an essay or an autobiographical story where they looked to capture how they see (or have seen) something about one or both of their parents—some habits, attitudes, or traits their parents have taken on. They were encouraged to give shape to their ideas and experiences in ways that went beyond their previous understandings and try things they hadn't tried in their writing. More a personal narrative than an essay. Todd's paper looks to capture one distinct difference in the way his mother and father disciplined their children. It is a rough draft that will be taken through one or possibly two more revisions. Readers were asked to offer whatever feedback they could that might help the writer with the next stage of writing.

17   This is a full and thoughtful set of comments. The responder, Jeremy, creates himself not as a teacher or critic but first of all as a reader, one who is intent on saying how he takes the writing and what he'd like to hear more about:

18   Good Point. Makes it more unlikely that you should be the one to get caught.

19   Great passage. Really lets the reader know what you were thinking.

20   Was there a reason you were first or did it just happen that way?

21   Would he punish you anyway or could you just get away with things?

22   He makes twenty-two comments on the paper—seventeen statements in the margins and five more in the end note. The comments are written out in full statements, and they are detailed and specific. They make his response into a lively exchange with the writer, one person talking with another about what he's said. Well over half of the comments are follow-up comments that explain, illustrate, or qualify other responses.

Figure 14-1

Todd

ENG 1

Rick Straub

Assignment 8b

"Uh, oh"

I like this paragraph. It actually lets the reader relate to you and also produces a picture in the reader's mind.

When I called home from the police station I was praying that my father would answer the phone. He would listen to what I had to say and would react comely, logical, and in a manner that would keep my mother from screaming her head off. If my Mother was to answer the phone I would have to explain myself quickly in order to keep her from having a heart attack.

When I was eleven years old I hung out with a group of boys that were almost three years older than me. The five of us did all the things that young energetic kids did playing ball, riding bikes, and getting in to trouble. (Because they were older they worried less about getting in trouble and the consequences of there actions than I did.) Good point. Makes it more unlikely that you should be the one to get caught

My friends and I would always come home from school. drop our backpacks off and head out in the neighborhood to find something to do. Our favorite thing to do was to find construction cites and steal wood to make tree forts in the woods or skateboard ramps. So one day, coming home from school, we noticed a couple new houses being built near our neighborhood. It was a prime cite for wood, nails, and anything else we could get our hands on. We discussed our plan on the bus and decided that we would all meet there after dropping our stuff off at home. (I remember being a little at hesitant first because it was close to my house but beyond the boundaries my parents had set for me. Of course I went because I didn't want to be the odd man out and have to put up with all the name calling.) I dropped my bag off and I headed to the construction cite.

What other things did you do to get into trouble or is it irrelevant?

Great passage. really lets the reader know what you were thinking

I meet my friends there and we began to search the different houses for wood and what not. We all picked up a couple of things and were about to leave when one of my friends noticed what looked to be a big tool shed off behind one of the houses. It looked promising so we decided that we should check it out. Tow of the boys in the group said that they had all the wood they could carry and said they were going home. The rest of us headed down to the shed to take a look.

Once there we noticed that the shed had been broken in to previously. The lock on it had been busted on the hinges were bent. I opened the door to the shed and stepped inside to take a look around while my friends waited outside. It was dark inside but I could tell the place had been ransacked. there was nothing to take so I decided to leave. I heard my to friends say some thing so turned back around to site of them running away. I thought that they were playing a joke on me so I casually walked out only to see a cop car parked near one of the houses under construction. As soon as I saw that cop car I took off but was stopped when a big hand pulled at that back of my shirt. I watched my friends run until they were out of cite and then I turned around.

Was there a reason you were first, or did it just happen that way?

The cop had me sit in the squad car while he asked me questions. He asked me if I knew those kids that ran off and I said "Noooooooooo". He asked me if I had broken in to that shed and I said "nooooooooooo". The cop wrote down what I was saying all the while shaking his head. Then he told me that I wasn't being arrested but I would have to go down to the station to call parents and have them pick me up. Upon hearing that I nearly soiled my undershorts. "My God. I'm dead. My mom is going to kill me."

What else happened at the police station? How long were you there?

At the station the officer showed me the whole station. jail cells and everything. An obvious tactic to try and scare me, which worked. That plus the thought of my mom answering the phone and me trying to explain what happened nearly made me sick.

"Waaahhhaaattt! You're where? She would say.

"The police station mom," uh oh, hear it comes.

"Ooooohhh my God, my son is criminal." so loud I would have to pull the phone away from my ear.

She had this uncanny ability to blow things out of proportion right from the start. She would assume the worse and then go from there. This was a classic example of why I could never go to her if I had any bad news. She would start screaming, get upset, and then go bitch at my father. My father is a pretty laid back but when ever my mother started yelling at him about me, he would get angry and come chew me out worse than if I had just gone to him in the first place.

Maybe you could say more as to why you think your mom is like this.

If my father were to answer the phone he would respond with out raising his voice. We would examine the situation in a logical manner and make a decision form there.

"Uhhmmm (long pause). You're at the police station."

"Yeah dad, I didn't get arrest they just had me come down here so I had to tell you."

"Uhm, so you didn't get arrested (long pause). Well (long pause), I'll come pick you up and will talk about then".

Did your dad get into trouble as a kid so he knows what it's like? Explain why he reacts as he does.

I feel like I can relate to my father much better than I can to my mother. He has a cool and collective voice that can take command of any situation. I always feel like he understands me, like he know what I'm thinking all the time. This comes in real handy when I get in trouble. *Would he punish you anyway, or could you just get away with things?*

I called home. Sweat beading on my lip.

"Hello", my mom said. Oh geez, I'm dead.

"Mom can I talk to dad?"

"Why, what's wrong?"

"Oh nothing, I just need talk to him, yes, this is going to work!"

"Hold on." she said.

I like the way you use dialogue in this section to illustrate how each of your parents would react and then explain to the reader what each of them is like. It works well.

"Hello," my father said.

"Dad, I'm at the police station." I told him the whole story of what happened. He reacted exactly as I expect he would.

"Uhhmmm (long pause). You're at the police station...

I really like the ending, it tells the reader what is going to happen without having to explain it step by step. Good paper. I like the use of dialogue. Perhaps more on your understanding of why your parents react as they do.

23   The comments focus on the content and development of the writing, in line with the assignment, the stage of drafting, and the work of the course. They also view the writing rhetorically, in terms of how the text has certain effects on readers. Although there are over two dozen wording or sentence level errors in the paper, he decides, wisely, to stick with the larger matters of writing. Yet even as he offers a pretty full set of comments he doesn't ever take control over the text. His comments are placed unobtrusively on the page, and he doesn't try to close things down or decide things for the writer. He offers more than he has already done, to extend the boundaries of his examination, in keeping with the assignment and the larger goals of the course, he calls on Todd in several comments to explore the motivations and personalities behind his parents' different ways of disciplining:

24   Maybe you could say more as to why you think your mom is like this.

25   Did your dad get into trouble as a kid so he know
         what it's like? Explain why he reacts as he does.

26   He is careful, though, not to get presumptuous and make
         decisions for the writer. Instead, he offers options and points to possibilities:

27   Perhaps more on your understanding of why your parents react as they do.

28   What other things did you do to get into trouble? Or is it irrelevant?

29   From start to finish he takes on the task of reading and responding and leaves the work of writing and revising to Todd.

30   Jeremy's response is not in a class by itself. A set of comments to end all commentary on Todd's paper. He might have done well, for instance, to recognize how much this paper works because of the way Todd arranges the story. He could have done more to point to what's not working in the writing or what could be made to work better. He might have asked Todd for more details about his state of mind when he got caught by the

policeman and while he was being held at the police station. He might have urged him more to make certain changes. He might even have said, if only in a brief warning, something about the number of errors across the writing. But this is moot and just. Different readers are always going to pick up on different things and respond in different ways, and no one reading or response is going to address everything that might well be addressed, in the way it might best be addressed. All responses are incomplete and provisional— one reader's way of reading and reacting to the text in front of him. And any number of other responses, presented in any number of different ways, might be as useful or maybe even more useful to Todd as he takes up his work with the writing.

31   All this notwithstanding, Jeremy's comments are solid. They are full. They are thoughtful. And they are respectful. They take the writing and the writer seriously and address the issues that are raised responsibly. His comments do what commentary on student writing should optimally do. They turn the writer back into his writing and lead him to reflect on his choices and aims, to consider and reconsider his intentions as a writer and the effects the words on that page will have on readers. They help him see what he can work on in revision and what he might deal with in his ongoing work as a writer.

Critical Reading Questions:

- **Rhetorical analysis:** Who is Straub's *intended* audience? How does he construct this audience? As someone in his *actual* audience, do all of his insights about "you" and imperatives to you actually apply to who you really are? Why or why not? How does Straub's direct address to his audience affect and construct his ethos?

- **Analysis:** When Straub talks about the teacher, he uses the pronoun "he"; however, when Straub discusses the student writer, he uses the pronoun "she." Is Straub simply trying to keep these two individuals easily distinguishable from one another by using these pronouns, or is there an element of sexism in this rhetorical choice? How does a person's gender factor into writing or responding to another's writing?

- **Analysis:** What are the most useful insights about responding to student writing that Straub offers? How could these strategies be implemented in class workshops? How could students use these approaches outside of class to help one another on writing assignments across the campus?

Mother Tongue

Amy Tan

Amy Tan starts "Mother Tongue" by emphasizing her love of language, while also acknowledging how complex it is for bilingual people. Tan is known as the author of the novel *The Joy Luck Club (1989)*, which was adapted into a film (1993). In this essay, Tan uses personal experience to examine the languages—the various "Englishes"—that she uses. As a linguist and storyteller, Tan uses "Mother Tongue" to illustrate the language differences among academic English, Chinese, simple English, and the "broken" English of her mother. Her narrative highlights the ways these languages interact, and how she navigates the world through them. Throughout the article, Tan argues that language can be defined culturally as well as socially and that this complexity provided a basis for her own education. Tan's article discusses the tension between the social ramifications of her mother's tongue and the way this "broken" language is familiar and "perfectly clear, perfectly natural." In her essay, Tan moves beyond the social complications of language use into public understanding, and in this way her work becomes a call to action.

—BLS

1   I am not a scholar of English or literature. I cannot give you much more than personal opinions on the English language and its variations in this country or others.

2   I am a writer. And by that definition, I am someone who has always loved language. I am fascinated by language in daily life. I spend a great deal of my time thinking about the power of language—the way it can evoke an emotion, a visual image, a complex idea, or a simple truth. Language is the tool of my trade. And I use them all—all the Englishes I grew up with.

3   Recently, I was made keenly aware of the different Englishes I do use. I was giving a talk to a large group of people, the same talk I had already given to half a dozen other groups. The nature of the talk was about my writing, my life, and my book, *The Joy Luck Club*. The talk was going along well enough, until I remembered one major difference that made the whole talk sound wrong. My mother was in the room. And it was perhaps the first time she had heard me give a lengthy speech, using the kind of English I have never used with her. I was saying things like, "The intersection of memory upon imagination" and "There is an aspect of my fiction that relates to thus-and-thus"—a speech filled with carefully wrought grammatical phrases, burdened, it suddenly seemed to me, with nominalized forms, past perfect tenses, conditional phrases, all the forms of standard English that I had learned in school and through books, the forms of English I did not use at home with my mother.

4   Just last week, I was walking down the street with my mother, and I again found myself conscious of the English I was using, the English I do use with her. We were talking about

the price of new and used furniture and I heard myself saying this: "Not waste money that way." My husband was with us as well, and he didn't notice any switch in my English. And then I realized why. It's because over the twenty years we've been together I've often used that same kind of English with him, and sometimes he even uses it with me. It has become our language of intimacy, a different sort of English that relates to family talk, the language I grew up with.

5   So you'll have some idea of what this family talk I heard sounds like, I'll quote what my mother said during a recent conversation which I videotaped and then transcribed. During this conversation, my mother was talking about a political gangster in Shanghai who had the same last name as her family's, Du, and how the gangster in his early years wanted to be adopted by her family, which was rich by comparison. Later, the gangster became more powerful, far richer than my mother's family, and one day showed up at my mother's wedding to pay his respects. Here's what she said in part: "Du Yusong having business like fruit stand. Like off the street kind. He is Du like Du Zong—but not Tsung-ming Island people. The local people call putong, the river east side, he belong to that side local people. That man want to ask Du Zong father take him in like become own family. Du Zong father wasn't look down on him, but didn't take seriously, until that man big like become a mafia. Now important person, very hard to inviting him. Chinese way, came only to show respect, don't stay for dinner. Respect for making big celebration, he shows up. Mean gives lots of respect. Chinese custom. Chinese social life that way. If too important won't have to stay too long. He come to my wedding. I didn't see, I heard it. I gone to boy's side, they have YMCA dinner. Chinese age I was nineteen."

6   You should know that my mother's expressive command of English belies how much she actually understands. She reads the Forbes report, listens to Wall Street Week, converses daily with her stockbroker, reads all of Shirley MacLaine's books with ease—all kinds of things I can't begin to understand. Yet some of my friends tell me they understand 50 percent of what my mother says. Some say they understand 80 to 90 percent. Some say they understand none of it, as if she were speaking pure Chinese. But to me, my mother's English is perfectly clear, perfectly natural. It's my mother tongue. Her language, as I hear it, is vivid, direct, full of observation and imagery. That was the language that helped shape the way I saw things, expressed things, made sense of the world.

7   Lately, I've been giving more thought to the kind of English my mother speaks. Like others, I have described it to people as "broken" or "fractured" English. But I wince when I say that. It has always bothered me that I can think of no way to describe it other than "broken," as if it were damaged and needed to be fixed, as if it lacked a certain wholeness and soundness. I've heard other terms used, "limited English," for example. But they seem just as bad, as if everything is limited, including people's perceptions of the limited English speaker.

8   I know this for a fact, because when I was growing up, my mother's "limited" English limited my perception of her. I was ashamed of her English. I believed that her English reflected the quality of what she had to say. That is, because she expressed them imperfectly her thoughts were imperfect. And I had plenty of empirical evidence to support me: the fact that people in department stores, at banks, and at restaurants did not take her

serlously, did not give her good service, pretended not to understand her, or even acted as if they did not hear her.

9   My mother has long realized the limitations of her English as well. When I was fifteen, she used to have me call people on the phone to pretend I was she. In this guise, I was forced to ask for information or even to complain and yell at people who had been rude to her. One time it was a call to her stockbroker In New York. She had cashed out her small portfolio and it just so happened we were going to go to New York the next week, our very first trip outside California. I had to get on the phone and say in an adolescent voice that was not very convincing, "This is Mrs. Tan."

10   And my mother was standing in the back whispering loudly, "Why he don't send me check, already two weeks late. So mad he lie to me, losing me money.

11   And then I said in perfect English, "Yes, I'm getting rather concerned. You had agreed to send the check two weeks ago, but it hasn't arrived."

12   Then she began to talk more loudly. "What he want, I come to New York tell him front of his boss, you cheating me?" And I was trying to calm her down, make her be quiet, while telling the stockbroker, "I can't tolerate any more excuses. If I don't receive the check immediately, I am going to have to speak to your manager when I'm in New York next week." And sure enough, the following week there we were in front of this astonished stockbroker, and I was sitting there red-faced and quiet, and my mother, the real Mrs. Tan, was shouting at his boss in her impeccable broken English.

13   We used a similar routine just five days ago, for a situation that was far less humorous. My mother had gone to the hospital for an appointment, to find out about a benign brain tumor a CAT scan had revealed a month ago. She said she had spoken very good English, her best English, no mistakes. Still, she said, the hospital did not apologize when they said they had lost the CAT scan and she had come for nothing. She said they did not seem to have any sympathy when she told them she was anxious to know the exact diagnosis, since her husband and son had both died of brain tumors. She said they would not give her any more information until the next time and she would have to make another appointment for that. So she said she would not leave until the doctor called her daughter. She wouldn't budge. And when the doctor finally called her daughter, me, who spoke in perfect English—lo and behold—we had assurances the CAT scan would be found, promises that a conference call on Monday would be held, and apologies for any suffering my mother had gone through for a most regrettable mistake.

14   I think my mother's English almost had an effect on limiting my possibilities in life as well. Sociologists and linguists probably will tell you that a person's developing language skills are more influenced by peers. But I do think that the language spoken in the family, especially in immigrant families which are more insular, plays a large role in shaping the language of the child. And I believe that it affected my results on achievement tests, I.Q. tests, and the SAT. While my English skills were never judged as poor, compared to math, English could not be considered my strong suit. In grade school I did moderately well, getting perhaps B's, sometimes B-pluses, in English and scoring perhaps in the sixtieth or seventieth percentile on achievement tests. But those scores were not good enough to

override the opinion that my true abilities lay in math and science, because in those areas I achieved A's and scored in the ninetieth percentile or higher.

15   This was understandable. Math is precise; there is only one correct answer. Whereas, for me at least, the answers on English tests were always a judgment call, a matter of opinion and personal experience. Those tests were constructed around items like fill-in-the-blank sentence completion, such as, "Even though Tom was, Mary thought he was—." And the correct answer always seemed to be the most bland combinations of thoughts, for example, "Even though Tom was shy, Mary thought he was charming: "with the grammatical structure "even though" limiting the correct answer to some sort of semantic opposites, so you wouldn't get answers like, "Even though Tom was foolish, Mary thought he was ridiculous:" Well, according to my mother, there were very few limitations as to what Tom could have been and what Mary might have thought of him. So I never did well on tests like that.

16   The same was true with word analogies, pairs of words in which you were supposed to find some sort of logical, semantic relationship—for example, "Sunset is to nightfall as _____ is to _____." And here you would be presented with a list of four possible pairs, one of which showed the same kind of relationship: red is to stoplight, bus is to arrival, chills is to fever, yawn is to boring: Well, I could never think that way. I knew what the tests were asking, but I could not block out of my mind the images already created by the first pair, "sunset is to nightfall"—and I would see a burst of colors against a darkening sky, the moon rising, the lowering of a curtain of stars. And all the other pairs of words— red, bus, stoplight, boring—just threw up a mass of confusing images, making it impossible for me to sort out something as logical as saying: "A sunset precedes nightfall" is the same as "a chill precedes a fever." The only way I would have gotten that answer right would have been to imagine an associative situation, for example, my being disobedient and staying out past sunset, catching a chill at night, which turns into feverish pneumonia as punishment, which indeed did happen to me.

17   I have been thinking about all this lately, about my mother's English, about achievement tests. Because lately I've been asked, as a writer, why there are not more Asian Americans represented in American literature. Why are there few Asian Americans enrolled in creative writing programs? Why do so many Chinese students go into engineering! Well, these are broad sociological questions I can't begin to answer. But I have noticed in surveys—in fact, just last week—that Asian students, as a whole, always do significantly better on math achievement tests than in English. And this makes me think that there are other Asian-American students whose English spoken in the home might also be described as "broken" or "limited." And perhaps they also have teachers who are steering them away from writing and into math and science, which is what happened to me.

18   Fortunately, I happen to be rebellious in nature and enjoy the challenge of disproving assumptions made about me. I became an English major my first year in college, after being enrolled as pre-med. I started writing nonfiction as a freelancer the week after I was told by my former boss that writing was my worst skill and I should hone my talents toward account management.

19   But it wasn't until 1985 that I finally began to write fiction. And at first I wrote using what I thought to be wittily crafted sentences, sentences that would finally prove I had mastery over the English language. Here's an example from the first draft of a story that later made its way into *The Joy Luck Club*, but without this line: "That was my mental quandary in its nascent state." A terrible line, which I can barely pronounce.

20   Fortunately, for reasons I won't get into today, I later decided I should envision a reader for the stories I would write. And the reader I decided upon was my mother, because these were stories about mothers. So with this reader in mind—and in fact she did read my early drafts—I began to write stories using all the Englishes I grew up with: the English I spoke to my mother, which for lack of a better term might be described as "simple"; the English she used with me, which for lack of a better term might be described as "broken"; my translation of her Chinese, which could certainly be described as "watered down"; and what I imagined to be her translation of her Chinese if she could speak in perfect English, her internal language, and for that I sought to preserve the essence, but neither an English nor a Chinese structure. I wanted to capture what language ability tests can never reveal: her intent, her passion, her imagery, the rhythms of her speech and the nature of her thoughts.

21   Apart from what any critic had to say about my writing, I knew I had succeeded where it counted when my mother finished reading my book and gave me her verdict: "So easy to read."

Critical Reading Questions:

- **Rhetorical analysis:** In "Mother Tongue," Tan recalls personal stories, which illustrate the effectiveness and limits of her mother's "broken" English in public spaces. Using evidence from these passages, reflect on the pathetic appeal of this piece. Who precisely is Tan's intended audience? How ineffective/effective is the language used?

- **Rhetorical analysis:** What are some of the many ways that Tan constructs her ethos? Tan holds both a bachelor's degree in English as well as a master's in linguistics, so why does she say that "I am not a scholar of English or literature"? What gives her authority in the eyes of her readers?

- **Reflection:** What are your thoughts on Tan's insights that "Math is precise; there is only one correct answer. Whereas, for me at least, the answers on English tests were always a judgment call, a matter of opinion and personal experience"? Does this resonate with your own beliefs about the objective or subjective nature of certain disciplines?

Sex, Lies and Conversation:
Why Is It So Hard for Men and Women to Talk to Each Other?

Deborah Tannen

In this short article from the *Washington Post* published June 24, 1990, linguist Deborah Tannen argues that men and women struggle to communicate not because they are biologically and inherently different but because they have been trained from a young age to participate in different discourse communities. She believes this means men and women value different types of communication and see its purpose differently; these factors lead to differences in conversational style and subsequent difficulties communicating across genders. Tannen further claims that these problems with communication can lead to marital strife and failed relationships. She provides evidence drawn from her personal experience as well as her professional research. Tannen has written many popular and academic books on the subject of communication between men and women. Though her books have received widespread acclaim, she is sometimes criticized within her own field for relying too heavily on anecdotal evidence and using "unscientific" research methods.

—PH

1   I was addressing a small gathering in a suburban Virginia living room—a women's group that had invited men to join them. Throughout the evening, one man had been particularly talkative, frequently offering ideas and anecdotes, while his wife sat silently beside him on the couch. Toward the end of the evening, I commented that women frequently complain that their husbands don't talk to them. This man quickly concurred. He gestured toward his wife and said, "She's the talker in our family." The room burst into laughter; the man looked puzzled and hurt. "It's true," he explained. "When I come home from work I have nothing to say. If she didn't keep the conversation going, we'd spend the whole evening in silence."

2   This episode crystallizes the irony that although American men tend to talk more than women in public situations, they often talk less at home. And this pattern is wreaking havoc with marriage.

3   The pattern was observed by political scientist Andrew Hacker in the late '70s. Sociologist Catherine Kohler Riessman reports in her new book "Divorce Talk" that most of the women she interviewed—but only a few of the men—gave lack of communication as the reason for their divorces. Given the current divorce rate of nearly 50 percent, that amounts to millions of cases in the United States every year—a virtual epidemic of failed conversation.

4   In my own research, complaints from women about their husbands most often focused not on tangible inequities such as having given up the chance for a career to accompany a husband to his, or doing far more than their share of daily life-support work like cleaning,

cooking, social arrangements and errands. Instead, they focused on communication: "He doesn't listen to me," "He doesn't talk to me." I found, as Hacker observed years before, that most wives want their husbands to be, first and foremost, conversational partners, but few husbands share this expectation of their wives.

5   In short, the image that best represents the current crisis is the stereotypical cartoon scene of a man sitting at the breakfast table with a newspaper held up in front of his face, while a woman glares at the back of it, wanting to talk.

Linguistic Battle of the Sexes

6   How can women and men have such different impressions of communication in marriage? Why the widespread imbalance in their interests and expectations?

7   In the April issue of *American Psychologist*, Stanford University's Eleanor Maccoby reports the results of her own and others' research showing that children's development is most influenced by the social structure of peer interactions. Boys and girls tend to play with children of their own gender, and their sex-separate groups have different organizational structures and interactive norms.

8   I believe these systematic differences in childhood socialization make talk between women and men like cross-cultural communication, heir to all the attraction and pitfalls of that enticing but difficult enterprise. My research on men's and women's conversations uncovered patterns similar to those described for children's groups.

9   For women, as for girls, intimacy is the fabric of relationships, and talk is the thread from which it is woven. Little girls create and maintain friendships by exchanging secrets; similarly, women regard conversation as the cornerstone of friendship. So a woman expects her husband to be a new and improved version of a best friend. What is important is not the individual subjects that are discussed but the sense of closeness, of a life shared, that emerges when people tell their thoughts, feelings, and impressions.

10   Bonds between boys can be as intense as girls', but they are based less on talking, more on doing things together. Since they don't assume talk is the cement that binds a relationship, men don't know what kind of talk women want, and they don't miss it when it isn't there.

11   Boys' groups are larger, more inclusive, and more hierarchical, so boys must struggle to avoid the subordinate position in the group. This may play a role in women's complaints that men don't listen to them. Some men really don't like to listen, because being the listener makes them feel one-down, like a child listening to adults or an employee to a boss.

12   But often when women tell men, "You aren't listening," and the men protest, "I am," the men are right. The impression of not listening results from misalignments in the mechanics of conversation. The misalignment begins as soon as a man and a woman take physical positions. This became clear when I studied videotapes made by psychologist Bruce Dorval of children and adults talking to their same-sex best friends. I found that at every age, the girls and women faced each other directly, their eyes anchored on each other's faces. At every age, the boys and men sat at angles to each other and looked elsewhere in the room, periodically glancing at each other. They were obviously attuned to each other, often mirroring each other's movements. But the tendency of men to face away can

give women the impression they aren't listening even when they are. A young woman in college was frustrated: Whenever she told her boyfriend she wanted to talk to him, he would lie down on the floor, close his eyes, and put his arm over his face. This signaled to her, "He's taking a nap." But he insisted he was listening extra hard. Normally, he looks around the room, so he is easily distracted. Lying down and covering his eyes helped him concentrate on what she was saying.

13   Analogous to the physical alignment that women and men take in conversation is their topical alignment. The girls in my study tended to talk at length about one topic, but the boys tended to jump from topic to topic. The second-grade girls exchanged stories about people they knew. The second-grade boys teased, told jokes, noticed things in the room and talked about finding games to play. The sixth-grade girls talked about problems with a mutual friend. The sixth-grade boys talked about 55 different topics, none of which extended over more than a few turns.

Listening to Body Language

14   Switching topics is another habit that gives women the impression men aren't listening, especially if they switch to a topic about themselves. But the evidence of the 10th-grade boys in my study indicates otherwise. The 10th-grade boys sprawled across their chairs with bodies parallel and eyes straight ahead, rarely looking at each other. They looked as if they were riding in a car, staring out the windshield. But they were talking about their feelings. One boy was upset because a girl had told him he had a drinking problem, and the other was feeling alienated from all his friends.

15   Now, when a girl told a friend about a problem, the friend responded by asking probing questions and expressing agreement and understanding. But the boys dismissed each other's problems. Todd assured Richard that his drinking was "no big problem" because "sometimes you're funny when you're off your butt." And when Todd said he felt left out, Richard responded, "Why should you? You know more people than me."

16   Women perceive such responses as belittling and unsupportive. But the boys seemed satisfied with them. Whereas women reassure each other by implying, "You shouldn't feel bad because I've had similar experiences," men do so by implying, "You shouldn't feel bad because your problems aren't so bad."

17   There are even simpler reasons for women's impression that men don't listen. Linguist Lynette Hirschman found that women make more listener-noise, such as "mhm," "uhuh," and "yeah," to show "I'm with you." Men, she found, more often give silent attention. Women who expect a stream of listener noise interpret silent attention as no attention at all.

18   Women's conversational habits are as frustrating to men as men's are to women. Men who expect silent attention interpret a stream of listener noise as overreaction or impatience. Also, when women talk to each other in a close, comfortable setting, they often overlap, finish each other's sentences and anticipate what the other is about to say. This practice, which I call "participatory listenership," is often perceived by men as interruption, intrusion and lack of attention.

19   A parallel difference caused a man to complain about his wife, "She just wants to talk about her own point of view. If I show her another view, she gets mad at me." When most women talk to each other, they assume a conversationalist's job is to express agreement and support. But many men see their conversational duty as pointing out the other side of an argument. This is heard as disloyalty by women, and refusal to offer the requisite support. It is not that women don't want to see other points of view, but that they prefer them phrased as suggestions and inquiries rather than as direct challenges.

20   In his book "*Fighting for Life*," Walter Ong points out that men use "agonistic" or war-like, oppositional formats to do almost anything; thus discussion becomes debate, and conversation a competitive sport. In contrast, women see conversation as a ritual means of establishing rapport. If Jane tells a problem and June says she has a similar one, they walk away feeling closer to each other. But this attempt at establishing rapport can backfire when used with men. Men take too literally women's ritual "troubles talk," just as women mistake men's ritual challenges for real attack.

The Sounds of Silence

21   These differences begin to clarify why women and men have such different expectations about communication in marriage. For women, talk creates intimacy. Marriage is an orgy of closeness: you can tell your feelings and thoughts, and still be loved. Their greatest fear is being pushed away. But men live in a hierarchical world, where talk maintains independence and status. They are on guard to protect themselves from being put down and pushed around.

22   This explains the paradox of the talkative man who said of his silent wife, "She's the talker." In the public setting of a guest lecture, he felt challenged to show his intelligence and display his understanding of the lecture. But at home, where he has nothing to prove and no one to defend against, he is free to remain silent. For his wife, being home means she is free from the worry that something she says might offend someone, or spark disagreement, or appear to be showing off; at home she is free to talk.

23   The communication problems that endanger marriage can't be fixed by mechanical engineering. They require a new conceptual framework about the role of talk in human relationships. Many of the psychological explanations that have become second nature may not be helpful, because they tend to blame either women (for not being assertive enough) or men (for not being in touch with their feelings). A sociolinguistic approach by which male-female conversation is seen as cross-cultural communication allows us to understand the problem and forge solutions without blaming either party.

24   Once the problem is understood, improvement comes naturally, as it did to the young woman and her boyfriend who seemed to go to sleep when she wanted to talk. Previously, she had accused him of not listening, and he had refused to change his behavior, since that would be admitting fault. But then she learned about and explained to him the differences in women's and men's habitual ways of aligning themselves in conversation. The next time she told him she wanted to talk, he began, as usual, by lying down and covering his eyes. When the familiar negative reaction bubbled up, she reassured herself that he really was listening. But then he sat up and looked at her. Thrilled, she asked why. He said,

"You like me to look at you when we talk, so I'll try to do it." Once he saw their differences as cross-cultural rather than right and wrong, he independently altered his behavior.

25   Women who feel abandoned and deprived when their husbands won't listen to or report daily news may be happy to discover their husbands trying to adapt once they understand the place of small talk in women's relationships. But if their husbands don't adapt, the women may still be comforted that for men, this is not a failure of intimacy. Accepting the difference, the wives may look to their friends or family for that kind of talk. And husbands who can't provide it shouldn't feel their wives have made unreasonable demands. Some couples will still decide to divorce, but at least their decisions will be based on realistic expectations.

26   In these times of resurgent ethnic conflicts, the world desperately needs cross-cultural understanding. Like charity, successful cross-cultural communication should begin at home.

Critical Reading Questions:

- **Reflection:** Tannen has been criticized for relying too heavily on anecdotal evidence and generalizations to support her arguments. Do you think these criticisms are justified in this article? Which of her anecdotes do you find the most convincing? Which of her generalizations do you find to be in the most need of support? What type of support could she provide that might strengthen these claims?

- **Reflection:** The concept of "discourse communities" that Tannen presents in her article has often been applied to academic communities such as university students and professors, different academic majors or professions, and graduate and undergraduate students. What discourse communities are you a part of? How do the topics Tannen describes here (purposes for communicating, turn-taking, body position, the role of participants in a conversation) apply to your own discourse communities?

Ain't I a Woman?

Sojourner Truth

Sojourner Truth, born Isabella Baumfree in 1797 in New York State, left her slave master after he refused to uphold the New York Anti-Slavery Law of 1827. She became an itinerant preacher, changed her name to Sojourner Truth in 1843, and worked as a staunch advocate for human rights. At the 1851 Women's Rights Convention in Akron, Ohio, Truth stood to respond to male speakers who claimed that women's inherent weaker natures and lower societal and religious stations precluded them from holding equal rights with men. When Truth rose to speak, her audience feared that she would detract from the subject at hand because she was an outspoken abolitionist who could neither read nor write. However, Truth's speech, later entitled "Ain't I a Woman?" was delivered with concise, powerful evidence and emotion, which enhanced her credibility so that, by the end of the speech, her audience were on their feet, applauding.

—DG

1   Well, children, where there is so much racket there must be something out of kilter. I think that 'twixt the negroes of the South and the women at the North, all talking about rights, the white men will be in a fix pretty soon. But what's all this here talking about?

2   That man over there says that women need to be helped into carriages, and lifted over ditches, and to have the best place everywhere. Nobody ever helps me into carriages, or over mud-puddles, or gives me any best place! And ain't I a woman? Look at me! Look at my arm! I have ploughed and planted, and gathered into barns, and no man could head me! And ain't I a woman? I could work as much and eat as much as a man—when I could get it—and bear the lash as well! And ain't I a woman? I have borne thirteen children, and seen most all sold off to slavery, and when I cried out with my mother's grief, none but Jesus heard me! And ain't I a woman?

3   Then they talk about this thing in the head; what's this they call it? [member of audience whispers, "intellect"] That's it, honey. What's that got to do with women's rights or negroes' rights? If my cup won't hold but a pint, and yours holds a quart, wouldn't you be mean not to let me have my little half measure full?

4   Then that little man in black there, he says women can't have as much rights as men, 'cause Christ wasn't a woman! Where did your Christ come from? Where did your Christ come from? From God and a woman! Man had nothing to do with Him.

5   If the first woman God ever made was strong enough to turn the world upside down all alone, these women together ought to be able to turn it back, and get it right side up again! And now they is asking to do it, the men better let them.

6   Obliged to you for hearing me, and now old Sojourner ain't got nothing more to say.

Critical Reading Questions:

- **Rhetorical analysis:** As an abolitionist who couldn't read or write, Truth's situated (extrinsic) ethos for this particular audience was weak. How do her words enhance her ethos so that her audience finds her credible and persuasive?

- **Rhetorical analysis:** As a spontaneous speech, "Ain't I a Woman?" operated within many rhetorical constraints. What were they? How do the rhetorical appeals work in Truth's few words to reach her audience?

- **Rhetorical analysis:** Consider the evidence Truth offers in support of her argument that women deserve equal rights with men. Why would this evidence be considered reasonable by her audience?

The Perils of Indifference

Elie Wiesel

Elie Wiesel's experience, as a fifteen-year-old boy, of the horrors of Auschwitz and Buchenwald has authorized him to speak and write extensively of the atrocities we know as the Holocaust. He was deported, with his family, from his home in Romania, separated from his mother and sisters, and shuffled among three camps before he and two of his sisters were liberated in April of 1945. His parents and younger sister died. The author of many books, a political activist, and Professor of Religion and Philosophy at Boston University, Wiesel has been the recipient of many honorary degrees and numerous awards, notably the 1986 Nobel Peace Prize, the Presidential Medal of Freedom, and the U.S. Congressional Gold Medal. He and his wife established The Elie Wiesel Foundation for Humanity, its purpose to fight indifference, intolerance, and injustice. Wiesel was invited to speak at the 1999 White House Millennium Lecture series on the subject of The Perils of Indifference. His speech was preceded by speeches by then First Lady Hillary Rodham Clinton and President Clinton and followed by a question-and-answer session in which guests who were present and those viewing via the internet contributed to the evening's discussions. Wiesel challenges assumptions about the necessity of indifference to maintain one's sanity, instead demonstrating the unnaturalness of the state of indifference to suffering of others.

—AMW

1   Mr. President, Mrs. Clinton, members of Congress, Ambassador Holbrooke, Excellencies, friends:

2   Fifty-four years ago to the day, a young Jewish boy from a small town in the Carpathian Mountains woke up, not far from Goethe's beloved Weimar, in a place of eternal infamy called Buchenwald. He was finally free, but there was no joy in his heart. He thought there never would be again.

3   Liberated a day earlier by American soldiers, he remembers their rage at what they saw. And even if he lives to be a very old man, he will always be grateful to them for that rage, and also for their compassion. Though he did not understand their language, their eyes told him what he needed to know—that they, too, would remember, and bear witness.

4   And now, I stand before you, Mr. President—Commander-in-Chief of the army that freed me, and tens of thousands of others—and I am filled with a profound and abiding gratitude to the American people.

5   Gratitude is a word that I cherish. Gratitude is what defines the humanity of the human being. And I am grateful to you, Hillary—or Mrs. Clinton—for what you said, and for what

you are doing for children in the world, for the homeless, for the victims of injustice, the victims of destiny and society. And I thank all of you for being here.

6   We are on the threshold of a new century, a new millennium. What will the legacy of this vanishing century be? How will it be remembered in the new millennium? Surely it will be judged, and judged severely, in both moral and metaphysical terms. These failures have cast a dark shadow over humanity: two World Wars, countless civil wars, the senseless chain of assassinations—Gandhi, the Kennedys, Martin Luther King, Sadat, Rabin—bloodbaths in Cambodia and Nigeria, India and Pakistan, Ireland and Rwanda, Eritrea and Ethiopia, Sarajevo and Kosovo; the inhumanity in the gulag and the tragedy of Hiroshima. And, on a different level, of course, Auschwitz and Treblinka. So much violence, so much indifference.

7   What is indifference? Etymologically, the word means "no difference." A strange and unnatural state in which the lines blur between light and darkness, dusk and dawn, crime and punishment, cruelty and compassion, good and evil.

8   What are its courses and inescapable consequences? Is it a philosophy? Is there a philosophy of indifference conceivable? Can one possibly view indifference as a virtue? Is it necessary at times to practice it simply to keep one's sanity, live normally, enjoy a fine meal and a glass of wine, as the world around us experiences harrowing upheavals?

9   Of course, indifference can be tempting—more than that, seductive. It is so much easier to look away from victims. It is so much easier to avoid such rude interruptions to our work, our dreams, our hopes. It is, after all, awkward, troublesome, to be involved in another person's pain and despair. Yet, for the person who is indifferent, his or her neighbors are of no consequence. And, therefore, their lives are meaningless. Their hidden or even visible anguish is of no interest. Indifference reduces the other to an abstraction.

10   Over there, behind the black gates of Auschwitz, the most tragic of all prisoners were the "Muselmanner," as they were called. Wrapped in their torn blankets, they would sit or lie on the ground, staring vacantly into space, unaware of who or where they were, strangers to their surroundings. They no longer felt pain, hunger, thirst. They feared nothing. They felt nothing. They were dead and did not know it.

11   Rooted in our tradition, some of us felt that to be abandoned by humanity then was not the ultimate. We felt that to be abandoned by God was worse than to be punished by Him. Better an unjust God than an indifferent one. For us to be ignored by God was a harsher punishment than to be a victim of His anger. Man can live far from God—not outside God. God is wherever we are. Even in suffering? Even in suffering.

12   In a way, to be indifferent to that suffering is what makes the human being inhuman. Indifference, after all, is more dangerous than anger and hatred. Anger can at times be creative. One writes a great poem, a great symphony, one does something special for the sake of humanity because one is angry at the injustice that one witnesses. But indifference is never creative. Even hatred at times may elicit a response. You fight it. You denounce it. You disarm it. Indifference elicits no response. Indifference is not a response.

13   Indifference is not a beginning, it is an end. And, therefore, indifference is always the friend of the enemy, for it benefits the aggressor—never his victim, whose pain is

magnified when he or she feels forgotten. The political prisoner in his cell, the hungry children, the homeless refugees—not to respond to their plight, not to relieve their solitude by offering them a spark of hope is to exile them from human memory. And in denying their humanity we betray our own.

14   Indifference, then, is not only a sin, it is a punishment. And this is one of the most important lessons of this outgoing century's wide-ranging experiments in good and evil.

15   In the place that I come from, society was composed of three simple categories: the killers, the victims, and the bystanders. During the darkest of times, inside the ghettoes and death camps—and I'm glad that Mrs. Clinton mentioned that we are now commemorating that event, that period, that we are now in the Days of Remembrance—but then, we felt abandoned, forgotten. All of us did.

16   And our only miserable consolation was that we believed that Auschwitz and Treblinka were closely guarded secrets; that the leaders of the free world did not know what was going on behind those black gates and barbed wire; that they had no knowledge of the war against the Jews that Hitler's armies and their accomplices waged as part of the war against the Allies.

17   If they knew, we thought, surely those leaders would have moved heaven and earth to intervene. They would have spoken out with great outrage and conviction. They would have bombed the railways leading to Birkenau, just the railways, just once.

18   And now we knew, we learned, we discovered that the Pentagon knew, the State Department knew. And the illustrious occupant of the White House then, who was a great leader—and I say it with some anguish and pain, because, today is exactly 54 years marking his death—Franklin Delano Roosevelt died on April the 12th, 1945, so he is very much present to me and to us.

19   No doubt, he was a great leader. He mobilized the American people and the world, going into battle, bringing hundreds and thousands of valiant and brave soldiers in America to fight fascism, to fight dictatorship, to fight Hitler. And so many of the young people fell in battle. And, nevertheless, his image in Jewish history—I must say it—his image in Jewish history is flawed.

20   The depressing tale of the St. Louis is a case in point. Sixty years ago, its human cargo—maybe 1,000 Jews—was turned back to Nazi Germany. And that happened after the Kristallnacht, after the first state sponsored pogrom, with hundreds of Jewish shops destroyed, synagogues burned, thousands of people put in concentration camps. And that ship, which was already on the shores of the United States, was sent back.

21   I don't understand. Roosevelt was a good man, with a heart. He understood those who needed help. Why didn't he allow these refugees to disembark? A thousand people—in America, a great country, the greatest democracy, the most generous of all new nations in modern history. What happened? I don't understand. Why the indifference, on the highest level, to the suffering of the victims?

22   But then, there were human beings who were sensitive to our tragedy. Those non-Jews, those Christians, that we called the "Righteous Gentiles," whose selfless acts of heroism saved the honor of their faith. Why were they so few? Why was there a greater effort to save SS murderers after the war than to save their victims during the war?

23   Why did some of America's largest corporations continue to do business with Hitler's Germany until 1942? It has been suggested, and it was documented, that the Wehrmacht could not have conducted its invasion of France without oil obtained from American sources. How is one to explain their indifference?

24   And yet, my friends, good things have also happened in this traumatic century: the defeat of Nazism, the collapse of communism, the rebirth of Israel on its ancestral soil, the demise of apartheid, Israel's peace treaty with Egypt, the peace accord in Ireland. And let us remember the meeting, filled with drama and emotion, between Rabin and Arafat that you, Mr. President, convened in this very place. I was here and I will never forget it.

25   And then, of course, the joint decision of the United States and NATO to intervene in Kosovo and save those victims, those refugees, those who were uprooted by a man whom I believe that because of his crimes, should be charged with crimes against humanity. But this time, the world was not silent. This time, we do respond. This time, we intervene.

26   Does it mean that we have learned from the past? Does it mean that society has changed? Has the human being become less indifferent and more human? Have we really learned from our experiences? Are we less insensitive to the plight of victims of ethnic cleansing and other forms of injustices in places near and far? Is today's justified intervention in Kosovo, led by you, Mr. President, a lasting warning that never again will the deportation, the terrorization of children and their parents be allowed anywhere in the world? Will it discourage other dictators in other lands to do the same?

27   What about the children? Oh, we see them on television, we read about them in the papers, and we do so with a broken heart. Their fate is always the most tragic, inevitably. When adults wage war, children perish. We see their faces, their eyes. Do we hear their pleas? Do we feel their pain, their agony? Every minute one of them dies of disease, violence, famine. Some of them—so many of them—could be saved.

28   And so, once again, I think of the young Jewish boy from the Carpathian Mountains. He has accompanied the old man I have become throughout these years of quest and struggle. And together we walk towards the new millennium, carried by profound fear and extraordinary hope.

Critical Reading Questions:

- **Rhetorical Analysis:** Wiesel makes use of definitional arguments to re-frame the concept of indifference in new ways. How does he define indifference in ways that are different from the norm, and how does this re-framing serve to invoke new emotional associations with the concept that are conducive to Wiesel's aims of moving his audience to action? How do these definitions then serve to warrant his arguments that follow?

- **Rhetorical Analysis:** Wiesel carries into this speech well-developed situated, or extrinsic, ethos, including first-hand experience, numerous awards, and a well-established reputation for his extensive work in the service of others. What moves does he make within the text itself to establish intrinsic ethos? Where do you find demonstrations of good will, good sense, and good moral character? What role do these demonstrations play in the persuasiveness of the speech?

ABOUT THE CONTRIBUTORS

Mia Alvarado (MA) is a Senior Instructor in the First-Year Rhetoric and Writing Program at UCCS. She has also taught at the University of Iowa, St. Michael Academy in New York City, the Lighthouse Writers Workshop in Denver, and Cincinnati's Seven Hills School, where she was a writer-in-residence. Alvarado is the author of *Hey Folly* (Dos Madres), a book of poems, and her nonfiction and poetry have been published widely. Her interests include urban farming and sustainability, printmaking, the relationship between humans and machines, urban planning, the essay, the novel, short stories, and poems.

Susan Finger (SF) is a Senior Instructor at UCCS. She graduated with a B.A. from Purdue University and went on to earn an M.A. in English Literature from Florida Atlantic University. Before teaching at UCCS, she was an Associate Editor at Unified Neighbors (now AngiesList.com) and freelanced for the following magazines: *Woman's World, Indianapolis Monthly, Indianapolis Star Sunday Magazine, Indianapolis Woman, Grand Rapids Magazine, South Bend Tribune Sunday Magazine, Indiana Business Magazine,* and *Today's Boca Woman.*

Denise Garrett (DG) received her B.A. in English from the University of Colorado Colorado Springs. During her study of English, she worked in the UCCS Writing Center and developed a deep interest in how students develop critical thinking and writing skills, an interest that led to her pursuit of an M.A. Degree in Rhetoric and the Teaching of Writing at the University of Colorado Denver. She currently teaches in the First-Year Rhetoric and Writing Program at UCCS. Her academic interests range from studying rhetorical theory to understanding student motivation. When not reading or grading, Garrett can be found hiking, practicing yoga, or with her grandchildren.

Catherine Grandorff (CG) serves as an Instructor for the UCCS First-Year Rhetoric and Writing program and teaches creative writing classes. As an educator, she relies upon feminist and classical rhetorical theory to foster inquiry communities that critically engage with a broad range of texts and cultural perspectives. Beyond the classroom, her research and writing focus on the intersections of cultures, genders, and language. Outside of the English Department, she co-chairs the Faculty Assembly Women's Committee and enjoys traveling everywhere from the Black Hills to Bogotá. She lives in Colorado Springs with her husband and their Siamese cat.

Phillip Heasley (PH) is an Instructor in the First-Year Rhetoric and Writing Program at the University of Colorado Colorado Springs. He has an M.A. in English from the University of Oklahoma and an M.A. in Teaching English as a Second Language from Northern Arizona University. He specializes in teaching second language speakers, writing assessment, and genre-based approaches to writing.

Keri Hemenway (KH) is a Senior Instructor at UCCS and has been teaching in the First-Year Rhetoric and Writing Program for nearly ten years. She holds an M.A. from the University of Colorado Denver in The Teaching of Writing and has taught various age groups as well as internationally. She has interests in ESL writing, computers in composition, and linguistics. She serves on the Executive Committee and as the Technology Specialist for the F-YRWP. She resides in Denver with her husband, son, and many pets.

Ceil Malek (CM), finishing her third year as Interim Director of the First-Year Rhetoric and Writing Program, is a long-time Senior Instructor at UCCS. She holds degrees in three writing intensive fields (B.A. in English studies, M.A. in journalism, and M.F.A. in creative nonfiction) from Colorado State University, the University of Colorado Boulder, and Goucher College as well as having completed extensive coursework in rhetoric and writing. She teaches creative writing courses and Advanced Rhetoric and Writing at UCCS while focusing on her own writing practice.

Omar Montoya (OM) is an Instructor of First-Year Writing at the University of Colorado Colorado Springs. He has completed the coursework and comprehensive exams for a Ph.D. in Rhetoric and Professional Communications from New Mexico State University. Montoya specializes in providing writing instruction for second language students and students of diversity. He currently teaches first-year writing, and his research interests include faculty training for teaching writing to second language students and writing across the curriculum. A first-generation college student himself, he acknowledges the importance of education for all students of diversity and is therefore actively involved in campus-wide organizations and initiatives that seek to improve access and education for second language students and students of diversity.

William Myers (WCM) joined the faculty of UCCS in 2002 after a long career in the financial services industry. He completed his graduate work at the University of Colorado Denver. In addition to academic concerns, Myers is an avid caver, a Graduate Gemologist, a field investigator for MUFON, and the author of a novel, *Welcome to Blackwater.*

Christine L. Robinson (CLR) is an animal studies scholar and rhetoric and writing Instructor at UCCS. She holds a B.A. degree in art with a comprehensive minor in prehistoric art history from Western Washington University and an M.A. degree in English with an emphasis in rhetoric and composition from Colorado State University. Robinson presents at conferences across the nation on the rhetorics of the human-animal binary and their potential effects on a diverse range of Others—human and nonhuman. Largely shaped by a posthumanist lens, Robinson defines rhetoric as a form of energy—something many species sense and use to persuade. She has an affinity for vintage jewelry, Airstream trailers, and the television show, *The Walking Dead.*

Kacey Ross (KGR) is an engaged member of the field of rhetoric and writing. She earned her B.A. in English with an emphasis in Rhetoric and Writing in 2009 from UCCS and then completed her M.A., also in English with a specialization in Rhetoric and the Teaching of Writing at the University of Colorado Denver in 2011. As a student, she worked as an undergraduate and graduate writing consultant in the UCCS Writing Center; she also served as the Interim Director of that center after completion of her master's degree. Ross' research interests include rhetorical theory, transferability, and the rhetorical work of classroom documents. She is an Instructor in the First-Year Rhetoric and Writing Program at UCCS, where she enjoys challenging students to read critically and develop a rhetorical lens through which to view the world. She serves on the F-YRWP's Executive Committee and works as the Placement Coordinator for the program. When she's not busy reading, writing, and grading, she enjoys spending time with family, hiking, camping, and playing cards.

Benjamin Lyric Syn (BLS) earned his B.A. in psychology and English (with an emphasis in film as literature) in 2004, his Graduate Certificate in Teaching English to Speakers of Other Languages in 2009, and his M.A. in Rhetoric and the Teaching of Writing in 2011, all from the University of Colorado Denver. His master's thesis focused on using the vampire film "Quarter de la Madeleine" to teach composition and rhetoric. Since 2012, he has been an Instructor at the University of Colorado Colorado Springs where he teaches rhetoric and writing with a focus on visual rhetoric and pop culture, especially in comic books and the works of Walt Disney. Syn is enthusiastic and passionate about teaching and his family. He lives with his wife and their two sons in Westminster, where he enjoys spending time with his family, playing games, taking walks, and watching and discussing films and television.

Richard Thomas (RT) is a second-year Instructor at UCCS who has also taught at CU Boulder, Pikes Peak Community College, and Colorado Springs Early Colleges. He graduated from UC Berkeley with his B.A. in English before the mountains of Colorado lured him to Boulder. While also skiing and hiking, he received his M.A. from the University of Colorado Boulder with a focus in nineteenth century ethnic literature. His research interests include compositional theory and pedagogy, identity production and agency, contemporary ethics, and emerging technologies. Outside of class, Thomas is an avid sports fan who enjoys watching and participating in a wide variety of sports, especially basketball; he can often be found playing pickup basketball games at UCCS's Recreation Center.

Justin Tucker (JT) received his B.A. in English from the University of Texas at San Antonio and his M.A. in Rhetoric and Composition from Texas State University. While he has taught at various institutions across the country, he believes he has found his academic home at UCCS. He currently teaches both English 1310 and 1410.

Andrea M. Wenker (AMW) is a Senior Instructor who has taught in the First-Year Rhetoric and Writing Program at the University of Colorado since Fall 2008. She received her B.A. in English Literature at UCCS and her M.A. in English, Rhetoric and Composition at Colorado State University, where she focused her studies on the teaching of writing, pedagogical and literacy theory, and writing assessment. Her academic interests remain on rhetorical theory as a means of teaching and practicing critical reading, thinking, and writing. She emphasizes close analysis of texts that represent diverse experience and challenge hegemonic assumptions about race, gender, language. She participates actively in departmental governance and has worked as a Program Assistant both in the office of the UCCS portfolio-based writing assessment project and in planning and implementing professional development. In her spare time, she enjoys gardening, hiking, cooking, and enjoying the outdoors.

CREDITS

Alexie, Sherman. "The Joy of Reading and Writing: Superman and Me." *Los Angeles Times* 19 April 1998. Print.

Angelou, Maya. "Graduation." *I Know Why the Caged Bird Sings*. New York: Bantam, 1969. Print.

Anthony, Susan B. "On Women's Right to Vote." 1873. Rpt. in *Historyplace.com*. The History Place, n.d. Web. 25 July 2010.

Anzaldúa, Gloria. "How to Tame a Wild Tongue." *Borderlands/La Frontera*. 2nd ed. San Francisco: Aunt Lute Press, 1999. 75-86. Print.

Barbur, Jonathan E. and Trischa Goodnow. "The *Arete* of Amusement: An Aristotelian Perspective on the Ethos of *The Daily Show*." *The Daily Show and Rhetoric: Argument, Issues, and Strategies*. New York: Lexington Books, 2011. 3-18. Print.

Bartholomae, David. "Inventing the University." *Composing Knowledge: Readings for College Writers*. Ed. Rolf Norgaard. Boston: Bedford/St. Martin's, 2007. 208-213. Print.

Bush, George W. "Address to a Joint Session of Congress and the American People." Rpt. in *archives.CNN.com*. CNN, 21 Sept. 2001. Web. 25 July 2010.

Carr, Nicholas. "Is Google Making Us Stupid?" *theatlantic.com*. Atlantic Magazine, July/Aug. 2008. Web. 25 July 2010.

Catt, Carrie Chapman. "Speech before Congress." 1917. Rpt. in *womenshistory.about.com*. About, n.d. Web. 25 July 2010.

Clinton, Hillary Rodham. "Women's Rights Are Human Rights." United Nations 4th World Conference on Women Plenary Session, Beijing, China. 5 Sept. 1995. Address. Rpt. in *americanrhetoric.com*. American Rhetoric, n.d. Web. 26 July 2010.

Crow Dog, Mary, with Richard Erdoes. "Civilize Them with a Stick," *Lakota Woman*. New York: HarperCollins, 1990. 28-41. Print.

Davis, Kevin. "Does Coming to College Mean Becoming Someone New?" *The Subject Is Writing: Essays by Teachers and Students*. 3rd ed. Ed. Wendy Bishop. Portsmouth, NH: Boynton/Cook, 2003. Print.

De Zengotita, Thomas. "The Numbing of the American Mind." *Harper's*, April 2002. 33-40. Print.

Douglass, Frederick. "Learning to Read and Write." *My Bondage and My Freedom*. 1855. New York: Barnes and Noble Classics, 2005. Print.

—-. "To My Old Master, Thomas Auld." 13 Sept. 1848. Rpt. in *cato.org*. Cato Institute, 19 June 1998. Web. 25 July 2010.

—-. "What to the Slave Is the Fourth of July?" Meeting sponsored by the Rochester Ladies' Anti-Slavery Society. Rochester Hall, Rochester, NY. 5 July 1852. Speech. Rpt. in *TeachingAmericanHistory.org*. Ashland University, n.d. Web. 25 July 2010.

Gerberg, Mort. "What Is a Cartoon?" *Cartooning: The Art and the Business*. Chicago: Quill, 1989. Print.

Hirschberg, Stuart. "The Rhetoric of Advertising." *Reflections on Language*. Eds. Stuart Hirschberg and Terry Hirschberg. Oxford: Oxford UP, 1999. 463-77. Print.

Irvin, L. Lennie. "What is Academic Writing." *Writing Spaces*, Series Edition: Vol 2.

Jefferson, Thomas. "The Declaration of Independence." 4 July 1776. Rpt. in *ushistory.org*. Independence Hall Association, n.d. Web. 25 July 2010.

Kennedy, John. F. "Address on the Cuban Crisis." 22 Oct. 1962. Rpt. in *Internet Modern History Sourcebook*. Fordham University, July 1998. Web. 25 July 2010.

Kilbourne, Jean. "Two Ways a Woman Can Get Hurt: Advertising and Violence." *Can't Buy My Love: How Advertising Changes the Way We Think and Feel*. New York: Simon & Schuster, 1999. 270-91. Print.

King, Martin Luther, Jr. "Letter from Birmingham Jail." 16 April 1963. *Why We Can't Wait*. New York: Signet, 2000. 64-84. Print.

King, Stephen. "What Writing Is." *On Writing: A Memoir of the Craft*. New York: Simon and Schuster, 2000. Print.

Lamott, Anne. "Shitty First Drafts." *Bird by Bird: Some Instructions on Writing and Life*. New York: Anchor, 1994. 21-27. Print.

Lincoln, Abraham. "The Gettysburg Address." Gettysburg, PA. 19 Nov. 1863. Address. Rpt. in *ourdocuments.gov*. Our Documents, n.d. Web. 25 July 2010.

Lutz, William. "With These Words, I Can Sell You Anything." *Double-speak: From Revenue Enhancement to Terminal Living—How Government, Business, Advertisers and Others Use Language to Deceive You.* New York: HarperCollins, 1990. Print.

Malcolm X. "The Ballot or the Bullet." Meeting of the Congress of Racial Equality. Cleveland, Ohio. 3 Apr. 1964. Address.

Malcolm X, with Alex Haley. "Discovering the Power of Language." *The Autobiography of Malcolm X: As Told to Alex Haley.* 1965. New York: Ballantine, 1999. Print.

Pollan, Michael. *"Why Bother?" New York Times* 20 April 2008. Print.

"Public Statement by Eight Alabama Clergymen." 12 Apr. 1963. Rpt. in *Stanford.edu.* Stanford University, n.d. Web. 25 July 2010.

Reagan, Ronald. "Address at Brandenburg Gate." Brandenburg Gate, Berlin, Germany. 12 June 1987. Address. Rpt. in *millercenter.org.* University of Virginia, n.d. Web. 26 July 2010.

Rodriguez, Richard. "Aria: A Memoir of a Bilingual Childhood." *The American Scholar* 50.1 (1980-1981): 25-42. Print.

Roosevelt, Franklin Delano. "The Great Arsenal of Democracy." 29 Dec. 1940. Rpt. in americanrhetoric.com. *American Rhetoric*, n.d. Web. 25 July 2010.

Rosenberg, Karen. "Reading Games: Strategies for Reading Scholarly Sources." *Writing Spaces*, Series Edition: Vol 2.

Smith, Zadie. "Generation Why?" *The New York Review of Books* 25 Nov. 2010. Print.

Standing Bear, Luther. "What the Indian Means to America." *Chief Standing Bear, Land of the Spotted Eagle.* 1933. Rpt. in *Great Documents in American Indian History.* Ed. Wayne Moquin, with Charles Van Doren. New York: Da Capo Press, 1995. 306-08. Print.

Stanton, Elizabeth Cady. "The Seneca Falls Declaration (1848)." AMDOCS: *Documents for the Study of American History.* Virtual Library, n.d. Web. 25 July 2010.

Straub, Richard. "Responding—Really Responding—to Other Students' Writing." *The Subject Is Writing: Essays by Teachers and Students.* 2nd ed. Ed. Wendy Bishop. Portsmouth, NH: Boynton/Cook, 1999. 136-46. Print.

Tan, Amy. "Mother Tongue." *The Threepenny Review* (1990): 7-8. Print.

Tannen, Deborah. "Sex, Lies and Conversation: Why Is It So Hard for Men and Women to Talk to Each Other?" *The Washington Post* 24 June 1990. C3+. Print.

Truth, Sojourner. "Ain't I A Woman?" Women's Convention, Akron, Ohio. 1851. Address. Rpt. in *Internet Modern History Sourcebook*. Fordham University, Aug. 1997. Web. 25 July 2010.

Wiesel, Elie. "On the Perils of Indifference." Millennium Lecture Series. White House, Washington DC. 12 Apr. 1999. Speech. Rpt. in *historyplace.com*. The History Place, n.d. Web. 26 July 2010.